The Surrealism Reader

The Surrealism Reader

An Anthology of Ideas

Edited by Dawn Ades and Michael Richardson
with Krzysztof Fijalkowski

Tate Publishing

First published 2015 by order of
the Tate Trustees
by Tate Publishing, a division of
Tate Enterprises Ltd,
Millbank, London SW1P 4RG
www.tate.org.uk/publishing

All translations are by Krzysztof
Fijalkowski and Michael
Richardson, except texts on
pp.122–7 and 322–7, translated
by Dawn Ades and pp.264–7,
translated by Haim Finklestein.

A catalogue record for this book
is available from the British
Library

ISBN 978 1 85437 668 8

Design concept by Matt Brown
Printed and bound in Great
Britain by T J International Ltd,
Padstow

Front cover: Details from Max
Ernst, *The Attirement of the Bride*
1940. Peggy Guggenheim
Collection, Venice. See p.368 for
complete image.

This publication is the result
of a joint initiative between
Tate Publishing and the AHRC
Research Centre for Studies of
Surrealism and its Legacies.

Acknowledgements
Thanks to Frédérique Audoin-Rouzeau, Annie
Dax-Rowling, Gail Earnshaw, Aube Elléouët, Mattias
Forshage, Guy Girard, Jean-Michel Goutier, Steven Harris,
Jean Jamin, Abdul Kader El Janaby, Annie Le Brun, Sylvette
Legrand, Michael Löwy, Claudie Mabille, Jean-Pierre
Mabille, Michiyo Miyaka, Marc Nahum, Geneviève
Sézille-Ménil, Bruno Solarik, Sarah Whitfield.

Contents

Introduction

Surrealism, as is generally known, took shape as a movement in 1924 after a five-year gestation period during which it emerged as the negation of the Dadaist negation, occasioned by the First World War and the crisis of consciousness of western thought that followed it.

It has been subject to a vast amount of critical literature, but one aspect that has been neglected is its intellectual basis and the extent to which it has engaged with specific issues in the intellectual history of the twentieth century. The aim of this volume is to make a major contribution to this gap by drawing together essays from the whole history of surrealism to illustrate the tenacity and consistency with which the surrealists have treated socio-cultural and political themes as they developed their critique of positivist and rationalist notions of reality and advanced their own understandings of questions of the construction of identity, cultural communication, freedom and poetry – issues that have become perhaps even more important in recent years and to which surrealism brings a distinctive perspective that deserves to be recognised.

The nature of surrealism is protean and it is impossible to give a simple definition of its precise nature. Maurice Blanchot has perhaps given us the most concise description, calling surrealism 'a pure practice of existence' (Blanchot 1993, p.407). This gives emphasis to the fact that surrealism is a total activity which cannot be confined within traditional frameworks. Indeed, it explodes most categories, as the surrealists refused to restrict their realm of engagement to art and literature, the fields with which they are most often associated. If most surrealists have been writers or artists, the movement has also drawn into its environs scientists, anthropologists, philosophers, musicians or even people who contributed to it by the simple fact of living in the spirit of Marcel Duchamp, who once, when asked what he did, responded, 'I breathe'. As a total activity, surrealism cannot be understood if it is treated piecemeal, and thus our understanding of its art and literature remains incomplete if we are not aware of its broader context.

Surrealism is above all a 'movement' – not only in the sense of being an association but also because it is constantly 'in movement', shifting its ground to meet different demands and never settling in one place. This anthology aims to do justice to both its protean nature and to the fact of its constant movement. To do so, in editing it, we have striven to take as a methodological starting point, in relation to the organisation of the material, some of the ways the surrealists themselves edited their own journals, their basic principle was to be responsive to the potential of techniques of collage and juxtaposition to create meaning in and of themselves, and give depth to and fresh perspectives on what a particular text or image on its own can express. In this way we hope that the texts and images in the book will speak to one another, as well as speaking to the reader, creating the inherent dialogic which has been an important element of surrealist practice.

Maurice Henry
Reproduced in
Almanach surréaliste du demi-siècle, 1950
[Portraits of members of the surrealist
movement, together with inspirational
figures both past and present. Surrealists
with spots on their faces were considered
to have been morally compromised in
some way.]

Since it is not possible in a single volume to do anything like justice to the full range of work accomplished by the surrealists over the past century, we have chosen four key themes around which to explore issues that are essential to a proper understanding of what surrealism means.

The first theme, documented in Part One, draws together texts that deal with different aspects of surrealist approaches to identity. This theme, which in recent years has become a central concern of social and cultural discourse, was one of the starting points of the surrealist adventure, a theme they addressed in ways that seem strikingly in tune with present day debates. We have given this Part the perhaps provocative title 'The Annihilation of Self-Identity'. This is a reference to André Breton's *Second Manifesto of Surrealism*, in which he argued that the ultimate aim of surrealism is 'the annihilation of being into an internal and blind diamond, which has no more the soul of ice than of fire' (Breton 1988, vol.1, p.782). This assault on the concept of being as it has been understood in dominant strands of western thought especially calls into question the individualism underlying the traditions of rationalism and positivism which surrealism targeted in its general will to demoralise the idea that the universe can be understood in realist terms.

The texts in this section address questions of identity from a variety of perspectives, including scholarly essays on the constitution of the person by Pierre Mabille, himself a practising doctor and scientist, and Paul Nougé, a practising bio-chemist; speculative anthropological essays by Michel Leiris and Vincent Bounoure; and powerful critiques of some of the assumptions underlying developments in feminism and technology by Leonora Carrington, Annie Le Brun and Bernard Caburet, as well as more creative explorations by René Crevel and Marcel Mariën.

Part Two addresses the related theme of otherness, which was equally central to surrealism from its beginnings. Surrealism discovered in the psychological investigations of Freud and the philosophical phenomenology of Hegel complementary scientific suggestions that gave substance in their eyes to Rimbaud's contention that the '*I* is *another*'. Freud was crucial here for his discovery of the unconscious, revealing that there is a domain of the human psyche that eludes the control of consciousness and remains largely unknown to us, while Hegel showed how the person is not an entity existing in and of itself, which establishes an identity unique to itself, but is rather formed through encounters in the world which are constantly changing. This offered a double sense of otherness: one internal, the other external. It is also why the collective aspect of surrealism is so important – indeed, the locus of surrealism is founded not in any common purpose but in the value of encounter. Too often André Breton is criticised in the literature for supposedly imposing a strict dogma and expelling those who did not conform to it. It is apparent, however, that Breton's primary concern was the opposite: to maintain a vibrant atmosphere of encounter within surrealism so as to prevent it from being reduced to a self-satisfied and exclusive club.

Simone Breton, Max Morise,
and Denise Levy in Breton's
apartment, 42 rue Fontaine,
Paris, 1929. Photographer
unknown

These perceptions were also sharpened as the surrealists engaged
with the realities which appalled them, in particular nationalism and
colonialism but also the arrogant human assumption (born in the
Enlightenment) of human superiority over nature: from early on, the
surrealists recognised the dangers of ecological imbalance which
have become such a vital issue today. The texts in this section
address various aspects of otherness, from critiques of Zionism
(Desnos) and attacks on colonialism (Viot and Crevel), to an
affirmation of universal culture in specifically surrealist terms by
Artaud, reflections on nature and ecology (Péret, Bataille, Sénard-
Duprey) and affirmations of oppositional cultural traditions (Breton),
supported by critiques of different attempts to assimilate such
oppositional forces to conformist agendas (Benayoun, Ménil, Le
Brun). Finally, a text by René Alleau brings together some of the key
themes of the section.

 Some readers may be surprised by the emphasis placed on
morality by many of the writers throughout this volume, since
there seems to be a tendency to see surrealism as advocating a
total freedom which goes beyond morality. Certainly surrealism
challenges – sometimes virulently – bourgeois and Christian notions
of morality. Yet it does so generally in the name of morality,
considering anything founded in respect for nation, family and
religion as having led to the debacle of the First World War and to
be morally bankrupt.

 Central to this moral concern is the nature of freedom,
something which has been surprisingly little discussed in the critical
literature, even though the surrealist understanding of freedom
is quite distinctive. This developed from the demand for a 'new
declaration of human rights' made in the first issue of *La Révolution
surréaliste*, although it moved away from this starting point as
freedom came to be seen neither specifically in terms of 'rights',
nor of 'human'. No doubt formed principally through Breton's and
especially Aragon's reading of Hegel (although Marx and Nietzsche
may also have been important here, along with Schelling and

Surrealists at the Désert de
Retz, Chambourcy 1960.
Photograph by Denise Bellon

1 A start on addressing this lacuna has been made by Georges Sebbag in his recent book, *Potence avec paratonnerre: surréalisme et philosophie*, Paris: Hermann, 2012.

Heraclitus – the philosophical underpinnings of surrealism are still little explored'), and consistent with the demand for the annihilation of the self, freedom came to be viewed generally in surrealism not as a property of the individual (something which would reinforce the idea of an individual self), but in its own terms and as related to the key surrealist notion of 'objective chance'. Freedom therefore needs to be viewed in relation to necessity, as its complement and condition. This is most strongly expressed by Aragon in his two short texts in Part Three, which assert that freedom can only be absolute: if any conditions are attached to it then it ceases to be freedom. Since it is absolute, however, a moral responsibility is placed upon me: I cannot be free if others are enslaved. In order for me to be free, I need to fight for the freedom of all.'

This provides the central theme running through this section, addressed in different ways in the texts by Aragon, Calas, Breton, Bataille, Henein, Lenk and Mabille. Of particular significance is the distinction between 'liberty' and 'liberation' made by Breton in his book *Arcane 17*, written in the wake of the Second World War, which raised different moral questions to that of the First World War and necessitated a reconsideration of the nature of surrealism's opposition to the dominant society. Nazism and Stalinism had revealed that the cancer was deeper than previously thought and could not be eradicated by changes of a political and social nature.

In the other texts of this section, Ristić's essay directly addresses the issue of morality in relation to humour, seen as a component part of any notion of freedom. Legrand is concerned to clarify surrealism's position within the western philosophical tradition, taking issue with the contention of the philosopher Ferdinand Alquié that it can be considered as part of a humanist tradition. Philippe Audoin, in contrast, draws our attention to the 'silent revolution' of managerialism that was occurring in the 1960s and has since become ever more apparent in our everyday lives, eroding our freedoms in insidious and often imperceptible ways.

The final section, Part Four, considers questions relating to art and poetry which will perhaps be more familiar to readers with a hazy knowledge of surrealism. Here what is crucial is the distinction made by Tzara between poetry as an 'activity of the spirit' and as a 'means of expression', something which was rejected by the surrealists. As we note, Tzara's argument in support of this distinction is tortuous and not always convincing, but the distinction itself is nevertheless key to understanding what the surrealists were seeking to achieve, which was a poetry that was free of literary artifice and would constitute a free engagement with the phenomenology of living. Poetry here is not to be understood as writing verses, but rather as a way of living, so that, as they often reminded us, one may be a poet without ever having written anything.

The principal means of this 'activity of the spirit' is automatism, even though what this actually consists of has been and remains controversial in the history of surrealism. First surfacing as the methodology by which André Breton and Philippe Soupault wrote *Les Champs magnétiques*, the 1919 book which is generally accepted as the initial starting point of surrealism, its moment of conception, it remained for Breton tied to this form of spontaneous outpouring, the result of which, he believed, would be to reveal 'the true functioning of thought'. There were enormous difficulties with this conception, however, which did not satisfy many of the surrealists; the essays by Salvador Dalí, Roger Caillois and Paul Nougé in our selection raise some of the problems. In his text, Adrien Dax brings a painter's perspective to the significance of automatism as it developed over the early decades of surrealism.

What is more broadly involved here is the nature of surrealist poetics, something that has surprisingly not really been directly addressed either by the surrealists themselves or in the critical literature, even if Breton's and Éluard's rather neglected text from 1929 and Nougé's 'Notes' go some way to providing a basis for its consideration. Antonin Artaud's essay here brings morality centrally into the equation by focusing on the social role of the artist.

Another central and related theme was that of language itself and the nature of representation. One of the tasks surrealism set itself was to reinvigorate language, to give it back a power of expression that was being lost both through positivist reduction and by the advance of a consumerist society devoted to twisting language to serve its own agendas. Ironically, this may have been one of the major failures of surrealism, since one of the effects of the most visible of surrealist manifestations – in particular the painting of Magritte and Dalí – has been to give inspiration to the very advertising industry that has done most to contribute to this degeneration of the enunciative power of language. Whether we see this as a failure of surrealism or simply as evidence of capitalism's ability to adapt oppositional discourses to its own benefit, the ambivalences of language to which surrealist painters above all have drawn attention remain resonant in today's debates concerning representation and its problematic. In Nougé's 'Inviolable Images' we have an early exploration of Magritte's painting which places it in a wider context of surrealist concerns, while the short text by Magritte himself helps us to appreciate the aims of the painter beyond the superficial appropriation to which his painting has been subject.

Language in its multiple forms has been a particular focus of surrealism in Czechoslovakia throughout its long history, as the texts by Teige and Effenberger reveal.

Note on the Selection of Material

In compiling an anthology of surrealism, one is faced with insuperable difficulties. Indeed, in order to do justice to the subject at least ten volumes would be required, as well as a team of researchers to engage with the vast range of material available. Surrealism has undoubtedly been the most complex intellectual movement of the past century. Active participants in it and those who have contributed on the margins number in the hundreds, coming from many different countries across the world and writing in different languages. Since our own expertise is largely limited to English, French and Spanish, we ourselves are largely precluded from engagement with important surrealist work written in Czech, Serbo-Croat, Greek, Romanian, Japanese, Portuguese and Arabic in particular.

Moreover, the scope of surrealist investigation is enormous. Surrealists have not considered any realm of activity to be outside their interest, and have engaged in significant ways with issues not simply related to art or literature, but have made contributions to anthropology, philosophy, sociology, social geography, political theory, the hermetic and occult sciences, and modern physics. Surrealist work is therefore cross-disciplinary in nature and, considering the number of artists and writers who have participated in it over what is now almost a century of continuous work, is of such a range that no anthology can hope to offer more than a fraction of its most important texts.

Anyone compiling an anthology based on this material is therefore faced with a dilemma which involves making far-reaching decisions about how to limit its scope, either thematically or historically. Our aim in this work has been principally to engage with the contribution made by surrealism to the intellectual ideas of the past century, an area which we believe no previous anthology has really addressed, certainly not in any systematic way. The texts and images have therefore been chosen to illustrate and illuminate surrealism as a set of *ideas*, and to seek to elucidate those ideas that have been most essential to surrealism as it has developed as a totality. Despite the vast number of people who have contributed to its ideas, and notwithstanding the heterogeneity of these materials, the surrealists have never been eclectic in their approaches and have generally adhered to a strong, if largely unspoken and intuitive, set of fundamental notions which nevertheless remain in need of elucidation.

We have also found it necessary to place methodological limitations on our selection of texts. As basic principles, therefore, we decided firstly only to include complete texts; there is a temptation for the editor of an anthology like this to expurgate texts so as to include more material and give a wider span to the selection. This, however, aside from doing violence to the original texts, limits their particularity and gives the anthology the feel that it is simply a 'sampling' of something greater than itself, which the interested

André Breton (centre) and
surrealists, plus three fashion
models, grouped around *The
Feast*, an installation by Méret
Oppenheim for the 1959
International Exhibition of
Surrealism (EROS). Photograph
by William Klein

reader can follow up later. We have sought, in contrast, to focus on
maintaining the integrity of the original text, which in turn, we hope,
establishes the integrity of the anthology as a text in its own right.
Although the reader is perfectly free to read individual texts
separately from the context of the whole book, we hope that it also
functions as an integral work that can be read sequentially. In
addition, to abridge texts structurally affects their architecture,
something that is very important for many of the pieces in this
volume, which were conceived as *essays* in a double sense, that is
as a study of a topic but also as a *test* or *experiment*.

Secondly, we selected texts originally published in periodicals,
most particularly of course in the surrealists' own journals, but also
those published by surrealists in other publications of the time.
Publication in a journal is to some extent evidence that the text has
been given a certain sanction in having been chosen by the author's
peers as raising currently relevant issues. We thus hope that through
this strategy, the anthology will give a sense of the vitality of surrealist
responses to the intellectual issues of the time during the different
periods of surrealism's history. We have selected images either
because they were reproduced in the original article, or more often
because we feel they reflect the theme of that particular text.

Thirdly, we chose to include (with very few exceptions), only
previously untranslated pieces; this means of course that we have
excluded many famous texts which might be expected to be included
in any surrealist anthology. When the translator has considered it
helpful to add an explanatory interjection for the reader, this is

indicated by 'trans.' at the end of the note; other notes are taken from the original texts. The full references for sources given in square brackets can be found in the Bibliography.

These were our general principles, although we have not strictly bound ourselves to them and in a few instances have not followed them. In addition we have tried to bring attention to some of the lesser-known (especially in the English-speaking world) but no less important voices within surrealism, as well as stress the dialogic aspect of surrealism and give a sense of the surrealists *in conversation*, not just among themselves but also in relation to the wider society.

MINOTAURE

Part 1

The Annihilation of Self-Identity

PHOSPHOR

a surrealist luminescence

2

Phantom Objects

Andrew Boobier • Eugenio Castro • Stephen J. Clark • Jan Drabble •
Guy Ducornet • Kathleen Fox • Michaël Löwy • Noé Ortega Quijano •
Peter Overton • Mike Peters • Franklin Rosemont • Bruno Solarik •
Jan Švankmajer • John Welson • John Hartley Williams

Autumn 2009   **Price £ 6.00**

Phosphor, Autumn 2009
Front cover

Introduction

Part 1
The Annihilation of Self-Identity

Part 2
The Challenge of Otherness

Part 3
The Moral Imperative

Part 4
The Tasks of Art and Poetry

Biographies
Journals
Bibliography
Index

Jacques Hérold
from *Almanach surréaliste du demi-siècle*, 1950

Being and its Reflections

Immutable man in his organic equilibrium detaches himself from absurd uniformity through the scandal of his dissymmetry. Symmetrical with his 'useful' body; head in two and so on, pyramids of reality like geological strata but dissymmetrical with his desire the object of his realisation, an object of his struggle, a glass of blood. Woman called and hostess, equally incomplete; woman and man, reflection of the other, coalescence of the sexes.

O masked flint, utter your magnetic cry!

L'Etre et ses Reflets

L'homme immuable dans son équilibre organique se détache de l'absurde uniforme par le scandale de sa dissymétrie. Symétrique de son corps « utile » : tête en deux, etc., pyramides de la réalité comme des strates géologiques mais dissymétrique par

stelfeR ses te ertE'L

son désir, objet de sa réalisation, objet de sa lutte, verre de
sang. Femme appelée et hôtesse, également incomplète; femme
et homme, reflet de l'autre, coalescence des sexes.
    O silex masqué, lance ton cri magnétique!

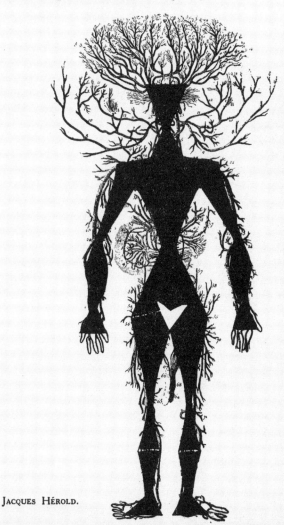

JACQUES HÉROLD.

The Annihilation of Self-Identity

Issues of identity and the constitution of the self run through surrealism. Long before Foucault announced the 'death of the subject' or Barthes proclaimed that the author was dead, the surrealists had implicitly taken both notions for granted. Indeed, an essential element of surrealism's coming into being was precisely the recognition that Enlightenment individualism had ceased to be a tool of human emancipation and was displaying increasingly oppressive aspects. Self-identity, that culmination of the Aristotelian 'law of non-contradiction', could therefore not be taken for granted but needed to be subjected to a rigorous interrogation, an emptying out. This theme runs through much surrealist work and yet has rarely been considered, or even recognised, in the literature on surrealism, notwithstanding usually fairly perfunctory references to the central importance of Rimbaud's '*I* is *another*' or 'it is incorrect to say "I think", one should say "I am thought"', or Lautréamont's 'poetry should be made by all, not by one' – statements more generally seen as poetic flourishes than as the declarations of war against the unity of the self that the surrealists perceived them to be.

The section takes as its starting point André Breton's opening paragraph from his narrative *Nadja*, in which he brought his own person into question. Breton has often been criticised for the apparently insensitive way he treated Nadja, that enchanted being he encountered one day by chance on the streets of Paris and later abandoned to her fate. However, it is only the honesty of Breton's telling that allows us even to know she existed, and we can judge Breton's treatment of her only through what he tells us. Any annoyance we may feel at his lack of responsibility should not therefore blind us to the fact that through the complex story Breton tells he is above all taking his own identity apart through the sense of 'disponsibilité' or availability that his encounter with this young woman has instilled within him. Nadja was for him a catalyst who enabled him to question what he was and to explore his relationship to the greater world.

This sense of the instability in the self was reflected in the socio-political, sociological and psychological concerns of the period when the disjunction between technological advances and the inexorable progress of modernism on the one hand and the sense of a world out of kilter with itself could hardly have been more acute. This was the context in which it appeared to the surrealists that everything was to be re-evaluated.

The reader should therefore not be surprised by the inclusion of Pierre Mabille's 'Preface in Praise of Popular Prejudices', even if this study of human development from a scientific perspective may not meet popular expectations of typical surrealist concerns. Yet the surrealists wanted to set their work within a scientific framework, even if this framework was very broadly envisaged, and tried as far as they were able to take account of the latest scientific findings and incorporate them into their own investigations. Mabille, who was trained in medicine and earned his living as a general practitioner, was able to combine knowledge of the natural sciences with interests in anthropology as well as in the occult sciences, drawing upon his vast knowledge of alchemy and astrology.

With the first of René Crevel's texts we move away from the empirical into the realm of speculation that may be more in keeping with what is expected of the surrealist imagination, as Crevel conceives of the mannequin as a being more living than the living. As in several of the texts in this section – and this is a perennial theme in surrealist writings – Crevel is also concerned to explore the nature of masking and disguise and to undermine the distinction between living and dead matter.

Paul Nougé is more interested in showing how the identity of any thing cannot be determined in itself and is always relational to whatever is perceiving it. This theme was perhaps a determining characteristic of the work of the Brussels surrealists, given its most striking manifestation in the paintings of Magritte, which play upon the ambivalences of representation as they depict objects in unusual relationship with one another. In his text in this section, Marcel Mariën, another member of the Brussels group, explores a different aspect of representation as he puts forward a ironic take on the fourth dimension, that place or no-place which is part of ourselves but a part about which, in a three-dimensional world, we can know nothing.

The other essay by Pierre Mabille in this section explores the nature of mirrors to show how our identity is tied in with our reflection to the extent that we would be unable to perceive what we are without the use of some form of mirror reflection. Related to the widespread myths found in many

Emila Medková
Cascade of Hair 1949

cultures concerning the uncanny quality of doubles, shadows, doppelgängers, twins and so on, the mirror is another element within the world that brings our sense of identity into question even as it helps us to form it.

Michel Leiris in his text is also concerned with reflections and masking as he enquires into the effect that the masks we wear – both literally and figuratively, both consciously and conconsciously – affect our personality and relation to others. Leiris would later become one of France's most distinguished anthropologists, but in 1929 he was still seduced by the idea of the exotic as he looked forward to leaving Europe as part of Marcel Griaule's ethnographic expedition from Dakar to Djibouti. In his essay, one of the most disturbing in the whole canon of surrealist writing, Leiris does more than simply bring our identity into question: he suggests that there is something frightful at its core.

Vincent Bounoure's essay is also concerned with masks. Bounoure, who believed we were living at the end of civilisation (or rather that what we called 'civilisation' was actually a form of barbarism), sought in the mask the key that would open the way towards a new sensibility.

The relation between the sexes of course is a central surrealist concern, and one might imagine that the surrealists, with their emphasis on revolt against the roles that society inflicts upon us, would welcome the emergence of the women's movement at the end of the 1960s and to an extent they did. However, many of the women associated with the movement soon became wary of what they perceived as totalitarian elements within some aspects of feminism. This was especially so when it came to questions of identity – which is perhaps not surprising if considered in relation to the theme of this section, since the women's movement was centrally concerned to assert rather than to question women's identity. Nevertheless, Leonora Carrington was one of those who from the beginning tentatively embraced the women's movement, and certainly all surrealists welcomed the way it opened up the possibilities for women to assert themselves, giving them more opportunities to express themselves. Annie Le Brun, on the other hand, would become one of the fiercest critics of what she called 'neo-feminism', equating it with totalitarian thinking, a 'Stalinism in petticoats', as it imposed upon women an identity she regarded as equally if not more oppressive than that to which woman had traditionally been assigned.

In the final text in this section, Bernard Caburet addresses the issue of identity in the light of the machine age and finds the intellectual responses being developed in the wake of 1968 (what we would now call 'post-structuralism') to be wanting, complicit as they were with the sense of dehumanisation at the heart of the technologisation of the world.

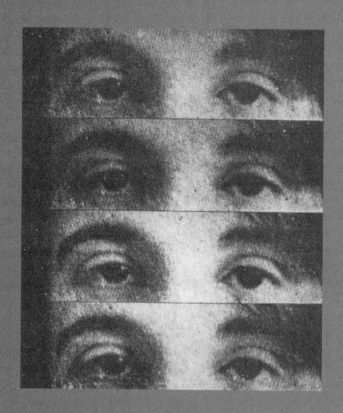

'Les yeux de fougère'
(Fern eyes) from
André Breton, *Nadja* (1928)

André Breton
The Haunting

The famous opening paragraph of Breton's *Nadja* sets up some essential elements of surrealist phenomenology: that one's existence is always contingent upon the existence of a complex 'other' so making personal identity essentially porous, in constant transformation and not admitting of an individual self, at least not in terms put forward by Aristotelian logic and elaborated by the Enlightenment. Opening with the mysterious (and impossible to translate) question 'Qui suis-je?', meaning 'who am I?', but also 'who am I following?', Breton was undermining his own stability of being. For him the world was indeed haunted, haunted above all by our presence within it. Breton's placing of himself outside himself was more than a personal statement: it was also marking out a surrealist phenomenology by which surrealism would oppose not simply those obvious facts of a realist attitude as descended from positivism and the Enlightenment, but also fundamental realist notions about existence in general.

First published in André Breton, *Nadja*, Paris: NRF, 1928.

Who am I? Perhaps I should for once rely on an adage: isn't it dependent on what I 'haunt'? I must concede how deceptive a word this is, tending as it does to establish relations more singular, inexorable and disturbing than I imagined between myself and certain other beings. It expresses far more than it denotes, casting me, while still living, in the role of a ghost, evidently alluding to the fact that to be *who* I am I must have ceased to be what I might be. Assuming a hardly excessive meaning, it hints at how what I consider to be objective and more or less deliberated expressions of my existence are merely what happens, within the limits of this life, in an activity whose actual scope is entirely unknown to me. How I imagine this 'ghost' in its conventional appearance as in its blind submission to certain contingencies of time and place is significant for me principally as a finite image of a torment which may be eternal. My life might possibly be just this sort of image, condemning me to retrace my steps just when I think I am exploring, trying to know what I should perfectly well recognise and learning a small part of what I have forgotten. This vision of myself only seems false if I presuppose myself, arbitrarily situating a completed form of my thought composed at a level of anteriority that has no relation to time and implies in this very time an idea of irreparable loss, of penance or a fall whose lack of moral foundation would in my view brook no discussion. What is important is that the particular aptitudes I slowly discover in this world do not in any way distract me from seeking a general aptitude, one particular to me yet not innate. Beyond any taste I am aware of, the affinities I feel, the attractions to which I yield, the things that happen to me and me alone, beyond the number of movements I am aware of making, the emotions I alone experience, I strive to know what my

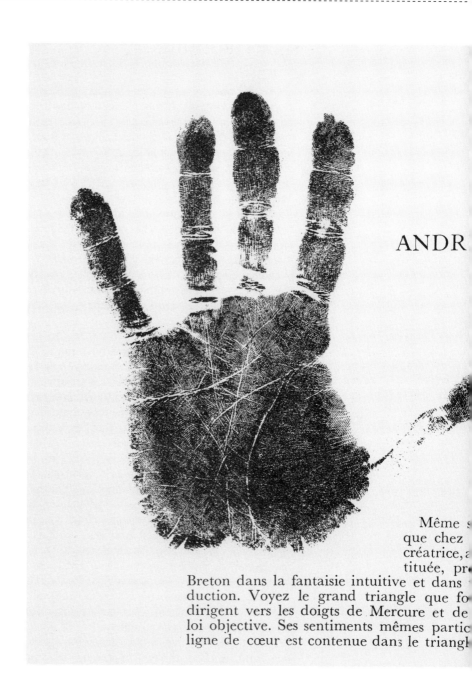

ANDR

Même s
que chez
créatrice, a
tituée, pre
Breton dans la fantaisie intuitive et dans
duction. Voyez le grand triangle que fo
dirigent vers les doigts de Mercure et de
loi objective. Ses sentiments mêmes partic
ligne de cœur est contenue dans le triangl

André Breton's palm prints,
from Lotte Wolff, 'Les
Révélations psychiques
de la main', *Minotaure*,
no.6, Winter 1935

RETON

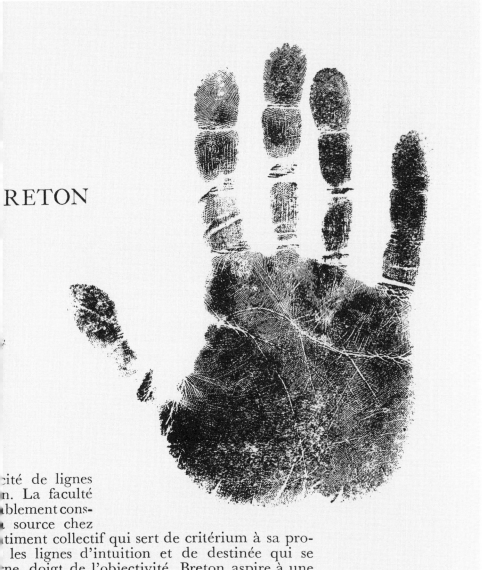

cité de lignes
n. La faculté
blement cons-
source chez
timent collectif qui sert de critérium à sa pro-
les lignes d'intuition et de destinée qui se
ne, doigt de l'objectivité. Breton aspire à une
à l'élaboration esthétique. (Une partie de la
ains de créateur et de révélateur.

differentiation from other people consists of, if not how it came about. Is it not precisely to the extent that I become aware of this differentiation from others that I will realise what I have come in this world to do and what unique message I bear, making me alone responsible for its fate?

Pierre Mabille
Preface in Praise of Popular Prejudices

As the surrealists extended their explorations into areas of phenomenology during the 1930s they welcomed into their ranks not just artists and writers but scientists, among whom the most significant from a surrealist perspective was Pierre Mabille, a practising general practitioner who had wide-ranging interests and had especially studied alchemy and the hermetic sciences. As a trained physician, Mabille was particularly interested in the interactions between phenomena and the correspondences occurring throughout nature – a human being's development was no different in principle from that of a plant, an idea or a society. Mabille clarifies some of the confusions which have often been repeated about the surrealist notion of the unconscious and the nature of automatism. For him the unconscious is not a repository of repressed individual memories, but a much vaster one containing the whole history of the universe which remains latent and acts through individuals. This study would later become part of his book *La Construction de l'homme*, published in 1936.

First published in *Minotaure*, no.6, winter 1935; reprinted in Pierre Mabille, *Traversées de nuit*, Paris: Plasma 1981.

The spermatozoid has encountered the egg in the woman's uterus. From that moment on, a construction begins, which goes beyond the human framework to reconnect with the vast natural elaborations. The structures will be furnished by the animal species and the threads stretched across geological periods. Not all living or extinct series repeat themselves in the developing embryo as one might too easily think. Only tendencies of edification that have found their realisation in distant periods in the forms of higher animals reappear outlined in the foetus, and in the state of intentions. These impulses, which are affirmed, differentiated or sought out over time, mingle here and link up as they dissipate. In the space of a few weeks the egg crystallises the gradual progress of adaptation over millions of years. But it very quickly attains its proper species and begins to resemble what it will be, and by slowing down the rhythm of this appraisal of time, with a greater anatomical precision concludes towards the end of pregnancy in the datum of close heredity. A film which resembles a dream in which desires and the creative imaginations of nature are superimposed, double-exposed, hazily, to reach a distinctness in the finalisation of the completed construction. This process is moreover identical in all elaborations, whether it is a question of a being, an idea or an act.

But as soon as the embryo has a material existence, from its very first moment it is subject to its own life. Its environment is first the maternal blood which for it is an alien universe, against which it must struggle even whilst taking from it what it needs to form itself. At birth, the contact with beings and objects becomes direct. Defence and adaptation to the surroundings impose a personality on it which will be established by more or less deforming the initial hereditary impulse. The being can then be represented as a relation whose two terms are the experience of time and self-experience. It must adapt, for itself and contingent on the environment, its person which is already a conglomerate of all previous adaptations.

These origins need to be recalled, because this order in the physical construction is replicated in psychological phenomena. Nothing here is very different. However, the study of psychological facts is rendered more difficult by the existence of consciousness. This appears to establish a barrier between two opposed realms: on the one hand, the intelligence fed by sensory contributions or memory leading to judgement and abstraction; on the other hand, seeping out of this narrow illuminated strip, the unconscious with its vast content whose exploration is primordial. It appears to be formed of two parts: a visceral unconscious, bearing witness to our internal life, and a more general one which could be called the unconscious of forgetting; it is at once personal and social. Let's try to discern its main lines.

Viscera, glands and circulation vessels form a system whose appeals, harmonies and discords establish a vegetative life, the very basis of our existence. From this alembic arise the stimuli, desires, needs and states of dejection or joy, discomforts or euphoria. Consciousness is generally not attained except when phenomena go beyond their usual limits, but these internal movements, the factors of our dynamism, impose their directions and their colours on intellectual concepts. The visceral play and balance of hormones determine our tastes and activity absolutely and lead our efforts, forming our passionate core which the intelligence may or may not realise in conformity with the surroundings. Consciousness has no other aim than to serve these passions, to garb or to deform them, to reduce them into the framework of the imperative limits of the external world.

Just as the higher animals have a rather similar visceral organisation, this unconscious is also similar in various species; it is a psychological reaction of living matter which, inherent to life, evolves from health to death. However, the individual aspect is not negligible, thanks to personal susceptibilities, internal formulas, humoral equilibrium and the variable thresholds of the conscious sensibility.

It remains overwhelmingly instinctive, by its very anatomical nature (the regulatory glandular balancing, the structure of the vegetative nervous system). Sickness, major disorders and

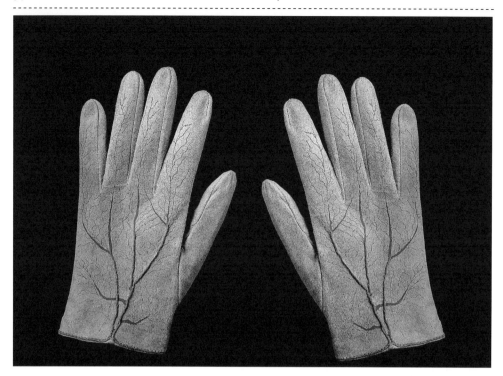

Méret Oppenheim
Pair of Gloves 1985
Edition for *Parkett* 4,
realising an original
design by Oppenheim
from 1936

modifications in the surroundings hardly manage to change the content of this unconscious, so narrow and stable are its limits. There is little hope that it will be greatly enriched in the future. Pledged to darkness, this central core of life, this witness of the combustions of internal fire, only really bursts out with pain, it speaks only to curse and to complain, its equilibrium and not its tumults is silent. The sexual element has an important but not a unique place there, being one of the components of this structure.

          * * *

The other element of the unconscious is made up of the mass of things learned during the ages or throughout life, that which was conscious and that by diffusion has been forgotten. Here the parallel with embryonic development or geological construction is particularly visible. All efforts, whether successful or not, are superimposed, a sort of slow and obscure stratification, a library in which the books are blended together and in which the titles have been rubbed away. A vast submarine reservoir in which all the cultures, all the studies, all the reasoning of minds and will, all the social revolts and struggles undertaken are brought together in a formless vessel in which the elements are digested, rot and mingle as they disintegrate. This constitutes a veritable spiritual geography in which, in layers, materials, casings and shells, leaves and flowers are deposited in the darkness. The emotional elements of individuals are withdrawn and extinguished. What lives on is only the data drawn from the external world that are more or less transformed and digested. It is from the external world that this unconscious is made and it continues its slow work by means of its passage through people's minds, gathering together, crystallising and neutralising itself at will and in accordance with the elective affinities of the materials laid down. Such is the march of ideas in the unconscious. Born from social life, this humus belongs to societies. The species and the individual count for little, the races and time are its only references. This enormous work carried out in darkness reappears in dreams, thoughts and decisions, especially at the moment of important periods and social upheavals; it is the great common capital, the reserve of peoples and individuals. Revolution and war, like fever, activate it more effectively. When it re-emerges seething, crossing the thresholds of consciousness to transform itself into acts or concepts, we only lend it our persons, which furnish it a means to take shape; it then exploits our personal material.

The visceral unconscious lends itself to analysis; one can follow its fluctuations from day to day through the control of dreams, the examination of mimicry or of gestures taking shape, and by the comprehension of our motives. Its vision is always strongly impregnated with a physiological and almost medical judgement.

The unconscious of forgetting, which each person carries within the self, can be perceived only by furnishing it with the means to burst out, if possible by lowering the threshold of consciousness or by seeking the means to facilitate its escape. Most often the effort of the intelligence is opposed to its release. We guess at how rich and confused, geologically rich and unfathomably deep it is. Consequently, there is no further mystery about Pascal rediscovering the books of Euclid than in the child poet, or in the mathematical genius or the musical prodigy. They are islands which emerge from the ocean of forgetting and not strange creations of curiously organised beings. They are the natural and normal protrusions of lands elaborated slowly by the ages and the corpses. All that is necessary is to study this internal fire and these underlying layers in the light, the eruptions and breakings; but let us not consider them as accidents or disorder when they are only normal processes. Earthquakes and volcanoes are habitual methods for the progression of things. Let's seek the timetable of internal tides. Individual psychology being surpassed, let's call upon a sort of natural history of volcanic rhythms and underground watercourses. There is nothing on the surface of the globe which was not once underground (water, earth, fire). There is nothing in the intelligence which did not once digest and circulate in the depths.

* * *

On the one hand stratigraphic analysis will reveal what this chalk, these sands and rocks of ideas are made of and where they come from. On the other hand, the laws and cycles of eruptions will indicate the date, place and conditions of these drillings of peripheral knowledge.

Such a programme of studies is not at all impossible to realise if one takes account of the great number of observations

PRÉFACE
à l'Éloge des Préjugés Populaires*

Par le DOCTEUR PIERRE MABILLE

LE spermatozoïde a rencontré l'ovule dans la matrice de la femme. Dès cette minute, une construction commence, qui dépasse le cadre humain pour rejoindre les vastes élaborations naturelles. Les échafaudages seront fournis par les espèces animales et les fils tendus au travers des âges géologiques. Toutes les séries vivantes ou éteintes ne se répètent pas dans l'embryon en formation comme on pourrait trop simplement le penser. Seules, et à l'état d'intentions, les tendances d'édification qui ont trouvé en des périodes lointaines leur réalisation dans les formes des animaux supérieurs reparaissent ébauchées dans le fœtus. Ces impulsions qui dans les temps se sont affirmées, différentiées ou cherchées, se mêlent ici et se nouent en se dissipant. L'œuf coagule en quelques semaines les recherches lentes de l'adaptation pendant des millions d'années. Mais très vite, il arrive à sa propre espèce, il commence à ressembler à ce qu'il sera et ralentissant le rythme de cette revue des temps, aboutit vers la fin de la grossesse, avec une plus grande précision anatomique, aux données de l'hérédité proche. Film qui ressemble à un rêve où les désirs, les imaginations créatrices de la nature se superposent, se surimpressionnent, floues, pour arriver à la netteté dans la mise au point de la construction achevée. Ce processus se retrouve d'ailleurs identique dans toutes élaborations, qu'il s'agisse d'un être, d'une idée ou d'un acte.

Mais dès que l'embryon existe matériellement, dès sa première minute, il est assujetti à une vie propre. Son ambiance est d'abord le sang maternel qui lui prenant les choses dont il se fait. A la naissance, le contact devient direct avec les êtres et les objets. La défense, l'adaptation au milieu lui imposent une personnalité qui va s'établir en déformant plus ou moins la poussée héréditaire initiale. L'être, peut se représenter alors comme un rapport dont les deux termes sont : expériences des temps et expérience propre. Il lui faut adapter pour lui et en fonction de l'ambiance sa personne qui est déjà un conglomérat de toutes les adaptations antérieures.

Ces origines sont nécessaires à rappeler, car cet ordre dans la construction physique se retrouve dans les phénomènes psychologiques. Rien ici de bien différent. Cependant l'étude des faits psychiques est rendue plus difficile par l'existence de la conscience. Celle-ci paraît établir une barrière entre deux domaines opposés.

D'une part, l'intelligence alimentée par les apports sensoriels ou de mémoire aboutissant au jugement, à l'abstraction; d'autre part, débordant cette étroite bande éclairée, l'inconscient avec son vaste contenu dont l'exploration est primordiale. Celui-ci apparaît formé de deux parts : un inconscient viscéral, témoin de notre vie interne et un autre plus général que l'on pourrait nommer inconscient d'oubli; il est à la fois personnel et social. Essayons d'en dégager les grandes lignes.

Viscères, glandes, vaisseaux de la circulation forment un système dont les appels, les harmonies, les discordes établissent une vie végétative, base même de notre existence. De cet alambic montent les impulsions, les désirs, les besoins, les états de tristesse ou de joie, les malaises ou l'euphorie. La conscience n'est généralement pas atteinte sauf lorsque les phénomènes dépassent leurs limites habituelles, mais ces mouvements internes, facteurs de notre dynamisme, imposent aux concepts intellectuels leurs directions et leurs couleurs. Le jeu viscéral, l'équilibre des hormones déterminent absolument nos goûts, notre activité, dirigent nos efforts, forment notre noyau passionnel que l'intelligence réalise ou non en conformité avec l'ambiance. La conscience n'a d'autre but que de servir ces passions, de les habiller ou de les déformer, de les réduire dans le cadre des limites impératives du monde extérieur.

VER, REPTILE, BATRACIEN, POISSON, OISEAU, MAMMIFÈRE A CORNES, HOMME SONT SUPERPOSÉS. EN 3, MASSE VISCÉRALE, FOYER DE LA VIE, CENTRE DE L'INCONSCIENT VISCÉRAL. LES VARIATIONS DES ESPÈCES SE PORTENT SURTOUT SUR 1, 2, 3, 4.

Comme les animaux supérieurs ont une organisation viscérale assez semblable, cet inconscient est lui aussi voisin dans les diverses espèces, il est réaction psychologique de la matière vivante, inhérent à la vie, il évolue de la santé à la mort. Cependant la part individuelle n'est point négligeable du fait des susceptibilités personnelles, des formules intérieures, de l'équilibre humoral, des seuils variables de sensibilité consciente.

Il reste soumis au plus grand automatisme, par sa nature anatomique même (balancement régulateur glandulaire, structure du système nerveux végétatif). La maladie, les plus importants désor-

* Ceci peut être encore considéré comme un résumé synthétique d'une étude de morphologie physique et psychologique qui paraîtra incessamment.

1

Pierre Mabille
Opening page of 'Preface in Praise of Popular Prejudices'. The anonymous illustration is captioned: 'Worm, reptile, batracian, fish, bird, horned mammal and man are superimposed. In 3, visceral mass, hearth of life, centre of the visceral unconscious. The variations of the species bear especially on 1, 2, 3, 4.'

1 Gaston Doumergue (1863–1937) was French President from 1924 to 1931. Mabille is referring to building work at the Ouest-Ceinture railway station in Paris [trans.].

2 Among individuals, memories of the early years reappear at times of great tiredness or on the approach of death. The same thing goes for ancestral consciousness when it becomes aware of very ancient layers, which is a signal that a mode of civilisation is ending or at the very least undergoing a very deep social disturbance.

3 There are certainly several still more distant phenomena of 'heredity', which rise through the course of ages. Tendencies and forms dating from man before the historical era are currently re-emerging. Let us point out that it is not by chance that we are writing in *Minotaure*. This very word is sufficiently characteristic.

already made. It is not illusory to imagine making contact with this unconscious of the forgotten, the primal terrain of our intellectual life, by contemplating its successive appearances.

The means for reaching it lie in the analysis of time periods and heredity. There is no question here of entering into long considerations about these subjects. Yet one can, it seems, furnish a brief idea of this analysis. Let's say first of all that heredity is closely linked with the notion of cyclical concordances. The scale on which hereditary phenomena are today studied (for instance through Mendelian observations) is too short. Let's also discern the existence of all the intermediary points among survivals and reappearances (some continually inflected positively or negatively, others tracing a sinusoidal appearance), because nothing which might reappear completely disappears. When we speak of emergence, we are still the victim of appearances. It would be better to speak of flowering, an impulse of activity on a dormant foundation and reduced to being no more than an outline, in other words almost a forgotten memory.

Survivals are superstitions, customs, habits and practices. Superstition of the 'super-stare', what remains after forgetting, that which lingers. These are gestures or judgements whose meaning has become diverted and which subsist. We live in the midst of a great number of such survivals. Foundation ceremonies, for example. When Gaston Doumergue, equipped with a small silver trowel, inaugurated the Ouest-Ceinture[1] works and set the first stone by adding a new ten-franc coin to the mortar, he was performing an act he would not have been able to legitimate. He was following social instinct. In reality, he was continuing those founding ceremonies using the placing of objects (tablets, rolls, coins) which are described in detail in the most ancient texts of Sumer and Akkad, dating from thirty centuries before our era. It is the same for baptism ceremonies using water, or white shrouds for the burial of the dead and so on... We might specify the extreme richness of customs of this order in Provence. Such are survivals, profound currents upon which all social systems and religious constructions regularly draw. A vast pool of social conservation which is only slowly augmented and hardly modified.

Still more interesting is the study of emergences or reappearances which, through their rhythms and tokens, form history – the history of the thought of individuals as well as peoples. Let us provide a few brief examples.

Today, newly flourishing philosophical systems have continued those of Plato and the neo-Pythagoreans. Some of the Greek and Alexandrian heredity again comes to life.[2] These are phenomena of distant heredity that are very difficult to isolate as physical morphological facts and that on the contrary are so apparent in the psychological realm. There is no genuine creation in modern thought of this order. These are old Greco-Asian layers which reappear after long remaining in the unconscious.[3]

Books and works of art have been left as seeds to germinate again one day, at the moment when the ancient breath surges up

4 Cornelius Agrippa (1486–1535), German magician, astrologer, and alchemist; Robert Fludd (1574–1637), English physician astrologer, mathematician, cosmologist and Rosicrucian; Paracelsus (1493–1541), Swiss physician, alchemist and astrologer; Jérôme Cardan (1501–1576), Italian mathematician, physician, astrologer and philosopher [trans.].

from the depths of beings. In the same way the forms reinvented by certain artists today – Picasso, for example – and which emerge from automatic drawings, are quite similar to ones traced in the pre-Hellenic era. From the clay of our potters rush forth inflections which, without the conscious will of their makers, are linked to those produced in the Middle East in ancient times. This long-term heredity makes the study of archaeology fascinating. It provides a fresh light on so-called mysteries. Although scholars seek the key to these phenomena in migrations and various invasions, the study of the cyclical tides of the unconscious easily allows us to understand these distant eruptions in time.

But shorter links bind ages only four or five centuries distant. We are witnessing a renewal of medieval conceptions, a re-flowering of astrology, conjectural sciences and significant attempts at synthesis; in the realm of politics attempts at international legislation, corporate tendencies and the struggle of vast semi-secret organisations bring us closer, with all these inherent differences in the change of surroundings, to the fifteenth and sixteenth centuries. The conceptions of modern physico-chemistry, mathematical reasoning and homeopathic medicine take us into the vicinity of individuals like Agrippa, Fludd, Paracelsus and Cardan.⁴ These might be called mid-term hereditary phenomena.

* * *

The immediate filiations are perceived with the greatest clarity. A close heredity joins our time with the middle-third of the nineteenth century, from about 1860 to 1880. Here Mendelian observations are rediscovered in their entirety: a re-apparition in the second or third generation of acquired characteristics. We know the link which generally unites grandparents and grandchildren while the direct filiation between father and son tends to be established as an opposition. In most cases there is a continuation with the grandparents and a defensive reaction, a change of sign with the parents.

Here stand phenomena indicated by sociologists. We know that for a new philosophical system, scientific theory or an attempt at innovation in art to become a component factor of social life, a half-century has to pass for it to be properly understood. It is generally said that people are slow to grasp their times, whatever the dissemination given to ideas or forms. There is a simple explanation for this: between creators and the mass at each moment there can be only simple contact, conversation, strictly external exchanges in which snobbery often intervenes, a purely intellectual absorption. The opposite is the case when things reappear in the generation after next which have become integral parts of individuals, digested within the unconscious; then a real dissemination and a genuine comprehension can exist. The case of Rimbaud and his surrealist filiation, that of Marxism and its social dissemination, and that of Nietzsche and fascism are sufficiently eloquent examples. The seed does not find the ground but creates it; its descendants form its soil.

These appearances naturally do not all have the same characteristics. The eruptions of ancient layers have a more general and impersonal appearance. They are freed from emotional moods. These are hard and stable rocks. The more recent reappearances are still warm with love and hate; these are heterogeneous granular marls. They are especially enacted in superficial forms of thought, in fashion or upon aspects of the sensibility. What we have just considered in human hereditary experience is similarly found at the limits of life. The same cyclical alternations cause experiences drawn from various ages to emerge from the unconscious. In their mingling, all of these terrains form the moments of our thought. Forgotten reasonings from childhood, classical readings and the work of recent years re-emerge and rush into me along these lines. The aspects of these internal tides of the unconscious can thus be summarised in a brief sketch. It is also necessary to embark upon the study of the coalescence of ideas during their dormant periods, the analysis of conditions which result in concepts plunging into the unconscious, the ripening which they then undergo and the factors by which they emerge into the light. It is impossible to attempt this in the framework of such a brief study. Let's limit ourselves to noting the attitude of the intelligence in relation to this double unconscious. We have already remarked that it is the plaything of visceral impulses: intelligence has no other aim than to obey these internal tendencies within the limits imposed by the laws of the external world. We clothe our needs and our desires in rationalisations and pretexts. Our lucid mechanism is destined to organise the search, ingeniously to develop the means of satisfying hunger.

As for the unconscious of forgetting, it is what resolves problems and takes care of creations. In it, solutions and discoveries are made. Thanks to it, the child reinvents his science. Our rational self, with the considerable pride that is its signature, takes on all of this work on its behalf. It swaggers about in this slow construction as though it was its creative agent. Generally by its stupidity, its deformed optic, its fear of the new and its desire to understand straightaway, it closes the door on these profound eruptions. By means of control, it becomes an inhibitor. Only true poets and artists allow the fire to surge up from the submarine depths within them. They lend themselves like tools, with pen and ink, to the internal dictation. They bring to what we call inspiration only the exertion of a technique or profession, necessary for fixation or assembling. Often they are even so far outside the phenomenon that they are unable to understand the precise meaning or significance of what escapes from them; they cannot follow the words which flow from their mouths. These successes assume a certain aptitude for automatism, a great sincerity, and an evident good will. In the social order, the individuals who become vectors of such facts assume an appearance of prophets and become symbols. During human stirring, the fire always finds a way out through certain beings who are involuntarily prepared for it. Such is the significance of poets and a few people. Such is the importance of the unconscious content of peoples and individuals.

André Masson
Mannequin at the International
Surrealism Exhibition in Paris,
1938. Photograph by Denise
Bellon

René Crevel
The Noble Mannequin Seeks and Finds her Skin

The surrealists had a particular fascination for mannequins, something which culminated in the famous street of mannequins made for the 1938 International Surrealist Exhibition in Paris. In this complex poetic text, Crevel draws out some of this fascination as he explores the shifting senses between living and dead matter, between seduction and indifference in these creatures fashioned, Pygmalion-like, to satisfy a desire for our own simulacrum. The demiurgic compulsion by which we create mannequins symbolises at once our freedom and our enslavement, something which Crevel explores here with subtle humour.

First published in *Minotaure*, no.5, February 1934; reprinted in René Crevel, *L'Esprit contre la raison*, Paris: Jean-Jacques Pauvert, 1986.

Looks shaped as shops, looks, intended not at all to see but to be seen, nothing but fragilities or confessions, even in your most opulent impudence.

No matter what their Jupiter does, these facades whose six, eight, ten, twenty, thirty, forty, fifty or sixty storeys crown the glances of the ground floor, no invulnerable Minerva is about to give birth to the marble's ambitions or the brick's neuralgia. On the contrary, the most mineral architecture, from the first incision, admits architectures halfway between the vegetable and the animal, halfway between what withers and what bleeds. In the tiniest details of a naivety as well as in the most resounding apotheosis of an eye-catching exhibitionism, the intrigues of the fabrics (wool which drapes itself, silk which flaunts itself, over-ornate linen with flirtatious curls) don't take long to make themselves more transparent than the windows protecting them. With a thousand twists and turns, the invertebrate sets out to fascinate what will allow it to take shape. Department stores, especially during sales of household linen, are showrooms of skin, miles of skin offered up to the Noble Mannequin's desires.

The Noble Mannequin?

Of course you know her, the Noble Mannequin, with her violet-sapped and violent iris, too violet and too violent to accept the shopkeeper hypocrisy set out on display everywhere with its crimson lies, faded cunning and velvety perfidy. Other gardens are needed than these flowerbeds whose hypocrisy claims to stem the rise of the avenues that are the most, the best committed to space. She is too untamed to resign herself to roles of pure display and attitudes with no resonance. The exploiters wanted to condemn her to imprisonment. The frost of a shop window, the angry affectations of the facades vainly tried to stop her impulsion.

Have they helmeted and armoured her into insensibility? Old fur nevertheless becomes a forest of papillae roused at the first stroke of her fingers. Rasping silk murmurs tenderly on her breast.

Old rags find their lost youth and life at her approach. They begin singing in every colour.

On sordid street corners, at the crossroads of European misery, she disports an African majesty and no skirt could ever hinder her long stride. With all of her radiance she calls to her lovers, her brothers and the dark-skinned men whom the hounds of the capital gnaw down to the bone. She leaps above the traps and fierceness of irony. She has been bundled up and imprisoned in old cast-offs as if for a sinister carnival. And yet here she is, still free, a witness of time but frugal towards it, a mirror whose reflections, a cluster of glimmerings that have already blossomed into tragic, decisive, demanding thoughts, will light tomorrow up. Thus, as always, she looms up from the most everyday opacity, a bouquet of precisions, a geyser of anger, flames of the future, a sun whose sulphur fist tears apart and strangles the lepers of sentimental dawns. But in her violence she is also gentle, the Noble Mannequin, this woman who is a woman twice over since she is the daughter of feminine apparel and nudity, the Noble Mannequin, this Antigone who for finery knows how to display oedipal complexities in such carnal smiles. It is thanks to the Noble Mannequin that her fatherly fabric can live a life as full as her own body, the cylindrical body of this beauty, the one perfectly turned out, perfect, so perfect that in her peregrinations she doesn't always bother to take her head, arms and legs with her. Legs, moreover, those scissors for cutting up space, are what she bothers with least of all.

So she embodies the dream of every infant Prometheus, whose appetite recreates the maternal body all the better to gorge on it, unifies it from shoulder to ankle and turns it into a playground of happiness, embellishing it with gentle, welcoming curves, too gentle and too welcoming ever to open up even as far as a precipice. But, above all, the Noble Mannequin could never be unsexed. Deficiency and ambivalence are hardly her accomplishment. She is able to disguise herself. As Hermaphrodite she is the caricature of neither Hermes nor Aphrodite. But she is both of them when, in essentially masculine form, she unites with her opposite, with silk, in an embrace so sweetly enveloping that from the rigid ensemble and flecked material, from the mannequin and her fabric, from the fabric and its mannequin, will be born a new, dual, total reality.

It will be a synthesis, a coupling, the rustling of a love song.
* * *

Because men expect so much from her, they are awkward and shy with the Noble Mannequin. They do not know how to offer her a choice of epidermis, which she changes more often than her blouse. They try to seduce her through bombast, but bombast is always macabre. Upon the shop in which she will be the most beautiful ornament, on the eye whose pupil she will be, grows an eyelid of really funereal, dismal draperies with heavy silken tears instead of lashes. But if she appears it is spring. A ball of flowers will be her head. Her brain is both a beehive and a bouquet. She has a breast for every bodice. Honey ribbons constitute her nerves and hair, they

André Breton
Object-chest at the
International Surrealism
exhibition in Paris, 1938.
Ubu Gallery, New York and
Galerie Berinson, Berlin

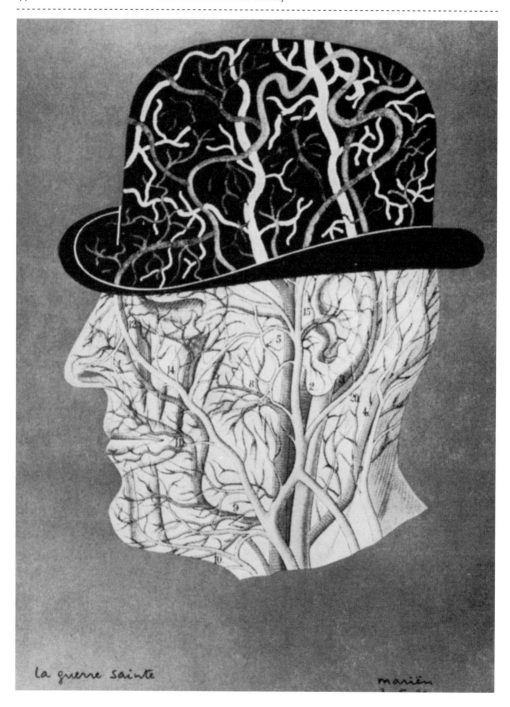

la guerre sainte

Marcel Mariën
The Holy War, reproduced in *Les
Lèvres nues*, no.9 (new series),
April 1974

dance upon her brains of small chattering leaves before descending in waves to the waist they encircle.

The Greek columns no longer know what to do with the daughters of the Parthenon. The haughtiest vestiges of antiquity are only too happy to attach themselves to her slightest whim. They enter the dance. A theatre right on the street opens for very strange ballets in which the shadow dares no longer to move, for the shadow listens to the song of silence.

The Noble Mannequin in the guise of a love song. But this love song won't become a standard. She knows how to come out of herself, like those seals (those seals worthy of being her animal familiars for she has their plenitude) which, according to the author of an ancient bestiary, can be dismembered by making a deep incision in the lower back; then, torturing and terrifying them until, in their precipitate flight, their bare and bloody muscles emerge from their oily skins.

The Noble Mannequin, the Orpheus of new skins of the skeleton, draws in her wake all the garments she had in turn inhabited. Bouquets of youthful walks. She is followed by what loves her. The rest dies. The shop windows become cemeteries, are littered with tombstones. Puddles of uselessness fall from vases of lamentation.

* * *

The Noble Mannequin in her charming little interior. She is not made for the ivory tower. Narcissism and the orchestration of egocentric niceties will soon take her out of herself.

But no one ever knows where they are with such a creature. She has already turned her back on her double and, on the threshold of night, has gone off, flying away.

At twilight, in vain does an iron curtain fall between her and the stroller, imprisoning her and condemning her to solitude. A lowering of the eyelid doesn't abolish the universe but on the contrary ripens with its sombre heat all the phosphorus scattered in the iris of love.

On the globe of the eye slips the Noble Mannequin in a Milky Way dress. Her antennae and her dreams will carry her straight to man's innermost secret.

Paul Nougé
The Light, the Shadow and the Prey

Paul Nougé engages more specifically with the idea of the subject as he further undermines the notion of a unified self in this essay. By refusing to accept the given in all of its forms, he cuts away the ground from under us by challenging our most obvious perceptions and assumptions about the true nature of the object, which he asserts only exists as an invention formed by the actions of our minds. It is thus different for each person who observes it. This sort of interrogation was especially characteristic of Belgian surrealism (think of Magritte's paintings, of which Nougé was one of the first champions). As we always find in surrealist work, the principle of identity is placed under assault as the world is shown to be a construction that is both unstable and deceptive. Nougé's text is also an unusual contribution to the surrealist discourse about the 'object' that reached a peak in the 1930s.

Written in 1930. First published in Paul Nougé, *Histoire de ne pas rire*, Brussels: Éditions de la revue Les Lèvres nues, 1956; reprinted Lausanne: L'Age de l'Homme, 1980.

It really seems that the familiar opposition between the object and the subject knows no limits. And in fact when it comes to objects, so handy and obvious, it would be difficult to think that the agreement made by common sense might be faulted. We don't find it easy to conceive that a cup for one of us might be anything other than a cup, a spoon a spoon, and so on. We move imperceptibly to more complex and less graspable things: an animal, a city, a given idea or reasoning. And when disagreement suddenly arises, explanations are offered almost as quickly as the accident they explain. The words used are abstraction, error, ignorance or subjectivity.

These opinions have a common foundation, namely that if the object escapes us it is due to negligence, ignorance or distraction. But it no less remains that this object is still the link in a defined and definable ensemble of qualities and properties on whose subject a little application would unfailingly reveal nothing but them, regardless of who enters into contact with it. We submit to the object and in the end we all need to submit to it in the same way. Any difference can boil down to how acute our observation is.

The scholar will here lend his support to the man of good sense.

The man of good sense will judge that mercury is a very heavy and shiny liquid. The man of science will only acquiesce before adding that it is *also* a good conductor of heat and electricity and that unlike most liquids it does not moisten glass... But the man of good sense who considers blood to be a red, warm, precious and terrible liquid will be amazed if the scientist considers it to be nothing but a circulating tissue which differs from muscular or bony tissue only by the mechanical independence of its constitutive cells. The sun is thus not the centre of the universe but a star like the most distant and least bright of those our eyes are able to see. And the woman who three men meet is for one of them the mother of his children, for the second an object of pleasure and for the last a receptacle of a mystery whose key he seeks through every form of the world and of himself.

Then, whatever the care the man of good sense takes to observe blood, even with the aid of a microscope, he will be unable to draw from it the image of a tissue in the way he would if he understood it as being a form of muscular flesh. The mother of the family will not be confused with the mistress tending to certain physical pleasures, and neither of them with the Muse and the Madonna.

Thus what appear to be the best-defined objects lose the identity which appeared inherent to them if one passes from one subject to another, and each of them is resolved in a series of actually irreconcilable objects. Or more accurately, they lose that quality of object that common sense discerned in them.

There is no longer an object, even the most basic one.

But here a difficulty arises which results from this observation: that however there would be something ridiculous and very dangerous in denying the external world, no matter what philosophers think.

And in fact, by responding to some vital necessity of our collective life, we save the object.

It could be pointed out that the distance between the mother of the family and the deft mistress is not so great, and that there is no great danger in speaking about a woman.

The existence of the object is therefore saved thanks to a compromise – a continually threatened compromise which results by some common feature of our particular inventions solely from coincidence.

Moreover, failures alert us to the nature of this compromise: the circulating tissue exists for the profane only thanks to a change, an adoption of the movement of the mind which is no longer that of someone profane and which allows him to *conceive* of blood in this way.

Thus the true nature of the object appears: it owes its existence to the action of our mind which invents it.

The *reality* of an object will depend firmly on the attributes our imagination has endowed it with; on the number and complexity of these attributes; and on the way in which the invented complex is inscribed in all that is pre-existing within us and exists in the minds of those like us.

Ordinary logical abstraction is habitually the fruit of a feeble imagination. There is little possibility of the abstract object being thrown out of the whole into which one has tried to integrate it. But its power over this whole will be feeble. It is endowed only with a paucity of *reality*. The sphere has less reality than the head.

It can still be noticed that the more powerful the reality of an object is, the more this reality has succeeded. Equally there are greater possibilities to be able to extend, enrich or upset it through a new invention, to draw a new reality from it.

Here one touches upon one of the reasons to trust poetic as well as scientific activity, both of which, by different paths, are applied to the invention of new objects.

We'll add that it is the success of objective invention that usually misleads us about the true nature of the object and that it is from an impressive assortment of successes that the most ordinary forms of the world resulting from the error made by common sense when it defines the object as having an actual existence, identical with itself and perfectly independent of the subject which invents and maintains it, is constituted.

But the mechanism of *objective success* deserves consideration.

We can conceive that every moment the world is offering us a collection of complex facts (sensations, feelings and so on). Thanks to constancy or the frequent reappearance of certain groups which within this collection *stand out* in some way we can conceive of ways we might accentuate these features to the point of finally being able to detach them from the whole. And so objects are born. But for them to subsist, the cut and accentuation needs to have been done *cleverly* so that the successive states we subsequently undergo do not conflict with the result of our invention. There is in this sense a whole series of degrees in objectivity and reality, whether of the cup or hand, or of God or of ghosts.

Scholars furnish us with a proposition which can become a favourable image of the invention of objects. They admit that Nature might be deceived about the genesis of animal species or more generally about living beings: which is where monsters, whose reality is annulled by their incompatibility with the group in which they try to insert themselves, come from. But their disappearance is so perfect that we are unable to doubt it and so believe in the infallibility of the process which engenders life in the world. Inventing species as variable and capable of evolution sufficed to alert us to nature's errors and failures – which especially illuminate certain failures of the mind when applied to the invention of reality.

A man uses chalk to draw a chicken on a wall. He gives it four feet. We laugh. He becomes angry until he discovers his mistake. He is a man of average faculties for whom a chicken is a familiar animal. But his familiarity with this object was still not enough to prevent him at a certain moment from adding two extra feet to it. Those who laughed obviously invented the bird in such a way that this proposition seemed unacceptable. But some of them would perhaps not have objected had he omitted the wings or given it two eyes on the same side of its head.

This anecdote could be compared with certain testimonies, and not only those which are said to arise from fable (sea serpents, siren, and so on) but from the most ordinary description of familiar objects, such as false recognition, divergent accounts of an event and so on. (We are so made that we *perceive* objects, in other words the sensation that we take from them and that can, for ease of discourse, be considered a means of passive reception; this sensation immediately becomes the object of a spiritual operation, of an *act* of our mind which gives a *meaning* to the object. The way we use words thus extends to all objects liable to affect our mind. Let's note in passing that here once again the characteristic feature of the mind, which is action, appears. The notion of mind and that of passivity are absolutely incompatible.)

And so here is an iron bar. For the judge, it is an instrument of crime; for the miner, a pickaxe; for the chemist, an ingot, and so on. Or at least it tends to be. Therefore we speak of professional 'distortion'. It is a way we have of evading the problem, or of reducing it. In fact, only one solution is admitted, which is that the object with the maximum of reality borrows the features of the one who experiences it, who thinks about it and invents it, according to the usual inclination of his mind.

Our negligence and the coarseness of the approximations with which our current life contents itself mean that our collaboration with the object ordinarily goes unnoticed.

One consequence of this state of things is that the fundamental principle of classical logic, the principle of identity, has only a *subjective* value, and here once more no great attentiveness is needed to wrong-foot it at each moment.

Pierre Mabille
Mirrors

This key essay, an influence on (as well as being influenced by) Jacques Lacan as he was developing his notion of the mirror stage, represents a further elaboration of Mabille's studies of human development, which he tenaciously refuses to consider apart from general ideas of development – even while differentiating it in terms of the relation we establish with mirrors as uncanny reflections of ourselves. Perhaps himself influenced by Otto Rank's pioneering study of the double, Mabille is less concerned than Lacan with the internal constitution of the ego and more with the mystery of that constitution as it has to divide itself in order to find itself, creating a double that materially has no relation to itself and yet is an integral part of its own perception of itself, to the extent that it is unable actually to perceive itself without the use of this reflection. The dialectic between 'self' and 'image' is thereby characterised, in typical surrealist terms, as central not simply to human becoming, but also as an aspect of phenomena itself, something which would become a major surrealist theme and provide the starting point for Mabille's later more extensive exploration of the 'marvellous' as something that is as much contained within being as coming to it from outside.

First published in *Minotaure*, no.11, Spring 1938; reprinted in Pierre Mabille, *Messages de l'étranger*, Paris: Plasma, 1981.

Mirrors, in the mystery of their polished surfaces resembling solid still waters, call up fundamental problems: the identity of the self and the characteristics of reality.

Facing the mirror, the animal has no conception of a virtual image, still less of its reflection. It sees a new arrival, immediately solicited to play with or to fight. Animal confidence in the senses is such that the hypothesis of an illusion never crosses its mind. Crashing against the glass amazes it and commits it to a prudent restraint.[5]

The child spontaneously acts in the same way. However, the particular construction of humans, the teaching of adults, the multiplication of experiences allow the child to overcome the initial confusion. Habit creates solid associations by which the projected image is recognised as our own. This association, essential for the

5 I am very grateful to Serge Roche, the well-known mirror dealer, for having given me some very interesting documents for this study. He recounted the following anecdote to me: an alley cat he had found when it was very young lived in his flat, which was well furnished with mirrors: the cat played endlessly with its image. When it was taken to the countryside, it caught sight of a stretch of very calm water in which it was reflected. As usual, it leaped at it, habituation having overcome the instinctive fear of water, which it did not recognise. Fortunately the water was not very deep; the animal escaped but, ashamed of itself, vanished forever.

6 This feeling is very individual. M.G., one of my friends, is often surprised when he observes the features of his father or his grandfather in the mirror, rapidly superimposed over his own personal image. The recognition of the self of this man is not completely lost, but is confused with a domestic relation.

mind, is nevertheless susceptible to alteration. There is no need to seek rare examples from pathology. Who among us, when we are tired or in an emotional state, has not been seized with a fleeting dread when noticing his features in a mirror that have become suddenly unknown, disturbing or absurd?[6] Habit being the only factor in our recognition, certain less common images more easily engender disturbance; those of our profiles are of this order. When I arrived in Paris as a young man, I recall my panic faced with the play of mirrors in department stores and hotels. Even today I still at times experience some disturbance between the tailor's arrayed mirrors. Such sensations indicate how painstaking the assumption of an awareness of the self is and how subject it is to the possibilities of regression.

On this primordial question, no help can be expected from classical teachings. On the contrary, traditional belief in an eternal soul inhabiting our perishable body conceived the self as emanating from a mental reality that has been definitively established even prior to birth. The idea of the progressive constitution of the being is relatively recent: it has followed separately the developments either of physics or of morality without perceiving the totality of human evolution. Mirrors, by revealing our person to consciousness, impel us towards an understanding of the stages of its construction.

* * *

The cutting of the umbilical cord in theory makes the child an independent organism. In practice, the independence is for a long time relative and the internal unity is very fragile. Regulatory mechanisms need to develop in the internal functions, they must become combined together before one might speak of an organic 'self', of a genuinely autonomous system of a personal life. Let's not say that this notion of physiological unity constitutes a speculative interpretation: balanced coherent activity, in the alternating rhythms of each part of our person in relation to the whole, is enough to prove the fact.

Yet this 'self' which lives does not yet know itself, or does so only in a very poor way. The perception of the intimate movements of the flesh has been called 'coenaesthesia'. This power exists, although in ordinary circumstances the majority of the phenomena remain non-conscious. In this respect it is useful to recall that if the unconscious corresponds to a realm of psychology, it is above all constituted by the forces in motion in our organism.

Mental development progresses to the extent that cohesion develops in the body. The activity of the five senses is the craftsman responsible for it. Each fortifies itself and the sensations received are associated together: the two coordinates of thought are simultaneous liaisons at each moment and a slow and successive stratification allowed by the memory. Psychic elements serve first of all to orient gestures and allow the satisfaction of needs.

Among the thousands of actions, the person soon perceives itself as the essential axis of all experience. The confused sensation of existing becomes a clear consciousness when it is translated into representations. But these result from sensorial images and by

Raoul Ubac
Untitled photograph
reproduced in Mabille's article

7 See the notes to my *La Conscience lumineuse*, Paris, Editions Skira, 1938 [reprinted in Pierre Mabille, *Conscience lumineuse conscience picturale*, ed. Jacqueline Chénieux-Gendron and Rémy Laville, Paris: José Corti, 1989 – trans.].

orientation; the senses are all directed towards the outside, towards the exploration of the external world.

The person clumsily applies such arms to knowledge of its person. It must link the diffuse internal coenaesthetic perceptions with clear sensorial perceptions received by its periphery. In this way a whole system of judgements is constructed, understanding a kind of dialectical play through judgement, a weighing up of two forces of the same order, but in opposite directions. This confrontation ends in an effect that for a long time is uncertain: the child readily situates its thought and dreams externally to itself and inversely endows the universe with voluntary and emotional aptitudes that are analogous to its own. A sort of frontier is imperfectly set up between the being and its environment; the psychological elements are all arranged in the functioning of an organic self as a centred building.

Each sense plays its particular role in the conquest of knowledge. Touch limits the individual and situates his movements in the certainty of space. The ear distinguishes between sounds emitted by us and transmitted through the bones, and sounds that are carried by the air. Thanks to this primitive experience, the child assimilates its thought over a long period into an internal voice. I have elsewhere insisted how sight furnishes[7] the fundamental elements of consciousness and poses the problems in which we will encounter the role of mirrors.

Without artificial assistance, we can perceive only a part of our bodies: our limbs and the front part of the trunk. This suffices to assure us that we are similar to other people. It allows for an effective management of our actions. Yet if we desire a complete representation of our person, we have to imagine it through the impressions of others. Similarly, the child sets great store in what those around it tell it about itself. It soon learns that these testimonies are fragile, and wants to have direct information. It needs to question the shadow it projects onto the ground and better still the image transmitted by a mirror.

There is no more curious a spectacle than that of someone in front of their mirror. From one angle, a living 'self' turns the warm, tense, shifting core, on which the multiple recorded sensorial experiences are cast, into a 'self', whose development we have already briefly noted – one which is ready to act, suffer, rejoice, and which constitutes its goal and extent. From the other angle, at an equal distance, perceived in a virtual space, is an individual we are able to examine externally as anyone else could. It is necessary for us to retain our distinctive signs contingent on the usual criteria of the race so we can recognise it.

I see among others this fellow who smiles when I contract a muscle, who becomes pale when I am sick, and habit assures me that he externalises my 'self'. I imbue him with the coherent whole I am; inversely, I make him participate in my life. In this exchange, consciousness of my being has been acquired. This duality corresponds well enough with the elements Freud isolated as the 'self' and the 'ego'. All reactions are possible between the two aspects of the person whose relative importance varies. The innumerable variety of individual psychologies is inscribed here. Sometimes the 'self' dominates with its spontaneity and the representative system is not very well developed, but sometimes, on the contrary, the external social image commands the stage. Such people are busy watching themselves live, concerned about their image. Civilisation, which tends to limit spontaneity, undoubtedly augments the value of the 'self'. The quantitative importance of these two aspects of the being do not at all prejudice anything of the attitude one takes in relation to the other. The reflection may dominate but be disturbing (one avoids mirrors) or loved (one multiplies the representations and displays), but whatever the particularities of each individual problem, the work of consciousness consists in resolving the duality of the 'self' and the 'ego' and seeking their unity beyond this conflict.

* * *

Mirrors, which have such importance in the psychological constitution, have become simple ornaments for our homes. The significance of this preference calls for investigation. In the seventeenth century in the west there was a taste for rooms entirely decorated with mirrors. In the Versailles of Louis XIV, a man who declared himself made in the image of God, from whom he claimed to hold his delegation of power, was unable to accept the boundary of walls. They had to reflect his features in a way that courtesans would later imitate. Equally, in gardens where nature had been rigorously pruned, mirrors of water reflected the man and his palace. This desire to demonstrate his power, and continuously assure himself of it, belongs to all civilisations. Imperial Rome also had palaces with polished walls and reflective surfaces.

The fashion for rooms made of mirrors spread throughout the eighteenth century in the country houses of Germany, Italy, Spain and Portugal, along with the taste for creating echoes in parks. These investigations were attached to the efflorescence of the Baroque. Romanticism soon transformed the need to see oneself, to look at oneself, into a systematic will to go further into introspection. The desire was to penetrate the image and reach the core of sorrows and dreams. At this point, poetic themes about crossing the mirror appeared.

Other houses aimed to take advantage of ornamentation by mirrors – that is, pleasure houses. But although amusement parks require an effect of surprise or sense of unfamiliarity whether by using deforming mirrors or not, brothels use them in other ways. If casual guests are seeking easy satisfaction of urgent needs, regular clients require the fulfilment of scenes that haunt their imaginations. Visual representation more or less linked to a genuine physiological exigency possesses an obsessive character. In the spectacle which unfolds, the real personality of the woman matters less than the role she consents to fill. Acting or not, the client is above all a spectator for whom the mirror is necessary. Leaving aside the whole question of deviation, it is certain that vice

8 Havelock Ellis (1859–1939), British physician and writer [trans.].

corresponds to a grave conflict between the 'id' and the 'ego', together with an overestimation of the image in relation to the need.

* * *

Among these phenomena, one which is recounted in the myth of Narcissus is particularly important. This ancient poetic theme has recently become the subject of detailed study. As a doctor, Havelock Ellis[8] first signalled an auto-erotic syndrome based on rather exceptional observations. Freud soon seized upon the idea of narcissism as a normal stage in the development of the person. According to him, a person orients his love towards two objects: himself and an individual of the opposite sex (generally the mother). But the question was also extended so that under this subject would be arranged various forms of egoism and even the instinct for self-preservation. In truth, by starting with the analysis of sexual preoccupations we have found this double perceptive current everywhere. One element is centripetal, leading towards the individual, personalising, isolating and crystallising it; the other, centrifugal, tending to dissolve it, diluting its being as much in its own terms as in its representations. No doubt narcissism finds its place in the alternating movement, but is this the meaning of the Greek legend?

Certainly, any genuine myth lends itself to endless interpretations and a botanical interpretation could even be made of this one without being apparently ridiculous. Personally I see the Narcissus story as an edifying apologue. It seems to be close to some Asiatic narratives, in particular those of the conquest of forbidden fruits in a paradisiacal garden. Let's recall the details. The son of a nymph, Narcissus is a fine specimen of youth in all its vigour. A horoscope predicts a long life and happiness for him on condition that he does not see himself. He is told to live spontaneously, like a fine animal. But this happiness is not accepted. The advances of the nymph Echo - this distant reflection of a being among the fields and forests - are repelled. Nemesis, the justice bringer, the guardian of the universal equilibrium, then punishes the unresponsive man, who sees his own image in a pool and falls in love with it. The intoxicating flower which provokes dizziness is evoked by the torpor into which the young man has fallen. His spirit lost, he drowns. Is this a case of sterile auto-eroticism, a vigour expended in vain, or might it not rather be the drama of human thought turned away from any external goal, letting itself be ensnared by the dizzy circle of gratuitous intellectualism which imagines itself to be its own object and end? The Greek, who loves above everything else a fulfilling life, stigmatises through this amorous theme not meditation but the dangerous self-absorption of the individual in himself. The disapproval extends right to the category of spoiled youth who, shielded from the needs of everyday struggle, become blasé and are interested in nothing more than lovingly contemplating their own person. I understand the Narcissus myth as an attempted trial against certain vain paths of the intelligence, against certain propensities for self-psychoanalysis.

Raoul Ubac
Untitled photograph
reproduced in Mabille's article

* * *

If, due to habit, we manage to recognise our reflection in the mirror, it no less remains that this image constitutes a mystery whose explanation we seek. What is this second person who suddenly appears at the same time as ourselves? We readily constitute it as a double in which we impart all the hopes of which reality deprives us. We wish to be eternal, weightless, invulnerable, always vigilant. The double will become these things for us. It becomes an improved, idealised representation of the 'ego'. It has taken centuries for people to be able to relate to themselves the image that seemed external, so they could incorporate it in their person.

In Egypt, being was apparently composed of five relatively independent parts: the perishable and tangible body; the bird soul (breath, which returns after death to the totality of collective life); the image (or Ka), the double enclosed in the portrait or the statue; the shadow, which follows the contours of the body and remains attached to the mummy; and finally, the name, which contains the person's essence.

On the shores of the Mediterranean, many customs and beliefs prove how vivid the idea of the autonomous reality of the image has remained. In places, it is forbidden to allow oneself to be painted or photographed – a precept inscribed in Koranic law. In others, there is the fear that the shadow could be threatened through some evil spell, by the steps of a stranger. The mirror in which we see ourselves is thought to contain an image; if it is broken, death will follow.

Actually, only a concern for simplification causes us to associate shadow and image. The confusion is never entirely complete. The shadow is a less intellectual notion; it is like the destiny of a body whose matter could be rarefied but which could submit to an inverse transformation (the Realm of Shadows for the Realm of the Dead, Elysium, various apparitions, ectoplasms, spirits). In contrast, the image contains an element of consciousness. For Platonists it becomes a sort of model, or matrix, for creation.

Christianity has tried to reduce these various components of humanity into a play of body and immaterial soul, in which ancient fragments (guardian angels, demons and so on) remain. But it has striven less to describe or to explain than to moralise. Its aim was to replace the individual image with a representation valid for all: the figure of Christ contained in each person and capable of becoming a collective model.

These systems elaborated by people do not have merely historical interest. Their multiplicity proves that the conflict of 'id' and 'ego' has over the course of the ages undergone numerous transformations. Consequently the oppositions, the current dualisms, the internal contradictions do not have any definitive character.

* * *

To endow the double with autonomy and glorious virtues would render the desire to demonstrate it imperious. From the beginning, people have sought to follow the contours of the shadow, to capture the reflection, to represent things and people. Thus art and magic were born together. The magical act assumes the substitution of the simulacrum for the person. It aims to submit the simulacrum to what one could not or would not dare to make the person do. Obstacles that stem from the distance in time and space, or from society, fade away as soon as one possesses the appropriate – in other words, the consecrated –representation and the ability to act upon it. Besides, the magician's ambition is to discover the name and image of natural forces whose presence in the universe appears evident to him (as Gods or demigods of rivers, places or the sky), but that the senses cannot reach. There is no superfluous curiosity in this, only the hope of an increased human power. The principle remains the same: to possess the representation, to act on it so as to rule over phenomena.

Since the mirror is capable of furnishing the image of the things one sees, it must also be capable of giving the image of things that are ordinarily invisible.

To obtain these exceptional representations, precautions and rituals are thought to be necessary. Various mirrors are therefore made using metals carefully chosen for their particular qualities. This is undertaken at astrologically propitious times: ceremonies are executed in the course of which the spirits of the dead or the absent, the greater powers of the world, whether friendly or hostile, are invoked. Today's experiments with crystal balls by clairvoyants correspond to the remnants of these ancient practices. No doubt the results obtained in such circumstances accord with an externalisation of the content of the unconscious. This modern explanation, if it has to be accepted to the exclusion of any other, brings clarity to the mechanism of data. However, it must be admitted that the mystery remains, for to extend the powers of the unconscious indefinitely only postpones the problem. In these magical preoccupations, whether they assume an official (that is, a religious)or a private, more or less occult form, the skill of the artist is sought. This individual is asked, outside any other decorative or aesthetic consideration, to be the true mirror which conserves the image. The practitioner must represent beings and things because in this way they will escape the threat of time. These representations should be traced with the maximum of character, associating them with emblems and symbols. Replacing the conjuring mirror, painters must be able to make the features of mythical characters, or those of divinities, perceptible to the masses. They must follow the indications given by ritual and tradition. Under these conditions, they can draw upon their own imagination. Freedom of expression is therefore limited, and only a margin of variety and deformation rendered necessary by perspective, taste and the personal sensibility of each craftsman is admitted.

Art, freed from these preoccupations, having become profane, is liberated. However, the artist continues to regard his representation as participating in reality, as being part of the reality which could be taken away. Devoting his life to making simulacra, he believes in their value.

Yet the public very strongly retains the old notion of the magic utility of art. Successive waves of iconoclasts have vainly swooped down on the world, in Byzantium, in Rome, with the adepts of Savonarola, then the Reformers; nothing succeeded. The first Christians mocked the pagan cult for idols – yet a few years later their basilicas were full of them. The habit of recognising oneself in one's personal image means that man spontaneously believes in the value of all representations. The great modern innovation comes from the way mechanical processes have made possible the automatic representation of things, so that the artist is freed from the social necessity by which he finds himself being a kind of common mirror. He can evoke emotions that are his alone, reproduce images which exist only in his head, such as dream visions. The abandonment of the object and the lack of concern for resemblance are regarded by the public with incomprehension and terror. The usual mission of art seems to have been betrayed. But there is more: considering the artist as traditionally charged with evoking and describing the world, with making it tangible, the spectator fears that, faced with contemporary efforts, the new living mirrors might reveal to him a universe different from that in which classical systems of thought enclosed it. He is afraid of testimonies which might bring everything into question.

* * *

The mirror being, as I have shown, the principal means of becoming aware of the 'self', causes us, because of this very fact, to worry about the true nature of reality. In fact, the phenomenon of reflection on polished surfaces constitutes the first example of an illusion – in other words, of a situation in which meanings are caught red-handed in error, where doubt can be born.

The glass deceives us by offering us an external reflection of our person that is ungraspable and is moreover reversed, while we feel we are within this character.

Likewise, as soon as it is a question of a secure or doubtful thing that may or may not be real, people think of the mirror as the creator of both consciousness and illusion. I regret not being able to analyse here the astonishing allegory that traditionally represents truth in the form of a naked woman climbing out of a well and holding a mirror in her hand. I would suggest that if we were to see this mirror as being held by a man unable to make use of it, we would have the precise symbol of philosophy.

After mystics, magicians and artists overestimated the value of the image and endowed each being with a double, philosophers, for their part, have insisted on the virtual and immaterial character of reflections. They finally had the possibility of easily constructing a realm in which nothing mattered and where descriptive contemplation alone was admitted. Arguing for the duality of the thing and its image, a crude duality however, they have constructed two universes, one of which would be the appearance of the other.

Sometimes tangible objects alone are equipped with existence and our mental representations are considered to be reflections without true reality: they are superstructures made of smoke. Sometimes, on the contrary, the external world is denied, to the benefit of psychological materials: swept along by logic, it ends up being said that the experimental and perceptible universe is only a momentary reflection of the grandiose and definitive thoughts of a divine central brain. We find the fundamental problem of the mirror in all of these theses which constitute the whole philosophical monument, whether they have remained simple or been rendered complicated, as well as in the inadequate conclusions drawn from the mirror's use. We see reappearing in these systems the transcended conflict of the 'id' and 'ego', which seeks to resolve itself by any means.

These debates would have little importance if they did not contribute, by fallacious reasoning, to accentuating a merely apparent duality in the world and in people. They are dangerous because they generally end up destroying hope. In fact the land of the marvellous is always to be found situated on the other side of the mirror and relegated to a virtual domain. I say it is time to put an end to the intolerable exploitation imposed upon phenomena of optical reflection. It is urgent to proclaim that Mystery and the Marvellous are not outside but within things and within beings, both transforming themselves at each moment, united as they are by unbroken links.

Behind the flat surface of the lake are not illusory poplar trees, but the intense life of the waters. Behind the mirror is the metal with its properties. And if it is possible to compare our mind with this mirror, its silvering is constituted by the red streak of desire. In any case, in this strange device the alternation of images, far from being gratuitous, marks out the first phase of the transformation of the universe.

Marcel Mariën
Non-Scientific Treatise on the Fourth Dimension

In this essay Marcel Mariën places a distinctively surrealist spin on then fashionable notions of the fourth dimension. Like the other writers in this section he seeks to undermine the idea that identity is constitutive of a fixed self. Not only does any *thing* have reality only in relation to other things, it also has a fourth dimension which is elsewhere and can never be seen or touched. The self exists only 'in the mind', but this 'mind' or 'spirit' is only partly present, since it is also part of the inaccessible fourth dimension.

Jean Benoît
*Costumes for 'The Execution of
the Testament of the Marquis de
Sade'* 1959
Photographs by Radovan Ivšić

This text was to have been published in a projected special issue devoted to the object by the group La Main à Plume in Paris in 1944. It has subsequently been published in Anne Verney and Richard Walter (eds.), *La Main à plume: anthologie du surréalisme sous l'occupation*, Paris: Syllepse, 2008.

Every object, thing and body has four dimensions. A pear, a house or a woman have their height, width, depth and i*mage* (or *surface*).

Therefore the eye always perceives only the fourth, the image-dimension, which is also mind, thought, dream, memory and that of which we speak.

The hand which holds a pear, the door-latch or another hand perceives a surface (flat or curved, no matter). It can perceive two surfaces, or several surfaces (holding faceted glass for example), but never the volume. The thickness of the object it encloses is just as indeterminable and fleeting as the air.

What is solid is in this way concrete; what resists is invisible, always inaccessible, always imperceptible. Because if one breaks, drills, pierces, smashes or penetrates the object, one does not reach its 'interior' but, by making a void in it, creates new images, touches unknown surfaces. Touch and sight conjoined, it seems that, when we slice a pear or penetrate into the house or into a woman, the three dimensions exist, logical and verifiable. They exist, yes – but not perceptibly, since the pear is only a stain on the table, the house only a stain in the landscape, the woman only a stain in the night. A mystery thriving on limited infinity...

...for thought develops through the eye or the hand, or the mouth, but not through immediate (integral) contact, from substance to substance. The heart does not know its neighbours, the stomach and the lungs. Images and surfaces alone make thought the centre of consciousness and exception. And even in the night of love the sensation is always a memory, an image, a hope of the time to come – never raw contact with matter, a perfect fusion, an absolute mingling although, this contact being made, the mind, curious about the void, wishes to be only matter stuck to matter.

Touch cannot reach the true depth of objects any better than the eye can. The universe is hermetic to them both. If I peel the pear, or take the bark from the tree, I create a new object: for the eye a new image, for the hand a new surface, has come onto the stage. But for each it is never volume they perceive. But always surface, or diverse image, going, succeeding each other, exploring at random. Moreover, everything we know about volumes is the realm of hypotheses and legends, of the beyond-those of before birth, and after death. Where the imaginary begins as well: where it is dealt with in the content and intimate behaviour of things.

The aromas of a rose are its colour. They are a support and an accent to its image. The same goes for any aroma, perfume or pestilence. Thanks to them, spring and autumn can exist for the mind. (A tree does not necessarily lose its leaves according to the season. It can wither, or benefit from artificial heat.)

The wind is the invisible rendered concrete.

Writing, speaking or simply thinking means to prove with certainty that the fourth dimension is the spirit [*esprit*].

Geography and cosmography, as people establish them, assume a possible control of the depth, more exactly of space. Perhaps... But let us make room for doubt as well, for the steps you

take when walking only transport you from image to image, from
surface to surface. Where are the depths?

Perspective? In the mind! Time? In the mind! Me? Again in
the mind...!

The universe is a fruit which ripens on a tree of the void.
Absolute reality, the completely full and concrete, the becoming is
the forest in bloom.

The anonymity of charnel houses

Me and my skeleton (or my heart, or my brain, or my leg) are
different things, strangers to each other and unknown. But there
are communities of skeletons, of hearts, of legs, as there are
communities of the 'Self'.

Towards another and possible dimension

Sometimes suffering is spoken about (sometimes we even manage
to speak about the mind). But rather than see suffering pinned to a
cross or disguised with a poem, we would like to see it (or the mind)
wear clothes, for example, and smoke a pipe.

Movement is also a body which contains the life of everything
– bodies, things, objects. But without depth, thickness or
localisation, it eludes any dimension, and thus responds best to the
representation of a world that is at once unlimited and finite, open
and hermetic.

The train from Brussels brings me to Paris, along with the
train, its carriages and its wheels. But the same materials also
constitute the City Hall in Brussels and Notre-Dame in Paris. The
difference here is still (always!) not in the content but in the images,
in the surfaces, always in the exterior. Vesuvius does not determine
Naples: its fire resembles fire, its rocky composition that of other
mountains, Vesuvius, Naples, Paris, Brussels, so many words, not
places; images, not spaces. Each step I advance is surrounded with
chasms.

Nostalgia for ubiquity

The child who is born emerges. Growing up, he learns to leave the
bedroom or the room in which he has taken his first steps. From
the bedroom he goes out into the street. From the street into town.
In this way our life is spent perpetually going from one object *into*
another. But it thus despairs at ever 'going back'; each second
brings changes. Nothing is ever the same. The mother, once left,
is an object like any other, a table, bird or oneself.

Death is the only access to three dimensions. Still it *does
not exist*. Not being able experimentally to be either controlled or
consciously 'lived', to believe in it is a falsehood. We are only what
we experience. Undoubtedly there is somewhere a cessation of
life – my 'self' must one day be terminated and will never see
tomorrow – but of death what have we but images: hard clay paths,
coffins, undertakers, cold white masks with closed eyes? But in this,
the reality, the 'depths' are only darkness, habit, submission and
conjecture.

The differences between the dimensions are like those between different worlds and thoughts: struggle between madness and reason, the known and the unknown, you and me.

The dream is the mind's mode of activity par excellence. There, images are really images, *only images*, and conceal no space and no time. The distinction from life stems from the fact that, being the quintessence of the images of life, the visions of dream are like real stains which bite and wound.

Superficial information is here enough to animate the dream to the point that it is able deliberately to neglect the concrete and its edges, all the dead weight of that which is not authentically *valid*.

The images of dream, of the spirit, are ideal surfaces, that is to say without a reverse side, without anything 'verso'. Their depth lies in their extent, their succession and their surpassing.

Michel Leiris
The 'Caput Mortuum' or the Alchemist's Wife

This extremely disturbing essay, which seems to respond to the 'war' Georges Bataille was conducting at the time on human dignity, and an essential feature of his contribution to the journal *Documents* in which this essay was published, also takes the surrealist purging of the idea of the self to an extreme which is almost unbearable. In some ways anticipating a theme Bataille himself would later address in his essay on the complicity of executioner and victim which can be found in Part 3 of our collection, Leiris (writing long before the reality of the concentration camps made such a connection inescapable) sees such complicity as an inescapable element of our own constitution of the self, which is also essentially implicated in the erotic relation. Based on a set of photographs (only two of which are reproduced here), which are in themselves extremely disturbing, the essay asks fundamental questions about what it means to be human, or even to be alive.

First published in *Documents*, no.8, 1930; reprinted in Michel Leiris, *Zébrage*, Paris: Gallimard, 1992.

At the start of the summer of 1930 the American writer and traveller W.B. Seabrook, then staying in Toulon (where he was working on the report on the journey he had just made to Tropical Africa, living with the Yafoubas of the Ivory Coast and the Habbés of the Bandiagara region) sent me the photographs reproduced here, which show a woman wearing a leather mask designed by him and executed according to his instructions in New York. I had come to know him only recently.

I saw him for the first and only time on 12 April, in the course of a conversation of little more than an hour, in a small café situated opposite the modest hotel in which he was staying, near the Théâtre de l'Odéon.

Introducing myself to Seabrook as the writer of a review of
The Magic Island, his strange commentary on Haitian blacks, the
sorcery practices of this country and the voodoo cult (published in
Documents, no.6, 1929, pp.334–5), I was immediately fascinated by
a marvellously cordial welcome, and by the attitude and manners of
this man, very attractive in their apparent roughness, because there
seemed to be, more than anything else, a really 'human' element
about him.

The conversation quickly went beyond the boundaries of
conventions and banalities. Seabrook and myself liked black
people, and both of us were passionate about occultism (myself
from curiosity, he as a practitioner), but more especially we were
both more than a little sceptical about modern western civilisation,
and fully convinced that one of the few valuable things one could
work towards was the abolition, by any means available (mysticism,
madness, adventure, poetry, eroticism...), of the intolerable duality
established, as a consequence of our present morality, between
body and soul, matter and spirit. Nothing else was required for us
immediately to feel we were friends and (today when before long I
will have the prospect of leaving Europe, and being away for a long
time) I realised that Seabrook would be one of the rare people I
would miss during this absence, and even one of those I would miss
the most.

Towards the end of the conversation, after I had spoken
to him about a number of mystical practices among the Tibetan
ascetics (from an article by Alexandra David-Neel published in
Revue de Paris of 10 April 1930, which my friend Marcel Jouhandeau
advised me to read), Seabrook told me the following story, which
had in turn been recounted to him during his journey through
Arabia:

In a Dervish monastery, a young ascetic was particularly
noted for his piety and mystical capacities. The old monk who
directed him in his exercises, noticing his progress, summoned
him. He said something like this: 'You have come a long way along
the mystical path, but not yet to the final end, the frontier you must
still cross. You are now ready: you can, if you want, see *the face of
God.*' He then advised the young man to spend the night in a ruined
mosque situated some distance from the convent, to recite certain
prayers and effect certain rituals: he would be certain to see the face
of God. Violently disturbed, the young ascetic refused. Each day the
old monk hounded him, the young man always replying that he was
not worthy, and not concealing the sacred horror with which the
idea of finding himself face to face with God inspired in him. By
force of his insistence, the old man finally overcame this resistance
and the young monk went to the mosque.

The next day, not seeing his disciple return, the old monk
went looking for him and, having finally found him, saw that he
was pallid, frighteningly haggard and ravaged.

When the old man asked him if he had gone to the mosque
and done properly all that had been prescribed, the disciple replied,
'Yes.' To another question, namely if he had seen the face of God,

LE " CAPUT MORTUUM " OU LA FEMME DE L'ALCHIMISTE

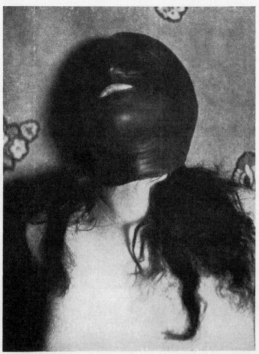

Photo W. B. Seabrook

MASQUE DE CUIR CONÇU PAR W. SEABROOK.

Lorsque, au début de l'été 1930, l'écrivain et voyageur américain W. B. Seabrook, séjournant alors à Toulon (où il travaillait à la relation du voyage qu'il venait d'effectuer en Afrique tropicale, vivant avec les Yafoubas de la Côte d'Ivoire et les Habbés de la région de Bandiagara), m'envoya les photographies ici reproduites, qui représentent une femme porteuse d'un masque de cuir conçu par lui et exécuté sur ses indications à New York, je ne le connaissais que depuis peu.

Je l'avais vu pour la première et alors unique fois le 12 avril, au cours d'un entretien d'à peine plus d'une heure, dans un petit café situé en face de l'hôtel modeste où il avait fixé sa résidence, près du Théâtre de l'Odéon.

[461]   21

W.B. Seabrook
Leather Mask
Reproduced in a page from
Leiris's article

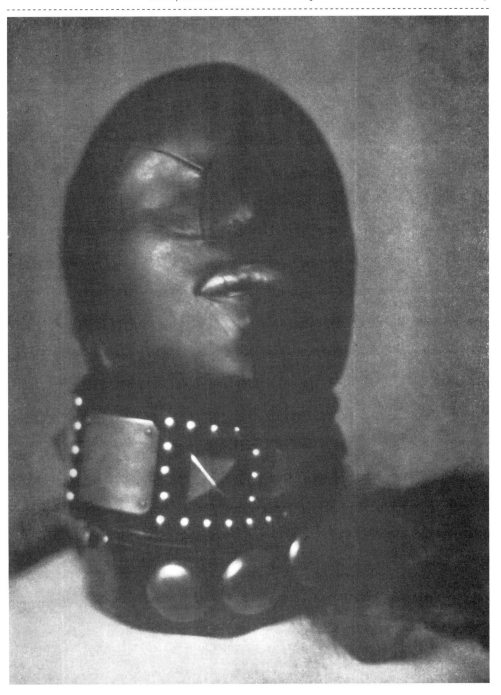

W.B. Seabrook
Leather Mask
Reproduced in Leiris's article

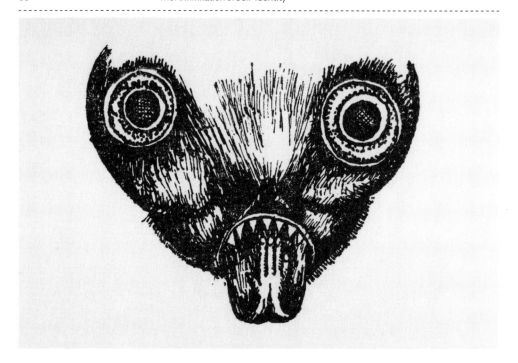

Anonymous illustration
reproduced in *La Brèche:
action surréaliste*, no.7,
December 1964

the disciple replied, 'Yes. 'Asked a third question – 'What is the face
of God like?' – the young Dervish was dumbstruck and began to
tremble. But, urged on by questions, shivering with terror, he finally
replied that he had seen the face of God but it was his own image,
and so he had found himself, in the course of this night spent in the
remains of the mosque, *face to face with God, in other words with
himself.*

I recalled this story – as beautiful as the legend alluded to by
Gérard de Nerval in *Aurelia*, in which a knight 'spends the whole
night in a forest fighting an unknown person who is himself' –
when I received Seabrook's photographs of masks and I
understood, thanks to this comparison, how such a profound joy (at
once erotic and mystical, like everything under the sign of total
exaltation) could be drawn from the simple fact of masking (or
denying) a face.

If there is an activity which has to constitute one of the first
levels among the innumerable human activities, it must be that of
disguise. From the simplest finery, the taste in dress or for uniforms,
to totemic disguises or tattoos and paintings, by way of theatre
costumes and masks, carnival fancy dress, clowns' rags, women's
make-up and the penitent's cagoule, it really seems that humanity,
barely having become conscious of its skin, most urgently needed
to change it, throwing itself head first into an exciting
metamorphosis which allowed it to free itself from its narrow limits
as it dreamt of another skin.

There is not a lot of difference between the attitude of the
savage who identifies himself with an animal, or another natural
species, by means of his totemic costume, and that of the person for

whom certain details of a woman's finery are powerfully erotic factors. In both cases it is a matter of an attraction exercised over us without our being aware of what is *foreign* to us within it. A detail like a disordered dress, an intimate accessory such as a garter or a mundane shoe, will exalt us by its character as a manufactured object, an object imbued with great social value, brutally opposed to pure nudity and drawing a profound strangeness from this contradiction. Moreover, one here touches upon the source of erotic fetishism, which is very close to religious fetishism and the cult of relics because it manifests the same type of magical thought in that the part is taken for the whole, the accessory for the person, and that the part is not just equal to the whole, but is even stronger than it – just as a drawing is stronger than the object it represents, the part or drawing being sorts of *quintessences*, more moving and expressive than the whole because more concentrated, and also less real, more external to us, more foreign, assimilable to the disguises by which reality – and, because of this ambience, humanity itself – is metamorphosed.

Returning to the masks we are concerned with, we first notice that they participate in these types of *disguises*. Thanks to them, the woman becomes unrecognisable, more schematic at the same time as the image of her body impresses itself with an increased intensity.

Like a phantom of flesh which is abruptly revealed in the shadowy recess of a room or on a poorly defined path passing beside a well, through them the woman is rendered so much more disquieting, so much more mysterious. Having become almost anonymous since her face is obliterated, she acquires a terrifying generality, with this hard leather or metal collar, a severe geometry which partly hides her.

It is no longer a matter of a specific person, but of a woman *in general*, who can equally well be the whole of nature and the external world that we are thereby directly ready to dominate. In addition to the fact that she is suffering under the leather, that she is upset and mortified (which must satisfy our desire for power and our fundamental cruelty), her head – the sign of her individuality and intelligence – is mocked and denied. Faced with her, the partner is no longer in the presence of a 'creature of God' whose face, hoist to the top of her shoulders, seems made to contemplate the stars or any other symbol of elevation and purity, but is in a position to use – with what sacrilegious power! – a simple and universal erotic mechanism. That same joy the young Dervish of the legend must have felt (no matter how innocently – or even hypocritically – he was terrified by it) in cancelling out the face of God and substituting it with his own face, the partner of the woman so masked must experience a satanic joy here, above all because it is sadistic and is then complicated by a crime of *lèse-divinité*.

Love thus reduced (very lucidly) to a natural and bestial process by the fact that the brain is symbolically obliterated due to

Emila Medková
Wind 1948

this mask, the fatality which oppresses us is finally subdued (since, thanks to this instrument, this woman between our hands is now simply nature itself, moulded by blind laws, without soul or personality, but, for once, totally enchained to us as this woman is enchained). The look – this quintessence of human expression – for a while blinded (which confers on the woman in question a still more infernal and subterranean significance); the mouth reduced to the bestial role of a wound (thanks to the thin orifice which makes it the only thing visible); the normal rules of dress entirely reversed (here the body is naked and the head masked, while ordinarily it is the head that is naked and the body masked) – these are so many elements which make these pieces of leather (a material from which boots and whips are made) marvellous contraptions admirably suited to what eroticism truly is: a means of emerging from the self, of breaking the lines imposed on you by morality, intelligence and customs, a way too of conjuring away evil forces and defying God or his substitutes, watchdogs of the world, by possessing and constraining the entire universe, their property, in one of its particularly significant places, but one no longer differentiated.

Placed on a living architecture whose bare feet remain plunged in a strictly sensual mire, the veiled head gradually becomes lost in the inflated clouds of metaphysical storms. It has now ceased to be a question of a woman endowed with an ordinary civil status, or even of a figure representing in our eyes the eternal feminine. Great alphabets of vapour pass far above the ground, dominating from on high the skyscrapers of New York (where Seabrook currently lives) and the old-fashioned buildings of Paris (where I, with pen in hand, am writing this essay for *Documents*).

As beautiful as the cow goddess Hathor, the woman masked like an executioner – or, like a queen, decapitated – rises up; and, standing upright before her with her face having become that of a God, the partner admires her body, rendered still more magnificent by the absence of face, which makes her at once more veracious and more ungraspable, transforming her gradually into a sort of obscure *thing in itself*, tempting and mysterious – a supreme residue that one can equally colour with a value that is the most ideal or the most sordidly material, the *thing in itself* – as enigmatic and appealing as a sphinx or a siren – a great universal matrix to which old Hegel, when he conceived it as 'the *product* of thinking, and precisely of the thinking that has gone to the extreme of pure abstraction, the product of the empty "I" that makes its own empty self-identity into its *ob-ject*' [Hegel 1991, p.87], gave the epithet of a *caput mortuum*, a term borrowed from the alchemists of old, who applied it to that phase of the Work in which all seems rotten when everything is regenerated.

Leonora Carrington
What Is a Woman?

The women's liberation movement, as it re-emerged towards the end of the 1960s, was not universally welcomed by women within surrealism, and certain aspects of it have been subject to withering criticisms, most harshly by Annie Le Brun in her book *Lâchez tout*, as noted below. Leonora Carrington, then living in Mexico, was one of those who did take inspiration from the women's movement, at least at first. This text, written in 1971, was one of her initial responses to the upsurge of female revolt then being witnessed across the world, and draws out some of the surrealist affinities with it.

First published in *Cultural Correspondence*, nos.12–14, Summer 1981, special supplement 'Surrealism Today and Tomorrow!': reprinted in Ron Sakolsky (ed.), *Surrealist Subversions: Rants, Writings and Images by the Surrealist Movement in the United States.* Brooklyn: Autonomedia, 2002.

Fifty-three years ago I was born a female human animal. This, I was told, meant that I was a 'Woman'.

But I never knew what they meant.

Fall in love with a man and you will see... I fell (several times), but saw not.

Give birth and you will see... I gave birth and did not know, who am I?

Am I? Who?

I am that I am, God the Father told Moses on the Mountain. This means nothing to me. *I am* may have been a dishonest invention meaning multitude.

Je pense donc je suis, but why? Some kind of pretension of Monsieur Descartes?

If I am my thoughts, then I could be anything from chicken soup to a pair of scissors, a crocodile, a corpse, a leopard, or a pint of beer.

If I am my feelings, then I am love, hate, irritation, boredom, happiness, pride, humility, pain, pleasure, and so on and so forth.

If I am my body, then I am a foetus to a middle-aged woman changing every second.

Yet, like everybody else I yearn for an identity although this yearning mystifies me always.

If there is a true individual identity I would like to find it, because like truth on discovery it has already gone.

So I try to reduce myself to facts. I am an aging human female now: soon I will be old and then dead. This is all I know as far as facts are concerned.

These facts are not particularly edifying or original.

However, out of the depths of this humanoid female a nameless apprehension is constantly present of a no I, no me, no it, but Is, limitlessly mysterious, but there – no doubt at all.

Pre-form, pre-light, pre-darkness, pre-sound Is.

Then in idle rumination I find pleasure in imagining that I am some kind of seed that must split and germinate into something so unlike what I appear to be that I could not imagine it in my wildest moment, but intensely convinced that once the split is complete the

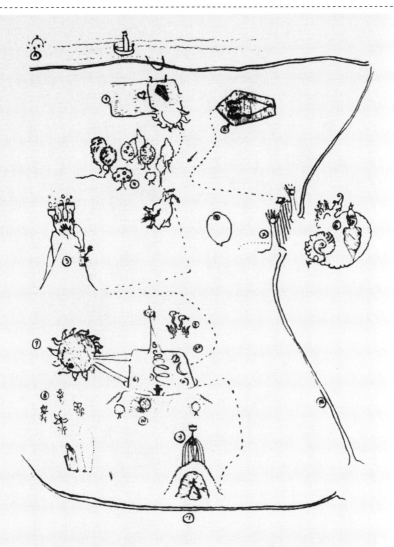

A.—A desert scene, Covagonda cemetery
B.—High wall surrounding the garden
X.—Gate of the garden
1.—Villa Covagonda
2.—Radiography
3—Villa Pilar
4—Apple trees and view of Casa Blanca and the valley
5.—"Africa".
6.—Villa Amachu
6B—Arbor

7.—"Down Below"
8.—Kitchen garden
9.—Bower and cave
10.—Don Mariano's "place"
11.—"Outside World" Street
a.—My room at "Down Below," the eclipse and the limbos
b.—The lair
c.—The library
   Wide "Down Below" alley

Leonora Carrington
Map of asylum, from
her book *Down Below* (1943)

Pierre Molinier
Portrait of Joyce Mansour
Reproduced in *Le Surréalisme,
même*, no.1, Spring 1958

absolute Other will take over in this field of doubting multitude I call myself and take a step further in evolution.

Perhaps I am talking of death or of those who are not yet born. Those we call woman, perhaps Men.

If the planet is still alive for people to be born.

I dare not say that I believe in evolution because I am not at all sure that there is such an I to affirm anything, but love of possible evolution feels sure as breath.

But will they give the chance to this seed to split and germinate?

On what does future organic life on this earth depend?

What induced the serpent to grow feathers?

A nameless force operating in the unknown psyche or pre-form of life that can perhaps perform miracles if miracles are allowed...

And the only one to give me absolute permission is myself.

Conscious deliberate permission to allow miracle.

Since civilisation is rolling quickly towards absolute destruction for Earth, blind inane mass suicide for all living beings, the last hope is an act of will to step out of the mechanical trap and refuse. This will could produce a medium for evolution. If all the Women of the world decide to control the population, to refuse war, to refuse discrimination of Sex or Race and thus force men to allow life to survive on this planet, that would be a miracle indeed.

Technology – or otherwise the clever extension of the human body, such as the caveman's club to a submarine or jet plane – is so hypnotically impressive of Man's Brainy Toys that we have passively allowed ourselves to be devoured by our own teddy bears. Surely it is time (if there is time enough) to become grown women and take away the teddy bears and other obnoxious toys that threaten to turn the nursery into a tomb.

It is a curious thought that the human cortex has been generally employed for make-believe, pretence, pretension. Pretending to be superior because of 'x' nationality, pretending to be better because I have television sets, a bigger house, a better car than you, pretending to be better than you a woman, I a man. Pretending that We Are Right because we have nastier and more totally destructive weapons than They Have.

Why all this deadly pretence?

Is it not possible that the cortex might have a real and positive function, such as a search for truth?

A will for survival of Life, a will for further mystery to unfold within the media of life?

The extraordinary and the horrible abuse of the human brain by other human brains is very difficult to explain, but to quote Professor Genoves: 'The same cunning that invented war could invent peace' (*Is Peace Inevitable?* by Santiago Genoves).

Pretension is, in fact, a blind alley that leads nowhere because it is a lie. I think we must try to look in through the smog in ourselves and ask who or what is this, and what within this we could evolve, live, grow. A maternal thought arising perhaps from maternal instinct – but instincts mothered consciously, or so they say. If through consciousness we could unchain our own emotional power, then we would no longer be the passive herd driven by mad shepherds into the slaughter-house.

In order to unchain our emotions we must observe all the elements that are used to keep us enslaved, all the false identities that we unconsciously embrace through propaganda, literature, and all the multiple false beliefs that we are fed since birth.

This is the only way to clear psychic territory for reality. Our emotions react mechanically to so much bunk that our own real emotions are practically impossible to decode. Some of us go to psychoanalysts in the hope of finding out; others try to find more and stronger illusions in the hope of never finding out; the rest accept what they are told and feel comfortable in order to conform, even if this conforming is slavery and destruction.

Emotional power, like electricity, can be manipulated in all kinds of devious ways; projecting Mickey Mouse on the screen, the electric chair, the subway or naturally by a thunder storm. However sublime, silly, or tragic expressions are manifested, the power is the same emotional force that is subject to change by manipulation, circumstances and also by understanding. We know that subliminal persuasion touches off stronger reactions than reason because it operates on the emotional centre which works on a stronger power system. What we ought to know as well is what we are going to allow to be fed into this mysterious centre.

However corrupt our emotional system has become, there is nevertheless a nucleus in all beings which knows basically that which is true and that which is false. Psychoanalysis, which is still fumbling in the unknown, has shown us that we can find a great deal of self-knowledge through our dreams, even if this science is in an embryonic state. Lies we live are shown to us in dreams. There appears to be a Knower in the unconscious that is never fooled and can rise to the conscious mind if the emotions are prepared to accept some elements of truth.

The idea that 'Our Masters' are Right and must be loved, honoured and obeyed is, I think, one of the most destructive lies that have been instilled into the female psyche. It has become most horribly obvious what These Masters have done to our planet and her organic life. If women remain passive I think there is very little hope for the survival of life on this earth.

Mexico, 6 September 1970

Annie Le Brun
Leave Everything

In the 1970s, Annie Le Brun's was one of the first voices to be raised against the normalising aspects contained within the new feminist movements, especially as they emerged in France. Her book *Lâchez tout* is a sometimes coruscating critique of the aggrandising and self-serving way in which some French theorists climbed on the bandwagon of female revolt to institute what she saw as new forms of psychic and social repression which limited rather than advanced the cause of woman.

Published as the Preface to *Lâchez tout*, Paris: Le Sagitaire, 1977.

I live in terror of not being misunderstood. (Oscar Wilde)
I would like to tell you cracked crystal howling like a dog in a night of beating sheets. (Benjamin Péret)

When I was sixteen I decided not to let my life be what it was supposed to be. Determination (and perhaps luck) allowed me to elude most of the inherent misfortunes of the feminine condition. If I am delighted that young women today are increasingly showing a desire to reject the models previously open to them, I just as much deplore their willingness to identify with the formal negation of such old models, or even to do no more than bring them up to date. Although everyone today takes pleasure in repeating that we are not born a woman but *become* one, no one seems to be even slightly concerned not to become one. Just the reverse, in fact. Unlike the eighteenth- and nineteenth-century feminists who sought to erase the illusory difference which bestowed on men real power over women, the neo-feminists of recent years have made it their business to establish the reality of this difference so as to lay claim to an illusory power supposedly denied to women. And they do so to such an extent that revolt against an *impossibility of being* tends to vanish under the impact of militant stupidity, instigating an *obligation to be*. Do we need to be reminded that when it comes to revolt we need no ancestors? But it should be added that we especially do not want technical consultants eager to exchange recipes for feminine insubordination from A to Z.

Confronted with the extent of crimes more or less legally committed not only against women but also against all those who refuse the social codification of sexual roles (in particular homosexuals), I consider this revolt too necessary not to want to disrupt the chorus of those men or women who aspire to abstract it from the individual obscurity which violently shapes it and from which it draws its overwhelming force. I insist that this revolt is always directed against collective morale, no matter what basis this might have. How can we then fail to see that today every woman is virtually dispossessed of this individual renewal, when her every escapade risks being hijacked to serve the construction of an

Toyen
Reproduced in *Almanach surréaliste du demi-siècle*, 1950

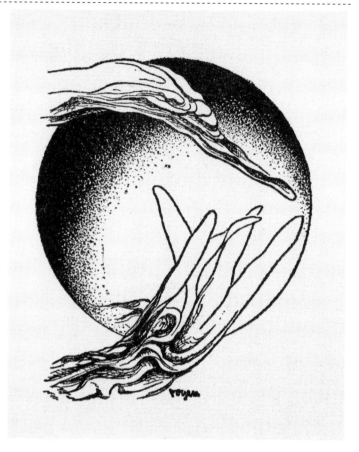

ideology as contradictory in its propositions as it is totalitarian in its intentions? Ever since the so-called 'women's cause' displayed the image of tame revolt in the net of the negative normalisation that our epoch is so good at casting over the most distant spaces of our horizon, she has even been more or less tacitly encouraged on all sides to exhibit the demands of her sex.

Having always scorned both masters who behave like slaves and slaves eager to slip into the skin of masters, I confess to having scarcely any interest in the ordinary conflict between men and women. My sympathy is more for those who desert the roles assigned to them by society. They never claim to be constructing a new world, proving their fundamental honesty by never imposing their interests on unwitting others, content to be exceptions which deny the rule with a determination often capable of overturning the established order.

Oscar Wilde interests me more than some bourgeois woman who agrees to marry and have children and one fine day feels her very hypothetical creativity being thwarted.

That's the way it goes.

I won't list my preferences in this regard: it would be pointless and overwhelming for the women's cause.

That I may have done all I could to restrict the grip of the

8 Elsa Triolet (1896–1970), Russian writer who became Louis Aragon's companion in the late 1920s and later his wife. The surrealists tend to hold her largely responsible for Aragon's drift away from surrealism and into Stalinism.

psychic, social and intellectual consequences of biological destiny is nothing to do with anyone else, but I will always refuse attempts to blame me in the name of all women so as to return me to the limits of this destiny. Such sudden and inescapable promiscuity in search for each woman's identity actually threatens women in the depths of their freedom when generic difference is affirmed at the expense of all specific differences. Let's just calmly consider what each of us has to contend with in the name of God, Nature, Man and History. As if this wasn't enough the banner of Woman has to be added to it. Specialists in coercion know what they are doing when all of a sudden they zealously proliferate the national and international organisations addressing the feminine condition while effecting no legislative changes. Moreover they could hardly go wrong, since Aragon, repression's apologist for nigh on half a century, announced that woman is 'man's future'. I have the gravest doubt about a future that could assume Elsa Triolet's features.[8]

In what is said and written in the name of woman, I see the return (under the pretext of liberation) of everything that has traditionally diminished women: they oppose the family but extol the triumphalism of the motherhood that is its foundation; they attack the notion of woman as object but promote the revival of feminine mystique; in the end, if relations between men and women are denounced as ones of power, it is in order to provide a starting point for theories about the most excruciating conjugal bickering. These just provide me with even more reason to be thankful for having definitively avoided the dead ends of a supposed 'feminine sensibility'. Moreover, nothing could make me renounce my natural aversion to majorities, especially when they are composed of part-time martyrs – most especially in the west.

The more deafening the clamour of the age, the more certain I am that my life is elsewhere, slipping along my love, whose forms entomb the passing of time. I look at you. We shall meet on the bridge of transparency before plunging into the night of our differences. We shall swim, whether near or far away, tense or distracted, going against the current of our enigma to find ourselves again in the uncertain embrace of our fleeting shadows. We are not the only ones to have been one day raised from the depth of our solitude to set off in anticipation of our ghosts, without worrying about whether they are male or female. And if not many men can easily recognise themselves in Picabia's declaration that 'Women are the agents of my freedom', it is perhaps because what is at stake is the triumph of a sense of the marvellous that men and women are yet to discover. This is why I object to being enlisted in the army of women fighting against biological accident alone. My frantic individualism has the precise extent of all that strives for the interchangeability of beings.

This book is a call for desertion.

Vincent Bounoure
Memory of the Last One

Vincent Bounoure considered that he was living in exile in the modern world, so strongly did he identify with the Polynesian and pre-Columbian civilisations whose study was his life's work. In this difficult text, he addresses the mask as providing one of the links between this and the other world, as something that exists between life and death and between living and inert matter. Even more than the mirror or the mannequin, the uncanny quality of the mask hardly needs emphasising: we are all aware, even if indistinctly, that donning a mask is a process that makes us *other*.

First published in *La Brèche: action surréaliste*, no.2, May 1962; reprinted in Vincent Bounoure, *Le Surréalisme et les arts sauvages*, Paris: L'Harmattan, 1999.

Since I have never been enthused by anything as much as faces, I regard the shadow enveloping them beneath a mask to be decisive. It is mortal. When the face vanishes, it goes through that stiffness which, perhaps provisionally, can only turn it into a ghost's skull. Associated with journeys beyond the grave in civilisations which evoke its vicissitudes beforehand, the mask at least transitorily conjures up a decease which in its fixity holds a funereal character: it celebrates a timeless passage in the most current way. Thanks to it, death has been envisaged as an everyday necessity, and not as a future terror. It is the most appropriate instrument to reduce this terror.

Whatever secret the mask arranges in its construction or in the drama it relates as it recalls to a second existence those it has started by putting to death, the exuberance of life has no less been reduced by its agency to simulating its end, which is nothing but its negation. But this transitory mineralisation affects life in its universal acceptance far more than in its personal incarnation. For some eminent beings, death lends such a peremptory immobility only in proportion to common destinies. The species prepares for its demise in the evening of its dazzling days. While ruins collapse into eloquence, the smile of the 'unknown woman of the Seine'[9] extends the grace of the child-woman into a durable accomplishment; Pascal still seems to be fighting against his epoch and against himself. As if in premonition of a sinister conclusion, the victory of nature illuminates the particularity of a great experience in the twilight. Historical development reveals each of its great stages against this background of a night in which we will lose our candles.

The mask evoking an end to the human species, the games in which it can partake occur at the far end of that horizon where any human consciousness is ruined: nothing suits it better than the game, in a light which sees through pretensions to seriousness. Its language is a *gay wisdom*, as it is given to the *last man* evoked by Zarathustra. What it proffers matters so much only because of the secret which is both silenced and denounced by this very silence, the secret of life which returns to icy materials and already admits the cries of the inanimate as its own.

9 A young woman whose body was found in the Seine around 1880 and whose beauty was such that it impelled the pathologist to make a death mask which became something of a cult among writers and artists, her enigmatic smile being compared with that of the Mona Lisa [trans.].

This detour is the only way the individual reaches such an exemplary value. The presence of a Jivaro shrunken head convinced me that small dialogues between appearance and reality, or between the face and thought, were interrupted when confronted with the preterition which so poignantly announced the end of a race when it simply seemed to want to perpetuate a physiognomy. This was necessarily that of a being who had finally understood. I accorded him this turn of wisdom that was more considerable for not having found a clear accommodation with that knowledge which is expressed in laughter, although it is sometimes tempted by the regressions, pilgrimages or dissolution in the futilities of humanism.

Hence fresh possibilities of individual expression appeared to me. That in the long term collective hopes might well result in an icy twilight rendered the affirmation of everything able to coordinate the human adventure to its end more urgent: as when serious illness impels you into heroism through an aesthetic appreciation of personal destiny, I took a view from the collective outcome which seemed to me to command each of its phases in an identical way, right down to the lowliest of them in which it could be given to me to take part. The antinomy between individual and collective was henceforth only a much reduced appearance. This was just another way of learning that faces are modelled onto their final insignificance and that their testimony, which is their assumed presence, cannot be expressed except as 'value'.

It is not very satisfying to have recourse to aesthetic criteria for personal peace of mind, criteria that are therefore necessarily inflected by a particular complexion, when it is a matter of the *face* of such a gifted species. I would say as much about other species, like those calosoma beetles whose mummies today fascinate me. Seeing them elude corruption, I infer that they have settled into a new form of existence such that the semblance of victory that nature had won over them did not defeat them. For at this point what is contested is their subjection to the natural order, and hence everything within their distinct existence as living beings that has scandalously done them wrong, something which saves them from dissolution in the cycles. Separated from the world by their needs, they were like us, without perhaps the adaptations which we found through subjectivity, when it allows us to interrupt our life. The revolt which is not only an aesthetic postulation but also an ethical decision, and responds immediately to the conditions imposed on human life, seemed to me no less justified in the face of the conditions imposed on all life.

Awareness of the ineluctable death of all species, and therefore of my own, reduces the terrors of individual death to nothing. It envelops in a single purview the multiple circumstances which could equally restore palpitations and joys to their mineral destinies. In this respect it should undoubtedly be seen only as a *sign of the times*, or a transmission into the gradual servitude of the spirit to the ends of laborious edification, as it insinuates itself into earlier societies as a common component in the provisionally most contrasting economic systems. This is an abyss to which nothing will ever make me consent, as this would represent the inevitable death throes of lost possibilities. The pirates' lantern will always carry the faces of the insubordinate towards the corals.

This would be to cede too much to the gods of shadows, if it did not deprive them of the signs and instruments of their power. In order to cross each circle of my hells, Ishtar lets fall her stones, her rings and her last veil. Ishtar become mine was better still than the *divinised vital energy*, and naked in the caverns she was the last one whose half-open eyelids might have let the pack-ice of the irremediable glaciations be reflected in her eyes. She, of whom I could say that I have a memory, if I believe the faces in which I thought I recognised the glaze of her lakes of dead water, I would always recognise beneath her Fuegian mask, in the last child of an ancient race, one never reduced even by nature. Never so naked, by virtue of the set stones of amber, than in having given life to feminine transparency, Ishtar stripped her mineral form at the approach of the shadows which covered her face in its eternal mask.

The resplendent one, all of her fires cast on the brow of women, descends further than the hypogeous realm where the blue vitriol or chalcanthite/*copper sulphate* sleeps. Her too presumable death ordains the masks she imprints on the beauties. Light, fleeing the too slow or too similar gleams of dawns, they elude the reflections of the sinister dial by bursting with all the appeals the aventurine ever uttered, true to this definitive mask to which they laboured to resemble with a dark and no doubt immemorial conscience. Never so perfect as in this operation in which their flesh comes together in the stone, they each form the scene in which the great gods confront one another. The shrouds of purple, the cyclamen horizon, the Prussian blues of a vacant evening are extenuated in mother of pearl, a cruel symbol of red moons.

I believe I am able, in what matters to me, to cast a little daylight on the conjurations of desire and death by reproducing, in spite of the slightly talismanic aspect they had donned, words by whose power metal and woman had at least once made me their accomplice:
CHANGED

There is nothing in desire that was not first in destinies.
(Charles Fourier)

Bernard Caburet
You Will Always Cherish your Failures, Machine-Man

Robots did not have the same appeal for surrealists as mannequins, lacking as they were in the uncanny element that constituted them as alike but unlike humans. As an extension of the human, created to serve human needs rather than to function as surrogates of human agency, they symbolised the conformism and alienation being increasingly fostered by technological development. Some may be surprised by Caburet's trenchant criticism of Bachelard's notion of 'surrationalism' and his collapsing of distinctions between science and poetry, especially given that the former concept was enthusiastically welcomed by several surrealists in the 1930s. However, the inadequacies of the theory from a surrealist perspective (especially the presuppositions upon which it was based) soon became apparent, and Caburet's response is consistent with later surrealist views which also informed their early distrust of postmodernism. Even though there are obvious correspondences between the surrealists and postmodernists in their respective rejections of Enlightenment notions of the self and the subject, for the surrealists postmodernism would do no more than displace these notions onto an equally oppressive stage, as Caburet's withering critique of Deleuze and Guattari here implies.

Published in Vincent Bounoure (ed.), *La Civilisation surréaliste*, Paris: Payot, 1976.

The revolt of the robots, very much like that of toys, would be nothing but a pleasant fiction, an effective joke, a witticism to inspire a delightful fear. So let's have done with this already archaic modern fantasy! Moreover, there are philosophers who, wishing to tame a reality constructed without them and to make up for their past misdeeds concerning modernity, busy themselves with dispelling this groundless fear. The illusion of danger, coming from the misunderstanding the majority still entertain, would soon be dissipated once, recognising machines for what they are (that is, matter organised by man so as to organise matter), their right to be accepted into contemporary culture has been recognised. In short, the phantasm of the revolt of robots (as in the patronymic work of Karel Capek, *R.U.R.*[10]) arises from the most basic anthropomorphism, and the progress of knowledge unfailingly effaces these vestiges of an anachronistic mentality awakened by the first great progress of science and technique.

10 Karel Capek, *R.U.R* (Rossum's Universal Robots), translated by Paul Selver, New York: Dover Publications, 2001 [trans.].

11 Bruno Bettelheim (1903–1990), Austrian-born American child psychologist. The reference is to his essay 'Joey: A "Mechanical Boy"', *Scientific American*, no.200, 1959 [trans.].

In our world saturated with technical objects and their waste, it is probably not very acceptable to continue expressing doubts. No more today than yesterday is there any place or recognition for anyone who does not live in his time, who does not adhere to it and in the end is not married to it! The pediment inscription reads: Consume, Function and Be Quiet. If not for his still problematic social profitability Joey, Bettelheim's[11] child-machine, might be considered a mutant announcing future generations precociously adapted to the new way of living. Let us have no doubt about it, tomorrow's great pedagogical aims will be, at the functional and pathological extreme, to bend the will without breaking it and to channel desire without extinguishing it. In this respect we are still in an age of transition, but soon we will no longer have to be afraid of machines: they are what we will be. And Joey will no longer benefit from someone's strange and subversive care: some smoothly functioning engineers will set him straight and on his feet. Correspondingly, psychologists will be subjected to revision (some have anticipated the call), and the most suitable will undergo the modifications necessary for their transformation into authorised mechanologists.

This spectre of a putsch by machines, to use a lurid expression – of an imperialism of the techno-structures in its most elaborated form – might be nothing but a childish fear, an infantilism, or the fad of the old-fashioned who are incapable of detaching themselves from their stale old humanist-romantic ideas, incorrigible individualists or poets blind to all novelty, viscerally hostile to progress and its benefits; this spectre – which some people manage to commute (a successful reactive training) into an artificial euphoria or, at least, a reasonable and relatively secure contentment – might be nothing but senility, debility, misoneism, cowardice and resentment if the 'idols of our time', so proud, so sure of having been best mecha-sodomised, are to be believed.

These days to think probably means to say yes, and tomorrow this could well be just to process correctly the information endlessly disseminated by a central computer fed by a few subjected people. Fiction-politics. Utopia. An unhealthy reverie. Unhealthy? Much less than all the Byzantinisms of bought-off intellectuals who are always ready to develop and then philosophically wrap up in swaddling clothes the latest socio-political promotion, the monstrous child of the regime.

Utopia? It would be congenitally totalitarian, would always once again reconstitute the project of a social organisation as totally rationalised, perfectly organised, planned out, and so eluding change, becoming and history. History is the irrational, imperfection and failure of rationalisation. And who still believes in the rationality of history, in the invisible hand which arranges everything, the ruse of reason whose ends would be realised unknown to us, through us and in spite of us – who believes in Hegel's romance? We are no longer the spoilt children of invincible progress, but we are certainly its maimed victims. Utopia: totalitarian or libertarian? Totalitarian: only the resentful, the embittered, the petty paranoiacs and the losers would resist. The utopian message can probably be considered in certain respects to be the fruit of current political impotence, if not of an insurmountable incapacity to insert oneself into the present so as effectively to construct the future within it. At best it is a long-term form of politics intended to dictate to us a tactic from one day to the next. So be it. But the truth of utopia cannot lie in the present, which moreover is always more the future promised by the present than

Nicole Espagnol in a mask by
Mimi Parent, and Alain Joubert
wearing a mask by Jean-Claude
Silbermann during a surrealist
meeting, Désert de Retz 1960.
Photograph by Denise Bellon

12 Gilles Lapouge, *Utopie et civilisation*, Paris: Weber, 1973.

13 Bachelard, whose quality of mind, as such, is not at issue, is invoked here only because of the alibi his work provides.

the actual edge of the past. Utopia is affectively of the order of a wish, not of a regret. It exceeds, admittedly in an imaginary realm, an unpleasant representation of the present and of the means the present offers for its own surpassing. It is the political phantasm of the desire for revolution which can be thematised and hardened into an image and then assume obsessive and totalitarian aspects. Its value therefore lies not in its systematic and doctrinal consequences but in its first movement. And the error of Gilles Lapouge[12] is certainly vastly to misunderstand this movement, this passion and this radical desire which animates utopian aims. His thesis, according to which all utopia promises a gilded cage – one not without some foundation – loses much of its force and pertinence when (thinking it is strengthening it) it radicalises and systematises it, by means of the same systematic spirit he denounces, with such constant success that it is then cast into doubt, even by utopians themselves. As though a prejudice for originality constrained him to judge all utopian expressions of political desire in an identical way, and to describe undeniably spontaneous expressions like those of May 1968 as anti-utopian: 'Beneath the pavement, the beach!' Is this quibbling over words? Let's end it by recognising that the word 'utopia' in its current usage has a strong libertarian connotation, and that it can only designate very inappropriately those totalitarian and ahistorical visions expressed in the past. In reality there is all the difference in the world between the forward-planning, therefore all technocracies, that seeks to submit historical disorder to an immutable and definitive rational level, and the emancipatory and rival utopian desire, with all the weaknesses inherent to desire alone, but which are the corollary of its strength and, sometimes, the hallucinatory manias of perfectionism.

Utopia therefore appears to us essentially to be the critical product of a practical and future-oriented reason which receives its inspiration from the imagination, and its force, conviction and truth from desire. This reason, this Reason, which they take pride in, which created the Enlightenment – a sovereign and long-lasting weapon against every obscurantism for every liberation – has become the prostitute of power and the scientifico-technical complex, and this double life keeps minds in a serious confusion which, as we shall see, favours duplicity and mystification. Thus we find Bachelard, who very well knew how to devote himself by day to the reason at work in contemporary science and by night to the imagination which inspires poetry, puts himself forward quite naturally as the ideal refuge of good conscience, as the alibi of a plenary dualism, as the exemplary and vibrant success of a happy double consciousness.[13] His double life and the very successful and balanced way he split himself in two is fortunate only for him and for those who, by way of identification, delight in recognising themselves within this. Yet here lies a quiet drama, a latent conflict which Bachelard apparently effectively resolved, that masks a problem which under the empire of reason was always repressed, or never even posed. Reason is not what has been said and it is not

14 Centre culturel international
de Cerisy-la-Salle, *Bachelard:
Colloque de Cerisy*, Union
Générale d'Editions, Paris
1974.

what Bachelard's apologists in fact make of it. Bachelardian
surrationalism functions, and will function objectively and
historically, as a humanist guarantee called upon to hide the
technico-rational hegemony of our age. For if Bachelard helps us
to understand the renewed means of reason, he does not urge us to
question the actual finalities of rational activity among scholars.
It is as though this lucid mind was seduced and captivated by
the achievements of the new reason which had broken with its
thankless Aristotelian, scholastic and Cartesian childhoods and,
extravagantly praising its new dispensations, vitality, conquests
and risks, neglected to question the political, that is to say human,
finalities of such a deployment of activity and constant assurance.
Technical concretisation is not otherwise suspected, and the
question of the subordination of scientific reason to technical
rationality, subordinated in its turn to political 'reason', is
ultimately never posed. This thought which isolates,
compartmentalises and separates, which contentedly incarnates
this separation and smoothly lives out the duality, is ultimately
revealed to be idealist, since it poses the terms of a conflict without
posing them as a conflict: Bachelard secures within himself the
cohabitation of the scholar and the poet as two sorts of people for
the admiration of all throughout his double life. One of these two
people is right because he has reason, while the other is not wrong
in not having it: each receives, separately and for himself, the
consecration he instigates.

    Bachelard's work therefore appears to rest on a cleavage of
images with a preservation and even reinforcement of the adaptive
sector – that, on the one hand, of the real and of science and, on the
other hand, of the insular arrangement of an anaclitic sector, that
of the imaginary and of poetry. But this dualism, this division, does
not control the propositions for utopia that Bachelard sometimes
sketches, since what is affirmed in them is nothing but the desire
for order. The Bachelardian utopia is a scholarly utopia, that of an
academia which is extended to the point of being stretched over
the whole of existence, or a scientistic utopia, that of the republic
of scholars achieving 'the union of evidence workers', imposing a
morality resulting from the professional ethics of scientific work.
The society of the future will be a school or a laboratory! If for the
edification of young minds we recall that Bachelard called his work
desk his 'table of existence', for my part I find this virtue somewhat
disturbing as it promises the completed transformation of the table
of existence into an immense work: the table as a utopia. Moreover,
in a paper which came into my hands and was given at the Cerisy
conference on Bachelard,[14] Michel Serres said, without beating
about the bush: 'What he wants to construct is a scientific edifice
whose fundamental characteristic will be the control of all by all.'
On the whole, we are not only promised generalised evening classes
and permanent training even beyond the third age, but also the
game of control of all by all, the game of suspicion and proof. In
the same way we read immediately after this that it might well be
that the 'fundamental code of training would then be a morality

Konrad Klapheck
The Spirit of Revolt 1964

15 Robert Stephenson Smyth Baden-Powell (1857–1941), founder of the Scout movement [trans.].

analogous to the diffuse ethic, protestant in inspiration, which underlay the university reforms of 1880–5'. Are you listening, Max Weber? Further on, a certain Pierre Thillet, who has a lot of happy school memories to tell us about, rapturously marvels at the reversal of finality effected by Bachelard between school and society, teaching and State. He is moreover even more manifestly amazed at the reversal itself (this astounding dialectic of means-end relations is always calculated to get a good university don salivating) than at what this operation and its results mean, and, more radically, at the value of the reversed pair. From now on we will be asking Kipling for lessons, and for recreation, if some may be granted, Baden-Powell[15] will probably need to be consulted. As for blessed Marie-Louise Gouthier, she must be seriously joking when, in the same work, she delights in reporting that one of her dear students 'very charmingly asked: "What's that? Bachelard was a leftie!"' Sic. Blessed Marie-Louise probably wanted to be crowned with a bucket of champagne, to borrow this expression from someone who would gladly have lent it on this occasion. Let's leave these old boys' reunions to carry on in peace.

On the agenda of thought is the question of the reason for the ever more extended power of reason, the question of its foundation and finality. In an abstract way we know that in the end reason is simply founded on itself, and finds its own end in its own realisation: this is the pure totalitarian tautology of reason by which it established its own right to power. This fraud found its first denigrator in Nietzsche, who forcefully dragged reason in absentia before another tribunal. The verdict: reason was led back to its 'grounding truth', which is not rational, to reveal a completely different reality, that of a subjection, just as the very idea of truth, and not only of a particular truth, is for the first time being radically attacked. Then, since the contrary illusion is always re-born, it needs once again to be affirmed that power is born, in the fact that reason, of itself and being as such self-sufficient, is solicited only so as to confer upon it a legitimate relation after the event, to procure for it a rational covering of complacency. This is therefore a re-doubled fraud since its real ancillary condition is hidden behind the vain pretension to self-legitimise itself and give itself autonomy. We shall see this off-beam reason in the end place itself in the service of the most vulgar pragmatism, in the service of the laboratory and industrial production, of management and bureaucracy.

In Peirce and James this new avatar of reason is at least perfectly clear: the work of reason is no longer that of the negative, it has ceased to be critical. Although in France people delighted in the providential Bergson, this is precisely what certain thinkers in Germany in the 1930s, who formed what came to be called the Frankfurt School, realised when they undertook a critique of reason and its servile use, founding 'critical theory' in order to restore the critique of its power. Thus Horkheimer and Adorno and, slightly less neglected in France, Benjamin and Marcuse, and even Habermas. All of them showed how reason was in collusion with

16 This question by which we call the Frankfurt School to account about the ultimate meaning of its rationalism can also be formulated in this way: why this refusal of the irrational if it is not by virtue of a normativity prior to the experience of life? It is never truly a question of this *a priori* normativity, a Kantian one on the whole, of which the Frankfurt philosophers in general (and Marcuse in particular) remain prisoners. But the fact that it might not have been questioned does not leave the debate without response. The refusal of the irrational, the appeal to the universal, leads them to a conception of art and its relations with revolution which amount to enclosing art in a definition it has long gone beyond, and deprives the revolution of forces that it might draw from sensibility. The fetish of purified reason constitutes an ostracism of the sensibility. As we know, the surrealist response is very different.

power, as philosophy and science were with politics, and they all denounced the most formidable ideology, that of the supposed anti-ideological weapon which is reason itself. The realisation of the rational is finally nothing other than that of world bureaucracy, henceforth the only effective outcome that might be acknowledged in it. And it is the instrumental functional rationality of means alone which ineluctably leads us to this end, without this consequently being posed as such by reason or, moreover, anything else. Because what characterises the current period above all, and in an essential way is inseparably the hyper-rationality of means and the total irrationality of ends: a perfect machine and perfectly crazy. 'The acceptability of ideas, the criteria for our actions and beliefs, the leading principles of ethics and politics, all our ultimate decisions, are made to depend upon factors other than reason', declares Max Horkheimer at the beginning of *Eclipse of Reason* [Horkheimer 1947, p.7]. Thus reason has become simply functional as it has become subjective and formal, and as such it 'conforms to absolutely everything' and can no longer claim to found anything at all. These latest avatars of the history of reason lead it to renounce its highest prerogatives, to arm its critique, to give in and sell itself off. But this destruction of reason is recognised only by a reason that has continued to be critical while it has nevertheless still laid claim to the determination of both ends and means. Moreover, such a critique draws part of its pertinence and importance from the idea that reason itself is historically alienated and becomes coarse, as though its virtue had been caught unawares, but that beyond its vicissitudes and confusions, recovering and becoming itself once more, it could again secure its role as a rector. There is in Horkheimer a nostalgia, expressed in a will towards restoration which we do not share, even though we fully recognise the historical necessity of the Enlightenment. This reason no longer illuminates but blinds and prevents any engagement with the neo-barbarism which has resulted from it. If 'being reasonable', as Horkheimer opportunely notes, means above all 'don't be stubborn', in other words to submit to reality such as it is, then it is not being reasonable that is required, but being even more unreasonable. What then can this de-rationalisation, this un-reason, be? Would it be equivalent to a conquest of the irrational, to a risky recognition of territories spared by the control of reason, of subjective territories that cannot be assigned to the pragmatic order of facts and functions?

One question seems to remain unresolved or held back within critical theory: that of understanding by which virtue reason, when it is not corrupted, if this was ever the case, is a virtue. What is this supposed virtue which never collapses? Why this continuing bad luck? Where is the virtue? This is a problem that is hardly ever posed but remains important to settle if we want accurately to weigh up the possible actions in order to prevent them from lapsing into the profits and losses of today's great machinery.[16]

Let's observe. On the one hand a wild hatred of a reason progressively but surely employed to speed minds along so as more effectively to take hold of bodies and bring them to heel – and, consequently, the reactive temptation of a wild irrationalism which exercises an instinctual terrorism against mechanised brainwashing by opposing it with the spasms of a dispossessed and uninhabitable body. On the other hand: the faith is retained in reason, but in a reason which would never have had to suffer the outrages of history, therefore in an idea of a purely regulatory, simple and indexed reason, one which nevertheless will never regulate anything, and on which humanity still relies to stigmatise its weaknesses! This would raise the question: can any arbitration of reason purely and simply be challenged without being thrown back onto the most dangerous irrationalism, that which we now know can result in rationalising and bureaucratising horror and penury? Idi Amin Dada is not a Dadaist! His insanity does not impel life under all its forms to extend itself through exultation; it is nothing but the work of death. The fine critical insouciance and the sublime cynicism of the Dadaists, if such they were in their heyday, would no longer be quite so appropriate today, as some of their number realised soon afterwards. Two-thirds of the way through the century we have fresh concerns which take over from the disappointed and then destroyed naiveties. Likewise this new evidence showing that the recourse to the irrational is not and can no longer be the recourse it was in the past, is no longer and can no longer be the Recourse. The irrational itself has become suspect, now that it has offered itself as an easy prey to every pragmatist undertaking and as a convenient alibi for every renunciation. This means at the same time that the old struggle against reason upheld in its positivist Procrustean bed is no longer operational, just as previously the struggle for an emancipatory, liberatory reason had ceased to exist. Such offensives no longer have an object and therefore mean nothing. The target has become mobile, and barely recognisable, at once omnipresent and omni-absent, everywhere and nowhere. As for the objective of defending the rights of the irrational, in other words the defence of human rights, it relies as much on the sustained denunciation of all of the breaches of trust for which reason is equally the pretext, the means and the object, as on the renunciation of any systematic disqualification, of any 'rational' approach to, and any glorification in principle of, what is set up as irrational.

A confused situation, apparently, in which the meaning of all action can be lost. Let's consider the situation once more. The reduction of reason to technical and technocratic rationality leads more generally to any thing being considered as a potential machine and soon, with the aid of cybernetics, as an actual machine. Life is a delight for the living, and a thought for thinkers, who see their activity reduced to the desirable standardised mechanical act: a living gadget, processed and lost (the idea that the individual is in the process 'of being liquidated' is still too optimistic, thinks Adorno). The last resources of the individual – those which, taking refuge in an ever narrower margin, have still eluded the general process of reification and uni-dimensionalisation – undoubtedly

17 Jean Baudrillard, *The Consumer Society: Myths and Structures*, London: Sage Publications, 1998 [trans.].

18 Viktor Tausk (1879–1919), psychoanalyst, a student and colleague of Freud's, mainly known for a paper on 'influencing machines', a delusion in which patients believe they are being persecuted by mystical machines whose workings they are able to describe in detail [trans.].

need to be consolidated, even if this might only be a matter of a simple reaction of self-conservation and defence whose significance is necessarily and already reduced, if not recuperated, if it is true, as Baudrillard forcefully shows,[17] that our society is balanced on consumption and its denunciation: that it is therefore reinforced by its very contradictions in so far as it succeeds in containing their destructive explosion. We must therefore recognise, in addition to the extreme lability of these reactions, their precise objective ambiguity. Besides the fact of the phenomena of massification and bureaucratisation, which today appear inescapable, any mass action is itself objectively constrained to abandon its ends by necessarily having recourse to the means which the current general situation imposes upon it. As a first approximation, the 'solution' can only therefore lie between the reification of consciousnesses and social massification, arising then from a fair estimate, to be constantly adjusted and readjusted, between these limits, of the momentary conditions of a genuine freedom of action. Without doubt naive conscience – good conscience – with its fine naivety that is commanded, created and maintained with the ideological chloroform it needs, will cry out and put a price on these various glimpses, in their summary state it is true, of the Machiavellian delirium of persecution. Yet we think it is reality itself which has become Machiavellian, and to a degree that goes far beyond Machiavelli's infamous realism. We estimate that the intoxication of consciences, and of increasingly younger consciences, by the 'spirit' of 'functional' rationality is something which arises from the initial observations in favour of a sociology of mentalities and aspirations.

In this present day of a twentieth century about to turn eighty, in which anomie is organised and renewed without any real change being achievable; in which the techniques of obsolescence immediately take hold of any innovation; in which initiatives, immediately amplified by the mass media, fall at the same time into a passive, indifferent and undifferentiated oblivion; in which the accumulation of knowledge makes all understanding impossible; in which bloated repletion is just as often called penury; in which desire is alienated in a system of purely ideological needs; in which the gratuitous use of signs (a human privilege according to the cyberneticians) manages to operate only in spite of the always greater primacy of system over word, denotation over connotation and representation over presence; in which everything is destined to pass through the strictures of 'functional' and bureaucratic rationality, pleasure as much as violence; when everything either is or is about to be turned into schizophrenia, and when we feel as if, like Victor Tausk's patients, we are the victims of the 'Influencing Machine',[18] and fear succumbing and abandoning ourselves to it; we wonder: is it still possible to escape this system of influences? What other delirium would release us from it?

But who is delirious at first? And why and how? Do I or the machines make *me* delirious? From what fissure do we emerge and for what other? Could it possibly be for no other? Who disturbs

19 It's clear that we do not fear giving in to fashion, which these days means that an allusion at least has to be made to this famed couple of stars who were so very well aware of how to take their places on the almost deserted intellectual stage in the wake of May 1968. Their well-known book, in other words one more misunderstood than understood, cultivates the confusion of genres (which naturally is still a genre), something which would not at all displease us if the semi-fiction with which most of their considerations are surrounded did not (deliberately it would seem) uphold an indefinable confusion. What is the point of these brilliant exercises in variable simulations, this interference, this mechanism of imported notions, this machinery of models, this finely tuned disorder maintained by contradictions between thinking and spontaneity, logic and intuition? This dithyrambic Bacchic rite of *anti-oedipal* desire and schizophrenia has not gone without scaring some people. This dog in their game of skittles was for them a disaster, a challenge to all their mediocre efforts at conserving and maintaining the fine French-style garden for which they love to be seen to be responsible. For them, civilisation was placed in danger, at the same time as the laws of intellectual progress consecrated by the university. This is not what we are afraid of! We fear, totally to the contrary, that it's not that at all and that Deleuze and Guattari, as they interminably disclaim, might have simply produced a thick if rather bizarre and Baroque book, all-purpose and for everyone's information, occasioning here and there, but principally in the Parisian region, a thrill or itch. Deleuze and Guattari, a fine symptom!

20 Diete Forte, *Martin Luther und Thomas Münzer oder die Einführung der Buchhaltung*, published in 1971; this work has never been translated into English [trans.].

what? Who is disturbed? Does not a local derangement reinforce the global arrangement? Who hatched the machinations; and for what conscious or unconscious interests? Are Deleuze and Guattari[19] crazy cyberneticians? What does their delirium (their delirious desire), as well as their logic, *mean*? How does their delirium oscillate between the two paranoid and schizoid poles? What makes these permanently widowed bachelor machines, and what then is the work and benefit of such mourning? 'The question to be asked', Deleuze and Guattari say, 'is whether schizophrenics are the living machines of a dead labour, which are then contrasted to the dead machines of living work as they are organised in capitalism' [Deleuze and Guattari 2004, p.416]. The question is to know what this question means and implies... Are there no other infernal machines against the empire of structure, and especially the Oedipal structure, than so-called desiring machines, or against familiarism than the mechanism of desire? And how should all these machines work? Is it in such a way that 'the social machine, the technical machine, the desiring machine closely marry and cause their system to communicate', as declared at the end of *Anti-Oedipus*? It cannot be a question of consecrating the identity of the social machine with the desiring machine, which resides in the fact that the first, as the second, is not limited by 'attrition, but rather [by] its misfiring; it can operate only by fits and starts, by grinding down and breaking down, in spasms of minor explosions. The dysfunctions are an essential element of its very ability to function, and is the least important aspect of the system of cruelty' (ibid., p.151). Has anyone ever died from contradictions? No, they have fed on them: so it is with capitalism. 'And the more it is disordered, the more it is made schizophrenic, the better it works, in the American style.' On the other hand, is it the motor-desire (the desiring machine) which requires this agreement of systems? And agreement under what system? And how (theoretically and practically, in praxis, in the order of causes) to realise it, in other words other than in a state of hallucination, as desire-aspiration? Can the system of the axiomatic bookkeeper of capitalism (whose beginnings are correctly clarified in the work of Dieter Forte,[20] *Martin Luther et Thomas Münster ou les débuts de la comptabilité*) enable him to admit in himself the manifestations of desire by re-encoding and finally repressing it, not seal off all ruptures? What failure can escape the functional law according to which 'a social machine must *not function well* in order *to* function'? This functional failure is nothing other than what is called the game – the soul of the mechanism, as has been precisely said. This game, but now just as much taken in all the other senses of this very significantly polysemic word, is nothing other than a very precisely controlled alienation.

What we need is a completely different game.

MACHINE-MAN, WILL YOU ALWAYS CHERISH THE SAME FAILURES?

MEDIVM

COMMUNICATION SURRÉALISTE

N° WIFREDO LAM

Nouvelle Série - Janvier 1955

4

Part 2

The Challenge of Otherness

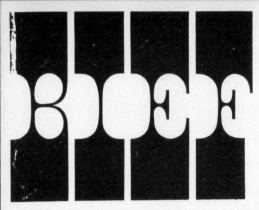

JONCTION SURRÉALISTE

Photo F. Drithon.

Les indigènes [des îles Marquises] qui étaient jadis les plus beaux et les plus virils de la Polynésie tropicale, et qui pouvaient compter quelque 75.000 âmes, ne sont plus qu'une poignée d'hommes, parmi lesquels on ne trouverait sans doute pas plus d'un millier de pur-sang. Ils languissent dans leur décadence physique et morale, tout en gardant leur fierté ; ils méprisent les institutions étrangères, qu'elles soient administratives, commerciales, ou religieuses, mais ils sont honorables et fidèles en amitié pour peu qu'on leur témoigne une estime sincère.

E.S. Craighil Handy, Ph. D.
Ethnologist of the Bishop Museum.

(Introduction à l'Art des Îles Marquises, par Willowdean C. Handy, Paris, les Éditions d'art et d'histoire, 1938).

N° 1. ● 15 Novembre 1958

Éditeur : LE TERRAIN VAGUE

The Challenge of Otherness

As documented in the first section, surrealism was founded in a challenge to the idea of the self, a challenge which involved confronting its own strangeness, its otherness, the fact that what is most familiar can also be what is most alien, something verified by what the surrealists learned from Freud, through the engagement with the unconscious, and Hegel, in the realisation that the self is constructed only through recognition and communication with an Other. In more immediate terms, such perceptions were put into practice politically in the anti-colonial struggle, initiated for surrealists by their opposition to the Rif colonial war in Morocco, in which French troops joined Spanish attempts to suppress revolts by the Berber tribesmen led by Abd-el-Krim. This conflict both concretised the surrealists' internationalism and fed their interest in non-western cultures, something they had already been concerned with at a theoretical level to the extent that they were inheritors of the many trends of modernism which extolled the 'primitive', from the largely aesthetic appreciation of African art, which in different ways inspired the fauvists or the cubists, to the respect for primitive ways of life that profoundly inspired artists from Gauguin onwards.

Almost from the beginning, however, the surrealists approached non-western cultures with a far more critical eye than any of their predecessors. If, during 1926 and 1927, they indulged in a certain exoticisation of other cultures through an exaltation of the 'Orient' as an alternative to western decadence with the spiritual resources to renew western culture or even to act as its nemesis, the return of the repressed that would purge the West of its hated capitalist and Christian presuppositions – this was merely a necessary stage to move towards a greater appreciation of the complexity of culture in an anthropological sense. Indeed, it was nourished by direct contacts with social scientists then constituting the budding discipline of anthropology.

The texts included in this section trace different aspects of the surrealists' engagement with 'otherness', which did not simply reflect a fascination with 'other cultures' but involved a broader questioning of the anthropological and philosophical relation of self and other. This reflected their fundamental concern with the nature of the encounter as the foundation of 'reality': the fact that for the surrealists reality is not something pre-existing into which we are cast at random, but is constituted dynamically in interaction between ourselves and the world.

Chiekh Tidiane Sylla
Reproduced in
Arsenal: Surrealist Subversion,
no. 4, 1989

The section begins with an early text by Robert Desnos published in *La Révolution surréaliste* and reflecting their Orientalist phase. In it he celebrates what he saw as most valuable in Jewish culture, that is as a culture of wandering and revolt in opposition both to the West and to the Zionism which he perceived as undermining this vitality. If Desnos's characterisation of Jewish culture may now appear naive, it sets down a marker of surrealist concern to oppose all forms of nationalist braggadocio and exclusionism, as embodied here for Desnos by the consecration of Jerusalem as a sacred place that could be claimed by a particular religion or culture.

Even more than Desnos, Antonin Artaud rejected western culture as a perversion of the human spirit. More than perhaps anyone in surrealism, Artaud placed his own self at stake as he sought to rediscover an authentic relation with the world which he felt had almost been lost. In the text here he asks us to reconsider the nature of culture as a universal sensibility which its bureaucratisation in modern society was, and is, in the process of destroying.

Jacques Viot was only a marginal participant in surrealism, but his 'déposition de blanc', the deposition of a white man or evidence of blankness, recounting what he witnessed of colonial piracy and exploitation as an art dealer in the South Seas during the late 1920s, was very influential in advancing the surrealists' critique of the colonial relation.

The distance the surrealists had come by the early 1930s in their understanding of the issues involved in the complex relation of self and other (as an anthropological, philosophical and psychological phenomenon) is shown by 'The Patriotism of the Unconscious', in which René Crevel equates the colonisation of the mind by psychoanalysis (or more specifically its application as a mode of psychological realism) with the exploitation of other cultures.

Benjamin Péret, meanwhile, had spent a lot of time in Brazil and Mexico and was engaging in his own extensive exploration of indigenous traditions, poetry and myth. This account of a trek through the rain forest complements his earlier text on ruins; there the focus was on the wreck of human hopes for permanence, here it is on nature's own inexorable and paradoxical struggle simultaneously to survive. His text on ruins introduces a further aspect of otherness – that of our own past as it continues to haunt us through the evidence of loss which the ruin represents.

In their texts René Ménil and Annie Le Brun are concerned to confront fashionable ideological positions which they respectively see as leading us along false paths. For Ménil, writing in the 1960s, it is the political doctrine of negritude as it underwrote the ideology of the emergent post-colonial regimes in francophone Africa, while Le Brun,

NUMÉRO 6 (Nouvelle série)   AVRIL 1973

LES LÈVRES NUES

RÉDACTION : MARCEL MARIËN, BOITE POSTALE 1186, BRUXELLES 1

LA CHAISE D'ÉCOUTE

Les cheveux ne poussent pas le lundi.

Une veuve de paix.

Le bon vieil espace.

A l'arbre nulle feuille n'est tenue.

Le guépard n'attaque heureusement pas le scutenaire.

Dieu n'existe pas le dimanche.

Le meilleur juge, c'est le coupable.

Plus de conscience ou plus de conscience, that is the question.

Atteint de marxisme-léninisme, Tarzan s'en fut mourir en Bolivie.

La goutte de sperme qui fait déborder le néant.

Le bourreau a toujours les larmes aux yeux.

A Sodome où les dames portaient leur derrière par devant.

Célèbre comme le soldat inconnu, franc comme le Masque de fer.

La chaisière est toujours debout.

La vie secrète de Salvador Dali : il n'en a pas.

La débauche des mineurs doit être l'œuvre des mineurs eux-mêmes.

Les ongles de François d'Assise.

Le sadisme et le masochisme ne sont que des moyens d'expression.

Belges ! encore un effort si vous voulez être républicains.

Il la caresse de l'anuk à la nuce.

L'avenir de la jeunesse, c'est la vieillesse.

Saint Joseph aimait les restes.

Il faut mettre le pompidur dans la pompidouce.

Et Job se réjouit : Au moins ce Salaud m'a laissé mon fumier !

L'aveugle pleure aussi.

LES ENTRETIENS DE LUZERNE-LA-BAIGNOIRE. — Louis Scutenaire et Paul Colinet en juillet 1956. *(Photos G. Thiry)*

drawing on Ménil to some extent, is concerned to tear the veil away from the supposed universalism of movements of multiculturalism and hybridity as represented here by the Creolism ideology in the Caribbean.

Jacques Viot's view that it was impossible for westerners to enter the enchanted castle of 'primitive culture' became ever apparent to André Breton during the 1930s but especially after the Second World War when he urged that it would be more productive to seek alternative visions of the world within hidden traditions of western culture. This initiated a particular interest in Celtic cultures, one of the results of which was Breton's own 'Embers in Ceridwen's Cauldron'.

The aftermath of the Second World War led many of those linked with surrealism to re-examine the relationship between the human and natural worlds and issues of ecological balance that still have resonance today. In his essay, Georges Bataille takes up a theme that had long interested him, that of our relationship to the horse in its double configuration as an exalted, noble animal on the one hand and wretched beast of burden on the other, which has a parallel equivalence in the human world. Jacqueline Sénard-Duprey, in contrast, is concerned specifically with the importance of maintaining an effective ecological balance, something which the surrealists became aware of in the 1950s, long before it became a central concern in general discourse.

Another issue that particularly concerned the surrealists in the 1950s was the emergence of a prevalent 'scientism' that, much like the movements celebrating hybridity criticised by Ménil and Le Brun, brought together disparate ideas into a questionable and confused unity that served as a smokescreen for a potentially dangerous ideology. This trend, exemplified by the work of Pauwels and Bergier who initiated what we would now call 'New Ageism' with the publication of their bestseller *The Morning of the Magicians*, is subjected to a witty critique by Robert Benayoun.[1]

The Romanian surrealist group (which was active only during the 1940s before its members became dispersed following the communist takeover of the country) engaged in some of the most intensive collective work in the history of surrealism and this delirious text, like much of their work, is included here both as an example of surrealist collective work and as a meditation on and exploration of the nature of objectification.

In the final text in this section, René Alleau brings together several of its themes as he calls for the reinvigoration of the notion of 'civilisation' itself by means of a fresh 'exodus' from Egypt.

1 This question has been fascinatingly explored by Gavin Parkinson in his *Futures of Surrealism: Myth, Science Fiction and Fantastic Art in France, 1936–1969*, New Haven: Yale University Press 2015.

Robert Desnos
Pamphlet against Jerusalem

This strange and rather obscure text was written at the time of the surrealists' Orientalist phase, when for a short time they became fascinated by the idea of the East as the eternal avenger against western excess. Desnos was especially taken with this notion[1] and the text retains interest as an aspect of the surrealists' anti-nationalist sentiments and their advocacy of social and cultural vagabondage, in accordance with Breton's injunction to 'leave everything' as a marking point of his own departure from Dada. For Desnos this sensibility is embodied by the peripatetic quality of Jewish culture, which he seeks to celebrate in opposition to its perversion into Zionism. Sadly everything Desnos warns against in this text would be enacted: the Jewish spirit in which he places his hopes will soon be destroyed by the Nazis and an oppressive Zionist State will later come to embody the very nationalism he abhors, while Desnos himself will personally feel its effects. Shunted between one concentration camp and another, he experienced the horrors of both Auschwitz and Buchenwald before dying soon after the liberation in Terezin.

1.

First published in *La Révolution surréaliste*, no.3, 25 April 1925; reprinted in Robert Desnos, *Nouvelles Hébrides*, Paris: Gallimard, 1978.

The Jews have always presented the spectacle of self-flagellation. They are the ones who recount the nastiest stories about Israel. It is they who make fools of themselves, who accuse and condemn themselves. Little old man Drumont,[2] you couldn't have done it.

Perhaps I would then be able to express with greater freedom than them my admiration for the sacred character of their mission and denounce, in writing which is not anti-Semitic, all the horror I feel for nascent nationalism and all the hope I place in them to defeat a certain desertion of the spirit.

2.

1 Desnos may have collaborated on a novel, *La Papesse du diable*, in which Oriental hordes led by a merciless princess lay waste to Europe. Written around 1927 this novel was not published until 1958 (Paris: Eric Losfeld) under the pseudonym of Jehan Sylvius and Pierre de Ruynes. There is some doubt about who its real authors were but Desnos and Jean Genbach seem most likely to have been involved in it. It is certainly a work that emerges from the surrealist environment of this period, perhaps providing its culmination [trans.].

If America had been discovered (in the sense in which the descendants of Columbus understand it) by Oriental navigators from the west, in other words from the Pacific, instead of by Westerners from across the Atlantic, we would probably not have to signal the danger run by the spirit in the fact that Asia, the citadel of all hopes, is being attacked from west and east. The American continent would then have been an advanced fortress, impregnable to people with narrow minds from the old world (as they call, speaking of this wasp's nest, Asia's wart, Europe).

At the current time, the question of taking sides in the great quarrel of mind and matter admits no further indifference. From the foothills of Tibet to the plump valleys of coloured rivers, to the elephant plains and alligator swamps, from the Himalayas to the Coromandel coast, from Amu Darya to Sakhalin, deep souls feel the storm, the Western epidemic, approaching like an ocean. Make

2 Édouard Adolphe Drumont (1844–1917), journalist who founded the Anti-semitic League of France and played a leading role in the persecution of Alfred Dreyfus [trans.].

Illustration reproduced
in Desnos's article

no mistake. Japan has been contaminated, westernised. Russia,
balanced between its two antagonistic fragments, has not affirmed
its will in a spiritual direction. Everywhere else everything holds
back the danger, but for how long? The battle for Africa has been
ardently engaged without a sound. Let no defections occur among
the defenders of the knot of the universe whose side one must take
in the name of infinity and eternity!

Among the Oriental races, the Jewish race seems to have
received a special mission. Delegated among the enemies,
consciously or not, they are not the servants of the primitive spirit.
A strange race. The Christians adore one of its individuals, crucified
by his compatriots.

Mystics can speculate on the strange circumstances of the
Passion on this poetic terrain, but it nevertheless remains that,
without lyricism, however legitimate it might be, the Jews were
introduced into Europe following Jesus. Once more the Red Sea

3 Tamerlane (1335?–1405), Turkic conqueror of most of southern and western Asia [trans.].

4 Leonidas (499?–480 BC), Spartan king slain in the battle of Thermopylae [trans.].

5 Place de Grève, square in Paris which was a place of execution during the Revolution [trans.].

6 Church in Paris, the scene of a barricade that witnessed fierce fighting during a republican uprising in 1832 [trans.].

7 *Isbas*: thatched cottages of Russian peasants [trans.].

opened for a magnificent conquest, but the persecutors had a notion of the drowning to which they were predestined. On the ocean, the cradle of Moses encountered a powerful liner and the air was full of supernatural storms on the point of breaking.

What then is their role, these scouts for a future Tamerlane,[3] what wind propels them, these new Spartans, after Leonidas's crucifixion,[4] going from defence on to the attack?

3.

Although they pretended to submit to the influence of the country in which they lived, the atmosphere was transformed wherever the Jews passed through. No doubt we do not see them leading revolts, proclaiming the truths necessary to the birth of revolutions but, in the crowd, look at those arched noses, the wavy hair, the velvet gazes. Emerging from the ghettos and peaceful shops, those one could believe intent solely on the pursuit of money revealed themselves to be the anonymous pillars of insurrection. They opened the doors of freemasonry in the eighteenth century to uneasy minds, they left the first baker hung in La place de Grève,[5] stimulating popular ardour and leaving on their counters gleaming with usury the assay scales for weighing gold. The church of Saint-Merri[6] saw them behind the famous barricade; the white plains of Siberia, the Russia isbas[7] sheltered them and their bombs. The last century saw destiny seize one of them and remind the French that they had to recognise themselves and find a place behind the two enemy banners of the Country and Freedom.

Others, burdened with less evident need, left to their brothers the thankless need for an agent provocateur of the spirit. And these are the bankers and these are the ministers still exaggerating the infamy of the enemy class which welcomes them. In their hands gold seems endowed with a reptile life, the stock exchanges rock on their neo-classical foundations, the course of Rio Tinto and the petroleum wells become certain instruments of demoralisation.

Colourless emigrants insensible to the blows of fate, migratory birds from humid ports, usurers in black, Levites from Fes and Nizhny Novgorod, Baron de Rothschild, Mr Dreyfus (whom others call captain), a trader in vodka and smoked fish from the rue des Rosiers, by different means, unknown to you perhaps, you pursue the same goal, you take part in the same cause.

Lost children! Cursed children! The Arab spits as you pass and you are the rampart of Mecca, the Buddhist despises you and you defend the Ganges, Lhasa is forbidden to you and you are among the servants of the Lamas, white ideas in a white sky.

Yet it's a fable, these political and useful hatreds in the fair accomplishment of the task you are assigned. Whether it detests or defends you, the West is prey to the elevated thoughts your trail entails; you are an element of disorder among the enemies of the Orient; the passions against which several millennia of Mediterranean civilisation have risen up are reborn, more profound and capable of impelling humans to extreme determinations. You are the most despised and sacrificed among the soldiers of Asia, the

8 We might also mention that unspeakable woman of letters who, as a delegate of this assembly, has assumed the mission of fighting obscene literature (!). [The identity of this woman is unknown to us – trans.].

isolated African foot soldier at the mercy of pogroms and cowardly vengeances – and yet you have never weakened, never has your activity been checked.

And yet, born from the League of Nations, we see a sentimental movement press towards the resurrection of Zion and the foundation of a Jewish State as ridiculous and artificial as Poland. Then all these impure ones, all these mixed brains which might weaken Europe, to Asia's benefit, would return to the sacred land, taking with them the worst sickness of the soul, the scepticism contracted during this two-thousand-year expedition into enemy lands. The confusion which they carry where they go they would take to the narrow valley of the Jordan, to the tragic banks of the Red Sea. This force will turn against what it has a mission to defend in becoming the advanced post of the western nations and as dangerous as the English and French colonies. By subsidising the Zionist expedition, the Rothschilds are going against the genius of the race.

I am well aware that it's rare to see those who desert and leave to find the famous Wailing Wall where imbecilic littérateurs have thought they saw the spirit of Israel returning to its cradle in the form of a few old men. Fortunately there is no doubt about the failure of such an attempt. The Monaco Monte Carlo of the Levant has not yet opened its casino and, if the reactionaries have not yet pushed the wheel of the old biblical chariot, nothing in their attitude suggests displeasure or worry. Quite the contrary: this quasi-silence should be seen as a mark of joy. These fine politicians rub their hands! Perhaps their territory will be evacuated.

But a current has been created. They must assume importance. The Israelites must remain in exile so long as the western cause is not yet lost, as long as this Latin, Greek, Anglo-Saxon and German mind, which is the most terrible threat to the spirit, has not been overwhelmed.

From Paris to Rome, from London to New York, from Oxford to Hamburg, every day the sickness becomes more acute. The old Sadist of Geneva claims to sequestrate the soul. The final freedoms are threatened. The right to opium, to alcohol and to love, the right to abortion, the right of the individual to dispose of himself, this is what the sinister monks of the League of Nations are in the process of destroying.[8]

And it is at the very moment when the world needs its thirty sacred pieces of silver, which you hold onto while claiming to shun! The very idea of a possible retreat should feed your revolt against the feeble and cowardly among you. The day approaches, your day. This time it is a question of life or death, for all that is worth being lived and defended.

Judas's thirty coins were not given in vain. You retained them in order to buy rarer ones which are worth taking the trouble to save. Don't squander them by reclaiming sentimental lands.

It is a treasure that all the gold in the world could not buy back for you.

Antonin Artaud
The Universal Bases of Culture

This essay, the text of a talk given by Artaud in Mexico in 1936, is a powerful assertion of surrealist identification with earlier forms of culture (for Artaud the only real culture), and especially emphasises the intensity of surrealist rejection of rationalist individualism. Artaud's assertion that the purpose of culture is not to modify man but to modify existence *within* man offers us a fundamental key to the surrealist attitude and the profound reason for it considering modern society to be decadent, since it has surrendered our essential being to individual advancement or self-development. His severe criticism of Hermann Keyserling's appropriation of non-western culture accords with several other essays in this collection (see those of Benayoun, Menil, Le Brun, etc.) and his comments on the commercialisation of education seem extraordinarily prescient in today's world.

First published in *El Nacional* (Mexico), 18 August 1936; reprinted in Antonin Artaud, *Messages révolutionnaires*, Paris: Gallimard, 1971.

In Europe today, culture, like training and education, is a luxury that has to be bought. This is the best proof that the meaning of words is being lost and that there is nothing like a confusion over words to reveal a now generalised state of decadence in Europe. This is really why, before discussing culture, the meaning of this word needs to be clarified. First I would say what everyone understands, or thinks they understand, by it, and then what it really means. We speak of a cultivated person and of the cultivated earth, and in this way we are expressing an action, an almost material transformation of man and the earth. One can be trained without really being cultivated. Training is clothing. The word 'training' signifies that someone has been dressed in knowledge. The word 'culture', on the other hand, signifies that the earth, the profound humus of man, has been *prepared*. Training and culture are generally confused, and in Europe, where words no longer mean anything, the words 'training' and 'culture' are used in current language to express a single and identical thing, although in reality they are two profoundly different things. And even if they are not confused, properly speaking, training and culture are situated on the same level and considered as going together, when everything we see around us proves that the contradictory scattered culture of Europe no longer has anything in common with the absolutely uniform state of its civilisation.

When I arrived in Mexico and I spoke about its ancient culture, the response from all sides was more or less the same: 'But there are a hundred cultures in Mexico!' Proof that today's Mexicans have forgotten the very meaning of the word culture and confuse uniform culture with the multiplicity of forms of civilisation. As distinct as its civilisations were, ancient Mexico in reality had only a single culture, in other words a unique idea of humanity, of nature, of death and of life; in contrast, modern

Jan Švankmajer
Bride of Ikarus 1990

9 Hermann Alexander Keyserling (1880–1946), German philosopher, opponent of German militarism [trans.].

Europe, having known how to make its civilisation uniform, has endlessly multiplied its conception of culture and, relative to the very idea of culture, it is, one can say it, in a state of complete anarchy.

If Europe conceives of culture as a gloss, it is because it has forgotten what culture was in those days when it genuinely existed. Words in fact have a rigorous meaning, and it is not possible to uproot the profound meaning from the word *culture* – its sense of the integral, one might even say magical, modification not of man but of the being within man, because the really cultivated person carries his mind in his body and it is his body that he works through culture, which means that he works his mind at the same time.

Europe has conceived of culture as what is contained in books, and every European nation has its books, that is its philosophy. In recent years a multitude of systems have been born, each corresponding to the appearance of a new book, and not only does each nation possess its own system, but so too does each political party. And inversely to what was produced in the great ages, when philosophers ruled over life and gave birth to politics, each new political system creates philosophers who woefully attempt to justify its demagoguery.

Marxism, a political system founded on a certain number of elementary confirmations as regards the economy, has produced a whole materialist conception of the world. Italy is so spiritually impoverished that it has been unable even to give rise to a single philosopher, yet Hitler's fascism has its philosophers whose system is a monstrous hotchpotch of Nietzsche, Kant, Herder, Fichte and Schelling. In Europe, alongside the prophets of the new west, we find prophets of western decadence, and alongside serious people like Spengler, Scheler and Heidegger, we find the minor masters of decadence who, like Keyserling,[9] are no more than travelling salesmen, lovers of a cast-off Hinduism and, beyond all measure, those who flit around the theme of the unconscious, from the Freudian form to the American form, this unconscious whose spectroscopy they imagine they can perform. For me, there could be nothing more odious than the philosophical snobbery of a Keyserling, especially when this snobbery, about beliefs on which humanity's primitive and hidden life is nourished, is just about good enough to turn it into something fashionable.

There is no sacred philosophy or great culture with which Keyserling has not meddled so as odiously to vulgarise its doctrines, even though, to demonstrate them, the ancient Indian Brahmins sometimes went so far as to sacrifice their lives. The case of Keyserling is aggravated by the fact that he presumes a system, I mean a personal dogmatism, from traditions which represented the collective and anonymous wisdom of whole countries and immense ages, at a time when the people who were the vehicle of these traditions and doctrines were careful not to allow them to be appropriated on an individual basis. In this Keyserling obeys the individualist and anarchic spirit of a Europe which currently counts as many philosophies as there are philosophers, and as many cultures as philosophies.

Two or three years ago there was grotesque talk of the United States of Europe. It would have been more profitable to speak of the total unbalancing of European culture, because the lamentable state of this dust of cultures which today represents Europe would have been for everyone the very proof that the United States of Europe was already no more than an obsolete buffoonery.

Jacques Viot
Don't Clutter Up the Colonies (fragment); Approaching the Enchanted Castle

The surrealists' uncompromisingly anti-colonialist attitude was established very early. In 1924, Paul Éluard and Max Ernst embarked upon their mysterious trips to the South Seas, about which they never spoke but which has been reconstructed with panache by Robert McNab in his magisterial book *Ghost Ships*, in which he shows how this trip had a determining influence on surrealist attitudes towards the 'primitive' and the oppresive colonial regimes that were in the process of extirpating it. This perception was reinforced through the more extensive voyages made by Jacques Viot to the same region in the late 1920s. Viot's view was uncompromising: for him civilisation was a sickness in need of curing, which could only be effected through a process of un-learning. Without it, we were forever excluded from the enchanted castle that is 'life'.

Published in *Le Surréalisme au service de la révolution*, no.1, July 1930.

[...] Ever since I approached New Guinea, stumbling and ludicrously armed with a fountain pen and thermometer, it has dominated my memory. It lies brilliant beneath the equator like a fortress that one could circumnavigate without finding its shadow and that could never be attacked except in the open, but from its heights the weight of its mystery falls on the assailant and if we are afraid of its strength it is only because its reflection has frightened us.

D'Albertis,[10] dying from fever, one day found a bird of paradise more beautiful than any of those he had so far come across: a black bird of paradise. He fled, overwhelmed. I want to be convinced that the only black bird was in d'Albertis's mind, but that he had been one of the only ones to cross the first stockades, beyond which one never knows what one might find.

Advancing towards the east, we would find other mountains, ones which would seem more accessible and vaulted, as powerful as an enormous musculature, and bare, denuded of forests: the Cyclops Mountains. Behind them the clear region of Lake Sentani opens up – a haven of grace, it seems, after Geelvink Bay – and one starts to believe, amidst its lighter landscape where it is easier to breathe, that the door is open and the path gentle, that you are an

10 Luigi Maria D'Albertis (1841–1901), Italian explorer especially noted for his explorations in Papua New Guinea [trans.].

expected and welcome guest. The lake, surrounded by small bright hills with pale green slopes, with such curious outlines, and scattered with islets to which the villages cling, bathes as though it were the retort, in New Guinea with its oppressive power, of a blue clearing in an overcast sky. The pure simplicity of the horizon, when I reached this lake after an exhausting march, the harmony with this nature of the gentle people who were waiting for me by the water, with their more regular features, with those long dugout canoes without poles, which are light in the water and elegant, as though they were the most perceptible expression of their souls, called to me – reminding me that elsewhere I had known the freshness, the dawn dew, the feeling of morning in which, such a long way from Europe, on this luminous lake, near these mountains covered by evening, under an enlarged sky that had become pale, I now found all hope once again.

As we arrived on the other bank, I kept watching the sky slip to the bottom of the lake, right to these final reflections as though of a pale child drowned under window panes and, when I returned to myself, terrifying New Guinea was once again there. Under the great breadfruit trees, I heard the flying foxes which fought the darkness with their terrible membranes. I plunged among the immobile gesticulation of leaves that were too big and of unknown trees, among the dark hollows, the forms and the nameless stains. I went towards a small light that awaited me. Insects started to screech with an acuteness born at once from exuberance and agony, and I could still hear the sound of the flying creatures' webbed paws. Suddenly I thought I had become blind. I took a step, stretching out my arms. One more step in New Guinea. The light reappeared.

When I reached it, butterflies were flying all around. One among them was larger than my two hands. Others were pearls. Some were cerise and white, like a summer dress, others were completely filigreed, bearers of mottos, and still others, simply, were like a little fresh leaf...

If God created man in his image so as to praise his creation, why do these butterflies fly at night?

I have spoken of occultism... But do they have occultism? It is in any case a word which doesn't really fit. Their occultism, if that is what it should be called, is not occulted.

It could also be said, more correctly, that they are haunted. They are even, certainly, haunted. On this point the tales of Catholic missionaries would make your hair stand on end, for we know how easy it is for Catholics to see the Devil. But in reality primitives are haunted in a delightful way. As for German scientists, if they speak about Papuans... You know the story of the lady with hiccups.

She asks her husband, 'Coco, frighten me.'

'Boo!' says her husband.

'Well, Coco, you didn't frighten me'...

German scientists cured hiccups.

Now that they are no longer considered to be idiots, great attempts have always been made to announce to the savages that they are unhappy. Come on, admit it! They do not admit it. Frequenting mystery leaves them perfectly happy.

'These rose bushes are very ungrateful, ' says the missionary.

Our philosophies have accepted the existence of a reality that is not present to our senses. Primitives do not make this distinction of two separated realms having at most a common frontier according to the latest information. They take a stone. It is a stone of mystery. This stone has a reality which extends into the extra-sensible: not a twin reality, not another reality of which it would be the appearance, but one and the same reality. In other words, matter and spirit are one.

This is why they do not explain the magical power of this stick. They do not say: it is Jupiter which… etc… But: it is a magic stick.

We have divided this stick up into: 1. stick; 2. Jupiter. Where is the stick now? We have mixed up all sticks; how do you expect us to recognise them all? And now Jupiter farts into the void. We think it can only end badly… How many philosophies have we not expended in order to recover Jupiter's stick! But how could they be expected to find it? They were the ones who divided it up. All they could do would be to divide and divide again… It is the only thing they know how to do.

All misfortune begins in that way. We were on the same line, like a starting line: people. But why did we think there was a starting point? That there was a race? There was no race. The proof of this is that we have not progressed. The first sages of the *Rig Veda* knew this as well as we do. This differentiation between mind and matter, the start of any civilisation, the artificial distancing from mystery, the appalling snare of an ideal which has to be merited, and there we are scampering along, with God in front of us, like a carrot on the end of a stick to hoodwink the soul. Millennia of endless perseverance! So have you not watched the termites, the bees, the social insects, all those creatures who believe in God? Where has it got them? How do they escape it? How will we escape it? We die…

Primitives have made friends with mystery. And they live it. Without controversy, without proselytism, without merit, without religion, without God. Primitives do not believe in God. They have no religion. Without it, there is no God. For God cannot do without praise.

Neither in fetishism nor in totemism is there a trace of religion. We spend our time trying to link primitivism with civilisation. We will not succeed. It is an egg. It is smooth and if we fracture it, it will have ceased to exist. But a tangled ritual exists and because there is a ritual we have inferred that it means religion, when it is really a question of magic. Fetishes and totems are mediums. Their ceremonies are the exercise of magic paths, used to obtain immediate advantages. They leap over dogma, faith, revelation and God. What is religion without one of these terms? From ritual to God, what are the degrees?

11 R.R. Marett, *Psychology and
Folklore*, Whitefish, Montana:
Kessinger Publishing, 2003,
p.66 [trans.].

And if we want to follow them, we also have to leap, but we cannot leap and cling on, as that Englishman did when he said: 'On the whole, ritual is the savage substitute for God' (Marett[11]). That's is too simple. I agree that the expression is elegant, but it is nonsense.

Primitives should be taken as they are. You can change nothing about them. The primitive soul is watchful behind its entrenchments; it will die rather than surrender. Not having 'evolved' (to repeat a word so dear to us), they are intact. They have never sought to flee their shadow. It belongs to them. They have not sold it. They are complete. They do not need to perfect themselves. Self-perfection is only a trick to make slaves push the wheel. They are free. They are saints. They push no wheels. They do not go anywhere. They have no goal. They have no hope.

When I came among them I did not find my place. They lived without me. They lived: we die. Living is the negation of God. Death does not exist. But if a powerful charm rots these arms and this day, they will return during the night to clasp me in their dreams. Eternity colours the feathers of birds. Hope alone is mortal.

'Suppose God was just fear of dying?' said Kirilov, the man who kills himself in Dostoyevsky's *The Possessed* – 'although to die is fear of God'. All civilisations have been nothing but flowerbeds of death. It blossoms there. We cultivate it. The incubation of death characterises us. It is what we call our culture. Because we believe there is a possible culture, as though the Future and the Past, having the same total of eternity, all experience had not already been accomplished, and as though it could contain another knowledge than ours. For the question is not to gain access to another knowledge, which is called dying, but to discover the one we possess. To know our knowledge, which is called living, and beyond which there are no questions because it is omniscience.

But what then are these veils that separate us from ourselves? They are the revelations, the false doors, which could only have been set up from within, because a world is closed when it is limitless.

And these revelations are the figures of time. Progress is a revelation like all others.

If time were suppressed there would be no more religion, no more goals, no more hope, no more God. There are no further changes. There is eternal continuation. Life. Our transmigrations coincide and this is omniscience. We will finally lose memory, that infirmity time has given us.

The colour we are painted is called temporal. Time is only a manifestation of space, but we have dissociated it from space. That was the first veil. After that we took the energy (gravitation, light, warmth) out of it and started to tangle ourselves up in all these dragnets. And the more we pull, the more appears. Now it's the ether... We no longer know if it is material or spiritual, but still we pull.

It's the accordion. Movement, space, it all comes at once. We'll never reach infinity... And it stretches, continues to stretch.

12 Grock (1880–1959), Swiss
clown, composer and
musician, known as 'the king
of clowns' [trans.].

Words, words that will have to be crossed out one by one.

Already time has had to be fastened back onto space but it hasn't been done properly. Instead of pushing back time, space has been pushed back. Grock[12] already did something like that with a piano and a footstool. It seemed so bizarre that they had to build another theory: relativity.

And so Einstein starts all over again. This time he stuck gravitation and electricity back together. One less fold in the accordion.

It's not over yet.

When the materialisations of space (energy) and its spiritualisation (time) have been crossed out, there will be no further movement which was the measure of time. For all that it will not be lost. Like the others it will retreat into its shell, into the same shell called infinity. And finally, so as to attain the life which does not express itself because it is omniscience, the very infinity of space and time will lose its meaning. And the Papuans, the idiots of Papua, will have gone before us, since, having learned nothing, in other words having known everything, they expected that we might have to unlearn everything in order to know all things. Note: To unlearn = Revolution.

And, Papuans or not, we will end up by no longer being people.

Come on, so much the better.

René Crevel
The Patriotism of the Unconscious

In this essay, René Crevel takes aim at the racism underlying the patriotism of the time as it was manifested within the French national unconscious, utilising the findings of psychoanalysis in a characteristically surrealist way. Like many of Crevel's essays, the effect is rather scattershot as he seeks to make telling points about the psychology of nationalism and at the same time experimentally to extend the essay form in a poetic, or allusive, direction.

First published in Le
Surréalisme au service de la
révolution, no.4, December
1931; reprinted in René Crevel,
L'Esprit contre la raison, Paris:
Jean-Jacques Pauvert, 1986.

In one of the most recent issues of the *Revue de Psychoanalyse*, the reviewer writes about an analysis of a black person that it 'tends [sic] to show that conflicts are the same in the white race as in the black race. Moreover the case is unconvincing,' he hastens to add, 'because hardly any consideration is given to unconscious conflicts'.

The author of this wishy-washy little summary is aiming, without any doubt, at scientific objectivity. He points to the work of a colleague and mitigates it because it remains vague, believing he has given sufficient proof of impartiality. And admittedly, this very subtle distinction would fall apart if it was intended to say that its

13 In 1929, an Armenian tailor named Almazian was arrested for a murder committed in Lille and tortured by the police although there was no evidence against him [trans.].

14 Dr Pierre Bourgrat, a prominent Marseilles physician, was sentenced to hard labour for life for the murder of Jacnu Itumebe in 1928. He escaped a few months after arriving in Devil's Island, one of only a small number of prisoners ever to escape from the notorious prison camp [trans.].

15 Psychological condition marked by an uncontrollable urge to wander [trans.].

imprecision is just one hair curler added to all the hair curlers of pretence, one hypocrisy more within which to wrap the classic vomit spouted about the inequality of races.

This is how, once the healers of the soul could no longer ignore it, psychoanalysis, which had been held in suspicion for a good number of years by the French medical corps, instead of forcing them to revise the idea they form of their individuals, of the more or less official state and role that they intend to play in it, becomes, on the contrary, a new pretext in the sophisticated whole with which they authorise themselves to pamper themselves, themselves and their self-satisfied prejudices. The opportunists thus use the very thing they condemn to open up a mine from which they can dig up whatever serves imperialisms, putrid ideals, religious obscurantism and their after-effects. Through this diversionary phenomenon, a recent discovery, one of Freud's as it happens, shores up everything it had been legitimate to think it had been about to reduce to dust. No sooner did opportunities for revolutionary leaps, already too rare in the history of the world, make contact with certain fingers than they trickled down the drain. This sauce is seasoned with extravagances that politicians and intellectuals have a mission to make those they administer or instruct swallow. This cuisine of well-brewed small and great lies is well known. The more or less sworn experts either understand it and would have the ear of every jurisdiction (the Almazian affair[13]), or they refuse it (the Bourgrat affair[14]) and the courts will take no notice of it. What does one false testimony more or less matter? Everything will turn out fine, the show will all end with a song, as long as good old bawdiness rules the roost. And she understands the art of using up the leftovers. If it is a question of the sexual instinct, quickly, she is expert in it, the smarty pants, she's in the know and, with a salacious smile, she spices up the scraps, carcases and giblets that have been sucked and sucked again from the reactionary old nanny goat. As she is in tune with her time, the dish of the day, soon enough, could well be the *Patriotism of the Unconscious*. She will sell the very expensive recipe to fashionable country inns and Pullman dining cars, piled up with so much foolishness and dromomania.[15] It may suggest Spartan gruel, but it is a gruel seasoned with Attic salt, a veritable feast for our youth when they graduate from the university colleges, faculties and secondary schools where the masters of cunning and satisfied liberalism will have whetted their appetite with this small stab at general culture which, in a single gulp, condenses the art of oratory ruses.

But if the well-brought up gentleman of the twentieth century, the worthy inheritor of the honest man of the seventeenth century, licks his chops at the succulence, he nonetheless retains his moderation, even at moments of supreme delight, because there is French harmony, and its Siamese sister French eloquence, and their twin, the French spirit, and their cousin, English humour, as well as their old flame, Slavic charm, and their hereditary enemy, German lies.

16 Henri Massis (1886–1970),
minor French nationalist
literary critic and historian,
mainly known for calling for a
crusade against the supposed
barbarism of the East which he
believed was threatening
European values [trans.].

Now, if the geography of good or bad qualities presents in an on-the-whole reduced space, that of a small continent, a number of differences and contradictions, all the hatreds which result from this parcelling up, as soon as they recognise a common interest, join forces, under the pretext of having civilisation to save.

Thus the patriotism of the unconscious would be a broad (let's call it European to please the League of Nations) patriotism, allied with America but Americans of pale faces rather than those of colour, since if a certain analysis 'tends to show that conflicts are the same in the white race as in the black race, the case is unconvincing because there is hardly any consideration of unconscious conflicts'.

So here we are back to square one, the circle is closed, the virtuous circle, people will say, to distinguish it from the great mass of perverts. Conformists of every stripe, in parliamentary kingdoms and conservative republics, will have a new rallying cry. And the age will continue to move towards the secular, the sole aim of which is to cultivate Christian ideology in greater peace, in a messianism which will give them the time of their lives. Hygienists of body and mind, in an official wave of goatees, pinces-nez, Panama hats, flannel waistcoats, support stockings, hernia belts, worn-out jock straps, chest protectors, false collars, celluloid cufflinks, and other accessories of the humanitarian ball, will be unfurled over Asia, Africa and Oceania. They will examine tribes deprived of a blessed state of innocence by their cassocked predecessors, for the pleasure of noting that they haven't had time to worry about the fiddle-faddle of those complexes worthy of metropolitans. Ages ago, over two or even three centuries, the evangelists might have vainly worked twice as hard without being able to obtain those lovely agonies which have so fetchingly stained the flesh of the Catholic world for two thousand years.

Then, stronger and better than ever, the white man is opposed to the coloured man. The ragtag of theological pretexts, the humanism which takes its vagueness for free thought, determine any given individual at all to recognise the exercise of faculties or professions towards and against others as a divine right. Of course, the more the country belongs to the supposedly civilised type, the keener the struggle between individuals will be. Capitalism takes delight in this state of concurrence. Christians will sigh. *Every man for himself and God for all*. The notion of the person, given the fact of its sacred character, is opposed to any research which would be dangerous for it (Massis[16] and his consorts). Freedom and will, as professors and priests conceive and teach their practice to their pupils and flocks, are nothing but means towards autocracy. When his philosophy class is over, the first whippersnapper will oppose, and continue all his life to oppose, the subjective and the objective, which allows him to recognise himself as the tabernacle of some eternal principle. The others he assimilates to things, to those things he judges as in essence inferior and fit only to be possessed and consumed. He thinks and conducts himself as though he was thinking himself, a noumenon among phenomena, as though

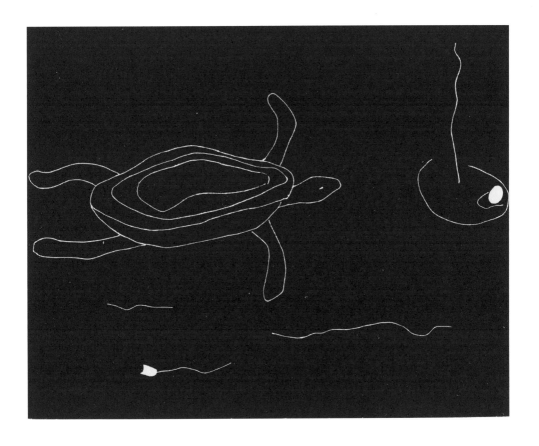

Luis Gayoso
To César Moro
Reproduced in *Le Surréalisme,*
même, no.1, 1956

17 The reference is to Clovis (466? – 511), the first king of France, who was persuaded to convert to Christianity despite hitherto being a committed pagan [trans.].

he was endowed with a sovereign thought in a dance of reflections – an aristocratic impressionism without anything living, perceptible or equitable under the daubings, a reign of young dandies.

Marx, in a definition of the human essence, embraced the 'ensemble of social relations' and Freud proved that this essence could not, in any circumstance, be reduced to the consciousness of it or to the idea that the veneer of reason laid down upon more or less accurate observations has constructed of it, both applied punches right in its belly allowing one to read behind the transparency of masks, behind the sophist grimaces, the fear of the approaching hordes.

And what a mediocre riposte when, in the name of psychoanalysis (against it, in truth), we are served up an observation whose ambivalent appearance implies that, in its author's opinion, conflicts could really be at the entire discretion of an unconscious that is variable from one race to another and from one individual to another, a faculty in itself and most specific to given races and individuals. There would then no longer be any need to take account of the external world and the circumstances which have furnished the occasion for some conflict or another to affect some unconscious or another, and one would be limited to the contemplative life, passivity, the arbitrary and the denial of justice – all luxuries exclusive to the plutocracy alone and in exchange for which it grants to each of its subjects the compensation of believing himself a normal man, an average Frenchman.

How touching, moreover, this charity appeared to whomsoever, denuded of distinctive signs, is willingly content with embodying the normal so as, in his turn, to despise the exotic.

* * *

'To the metaphysician,' says Engels [Engels 1968, p.411; translation modified to conform with the French], 'things and their mental reflexes and ideas are isolated, are to be considered one after the other and apart from each other, are objects of investigation, fixed, rigid, given. He thinks in absolutely irreconcilable antitheses stripped of any happy medium, communicating only by a yes and no. Anything which is beyond is colourless. Negative and positive exclude one another absolutely.'

This speculative principle is translated in practice by the infamous dictum of 'divide and rule'. The creature that detaches ideas and things from their living contexts has no curiosity or sympathies except for what is or can become its achievement. According to the state of the liver, it is the full-blown couldn't-care-less attitude or the fanaticism which moreover offers the alternation of its contraries to every Clovis[17] whom the first bishop to come along knows how to convince to burn what they have adored and to adore what they have burned. But no one will ever fail to have a good opinion of the self and the most banal will consider his very banality as a characteristic. Everyone must build themselves up, without any risk of realising what Feuerbach recorded as obvious: 'I am a psychological object for myself, but a physiological object for others'.

From this stems individualism, self-love and self-respect, which they say, as if the other, the true and the unique were dirty, means the taste for propriety and its sanctification for it is a question, above all, of making a showcase for that little jewel we see ourselves as being. In consequence, there is not the slightest hope of synthesis, but a piling up of specialisation which recalls the metaphor of herrings in the tin of sardines.

In the midst of these jumbles of interests, that middle-class sufficiency, after having elbowed its way in and found a nice little nook, might doze off and, in its dream, as in the hours of distinguished satisfactions, raise a little finger, that lousy blood-sausage little finger, which it will crown as if it were the finest phallus.

So it will be, through fear of risk, ignorance or congenital stupidity, those gentlemen the intellectuals will refuse the dialectic, which views objects and notions in their movement, their development and their demise. All these canaries then continue to demand cages so as, once between their bars, to make everything all nostalgic for us, as though they were eagles. In the cellars in which the gloom thickened each day, people with the complexion of chicory tried to make themselves dizzy by contemplating their navels. And they deified their navels. And they sought the chain of vainglory, no less extravagant than the male clergy, when, at the height of its antiquated triumph, it convened in council to decide whether women had a soul.

In this tradition from the Haute Epoque, to cite this son of the Holy Mother Church, a Dominican, whose sister (herself a woman priest who told me this when she looked after me during a childhood sickness) reported, for the greatest satisfaction of family and confessional pride, that from the ground, head raised to spit into the air, with all his strength and heroism, without fearing that it would fall back down on top of him, he baptised the idolatrous climbers whom the spectacle of his pale person did not convince to descend from their coconut palms, with these words: 'I baptise you as long as you have a soul.'

That black man about whom the ecclesiastical circles of 1905 were unable to decide whether or not he had a soul, or a 1931 journal specialising in mental health whether his unconscious might be susceptible to conflicts as distinguished as those patterns the psychoanalytical cashiers at head office considered standard (and note that the French doesn't say much so as to imply a lot) when it comes to forced labour and petty squabbles, can be recognised as a brother, a younger brother, of course, and therefore to be led with a firm hand. His rights, one affirms, are recognised. Then, that he, in his turn, and a little quicker than that – strewth! – give unto Caesar what belongs to Caesar. And of course, the putting into practice of this reciprocity of obligations will sanction the preliminary axiom, namely that what is given to the black man is nothing at all, while Caesar (imperio-capitalist society) possesses the universality of

18 Galaye M'baye Diagne (1872–1923) in 1914 became the first African to be elected to the French National Assembly [trans.].

19 This reference is to François Coty, perfumer and publisher, an anti-Semitic right-wing extremist and author of *Sauvons nos colonies: Le Peril rouge en pays noir*, Paris: Grasset, 1931 [trans.].

20 *Ronds de bras et porte de jambes* is a ballet dance [trans.].

21 Maurice Barrès (1862–1923), French novelist and politician, known for nationalist and anti-Semitic views. In 1921 the Dadaists famously put him on trial for 'crimes against the security of the spirit' [trans.].

22 Raymond Poincaré (1860–1934), French Prime Minister at various times and President from 1913 to 1920 [trans.].

rights, among which, of course, are those of life and death.

A secular state of affairs boosts the betrayal of anyone who, among the colonised, agrees to and serves the colonisers' ideologies.

Jesus, the first in line with this Giving unto Caesar…, his bright idea, will beat a path for anti-Semitism. The France whose (internal and external) governmental mystique perpetuates Roman drill-sergeant mentality, offers a portfolio to M. Diagne,[18] while it allows its Coty to cover the walls with the abominable poster 'Save our Colonies: The Black Peril in Red Countries'.[19]

Pogroms of orthodox and Tsarist Holy Russia, massive numbers of executions of Indo-Chinese rebels, punitive expeditions here and there – when Church and State connive (even and especially through a simple tacit agreement, under cover of a sham separation) it's a jolly fine work. But let no one complain, since the ministers of God on Earth have wanted to place the hope of a better world in everyone's mind. As for this world, the one down below, as long as they are left to make the law in it, the lack of the most elementary justice will constantly lead us to despair of knowledge.

* * *

Frustrated by their movement, objects and their mental reflections, ideas, are no more than mummies. Thought has shrivelled and petrified. A charming prom party at the charnel house of entities. To their scraps of bravery and various capers science and art bring gracious and comforting presence of mind, of which, to dream of *ronds de bras et jambes*,[20] would bear witness to a legless one-armed amputee, sole survivor of a catastrophe, its work, which left no creature in its detritus but an empire of dust. A singular negative mirage, the eyes of this megalomaniac, which, as small as they appear, were no less piercing, these tiny eagle eyes, which have delved through their desert, have not seen that it was populated with a confraternal neighbourhood of cripples, all of whom, moreover, are in the same boat as far as agility and perspicacity go. Thus, from this landscape of ashes, each dismembered gnome believes himself all the more absolute a sovereign for being without subject. When evening comes, they thank God for having metamorphosed their *becoming* into *staying put*. God is the motionless one since he occupies all of Time and Space and so does not have to move either in Time or Space. For the ecstasy of feeling that they are in the image of the Motionless One, who wouldn't therefore give up their feet and hands? To know what to be satisfied with, where to stand once and for all, that is faith. Faith is once and for all. As for the body, it matters little what it strikes out of it or reaches within itself to attain or receive beings. The flesh is only the momentary vessel of the eternal principle, the soul. Physical and temporal reduction pays the insurance on the life to come and eternal. The deal concluded, the Church beatifies cankers and penury, wounds and ulcers. It kills life to exalt death, pampers the necrophiliacs (of whom Barrès[21] is the prototype), who turn it to their advantage from anarchic degeneracy to the ultra-conformist dream (and in its realisation) of state funerals. And what a gamut,

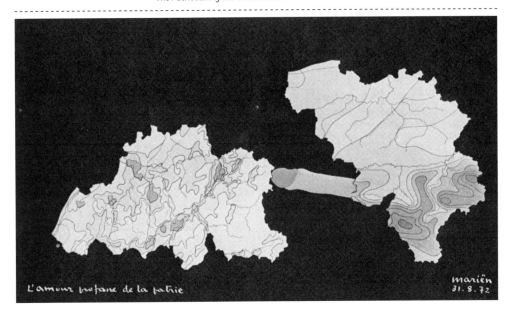

L'amour profane de la patrie

mariën
31.8.72

Marcel Mariën
Profane Love of Country 1972
Reproduced in *Les Levrès nues*,
no.6 (new series), April 1973

from Poincaré,[22] the man of the cemeteries, to that poor fool stupefied by more than half a century of servitude who I heard lament: to kill the living, fair enough, but to bombard tombs!

So the first revolutionary jump leaps straight to these tombs that have to be profaned, some to cast their symbol-corpses onto the dung heap, others to bring to light what was dying, buried alive. But alas, each of them still rejoices in being his own coffin. Freud was the first systematically to tear away the cover under which rotted that by which the emasculator had been emasculated. Psychoanalysis gives our amputee back his arms, legs and sex, which has to hang free between his legs. And as a result he enjoys himself, stirs, thinks, no longer dreaming of the Motionless One, he who, from one orison to the next, had only his bad smells to distract him.

Rancid virginities, urine-soaked celibates, regular or secular clergy of both sexes, in the depths of its chapels and cathedrals, can sing the Breton song:

> *Everyone stinks there*
> *It smells of carrion...*

* * *

Man has lowly cursed certain parts of the self only in order to take crafty delight in them, just like the Motionless One from whom creation, given its religious and metaphysical attributes, is conceivable only in the form of a faecal amusement. In practice, he condemns himself to the grossest *materialism* which accepts the dogma of Spirit become matter and of the word made flesh. Squeamish, fallen from the most nebulous of nebulae into a barrel of sewage, he nonetheless despises the materialist for whom, since being conditions thought, there is a passage from matter to the mind: therefore, according to the qualitative judgement of the idealist, there is progress instead of this orthodox and disheartening fall of the Spirit into the midst of matter. Here the religious man protests, because transubstantiation is for him the miracle, the exception which confirms the rule. As a consequence of all the idolatries whose causal and final principle is the negation of movement, the only thing which psychology considered about thought was its interruption, the consciousness it grasps of the self at the end of its course and without remembering the path which led it here or there. No one suspected that there was a thread in the labyrinth. It was like taking the dial for the watch and then being amazed at not knowing the time.

And now, because the tooth of old prejudices still and perpetually wants to take a bite out of revolutionary work, because the threat of obscurantism is never dispelled, because the method is not at all clearly enough denounced, the method whose flaw forbids going from night to day via a dawn illuminated by dreams, because the specialists ceaselessly drone on about reality, because the aesthetic convention and the moral apriorism are reborn from their ashes, it is important to recall, not by way of conclusion, but as a signal for a departure, the definition given by Breton in his first surrealist manifesto:

> Surrealism, n. Psychic automatism in its pure state, by which one proposes to express – verbally, through writing, or in any other manner – the actual functioning of thought. Dictation of thought, in the absence of any control exercised by reason, outside of any moral or aesthetic concern
> [Breton 1969, p.26, translation modified].

Benjamin Péret
Ruins: Ruin of Ruins

The theme of ruins, so central to romanticism and the gothic novel, is here taken up by Péret, though not to be treated as something sublime but as a remnant of ultimate human failure or loss. Rather than romanticising ruins, Péret eyes them from an anti-humanist perspective, weaving history together with the notion of the wreck of an individual life, haunted by nostalgia for childhood and the womb, the body decaying. The text is a kind of memento mori, in which the loss of culture to nature is not mourned. Everything that subsists is a ruin, a fossil of what once was, testifying to the fragility of all things and especially to that human arrogance that thinks it has the capacity to triumph over nature as well as over the ravages of time and corporeality.

First published in *Minotaure*, no.11–12,1939; reprinted in Benjamin Péret, *Oeuvres complètes*, vol.7, Paris: José Corti, 1995.

Man emerges howling from the unforgettable darkness of a castle, driven out by a thousand obsessive ghosts which will haunt him for the rest of his life until, once dead, he is shut up in another castle, a ridiculous bogey this time, and built to the scale of the worms that gnaw him. But here is man, a ghost for himself and castle visited by his own ghost. However far away he may be found, however young he might appear, his desire takes the form of a castle: a cavern in which he contends with bears or a tiny construction of which memory retains only the image of aventurine.

Certain cave-dwelling Indians of New Mexico make dolls whose heads outline a castle they have never seen and will never know.

Man envies the dumb contentment of the oyster and the snail, aspires – if he is a pathetic petit bourgeois – to a hideous suburban villa; if he is a nomad to a straw mattress; if he is an artist to some velvety ruin over which he will have to contend with vegetation and rapacious birds, a ruin he will transplant onto his own land if the sausage industry makes him rich.

Man, the hermit crab, sees nothing of life but the ruin in which the animal he denies still being is hiding. But the animal has been transformed. From a tiger, it has become a wolf, and the wolf has often mutated into a dog. The dog born of a dog barely recognises the wolf's ruins, but those of the tiger are for him no more than a trace in the sand, this sand whose ruins he has forgotten, derisory images of those he fails to recognise.

This dirty beast, man, has no other soul than the phantoms of his childhood, which, without his knowledge, will keep him in subjection for his whole life. There is nothing in that childhood to disown, except by someone who has become unworthy of it. Nothing in collective childhood should be disowned except in the case of societies which have become unworthy of it and glorify it all the better to deny it. Mussolini celebrates ancient Rome even though his actions oppose the progress it brought the world. Stalin tries to make Lenin a dead ruin, the better to betray him. It is the same everywhere. Ruins are denied by those whose lives are already just a ruin of which nothing will remain but the memory of a blob of spit.

The ruin is only endowed with a sulphurous lustre if it is immediately preceded by a real life of which it becomes the legendary extension, until that survival disappears in its turn, for want of an echo in human feelings. Classical literature idealised an antique society which had long since disappeared. Neither the French romantics nor the English pre-romantics were so patient. Hardly had feudal rule been torn down than poets were moved by the spectacle of a past forever gone. The king's severed head symbolised the capital execution of a society and at the same time released waves of florescent ink so vigilantly gathered by poets.

The caverns of prehistory are the fossils of ruined castles once more become castles thanks to the unslaked desire of their former inhabitants and the unbridled imagination of nature which

Alberto Giacometti
Dumb Mobile Objects
From *Le Surréalisme au service de la révolution*, no.3, December 1931

Text reads, top to bottom, left-then right-hand page:

All things near or faraway, all those which have gone by and the others, ahead,
[*images*]
which move and my girlfriends – they change (we pass very close, they are far away), others approach, rise, descend, ducks on the water, there and there, in space, rise,
[*images*]
descend – I am sleeping here, the flowers of the wallpaper, the water from my tap that hasn't been properly turned off, the design on my curtain, my trousers on a chair, someone speaks in a room further on; two or three people, from which station? The locomotives which whistle, there is not station here,
[*images*]
orange peel was thrown from the top of the terrace, into the very narrow and deep street – at night, the mules brayed desperately, towards morning they were slaughtered – tomorrow I leave –
[*images*]
she brings her head close to my ear – her leg, the large one – they speak, they move, there and there, but everything has gone.

OBJETS MOBI

Toutes choses... près, loin, toutes celles qui sont passées et les autres, par devant,

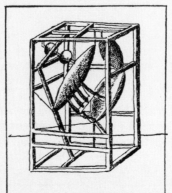 

qui bougent et mes amies — elles changent (on passe tout près, elles sont loin), d'autres approchent, montent, descendent, des canards sur l'eau, là et là, dans l'espace, montent,

 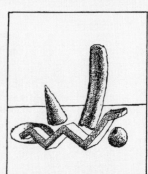

descendent — je dors ici, les fleurs de la tapisserie, l'eau du robinet mal fermé, les dessins du rideau, mon pantalon sur une chaise, on parle dans une chambre plus loin ; deux ou

18

MUETS

trois personnes, de quelle gare? **Les locomotives qui sifflent, il n'y a pas de gare par ici,**

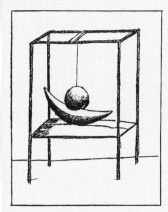 

on jetait des pelures d'orange du haut de la terrasse, dans la rue très étroite et profonde — **la nuit, les mulets braillaient désespérément, vers le matin, on les abattait** — demain je sors —

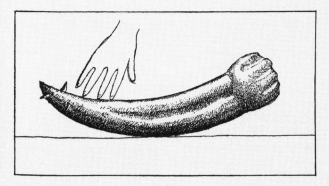

elle approche sa tête de mon oreille — sa jambe, la grande — ils parlent, ils bougent, là et là, mais tout est passé.

ALBERTO GIACOMETTI.

19

has sometimes lit them up or even peopled them with stalactites, phantoms of phantoms and frozen fairies in an invisible glass palace, and sometimes nature extracts from its blood the demons of stalagmites which threaten the former with their gaping jaws, their fists or their lances in a perpetual state of becoming.

The ruins of antiquity, sarcophagi without mummies from a society lacking any emotional contact with ours – for its dust has been scattered to the four corners of the world – offer only 'here lies' to the meditation of necrophiliacs. Too young to harbour human mystery, too old to participate in the life of nature, they are now scarcely anything but anatomical parts conserved in the denatured formaldehyde of museums, skeletons reconstituted from the navel or the coalmine which bears witness to the former existence of a forest.

One ruin drives away another, the one that preceded it, killing it. From the crumbling fortresses of feudal lords flows a thick lava stifling the Roman arenas and circuses for ever.

In the sun, the flash of armour remains suspended above the moats while the constructions of antiquity – which the phantoms have left, their mission ended – have become stone Saharas whose desiccated lions decorate, as bedside rugs, the nuptial chambers of chemists.

Apart from the churches embellished by the moss that covers the traces of the fire and the ashes of the priest who perished with them – castles whose lichwort has eaten away the crenellations, whose armour-clad ghosts have clashed and made the halls crumble, seeking in vain to bury themselves beneath their debris – what is left of the Middle Ages are the childhood memories of the grandmother who lived in the sun with the fairies and, trembling with fear, escaped the vampires in the night of their underground passages.

Revolting Versailles, incapable of producing a ruin because it is bereft of the ghosts it couldn't give rise to, is as opposed to the ruin of the Middle Ages as the waterfall is to the electricity station. Enemies to the death because the first is killed by the second which springs up from it! Versailles is nothing but the decadent product of degenerate feudal society, already gnawed away by the society to come, while the medieval ruin remains its fresh dawn. Passionate love, enemy of all the constraints imposed by the family and religions, that wrecks marriage, was born in the castle strongholds while Versailles produced only the passionless dalliance of old men, the corruption of any love.

But that epoch lived. All that remains of the old men is the memory of their senility and of the children, their innocence and games. The Versailles of feudal decay is razed out and returns to the earth from which it should never have emerged, to punctuate the horizon with donjons from which love fled through every machicolation. The world that was then about to be born and which threw Versailles into the common ditch will soon disappear in its turn. What ruins will it leave for the exaltation of the poets of another age? Not the churches that have survived the past only as complements to prisons, nor the banks without which neither would have survived; but perhaps one day, when its memory will have been effaced from human recall, the gigantic fossil of a unique animal, the Eiffel Tower, will be recovered. Perhaps some great station, long deserted, will see its rails covered in buttercups, and hares, abandoning their burrows, will seek a home in an abandoned booking office there, perhaps too the Grange-Batelière, recovering its rights, will flow through the Opéra from wings to entrance, bordered with cress and iris and criss-crossed with kingfishers. And the passer-by who saunters along it looking for a ford, catching sight of this ruin bristling with brambles and chirping with birds, will remember that in other times trifles for the luxuriously dressed dead were performed there, and will say:

– What a lovely spring, the Opéra is in flower as never before!

The Bucharest Surrealist Group
The Nocturnal Sand

The Bucharest surrealist group, active between 1940 and 1947 in highly unfavourable conditions, produced some of surrealism's most intense writings. Marooned in a far corner of Europe, they contributed to the 1947 international surrealist exhibition in Paris an unrealised proposal for 'a room of great black silence', a completely darkened space in which to encounter unknown erotic objects, for which the following text was reproduced in the catalogue.

Published in the catalogue for the international surrealist exhibition *Le Surréalisme en 1947*, Galerie Maeght, Paris 1947.

Condensing the traces of the bloodstain at its liquid extremities, we deliver its sumptuous coloration beneath which, in its inexpressible shudder, floats the angular finger expressed as a form made of air floating within the room full of air.

Moving bare-armed through the object, desire finds itself enhanced by yet another blinding. The tips of the palms, the tips of the eyelids of total vision put desire in touch, in a supremely hysterical way, with its infinite possibilities of becoming.

Lips glued to the unpronounceable words we kiss, we move in a bedchamber in which there are an infinite number of lascivious, gigantic and delicate sets of scales, made of some diaphanous substance, which invents the flight of a bird wounded by the cruel curiosity that will tear apart even its air.

The curve begins before the sign, it *comes* and you can bump into it with your eyes open without seeing it. There are far more accidents, accidents everywhere, whose destiny constantly intoxicates us, lubricates us, accidents equivalent to necessity, to movements, to ubiquity and the embrace. In a layer found beneath the accidents, there flow the initials, and beneath their matter and the blood is saliva, remote amputation, the traces left by fish in the water, one accident piled on top of another like a multiple monolith upon a distant sky.

The eruptive disintegration of the beloved matter, the fact of passionately stealing away with it to its physical limits and the forms imposed by the unbearable evidence of any external object, its fleeting dematerialisation aiming at an astounding materialisation – all of this completely changes its pernicious inclusion in the forms that still smoke along the vanished line under the final intransmissible point, double length, bathed in the looks inverted in the water: that same water which, when inverted, reveals its secret double bottom, and beyond the bottom, only the secret, only this one, which has the form of the magnetic viscera of the woman upon whom the hand performs its energy-absorbing passes.

Knowing through misunderstanding – it is by closing and opening the doors of our bodies one after the other that the wind will be able to bring them its evasive mirror at the very moment of a total opening up. The trickle of wind on the face of the beloved can easily be torn away by using a cyclone. One hand is stretched towards the invisible hips, another towards her fully formed lips, we displace the bodies and the tempests onto the thin lacrimatory layer to varnish the gaiters covered in hair, orchids and lazy kernels, in the lapsing of days hung from the mountains, disappearing behind them like a bruise that must be sought below the gaping flesh.

There are nothing but loving concretions in the jealous night that guards and delivers them without the slightest concern for their invincible debauchery. The debauchery of smiles, of trembling, of shortness of breath, of the slipping of a knee towards a cold wall, and in general the indescribable debauchery, too wild to be able to replace the furrowed winding of tears, that takes place between all the unnamed objects every night at 11 o'clock.

The door opens in the water, hampered by the submarine tresses, by a suffocating abundance, and the first one to enter is drawn by the currents towards a new door, open for love, a door that opens onto the thousand dense and diffuse corridors, a door of smoke and vice, of vice and multiplicity whose aromas, slumbering in breasts traversed by a carnivorous fluid, reject the equilibrium towards the vertebrate as the very ossification of the vertebra in its organic crux, vitrified by unknown time.

The evidence of the unknown must physically (materially) penetrate your bodies, oh hateful mortals, the unknown in grains of sand beneath the transparent skin of your whole body, like the stones borne by vultures over the waterfalls.

The water vultures have learned to bite the flames. The flame vultures are in the water. Able swimmers between the two layers of earth, as though in a conquered element.

In perpetual search of the found, present woman.

For the complete unblocking of the idea of an encounter between the woman and the man.

We are maniacs of their encounter so that, palpitating, we try to flee towards the divisible fragments of our own flight, infesting the solid domain with an efflorescence of mould, extending its course, diverting it, annihilating it or else crushing within it what is stationary, crushing the escape of hot air towards the regions occupied by cold air, impossible to find even for just a second, and found again at the very place where it began.

For the loveliest breasts are those the night wind brings us on the shoulders of thighs, with the eyes' mouth pressed shut by the finger of silence.

And through them, down with vision which is the exhausted oppressor of our senses.

The beloved's skin even stretches beyond her body, it covers the women and the objects that may or may not surround her, it reaches out to embark upon the entire universe, in a fur of flames.

* * *

A sur-automatic description of sixteen objects encountered in the nocturnal sand.

1. The insatiable wave slowly traversed by corrosive droplets.
2. Anguished breathing doubling, tripling and becoming blind under forgotten conditions.
3. A shadow cast by eyes floating around the rims of this bowl.
4. The lignification of touching subjected to freezing in the furthest corner of the room.
5. Underground mercury palpitating on the edges of equilibrium.
6. Compressed air, half-covered in silk, alone.
7. An immense crystal, impulsively scented, on the face of a feather.
8. The ebb of the look brushing against the level of the clouds above the lips.
9. The adornment of languor or even its interior at the entry to the cave.
10. A vertiginous corridor surprised in a succulent light at the heart of the breast.
11. The secret gestures of hysteria dominating the consistency of the lungs.
12. Deep fold balanced by blood.
13. Rays of darkness suspended over the simplicity of small dimensions.
14. Adhesive snow, uselessly coloured by the wind.
15. A vertiginous smile or that which attracts lovers on every wall.
16. An apparition of a hallucinated, absolutely unknown head of hair.

Gherasim Luca, Gellu Naum, Paul Paun, Virgil Teodorescou, Trost

Georges Bataille
The Friendship of Man and Beast

This essay, written at the time when Bataille was reappraising surrealism, feeds into central surrealist concerns, which would become especially prominent during the 1950s, about the relationship between man and nature. More especially, and a particular concern of Bataille, is the nature of the human and what separates us from pure animality. In this complex essay, Bataille is concerned above all to explore the will to command and the willingness to obey – and the consequences that follow from this dual imperative, which defines relations between humans and animals as well as those between humans, yet does not exist elsewhere in the animal world.

First published in *Formes et couleurs*, no.1, 1947; reprinted in Georges Bataille, *Oeuvres complètes*, vol.11, Paris: Gallimard, 1988.

The bestiality of barracks, the boredom of offices, burdened with impoverished inanity, the skilfully veiled sufficiency of human beings, what is expressed by 'a lapdog' that is weighed down and shameful, in a word the dispersed but general *flight* towards the least semblance of a way out... is all this the result of immense effort?... We have bent the most unruly forces; animals and waters, plants and stones have responded to our desires. But at the summit of power we succumb to an indefinite unease and flee: the whole work of nature we have at our disposal is lost in the affected vulgarity of some and in the boredom and play-acting of others. What do these accumulated resources, these shops, these buildings and these services, mean? We would like to remain sheltered not only from need but also from everything which upsets, awakens or arouses us; we would like to avoid the shocks which, suddenly revealing what we are to ourselves, would make us equal to the immensity of the universe. We have reduced nature to our power, but we go by ourselves, crawling along like limited things, resembling turkey-hens, sweets and ledgers. We can laugh nervously, distance ourselves from the vulgar and puff ourselves up, and what is given the name of nobility is just as oblique as the rest; if vulgarity turns away from a possibility assumed by nobility, nobility has fled the work assumed by the humble and confuses the fear of having dirty hands with pride. This resembles a ballet in a bad dream: a curse unites the street urchin and the old lady in common anxiety about *what exists*.

Would this 'existence', or more accurately this unknown within us which we prefer to see in a prejudiced way, in a fleeting way (just as our eyes see the fire of the sun), be horrible or embarrassing in itself? Possibly it is. The 'I am', the 'being' of philosophers is the most neutral thing, one most devoid of meaning, having the innocent blankness of paper. A slight shock nevertheless changes it into frenzy: this 'being' which sees red, insensitive to the clear and distinct calm of the objects it knows how to name (in which a sudden indifference revives the possibility of torrent, of brilliance and cry, *that it exists*), is at the same time this energy being able to discharge itself as the flash and the consciousness of mortal dangers resulting from the discharge of energy. To exist, in the strong sense, is not in fact to contemplate (passively), any more than it is to act (if by acting we renounce free conduct, with a view to ulterior results), but is precisely to *break loose*. Thus for most of the time we prefer to know nothing and timidly distance ourselves from ourselves, as we do from primed mines. But for the same reason we are touched by the outburst we see, which is not ours, but which lets us know that it could be.

* * *

The dumbfounded child who sees a bolting horse, whose mouth emits a white foam, slipping by in a passing storm on the paving set with rails, and which mothers' cries accompany with derision, has received an ineffaceable image from the possible outburst of beings. This image obviously means little. The child is unable to insert it into the world of efficacy and ordered action which will be imposed upon him. But off-stage a crash of hooves will constantly announce the black possibilities of non-sense to his tremblings. These animal possibilities would be the object of no favourable commentary but at the same time would not be denounced as dangerous: because the dazzling aspect of the unchained beast is situated beyond human limits. This unlimited discharge belongs rather to the realm of dream: it defines a *divine* possibility. Did a god not oppose, in the most ancient times, animal mystery to human measure? Its essence is to be *sacred*, terrible and ungraspable: it is founded by a tragic generosity, which provokes, leads to death and goes beyond it. The majesty of the storm and the absolute frenzy of the horse alone have this power to go to the end of the light, of the brilliance and of the immeasurable loss.

Bolting horses do not generally have this eminent dignity in human life. The horse is habitually reduced to the condition of a servant harnessed to the cart... No matter to what state of degradation it would have descended, a lasting preserve still endures in the attitude of man, of which it is *the most noble* of conquests. It is the least humiliated and most skittish of animals that man has enslaved: even its master often associates it with his glory. The Bible has God say to man, to Job, wanting to show the extent of his power: 'Do you give the horse his strength or clothe his neck with a flowing mane? Do you make him leap like a locust, striking terror with his proud snorting? He paws fiercely, rejoicing in his strength, and charges into the fray...' (Job 39: 19–25, New International Version). This quivering and pretty insane sensibility which for a shadow is resolved in frenzy is what assures the horse of a nobility that the weight of servitude cannot reduce. So much so that it has a privileged status in the human world. On the whole the domesticity of the animal results in decline. And savagery shies away from knowledge. In the midst of humans, the horse has the privilege of maintaining an essence of animality, more precisely of living being, which is that of being irreducible. To the very extent to which we have enslaved it, the truly domesticated animal has

Leonora Carrington
Horse 1940
Collection Horacio Amigorena,
Paris

become, so to speak, a thing, and the wild animal is inhuman. The horse is itself debased and does not assume its dignity from power, still less from moral value; it is on the lowest degree of the ladder. But be it harnessed, in which it is like people tied to their tasks, it can, by stupidity and in a tremor, break the established chain. Its refusal is thus irreducible: it does not come from taking account of effort and salary (the error can be rectified) but from a difference of nature between a cog and the machinery which employs it. Even if this truth might only have a mythic sense (similar to that of a work of art) in a fundamental way, a horse is a charge of energy that is dangerous to handle, capricious, ready at any moment for the blinding explosion. It is a beast of burden in one sense only. If man is a 'fallen god which remembers...', the clumsiest horse participates at one point of the unchaining. Its work strength can be calculated and used: the warlike impetuosity, the charge, the sudden and total expenditure of energy which nothing can stop are no less linked, if not solely to a particular individual, then at least to the genus it incarnates. The horse undoubtedly succumbs under the weight of human tasks, but it maintains the principle of being, which is nothing if it is not unchained, in the world of calculation and decline.

This image of being as a searing movement of power (and not as a static screen) is perhaps paradoxical. It is paradoxical also to state that, if not the clear and distinct consciousness of objects, the sharp consciousness of what exists, of the game that being plays with the world, is linked to the possibilities of explosions. The profound sense of friendship between man and beast can no less be founded in these shocking truths. The preserve, the brakes and the flight to the end in some closed futility are obstacles which give human beings that gaze which slips away, that poverty of hands and teeth, which announces the common abdication. The pacts sealed between horse and man at least maintain life under the primacy of a tension of explosive forces. Horsemanship does not ensure a virtue which would be inaccessible without it. But it is true that to be an integral part of the animal subject to terrific bolting, if it is not itself contained by some sudden discharge, even if he might have been fundamentally afraid, the rider remains open, continually, to its possibility. Its horizon is even this opening and perhaps this gives cowboys and gauchos, like Cossacks or horse guards, their eminence above foot shepherds: but does not the eminence here belong to the horse rather than the man?

The human attitude is at best very ambiguous: a concern to master is always dominant. The calm consciousness, in which objects become ungraspable, detaching themselves as though on a screen and requiring that we do not give in to frenzy. If we do, we miss the possibility of acting upon things. And we are no more than animals. But if we act, if we reflect on these successions of objects whose relations order the intelligible world in a consciousness that has become clear, we leave life suspended within us. We then accumulate the reserves, which are only the expenditure of these reserves, useful to life without really living, or at least live only halfway. Thus the chlorosis, the boredom, the futility, the falsehood and even an affected bestiality are given in the essential human attitude which hides being, as much as it can, from the possibility opened before it. This is why value still participates humanly in the misdemeanour. It is why remorse is to man what the air is to the bird, and in *two senses*. In these conditions, morality is never a rule and in truth can only be an art: in the same way an art can only be a moral, and of the most demanding type, if its end is to open some possibility of unchaining. But art being thus the purest moral exigency, it is also the most deceitful: the possibility it opens, it in fact opens only as an 'image', for the 'reflection' of spectators. And it is vain to protest against this snare; these men in frock coats and these affected women, gleaming with diamonds, acknowledged accomplices of laws opposed to our unchaining, if they witness the 'representation' of a tragedy unmoved, are not the obstacle to art but its condition: calm witnessing is nothing less than *clear consciousness* in the end *reflecting the very being* that, to be clear, it had excluded. This is the realm of falsehood, to which a desire for simplicity is opposed, but man is precisely this realm and to flee it is still a way of slipping away: the hatred of art is most often the result of tiredness and art has no worse enemies than vulgarity and vapidity. It is true that, in wanting to respond to the exigency he has received, the poet is at least open to frenzy, but his frenzy, for all that it is not feigned, is still addressed, from the outset, to the consciousness of he who is not frenetic; it calls above all for this calm consciousness, its contrary, which would not exist if it had fled. From this, in spite of everything, emerge the remorse and the comic character of 'Pegasus', who is not the *true* horse, whose absolute unchainings aim at nothing. Dada clearly played an agreement with itself on this remorse, but was Dada Dada? Or was it just a play-acting of it? Its extreme opposite is no more accessible to man than the nudity of the animal.

Jacqueline Sénard-Duprey
Cat = Clover

This text reflects an ecological interest that became an important strand of surrealist activity in the aftermath of the Second World War, especially as relating to maintaining the balance of nature against the human conceit that we can act with impunity upon it. The essay raises concerns about the environment in ways that were rarely recognised as a matter of consideration in the 1950s but have become matters of vital interest today, even to the appreciation of the importance of bumble bees in the chain of life.

First published in *Le Libertaire*, 23 May 1952; reprinted in José Pierre (ed.), *Surréalisme et anarchie*, Paris: Plasma, 1983.

If one March night some tyrant, prevented from sleeping by their miaowing, decreed that all cats should be put to death, the result would be a less abundant harvest of clover. And some Darwin is hardly likely to come along to tell the tyrant about the subtle chain linking the cause to its effects.

Darwin in fact noticed how the presence of cats conditioned the abundance of clover, and this is how: in the absence of cats, field mice proliferate; field mice are fond of bumble bees, but the bumble bees fecundate the pistils by transporting the pollen from one flower to another; therefore, the more cats = the more bumble bees = the more clover.

The use of vaccines, prophylactic measures and drastic medication has considerably reduced mortality and so we perceive the rise in polio as probably due to the fact that, shielded from numerous relatively benign sicknesses, the organism, unused to struggling and stripped of certain microbes, is poorly adapted at resisting the former, whose form it bears in a latent state.

And so, if we consider the constructions which punctuate the path of knowledge, and which falsely appear to increase in size the closer they come towards us, we can ask what they have in the end brought to man and whether we ought not to be afraid that some stimulus, of unknown origin, will topple its only just completed buildings. So it is that when certain species of fish proliferate excessively they are suddenly decimated as if by a decree of occult forces.

It is the same for the human species for which in certain regions famines and epidemics tend to re-establish biological equilibrium when it is threatened.

In another realm, we notice how the descendants of revolutionaries re-establish for their own benefit the titles their fathers abolished, and that there is no director or department chief who, just like the past use of 'My Lord', does not require us to address him as 'Sir'. Castes tend continually to reconstitute themselves and, to distinguish themselves sharply from everyone else, adopt the language of the specialist or the initiate. Each branch of knowledge has its own jargon and, with its passion for Latin or Greek, burdens a language ordinary people had made responsive, suggestive and alive. Public schools reflect these tendencies by adopting their own private lingua franca, brimming with passwords, and even certain linguistic habits or wearing a cap may be part of a class attitude.

Man is a being which knows itself to have three dimensions: the universe admits perhaps an infinity of them. In general, human intelligence, according to the being in question, projects a few more or less perforated grids on the cryptogram which the universe offers it. Everything that passes through it is intelligible; anything that does not is not only unintelligible but remains totally unknown. And yet, what does not pass through exists all the same, lies and acts no less within the very substance of the human. Here is an unknown which no Darwin could illuminate.

We can then anxiously wonder what a world in which many blind relations are established has in store for us. For example, machines that put an end to emotion are interposed between man and objects that really are neither wanted, chosen nor worked for. Having become anonymous, forms are projected by an automatic gesture which, excluding all intervention, disinfects the environment to the point of absolute void.

Opposite:
Toyen
Reproduced in
*Almanach surréaliste du
demi-siècle*, 1950

Elsewhere contacts are suppressed: mystery is hounded out of every space and object, hounded at the very heart of the forest swept by tracks along which maniacs of the 'ordinary' stupidly throb, forests are pointlessly cut down and stripped of does and wolves by the automaton imbecility of hunters. This actual world where sorcerers' apprentices, so proud of their rudiments of knowledge, enact and promulgate for the benefit of their own private plan and, having done so, gloriously ignore the unforeseeable consequences of the reactions provoked by their decrees, certain as they are, moreover, to be always in a position to restore order to Warsaw.

Mankind, they say, is still too close to the prehistoric age for ancestral impulses not to be coiled springs; and many modes of activity are really only a reminder, a simulacrum, of those of another age. Seeking profit is the current form of the prey and appetite for power. Battles are mimicked in stadiums and rings, which serve as outlets for a fascinated public.

But is it impossible not to have to submit to this filiation, and to push back the bounds of memory by imagining that it is arbitrary to stop at the prehistoric age rather than at any other moment of the unlimited past and that finally the pithecanthropus may be only a cousin?

No doubt, by reconsidering our ascendancy which, it should not be forgotten, is identified with the infinite, and consequently contains every 'possibility', we will find the incandescent dots where the points in the tracks that need to be rediscovered are lying.

Benjamin Péret
Light or Life

Benjamin Péret lived at various times in Mexico and Brazil, studying the local culture and landscape, about which he wrote many little-known essays of great insight and incisiveness. This account of a walk into the rain forest in Brazil gives us a vivid impression of life fighting for survival in an extreme environment where no mercy is given or expected and it provides an interesting contrast and complement to his essay above on ruins.

First published in
Le Surréalisme, même, no.5,
Spring 1959. It is part of a
longer work, *Visites aux
Indiens*, unpublished in Péret's
life, included in his *Oeuvres
complètes*, vol.6, Paris: José
Corti, 1992.

23 André Le Notre (1613–1700), French landscape architect [trans.].

On the shores of Rio Coluene we go into the forest from the Capitão Vasconcêlos outpost as we would go into the street from any house in the city. We find it everywhere, silent and dark, a great maw ready to close over the intruder. Compared to the tropical forest, the densest French forest gives the impression of being a park arranged by Le Nôtre.[23] Here, everything recalls bygone geological ages from which man was still absent. It is a silent and dark swarming of the vegetation which kills and crushes, perishes and is brought back to life in other species.

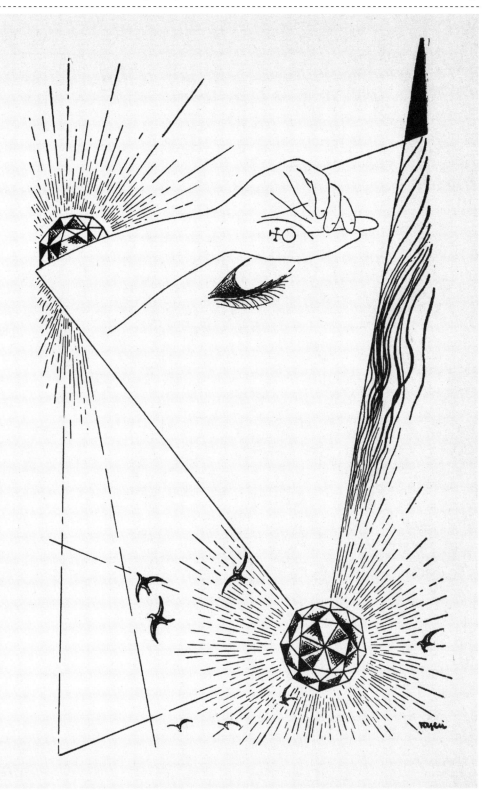

Max Walter Svanberg
Reproduced in
Médium, no. 3, May 1954

Past the first thickets which the hand of man has cleared, tracks traced by the feet of the Indians offer themselves in every direction. The majority however stop, breathless, one or two hundred yards further on in front of the impenetrable copse or will stumble on the mass of rotten trunks whose fringe is sometimes criss-crossed with flowers which have the disturbing appearance of slices of rotting veal liver, haloed with a cloud of midges which abandon them immediately for the face of those curious enough to bend over them. But are they flowers? A violent smell of mould emanates from them, unless it is coming from the soil itself and impregnating the whole vegetation. If it was not for the long spear-shaped leaf which seems to support the flower, one would be tempted to think of a cryptogram harbouring a mortal poison.

We have to retrace our steps. Another track appears which emerges onto a clearing bristling with termites' nests. Here all of the trees carry them like monstrous parasites, hideous excrescences, repugnant goitres, but are seemingly unaffected by them. On the contrary, freer in spite of the enormous bulbous forms which appear to eat into them, bit by bit, they find the sun again more easily. Several tracks leave the clearing to creep, like watchful burglars, into the forest where the sun gives way to a hostile twilight. Neither trees nor ground have managed completely to absorb yesterday's downpour. A drop of water falling from leaf to leaf breaks the silence which shatters like a window under the impact of a pebble and fills your head with a prolonged humming which seems to go on for ever. Then silence falls again like a soaked sheet, not even troubled by the sound of my steps on the thick carpet of vegetation which will soon be humus.

No life, except that of plants! Has the very close presence of people chased the animals away from their dwellings? Here the forest resembles a nest empty so long that the plants have tried to make up for the clamour of the absent bird with their immobility. And still this suspect half-light in which all the leaves shine darkish green, as if the absence of light allows the plants only those tones peculiar to the shadow and liable to accentuate it. And still this limp and sticky silence, a hideous slug which there would be no point in crushing under the impact of the foot putting all of its weight on a trunk, since it absorbs the sound in the way a sponge fills with water. And yet, a miracle! What is this barely perceptible perfume, light as an adolescent's head of hair, and where is it coming from? I seek with my eyes and see nothing; but yes, there, three steps away, some corollas like morning glory, of a pastel-hued mauve, so delightfully fresh that they proffer an indictment against their hostile surroundings by their presence alone. Here are half a dozen of them, fallen onto the spongy ground and spreading a weak dawn light into this twilight of dread. They have fallen, but where from? I look all around the forest and finally discover more than twelve feet up the delicate garland of a fine creeper which runs between the great trees to carry its message of light, freshness and perfume. So unwonted, these flowers! One would speak of a little girl playing with her hoop before a burial, a baby wailing in a charnel house!

The already narrow track becomes even more constricted. It is no more than a tunnel in the rotten forest into which one advances at times bent double, slapped at each step by a bouquet of leaves, hooked by a dead branch which breaks with the sound of a cocked pistol, slipping on the soaked ground where one avoids falling only by holding on to a trunk or creeper. Some dead trees which are reduced to spongy dust have collapsed across the path. They have to be cleared almost on all fours in spite of the repugnance one feels in putting one's hands into this indefinable material which is no longer wood and not yet earth, which perhaps hides in its gaping wounds a venomous insect or an even more dangerous reptile.

Finally one observes tinges in the half-light, gleaming to the right, dull to the left, elsewhere dense like a suspect fruit. It sticks to the skin like a leech. One would say that one was sinking into a slimy shadow in which one would by some miracle manage to keep one's head above the mud. The tunnel, however, widens. It even becomes possible to stand up again. One has the feeling of regaining a foothold on earth that is fairly firm and reliable and, suddenly, at the turn of the track, one glimpses a great patch of clearness which shines in the gloom and fascinates like the eye of a huge wild animal. A rustling of cattleya rushes down from a dead tree supported by a living one it had bent over under its weight. How many flowers gleam in the half-light? A hundred, a thousand, perhaps? It is a cascade of light which descends towards the ground where it will soon arrive. And still not a single presence: the total immobility of mummies in their sarcophagi.

Where are the shrill macaws which flock and chase each other at dusk above the outpost? Where are the little monkeys, those *macaços prêgos* that start moaning at nothing and whose shrill cry the Indians seem to amplify so as to welcome the return of the hunters every evening? Where are the little green parrots, hardly bigger than a blackbird, which chatter from morning till evening, and the *mutums* and *pasas* and the roebucks the Indians sometimes succeed in shooting? Do the animals here emerge from the gloom only at dawn or in the twilight to furnish their needs? Does the Indian find life where my unpractised eyes fail to notice any at all? I have difficulty in believing that any living being could haunt this blue-green darkness whose humidity oozes everywhere. No bird song at all! One begins to long for some manifestation of animal life; even if this would only be the furtive slipping of a fleeing reptile, but no, there is nothing. Whichever track one takes, one always ends up at the same spectacle of tragic immobility, half-light and mould. The 'great trees full of silent birds and monkeys' evoked by Apollinaire are not here. One feels, in this forest, that everything is diluted, dissolves, is worn away right down to the stones. Moreover, none of them are to be seen. If any animals are there they must ultimately melt under a thick bed of humus in the process of fermentation. If a man were to be struck with a sudden lethargy in such a place he would never awaken: he would dissolve before recovering his senses.

For hours I wandered in the forest without suspecting the slightest presence in it, no matter how much I expected it at each step. As high as the eye could see towards the hidden sky and invisible sun was nothing but a vegetal mêlée: here an endless battle takes place without respite. Every species is caught in a ferocious combat whose immediate stake was, high above, the light, in which it is forbidden to touch the ground for fear that the weak will perish. To this mêlée is added another in which the victors of the first are often crushed: that of trees and creepers. Rare are those that no one grasps by a branch or some point on the trunk. At times some creepers of different species even fight over the same tree they have condemned, at the same time as they grab each other in a merciless struggle to suppress one another. A silent, harsh and tenacious battle, every second, in which one guesses that even the night itself (it must be hardly different from the day) is turned to account to win an advantage, to mount by a millimetre or tighten a grip.

And the earth which takes revenge, sticks its tenacious humidity to the trunks that it eats away bit by bit, until the tree that is perhaps the victor at the top, tumbles, consumed at its base, in a rout of creepers and vegetal parasites of every variety, to receive, on the day when it will be no more than a skeleton eaten away by humidity and mould, its triumphal crown of orchids whose brilliance insults its defeat and death. No pity! People here have no pity for the trees and the forest repays them their hostility a hundredfold.

André Breton
Embers in Ceridwen's Cauldron

One of the most fruitful surrealist explorations during the 1950s concerned Celtic culture, undertaken in collaboration with historians Lancelot Lengyel and Jean Markale. Breton, who was born in Brittany and whose very name symbolically seemed to imply an almost primordial link with it, felt, like many surrealists, a particular empathy with Celtic culture, in which he perceived the possibility of a revival of values with the power to challenge the Greco-Roman heritage that Breton considered had been inflicted on European culture for two millennia, corrupting it in its roots.

First published as a preface to Jean Markale, *Les Grands Bardes gallois*, Paris: G. Fall, 1956; reprinted in André Breton, *Perspective cavalière*, Paris: Gallimard, 1970.

An interpretation deserving of the name being reserved for books described as 'sacred', the poetry that soars highest in our days which they claim to make accessible to the vulgar is treated as an object of education and is hence submitted to the ultra-debilitating regime of the 'textual explanation'. Depending upon how one feels, it is amusing or confusing to observe (when all those who know anything about it agree in proclaiming that a poem's virtue also partially depends on what it literally 'means', or appears to mean, just as a painting is judged by what it 'represents') that manuals, constrained by the *perceptible* trend for making ever more room each day for more or less hermetic works, are increasingly overburdened with glosses aimed at all costs at re-establishing the primacy of the intelligible over the perceptible. One could no more deliberately inscribe oneself against the will which commands the whole poetic attitude over more than a century and which has, willy-nilly, profoundly fashioned us all. The Nerval of *Les Chimères* and *Aurélia*, Baudelaire, Corbière, Lautréamont, Mallarmé, Jarry, the Apollinaire of *Onirocritique* or *Cortège* distil and diffuse a light coming from afar of which only those blind to this light could seek the ersatz in a banal and illusory clarity. The word of Rimbaud gleams at the centre of this chain, assuming value from the command: 'Therefore the poet is really the stealer of fire. He is answerable to humanity, even to animals; he must make his inventions tasted, touched and heard; if what he reports from over there has form, he gives form; if it is formless, he gives formlessness. Find a language'. So imbued was Valéry with the Mediterranean and docile spirit that he might reach for the powers of 'reason' that he was very careful to set aside so as to honour this considerable part of creation which assures the poet of quite different help than that of directed thought to which an aberrant critic, after the event, would wish to submit everything. Shortly before his death, he insisted on the fact that the 'blessed formation', highly complex in nature, which puts an end to the poet's expectation by fulfilling his desire,'is not a constructed expression, but a kind of propagation, a matter of resonance. Here language is no longer an intermediary annulled by understanding, once its effect is accomplished; it acts through its form, and the effect is to be immediately reborn and recognised as itself.' He is not afraid to call it the 'language of the gods' [Valéry 1958, p.301].

It was inevitable that those who understand the meaning of such a language would have no interest in its preliminary and integral unveiling and, to benefit from its substantial value, experience the need to return to its sources, so as ever more avidly to study the message bequeathed to us, for a long time to no avail, by remote ages. Do we need to be reminded that, well before it was reduced to nothing more than a utilitarian means of exchange between people, language was entirely penetrated by the unknown, making a breach in the azure? The accession to the highest levels that the human condition balances precariously above it and which cannot be expected except from a common leap of the mind and heart that began by finding its spontaneous and elective life in the poem, given wings by its rhythm alone. Even when imperatives intervened as a result of religious pressure, it was a long time before the sap of language lost its vitality. Centuries of 'logical' dictatorship were needed so that (with the sovereign light, that of *illumination*, kept hidden under a bushel) people were reduced, whenever they wanted once more to make contact with the old texts, to the recourse of the precarious gleams of *elucidation*...

A consequence of the poetic revolution, which has culminated in our time, has been to reveal the fallacious character of modes of the (I repeat) literal apprehension of a language that has yet to

24 'L'Esprit moderne et la Tradition', introduction to Paul Sérant, *Au seuil de l'ésotérisme*, Paris: Grasset, 1955 [trans.].

25 *Le Livre de Chilám Balám de Chumayel*, Paris: Denoël, 1955.

abdicate or aspire to reconquer its initial destination. They should be opposed with everything which can be developed in the direction of the greatest permeability for what emanates from it and to do so by virtue of intuition and perception through analogy. This alone can make a valid critique apparent, finally acceding to the complex symbolism which, unknown to its author, forms the poem's frame, the solidity and finesse of which depends, in the final analysis, on its force of impregnation... Nothing more penetrating has been said on this subject than by Raymond Abellio in his study 'The Modern Spirit and Tradition': 'The force of evocation a symbolism possesses proceeds from the implicit structuration which supports its convergences and confers a power of integration on them that is independent of the "letter" of the symbol, a power which announces that each symbol is itself integratable and is only a centre of meaning provisionally isolated in a vaster centre which has still to be named'.[24]

Still only half open to this truth, the fresh eye begins to enjoy a completely different power of inveiglement. Affective communion is (already) expected more than seamless comprehension. The essential fact is that on the fringes of the other the thirst would be felt for a language 'from the soul for the soul... thought pinning down thought and firing' (Rimbaud, 'Lettre au Voyante').

If the need to go back as far as possible to the places from which it sprang up has been experienced, it is in the hope of finding the harmonic key to this language, the most slender of secular conventions which govern our culture. We have asked for it by turns in Sumerian chants, in the great nocturnes of the music of the spheres brought to us by the Books of the Dead of the Egyptians and Tibetans and in what, from their most profound depths, the pre-Colombian civilisations emitted before extinguishing themselves (see in particular *Le Livre de Chilám Balám de Chumayel*, which Benjamin Péret has translated[25]). None too soon it was realised that they could well have continued the same vibrations wherever our stride takes us, where we find ourselves in direct telluric relation with it. In order to do this it was necessary to attack everything in the westerner that conspired in the 'shameful' repression of his past, a lasting consequence of the law of the strongest imposed nineteen centuries ago by the Roman legions. Historically there is no doubt that this operation was made possible by the feeling, which very quickly became generalised, of how flagrantly inadequate the newly defined conditions of life for this planet were, beginning with the liberation of nuclear energy, compared to the modes of thought of a bygone era. Henceforth, an atavistic burst led us to ask questions about the deepest aspirations of mankind in our countries as it might have been before the Greco-Roman yoke brought its weight to bear on it. Decisive in this respect was the very recent full revelation of Gaulish coins. Masterfully (notwithstanding that some objection might be made to details of his argument) Lancelot Lengyel, in his superb work *L'Art gaulois dans les médailles*, has been able to unlock the *spirit* in which these tiny masterpieces were conceived and at long last make

26 Catalogue of the exhibition *Perennité de l'art gaulois: l'art gaulois et l'art occidental*, Musée pédagogique, Paris 1955.

27 Jean-Baptiste Colbert de Beaulieu (1905–95), leading French numismatist and expert on Gaulish coins [trans.].

it a subject of exaltation for us. No lesson threatens less to be wasted, as one could judge by the reception afforded the exhibition *Permanence of Gaulish Art* which, at the beginning of this year, provoked innumerable commentaries in the press and attracted visitors in droves to the Pedagogical Museum.

For all those who have been studying them for a long time it is the Armorican Gaulish medals which stand out as worthy of attention and admiration. No doubt Lancelot Lengyel was thinking about them when he was impelled to state that 'the originality of the Gaulish art on the medals resides in its distance from the Greek essence of a beauty limited to terrestrial matter and distinguished by seeking another, eternal and imperishable, reality hidden behind appearance, without for all that getting lost in the clouds of the unreal'.[26] In order to hold their own at the foremost level of interest, these coins have for many years been the object of the scholarly work of Dr Colbert de Beaulieu[27] in a way that is moreover all the more auspicious.

For the majority, the revelation of Celtic art, which is given free rein in the medals and continues after the conquest in sculpture with, in the background, that of the megaliths as they are employed in splendour in the tumulus of Gavrinis, makes us bitterly deplore the lack of contemporaneous written documents, which might give us more precise information on the organisation of the key ideas affecting them. The great tree has been cut down, reducing us, on the river's surface, to watching its leaves of gold or silver sparkling as they pass and to imagine, from their tracks, the noble presences which surrounded it. Fortunately what does remain for us is an enduring offspring against which the perfidious Mediterranean blade could do nothing, which is what emerges from the ancient Breton or Cymric poetry, the frail hull of a very battered boat but of which we retain everything which could be saved, in terms of wisdom and the possibilities of native *dépassement* during the first centuries of the Christian era, through the oral tradition. This treasure resides in what has reached us from the texts by Aneurin, Llywarch Hen, Myrddin and especially Taliesin. It should be said that it is offered like those of our childhood, buried in a chest streaming with algae and spangled with shells, creaking on its hinges as soon as we try to do more than half open it. But then it lets some rays from King Arthur's shield filter out and, from our perspective today, we are still gathering around it on the shore. It has quite correctly been observed that the Celtic sculptor 'sees in the face only a reflection of internal, spiritual tension. The mask of its heroes probably resembled their carnal features only distantly: it expressed the impulse of their courage more than a war song' (André Varagnac). The exalting courage even of its collapses, re-immersed in the death of each brave man, is the pedal of this poetry in which the 'I' is already intensely an 'other' since it assumes every condition, including that of the inanimate, and consents to be conceived only as their global consciousness. Strained towards the resolution of the enigmas of the universe, it shares with that of the Icelandic *kenningar* the gift of arousing

28 'Kenningar', an essay by Jorge-Luis Borges, first published in the collection *Historia de la Eternidad* (1936); it does not appear to have ever been translated into English [trans.].

29 See, for example, *Kat Godeu ou le Combat des arbrisseaux*, Rennes, 1953.

30 The 'gay wisdom' or 'language of the birds' of medieval thought that Nietzsche invoked in one of his last books [trans.].

within us that *lucid perplexity* of which Jorge-Luis Borges has spoken, telling us that it is the 'unique honour of metaphysics, its recompense and source'.[28]

The time in which we live would be enough to cause us to oppose entirely such perplexity to the ridiculous assurance that some people believe they are able to found on the thinnest beam of light.

From the high places he haunts each year, between the Barenton Fountain and the Val-sans-Retour, not far from the disturbing village of Folle-Pensée, in the heart of the fabulous forest of Brocéliande where flashes from Perceval's lance still gleam, no one could be better designated than Jean Markale to present to us, with all the care required, the songs of the ancient Gallic bards. That up to now the old translators or compilers have treated these difficult texts too casually is the least that can be said.[29] Be this only to divert the nonsense and intercept interpolation where it had slipped, but even better to revive them for our use, nothing less was needed than what Markale possesses of '*gay sçavoir*'[30] and fervour.

Robert Benayoun
The Twilight of the Wheeler-Dealers

In this essay from 1961, Robert Benayoun separates surrealism from what has since been vaguely defined as 'magic realism', by which diffuse ideas (generally drawn from sources of the fantastic) are brought together with no overarching rationale to justify their linkage or provide a consistent grounding for their association. The book by Louis Pauwels and Jacques Bergier to which he is refers was in its time a bestseller, introducing many of the themes and the methodological sleights-of-hand that would later come to characterise New Age ideologies. Making a distinction between the obscure and doubtful, as celebrated by Bergier and Pauwels, and the shadowy and latent, Benayoun clarifies a crucial aspect of the surrealist understanding of the marvellous as being inherent to reality rather than distinct from it.

First published in *La Brèche: action surréaliste*, no.1, October 1961.

Some people would be tempted to interpret my title as a paraphrase of the recent work published by Louis Pauwels and Jacques Bergier, namely *The Morning of the Magicians*. They would be perfectly right. The advantage of such a title is that it summarises this essay accurately enough, whereas *The Morning of the Magicians*, with its promises of dawn and enchantment, unfailingly arouses a vague frustration in the reader – as can be procured by any vague book, but a frustration all the same, furnished with suitable conclusions.

Louis Pauwels and Jacques Bergier: when an association is based on two such diverse, I dare say inverse, terms, you can expect

31 The 'Manifesto of French Intellectuals' (issued in response to the Manifesto on the Right to Insubordination). [Benayoun is referring to a manifesto signed by right-wing French intellectuals and published in *Le Monde* on 7 October 1960 in support of the French government's colonial actions in Algeria. The famous 'Manifesto on the Right to Insubordination', which was drafted by the surrealists, called for mass mobilisation against the war; see José Pierre (ed.), *Tracts surréalistes et declarations collectives*, Paris, Le Terrain Vague, 1982, vol.2, pp.391–2, which can be found in translation in Krzysztof Fijalkowski and Michael Richardson (eds.), *Surrealism against the Current*, London: Pluto 2001, pp.195–7 – trans.].

32 A notable gap is the unexplained absence in the body of the work of a series of 'considerations by René Alleau on the state of superior consciousness', even though it is included in the Table of Contents.

33 Denis Saurat (1890–1958), professor of literature at the University of London who wrote *Atlantis and the Reign of the Giants*, tracing the location of Atlantis based on a dream [trans.].

34 Hans Hörbiger (1860–1931), Austrian mining engineer who expounded a bizarre 'Cosmic Ice Theory' adopted by the Nazis after his death – Heinrich Himmler was one of his followers.

35 Edward Bulwer-Lytton (1803–1873), popular English Victorian novelist; H.P. Lovecraft (1890–1937), author of horror fiction; Jorge Luis Borges (1899–1986), Argentine short-story writer, poet and essayist; Arthur Machen (1863–1947), Welsh writer of horror stories, best known for *The Great God Pan* (1890); Hanns Heinz Ewers (1871–1943) German actor and writer of short stories and novels; Gustav Meyrink (1868–1932) Austrian novelist, most famous for *The Golem* (1913) [trans.].

to generate surprises. Some will also say that the said terms, as diverse as they appear, are combined without great fortune among the signatories of a manifesto wrongly known as 'the manifesto of Marshall Juin'.[31] But I will answer that it is mean as well as superfluous to find fault from the outset with generalities when a book of 512 pages and a few gaps[32] offers the observer of good faith a sufficiently firm ground for possible argument.

What is *The Morning of the Magicians*? According to the method dear to Pauwels it is a succession of rather parsimonious individual thoughts, annotated anecdotes and long quotations interrupted at a rate of almost one chapter in every two by extracts from novels, summaries of lectures or complete stories, preferably borrowed from science fiction – in short, a sort of foraging anthology in which very disparate subjects are approached at top speed in an attitude of patient bewilderment called 'fantastic realism' ('doors open onto an *other* reality'), which seems a second form of that adage according to which 'truth is stranger than fiction'.

To begin with, the authors suggest that secret societies, as depositories of immemorial techniques, will undertake the total domination of another world over civilisations to come. Bergier reports a not very convincing conversation he claims to have had with Fulcanelli in 1937 in which the author of the *Mystery of the Cathedrals* apparently warned him about the grave danger of nuclear experiments. A brief panorama of alchemy soon unveils the authors' superficial, almost exotic, curiosity: 'When closely considered, it appears to us reasonable to regard, alongside technical texts and those of wisdom (of alchemy), demented texts as demented texts... Mercury was frequently used by alchemists. Its pungency is toxic, and poisoning provokes delirium.' After a digression about Charles Fort, whose intentions as we shall see they completely betray (the book readily goes from parenthesis to digression), the authors repeat on their own account Saurat's hazy conclusions about Atlantis and its giants,[33] then devote ten of their most coherent and sustained chapters to Hörbiger and his Nazi disciples.[34] Finally, after a rapid glance at parapsychology, they attribute the discovery of Breton's 'supreme point' to mutants coming to the earth, which they moreover identify with the 'great transparents', which in turn they greet as the birth of a collective being. Of course, such a summary analysis does not account for nuances and tends to dispel the transitions by which the authors arrange their cultural tracking shots. But I am forced to convey the almost incredible loose ends of the whole as I understand them, in which non-committal reflections ('we think that at a certain level intelligence itself is a secret society') are punctuated with an almost exhausting recourse to authors as contradictorily dubious as Bulwer-Lytton, Lovecraft, Borges, Arthur Machen, Hanns Heinz Ewers or Gustav Meyrink.[35]

I have mentioned authors. From the very first pages it clearly appears that Pauwels assumes sole responsibility for the editing – in which, moreover, we have little difficulty recognising his

36 Jean d'Agraives (1892–1951), French writer of adventure stories, mostly for children; Gaston Leroux (1868–1927), French popular novelist and journalist, author of *The Phantom of the Opera* [trans.].

37 Lobsang Rampa (1910–1981), writer whose book *The Third Eye* (1953) recounting mystical experiences in Tibet inspired a cult interest in the country; in 1958 an investigator uncovered the fact that 'Rampa' was in fact Englishman Clifford Burgess, who had never been to Tibet [trans.].

infinite sadness, his astonishing verbal gift, and that gloomy condescension beneath which, before television cameras, he buries the great of this world. Bergier bears all the initial costs of the operation (but we will see where he takes his revenge): Pauwels presents him to us as 'a little Jew...' with a 'pointed nose, wearing round glasses behind which agile and cold eyes gleam'. On the other hand, he corrects the sardonic precision of this sketch with the very real feeling of admiration inspired by the brilliant culture of his collaborator to whom, as he makes clear, he owes not only the basic idea of their work but also its initial material: 'In a single span, Bergier has saved me twenty years of active reading,' he writes. 'A formidable library is in service in this powerful brain. The selection, the classification and the most complex connections are established at electronic speed.' I would not raise the problem of sources, apparently a secondary issue in the case of a speculative work, if the fragility of his bases did not arise from the outset. In page after page Pauwels will yield to the pleasure of citing works he has not read, but whose seriousness is guaranteed by Bergier. This explains why the most solid arguments of the enterprise are borrowed, without qualitative control, from popular novelists like Bradbury, C.S. Lewis, Merritt, Van Vogt, Walter Miller or Arthur C. Clarke. The phrase 'centre of energy', Pauwels's leitmotif, comes from John Buchan, a sort of English Jean d'Agraives crossbred with Gaston Leroux.[36] Bergier might, for the same reason, have directed his credulous partner to James Hilton's *Lost Horizon*, *The Hesperides* by John Palmer, *New Crete* by Robert Graves, the novels of Rider Haggard or the adventures of Fu Manchu. Let's add that Bergier and Pauwels often rely on works of demystification such as *Fallacies in the Name of Science* by Martin Gardner (New York: Dover Publications, 1957), but only so as unhesitatingly to adopt all the fables they ridicule or dismantle, finally taking as their bible journals as frivolous as *Astounding Science Fiction*, and reproducing without verification extracts from the popular press.

What then is the role of Pauwels in this volume? The very elegant, but not very glorious one of a transmission system. He is amazed, he palpates, enthuses or worries over the tireless availability of his tame Huron scout. This man who casts a single glance on the prefect of police, and immediately recognises his spiritual brother, is stupefied by a little pre-Inca quipu, respectfully cites an anecdote by Cocteau, and ratifies Lobsang Rampa.[37] In the avowed desire to write a Fortean book, he gives in to the most summarily fallacious temptations of pastiche: 'We refuse to exclude facts on the grounds that they are not *suitable*... Our methods were those of scholars, but also of theologians, poets, sorcerers, magicians, and children. We have behaved like barbarians, preferring invasion to evasion. We are among the strange bands, the ghostly hordes... of the transparent and disordered cohorts which begin to be unfurled across our civilisation. ' Here is how this relates, with such sinister platitudes, to these passages by Fort: 'My methods would be those of theologians, savages, scholars and small children... We hold a

Kathleen Fox
Man and Bird - Assemblage
2010
From her exhibition *The Spaces of the Unconscious*, Freud Museum, London 2010

38 Ludwig Achim von Arnim (1781–1831), German Romantic poet and novelist; Petrus Borel (1809–1859), French Romantic novelist, mainly known for *Madame Putiphar* (1839); Charles Robert Maturin (1782–1824), Irish gothic novelist, author of *Melmoth the Wanderer* (1820) – all writers greatly admired by the surrealists [trans.].

39 Jean-Jacques Susini (born 1933), French politician, founder of the notorious OAS, a terrorist group opposed to Algerian independence. Twice sentenced to death for various attempted assassinations (several against Charles de Gaulle), he was reprieved by de Gaulle in 1968 and by François Mitterrand in 1983. Later a member of the National Front, he was elected to the French Parliament in 1999 [trans.].

40 Marcel Schwob (1867–1905), French symbolist writer greatly admired by the surrealists and uncle of the surrealist artist and writer Claude Cahun [trans.].

procession of all the data that science has judged should be excluded. Battalions of the damned, led by pale data I will have exhumed, will start marching'. We cannot even speak of plagiarism without insulting Lautréamont. It is a question at most of darning, or knitting.

Charles Fort, starting with precise data, labelled and controlled, applied to them a lyrical form of doubt, and poetically reached the surreal. Pauwels, inversely, starts with fine fictions and examines them with an indecisive good faith, and finds a certain realism in them. 'For the methods and apparatus of surrealism', he writes with modesty, 'we have tried to substitute the humbler methods and more weighty apparatus of what we call scientific realism'. This might more accurately be stated as: instead of discerning a quotient of surreality in reality, he examines the fantastic, in its most flaky forms, and finds a verisimilitude in it.

To those (the same ones every time) who believe they scent in this new practice of obscurantism a reactionary method, I will offer only a weak denial. I mentioned that Pauwels paid a very particular attention to the analysis of Nazi scientific theories. But we should speak about nostalgia. At the Nuremberg trials, Pauwels painfully registered the triumph of materialist thought over magic thought: 'It should not be thought that we would dream of denying the benefits of the Nuremberg enterprise. We just think that the fantastic has been buried with it.' Pauwels is certainly not the only person to deplore these funerals, but I get the idea that the fantastic he is talking about is not ours. It is not that of Borel, Arnim, Maturin, or even Nerval or Poe.[38] It would rather be that of the emblems of fire, the cheap junk of cowls, crosses scrawled in chalk on doorsteps and watchwords given from on high. Those who mourn the defeat of the Great Unknown or the thawing of glacial cosmogony have really turned with hope towards flying saucers. They are able to invoke the 'ultra-consciousness' with the same wily volte-face that characterises Susini's 'National Socialism'.[39] They will not succeed in relegating the black to the black shirt. The summary rigour of their work in the grip of inadequate digestion, their quest for the most univalent processes of mental seduction, their vain regrets for eras of intellectual panic indicate the decrepitude of their attitude which is closed to the most obvious ideas of the century (delirium of interpretation, lyrical automatism, paranoiac critical activity and so on). Permanent exiles from the poetic domain and its various realities, alien to the innocence of clairvoyants as to the desperate humour of mythomaniacs, they pulverise the shadow, and without even giving in to the cunning temptation of 'imaginary lives', as recorded by Marcel Schwob,[40] embellishing history from its denials, they identify their analysis of Nazism with the retrospective wishes that the lacunae of the record inspired in them. The systematic option they assume in favour of the obscure and the doubtful, to the detriment of the shadowy and the latent, forcefully links them to the stereotype of a theme which from the beginning is waiting for the highest bid. This lack of care completely betrays their ambitions: seeking to impose themselves

41 See Bergier's interview on the subject of Gurdjieff, *Médium*, no.2, May 1954.

42 See 'Here One Disintegrates' by Jacques Bergier, in *Fiction*, no.9, August 1954.

as the prestidigitators of a possible 'new order', they see from their balcony the sun of the illusionists, the deluded and false adepts setting.

Strangely, this failure seems to result from a subterranean conflict of personalities: when the blithe and paradoxical theses of a deadpan joker are developed by a pundit as grave as a marble statue, the hidden mines have a tendency to explode as if they were only crackers. The views of Gurdjieff, who impressed Pauwels to the point of nervous breakdown, were not so long ago considered inoffensive and overrated by Jacques Bergier.[41] Saurat's theses about Atlantis inspired in him the same disdain: 'We appreciate the hoax as much as the next man', he wrote, 'but to continue a hoax to the extent of writing a book like this is unacceptable. It is regrettable to see the worst rantings of Hitlerian pseudo-science reappearing in this way.'[42] Someone else inadvisedly arranged the variegated material he seems to have furnished in this game. It had to be someone as devoid of humour as Pauwels to be terrified for more than half a second by the monotony of Martians, necromancers, androids, poltergeists, zombies and crazy scholars which punctuate his friend's everyday conversations like a cough – and especially to pull from them such a rickety breviary.

As you read this book, and there file past, in the authors' waiting room (we wager), all the fortune-tellers, suburban spiritualists, sub-prefectural theosophists and Irish Swamis of the hemisphere; we express the candid wish that such a celebration might henceforth be pursued without the slightest hindrance. For every Louis Pauwels one should send in his Jacques Bergier.

René Ménil
The Passage from Poetry to Philosophy

This important text makes a number of points which are central to surrealist attitudes towards cultural identity and the effects of post-colonialism. But in elucidating the distinctions between negritude as promulgated respectively by Aimé Césaire and Léopold Sédar Senghor, Ménil raises questions that have a more general importance for our understanding of surrealism in terms of the uses of language – and especially the subversive value of poetic language as it challenges meaning, in the process transforming language itself and the meaning resulting from it.

1.

First published in René Ménil, *Tracées*, Paris: Robert Laffont, 1981.

Historically, black poetry preceded the philosophy commonly called negritude.

A remarkable fact. It will so happen that black philosophy will be essentially constituted from a prime material which is poetic. It will so happen that the maxims, proverbs, metaphors and images, hyperbolic amplifications, lyrical cries and ironical antiphrasis will be transferred unaltered from the realm of poetry to that of philosophical discourse.

It was in *Orphée nègre* (Black Orpheus) in 1948 that Sartre inaugurated this method of ambiguity: with the poems in the *Anthologie de la nouvelle poésie nègre et malgache* he constructed the first theorisation of negritude. Senghor will practice the same method and take up the conceptions to which this method logically led (see the 'Interventions aux congrès des écrivains et artistes noirs', 1956 and 1959, and other francophone discourses).

2.

If we were to compare the *Cahier d'un retour au pays natal* by Césaire (the official poet of negritude, its principal evangelist, according to Sartre) and the philosophy of Senghor (the official philosopher of negritude), who insistently and repeatedly uses the *Cahier* as authority, we would be in a position to measure within specific texts the margin which separates two languages and two orders of meaning: poetic language and meaning on the one hand and philosophical meaning on the other – all that until now has been amalgamated and awkwardly mixed up under the same denomination of negritude. (It is true that the poet of negritude, just like Molière's Maître Jacques, changes his overalls to act as theoretician-philosopher of negritude without much warning.)

3.

Let us therefore without delay read the *Cahier*, and then Senghor's philosophical presentation.

One striking thing is the difference in climate, language and thought.

What is apparent everywhere in the *Cahier* is the lightness of spirit at work, meaning that there is a vivacity and vitality of spirit which ensures swift displacements and reversals of thought and feeling.

In contrast, which is another aspect, in Senghor's philosophical texts we find an amazing awkwardness of conceptions.

More precisely, Senghor takes the *Cahier* as authority and here and there will draw upon a Césairian poem to define his black African. But how do the deduction and genealogy of the concepts operate?

From the outset we note a flattening out of the poetic text which, as it passes through Senghor, is divested of humour and of the inherent ambiguity of poetic meaning and conditions.

Many of the affirmations which in the *Cahiers* are ironic are found again with their meaning reversed in Senghorian doctrine, because they are taken literally and 'too seriously'.

Let's note in passing that Senghor's misunderstanding (his misreading) is shared by the friends of blacks in the West and by many blacks in Africa and the Caribbean.

43 Joseph Arthur, Comte de Gobineau (1816–1882), French novelist and man of letters credited with developing the theory of the Aryan master race in *An Essay on the Inequality of the Human Races* (1853–5) [trans.].

The Senghorian doctrine absurdly lays claim to just such a racist conception of the negro, which in the *Cahier* was borrowed from the white racist in order to throw it back at him in an ironic mode, and assigns it an inverse coefficient of positive value.

Here are the negroes as expressed by Césaire in the *Cahier*. But expressed by Césaire as white racists love and want them to be:

> *Gay and obscene, and to be rid of boredom, very hot on jazz,*
> *I can do the soft-shoe, the Lindy-hop and the tap dance.*
> *And for a special treat the muted trumpet of our cries wrapped*
> *in wah-wah.*
> *Wait… Everything's in order. My good angel grazes in neon*
> *lights.*
> *I swallow sticks. My dignity wallows in vomit.*
> [Césaire 1969, pp.64–5]

It so happens that the inconsistent negro absurdly denounced here in the style of tragic irony and by means of antiphrasis ('everything's in order') becomes in Senghor the very consistency of the negro of negritude.

The humour of the text has been ignored. And it is in the light of this inconsistency that Senghor obstinately insists on measuring negro value in the world. Thinking that he is outwitting Descartes he will direct this statement at the Europe-of-colonisation-and-racism: 'I feel, I dance, and therefore I exist!' But it works out really badly or comes at the right moment – it depends – since it was white racism that formed this devalued image of the negro as uniquely devoted to the practice of amusement (see Gobineau[43]). And in this vein, we have this profession of faith: 'Let Europe be the orchestra conductor, we other negroes, we would be content with drums (!)… All we will have to do is imperiously to mark the basic rhythm by stamping the ground with our feet.'

We see Senghor's humour here, but unfortunately it is objective humour, without the benefit of self-understanding.

4.

In the *Cahier* the antiphrasis and the ellipsis are continuously put in the service of the poetic digest. Ceaselessly the poet distances himself from what he is and what he says so as to produce *the literary effect of derision*.

The reader of the *Cahier* notices very quickly, in fact, that what is said is meant sometimes literally – and sometimes the meaning is the opposite of the literal.

This play in the poetic discourse of the *Cahier* is explained by the very situation of Césaire's discourse. In the *Cahier* there is a Césaire who speaks. But Césaire's constant return towards himself in order to contest himself, to contest the colonial subject within him, brings forth an other-of-Césaire. A duality. But the principal interlocutor who will (explicitly or implicitly) continually be interpolated so as to settle accounts with them is the personification of colonialism and white racism.

The poetic language of the *Cahier* is thus not simple, because the same language expresses three voices.

These three voices are to be understood in a continuous discourse without an explicit designation of the identity of the one who speaks – Césaire utilising the *literary process of collage* which consists of pasting the word of the other into the sentence without recourse to inverted commas and without announcing the entrance of this other onto the stage.

Senghor is blind, or wants to be blind (for the needs of his cause), to these 'leaps' in the writing.

Insensitive to the specific nature of the poetic enunciation which is floating, polyvalent, in perpetual drift and in full fixed explosion, he does not notice, or means to ignore, a whole world of Césairian aversions which are only implied, but which are readable between or behind the written lines. For this it is enough to take into account the context of the *Cahier* and its stylistic processes. Without forgetting the context of Caribbean culture arrived at by intellectuals around the 1930s in relation to modern modes of the sensibility (note in *Légitime défense* a refusal of folklorisation and of rural sluggishness).

5.

In different scholarly studies of negritude, the analysts presently agree on distinguishing between two types: one Caribbean, that of Césaire; the other African, that of Senghor.

It is the start of a clarification.

To evoke here two mentalities to explain the differences would be to take inspiration from a 'spontaneous naturalism' itself masking a form of racism within the black world itself.

It is preferable to refer to the historical evolution (the historic social formation, that of social classes and intellectual elites, the social struggles and their ideological content, the development of the sensibility – ethical and aesthetic taste and distastes – as a function of the way of living, of social movements and so on) in the Caribbean and in Africa.

In summary, Césaire's rhetoric and his thought, the regime and register of his sensibility, can only be defined with reference to a Caribbean intellectual history – in particular a stronger liaison with the critical spirit of the 'Enlightenment' (Voltaire, Diderot, Helvétius) than in Africa, with the ironic, irreverent and revolutionary French movement (for decades the Caribbean populations have been impregnated with a rationalist, secular and atheist ideology, that of Schoelcherism, the sharp end of anti-colonialism until recently), and with the progressivism of Jaurès and the thought of Marx, without forgetting western literary movements (romanticism, symbolism, surrealism) which echoed immediately among the Caribbean intelligentsia.

We note a difference in Senghor: the marked influence of the 'good missionary fathers' and western anthropologists suggesting to him an idealism attached to the past and the belief in a 'pre-logical' negro mentality, an academicism of thought which does not succeed in disturbing folkloric idiosyncrasy, a naturalist metaphysics which is afraid of movement and which evokes history only to immobilise it in archaisms and traditions when this is not simply part of 'negro physiology'.

Fear of movement is such that a resolution of the problems of the black world today or tomorrow by means of effective social and human transformations is felt, according to Senghor, to have already been achieved in the Africa of the past (the renowned African socialism of primitive communities) or in negro 'nature' and 'mentality' (surrealism is alleged to be a feature of the negro-African mentality).

6.

A passage of the *Cahier* was dedicated to Breton under the title 'In the guise of a literary manifesto'. By passing into negritude, this passage will serve to establish in the most serious way that negroes are deprived of conceptual, analytical and logical reason, but in compensation are endowed with the 'gift of emotion'. Let's quote:

> *Because we hate you, you and*
> *your reason, we claim kinship with*
> *dementia praecox with flaming madness*
> *with tenacious cannibalism*
> ...
> *And you know the rest*
> *that 2 and 2 make 5*
> *that the forest mews like a cat*
> *that the tree pulls chestnuts out of the fire... and so on.*
> [Césaire 1969, p.55]

This passage is evidently a proud charge made against the civilisation of colonialism and its 'reasons'. And evidently what is challenged is 'colonial reason', not negro human reason.

Moreover, what negritude will take for an anthropology (a description of negro mentality) is, at the same time, only the expression of political anger, essentially an aesthetic: a poetic art of word and image.

7.

A translation exists of the *Cahier* into prose – let's say, rather, an equivalence in prose since, properly speaking, it is impossible to translate poetry into prosaic language. Isn't the characteristic of poetry to express what prose cannot?

> *that the tree draws the chestnuts of fire*

And this equivalence is not the Senghorian prose of negritude. It is the prose of Césaire himself in the *Discourse on Colonialism* (1955).

In this blazing pamphlet we find the best of the philosophy and the concepts which underlie the *Cahier* – a responsible and rational vision of the destiny of the colonies in the modern world.

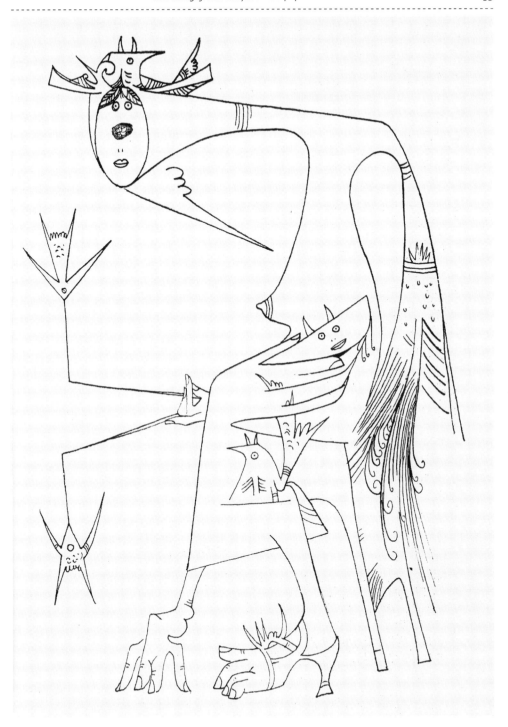

Wifredo Lam
Reproduced in *Médium*, no.4,
January 1956, p.3

The project of the negro without retardation, without diminution, which takes on its shoulders its whole human burden, the burden of all humanity, of the whole human species.

8.

In the *Cahier*, poetry lays bare Caribbean reality, situated and dated in the chain of historical events.

Let's quote at random this passage:

And I laugh at my old childish imaginings.
No, we have never been Amazons at the court of the King of
Dahomey, nor Princes of Ghana with eight hundred camels,
nor doctors at Timbuktu when Askia the Great was king, nor
architects at Djenné, nor Mahdis, nor warriors. We do not feel
in our armpits the itch of those who once carried the lance. [...]
I want to confess that we were always quite undistinguished
dishwashers, small-time shoeshiners, at the most fairly
conscientious witch-doctors, and the only record we hold is
our staying power in wrangling over trifles...
[Césaire 1969, pp.66-7]

What is shown here is an avatar of Caribbean colonial history. What is shown here is a historically situated misfortune, already surmounted through anger and indignation, already surpassed through poetic vision.

In the Senghorian expression of the presence of black people in the world, we will be there at the transformation of the colonial misery described above – a historical and thus passing misery – into a congenital misery due to some negating features of 'psycho-physiology', in other words of the 'nature' of blacks (that they are non-technical, incapable of taming nature, devoted to sensuality, abandoned to the cosmos, and so on).

The historic sense of the *Cahier* (the negro who is sometimes lazy or gives up, sometimes in revolt or reliant on others), by passing into negritude, becomes the absurd and stupid non-sense of the natural black body.

9.

Césairian grammar and Senghorian grammar. A dynamic versus static use of the word.

In the *Cahier*, Césaire makes words say what he wants them to say. Words are thus called up in the *Cahier* to enunciate feelings and vision in proportion to the poetic work. And if they did not exist as such, well, then the poetic word creates them!

Senghor is respectful of words – which make him say what they want. He kneels down before etymologies and asks their opinion.

This withdrawal to the root of words, this scholarly terrorism of prefixes and suffixes is probably not the best method of inventing new feelings and conceiving a historically conceived future for the black world. On the contrary, it will favour the return into the past, the enclosure in archaisms, the re-birth of traditional conformisms, which amaze the West in precise proportion to how bizarre they are.

The *Cahier*, hewn from the Caribbean imaginary, has sought to be the historic contemporary of the modern negro.

Senghorian negritude will be the definitive mythological contemporary of the African past.

10.

It is not that in the *Cahier* Césaire does not make a significant contribution to the elaboration of negritude.

What must be questioned is the *how of the operation*.

It can be seen that poetic density and modulation of tone are not the same throughout the *Cahier* – which can be explained by the additions made to the original text of 1939.

Yet the final part of the poem hands down a message of a pedagogic and political character whose expression is close to prose. It may be thought that in this part of the *Cahier*, the political consciousness of the situation of black people in the world has taken precedence, 'in the heat of revolution', over poetic consciousness, and has partly dismissed aesthetic reverie.

We then have a means of defining the 'negro of value' as opposed to the 'old negritude which turns itself into a corpse'.

It is this part of the *Cahier* which will constitute the most substantial content of negritude mythology, in passing intact from the poem, where it is situated in spite of everything, to the realm of philosophical prose. It will be considered literally without regard to the inherent inflections of context and the coefficient of uncertainty which, as we have said, characterises any text interpreted as a poetic text.

Several concepts then appear that we state *in neutral writing, in other words by freeing them as much as possible from the metaphorical impregnation of the* Cahier *as much as from the mythological garb with which Senghor clothed them.* In short, we will try to name these concepts simply:

- communication with the universe; human participation in and of the universe;
- non-science, non-denomination techniques of colonised blacks;
- a grasping of the essence of things (?);
- pride of the omniscient white victors and rehabilitation of those (the blacks) who were unable to invent anything under the conditions of colonisation;
- a will to and guarantee of regeneration, liberation and blossoming of the black world;
- universal love of the human species and anti-racism (humanism) linked to the necessity to 'cultivate' the black race.

And now what does the transposition of these concepts in a philosophical systematisation which will occur after the event give us?

To uproot a sentence from a poem in order to introduce it unchanged in a philosophical and political talk, as Senghor does (as, it should be said, does Césaire himself when he lays out negritude's theses) poses problems.

The constitution of negritude by Sartre and then by Senghor brings elements which are not negligible for the way these problems are approached.

In his work of theorisation Sartre, who is a philosopher, visibly has scruples from which he divests himself by turning negritude into a phantom, after having taken the trouble to give it consistency with the substance of black poems: negritude, he concludes, is the point of crisis in a dialectical progression. It needs to 'destroy itself' in the humanism of a 'society without races'.

Senghor, who does not subject himself to any rigour as he produces his concepts, since his 'truths' are 'intuitive', is anxious to repeat that his conception of the negro and negritude are as eternal as God the Father, which reveals the mythological dimension of the doctrine.

To establish his timeless conceptions, he submits the statements of the *Cahier* to a treatment which recalls the way the Egyptian Pharaohs embalmed the dead. The meaning which, in the poetic writing, was as mobile, floating, ambivalent and elusive as it should be in poetry, in short the meaning which was in suspense, is suddenly petrified in full flight and lapses into clumsy axioms. The richness of the potential connotations evaporates to subside into depressing and meagre sentiments: 'the negro is emotion'; 'the negro is rhythm'.

The *Cahier* had stated:

> *Heia for those who have never invented anything*
> *those who never explored anything*
> *those who never tamed anything*
> ...
> *Heia for joy*
> *Heia for love*
> *Heia for the reincarnation of tears and the worst pain brought*
> *back again...*
> [Césaire 1969, pp.75-7]

To depart from this text in order to conclude, as Senghor does, with the congenital non-technical nature of blacks, to proclaim the positive value of this non-technical nature, and to affirm, finally, the radical opposition of mental faculties of blacks (emotion) and whites (reason) – this arises from a misunderstanding. Because no precise analysis will reveal in this passage of the *Cahier* a definition and description of black mentality as excluding an aptitude for logic and the use of technology. No precise analysis will see non-technical nature erected as a value in it and proposed as an ideal of life. Quite the contrary: in establishing the poetic meaning of the text, such an analysis places us before a historic fact, nothing more, and not before a required value. It reveals that this avatar of the history of colonised black peoples is accepted in a consciousness which authenticates itself, but that the avatar is finally accepted *in the form of a challenge*, that the irony and bitterness which underlie the discourse signify that the deficiency (the non-technical quality) which is formally acknowledged has already been surpassed in the generosity of a voluntary historical project.

11.

A black person appears in the *Cahier* whom the reader knows is constituted by means of literary amplification and poetic hyperbole.

But these blacks 'who give themselves up to the essence of all things/ignorant of surfaces but struck by the movement of all things' [Césaire 1969, p.77] – who are they?

Among blacks, the man in the aesthetic attitude is not to be doubted. *Homo estheticus*: the white person or black person seized by emotion and gently drifting into imaginary worlds. Man in aesthetic practice.

Negritude is an a*esthetic which is mistaken about its own identity* and which considers itself to be an anthropology – for the realist truth of a mentality.

Conceived as it was by three poets – Césaire, Damas and Senghor himself – this is not surprising.

12.

A poem like the *Cahier* – which expresses a historic vision of the drama of black people in the world and which is commanded by a vigorous creative imagination – finally contains more objective truth than philosophical prose, which invents stories logically through the aligning of dead concepts.

The terrorist dogmatism of Senghorian negritude (peremptory affirmations, rigid axioms) should not fool us. The function of dogmatism is to hide what is to be discussed and it presents the problem itself as the solution. Negritude insistently poses problems which expect no solution because these are – beyond real problems – illusory problems. To follow Senghor and wonder whether the negro is emotion is, as in the fable, to follow the Pied Piper out of the city.

The fact is that negritude is a mythology which, as such, should be *read as imagery and in the very terms of its mythological functioning*. Senghor's negro should be *read* not so much within verbal discourse as in the visual register of advertising metaphors.

Annie Le Brun
A Creolism Sewn with White Thread

This essay by Annie Le Brun was published in the anthropology journal *Gradhiva* and demonstrates the continuity of surrealist positions in relation to changing circumstances. Le Brun's attack on multiculturalism through the Caribbean doctrine of Creolism – and especially her defence of cultural tradition – may surprise some, but it is fully consistent with the earliest surrealist positions which, as much as they may have led an assault on received cultural heritage, were always responsive to the need for cultural grounding. Indeed, her essay clearly draws upon the one above by Ménil, written in the 1960s and also defending Aimé Césaire (although from a very different form of misunderstanding).

Text of a lecture given at the Hautes Études en Sciences Sociales in the framework of the Centre d'anthropologie des mondes contemporaines, Paris, 8 January 1997; first published in *Gradhiva*, no.24, 1998. Bibliographic references appear at the end of the text, on pp.171–2.

If I find myself speaking here about Aimé Césaire, the Caribbean and Creolism, it is due to a series of chance events. But chance events which in the end are nothing of the sort, so much less so in that everything in this matter turns out to be the very opposite of what it might seem, which has led me to consider a little more closely what is today identified as multiculturalism, métissage and diversification.

But the simplest thing is first of all to begin by telling you how this came about.

In June 1993 a producer at France-Culture asked me to participate in a programme for Aimé Césaire's eightieth birthday. I immediately refused, since I have no taste for this kind of celebration, one which Aimé Césaire, who I consider to be one of the greatest poets of the age, seems to me not to need. My correspondent was thrown into panic, telling me he couldn't find anyone to speak about Césaire's poetry. From what he told me, people like Yves Bonnefoy and Michel Deguy, who are usually quite willing to appear on France-Culture, had also refused, but for other reasons.

According to him, these official poets were reluctant because of Césaire's non-literary paths. I was immediately convinced that I should change my mind. I reread Césaire's poetry, and especially the *Cahier d'un retour au pays natal*, whose intensity of revolt and nobility of theme had overwhelmed me when I was seventeen. Thirty years on, the text was just as dazzling. I bear witness to this, insisting on the fact that Césaire is one of this century's really rare individuals not to have forfeited the revolt of his youth, and perhaps even to have tried to practice poetry.

Some months later, the publisher Jean-Michel Place asked me for a preface for the republication of the review *Tropiques*, published in Fort-de-France by Aimé Césaire and René Ménil from 1941 to 1945 and moreover undertaken at the time France was Pétainist and the French Caribbean had come under the authority of Admiral Robert, who zealously applied the colonialist and racist directives of the Vichy government.

To get an idea of the unhealthy atmosphere then reigning in the Caribbean as well as the strength of subversion constituted by *Tropiques*, which was conceived by these West Indians in search of themselves, one should reread *Martinique, charmeuse de serpents*, in which André Breton, arrested in Fort-de-France by the French authorities while on his way to the United States, painted a sinister picture of the political and social situation on the island. But at the same time, he recounted how dazzled and reassured he was by the chance discovery of *Tropiques* and in it extracts from the *Cahier*.

Fifty years on, the importance and novelty of the problematic of *Tropiques* are still striking. Nevertheless, now busy with examining nine boxes of unpublished writings by Raymond Roussel, I thought I had neither the time nor the energy necessary to assess what was at stake poetically and politically for Césaire and Ménil during the adventure of *Tropiques*. So I refused the invitation.

But, some weeks later (in December 1993), by chance once again I came across the book by Raphaël Confiant, a name I was not familiar with, entitled *Aimé Césaire, une traverse paradoxale du siècle* (1993), a volume of three hundred pages of systematic demolition.

This crushed me. In it Césaire's poetry was subjected to a kind of police investigation aiming to show that it contradicted his political work. I felt I was reading the minutes of a Stalinist trial. The same falsifications and baseness were here in the service of an ideology whose existence I was just becoming aware of: *Creolism*.

Without knowing what I was getting into I wrote a defence of Aimé Césaire in ten days, discovering on the way the theoretical haziness on which Creolism was based but also how firmly anchored in the media were its ideologues, Jean Bernabé, Patrick Chamoiseau and Raphaël Confiant, co-signatories in 1984 of an *Éloge de la créolité* published by Gallimard in 1989 and vaunted by the critics. I also became aware (which I hadn't known prior to this) that Patrick Chamoiseau had been awarded the Prix Goncourt the year before, and, like Confiant, was well known among the Parisian literary chattering classes.

This helped to explain the generous welcome accorded to Confiant's attack on Césaire. Nothing was more natural in this narrow world than for Césaire to be adjudged off limits, and in the worst possible way: he had had his day and now the new Martiniquan generation should take over. At best, they appealed to the most devious objectivity so as to put the two sides of the argument back to back. I had not yet realised that Creolism was a fashionable ideology, more exactly a particularly successful example of one of those new cultural products in which multi-culturalism, *métissage* and the search for identity paradoxically serve to accelerate a process of generalised indifferentiation, day by day insinuating a little more denial into ways of being and thinking.

Still, if this was so, why attack a poet like Césaire, who had long been silent, in such an apparently disproportionate way? Why were French critics so tacitly acquiescent to what amounted to a mugging? Why, in the name of this new Creolism, had Césaire suddenly been found guilty of every misdeed?

The epoch steers clear of asking any of these questions, the better to forget who Césaire was and what his invention of negritude represented. Let us briefly call it to mind.

Aimé Césaire was born in 1912 in Basse-Pointe, Martinique into a large and impoverished family. His father was the grandson of a slave, at first a plantation treasurer then a tax employee, who, according to one of his sons, 'scorned money and well-connected people'. For his part Aimé Césaire was more precise: 'two family traditions influenced me. One was that of political struggle and another was the racial struggle' (quoted in Henry-Valmore et al. 1993, p.27). Of his career in education on a scholarship there is nothing to say except that he was an excellent student who arrived in Paris in 1931 to prepare for the École Normale Supérieure, which he entered in 1935.

But the most important thing was that during the preparatory class he met the Senegalese Léopold Sédar Senghor, who came to symbolise Africa for him, so that during the course of the 1930s he acknowledged having come under three determining influences: 'The first was French literature through the work of Mallarmé, Baudelaire, Rimbaud, Lautréamont, Apollinaire and Claudel. The second was Africa [...] and the third was that of the Harlem renaissance which did not influence me directly but made me aware of the solidarity of the black world' (ibid., p.40).

A posteriori, we can in fact see how, consciously or not, Césaire then took charge of everything that would help him to become aware of himself. Unfortunately I do not here have the space to evoke how Paris in the 1920s and 1930s was at a crossroads of African, American and Caribbean expressions in the course of which anti-colonialism joined with anti-fascism. But I will recall that from 1932 a group of Caribbeans, invoking Marx, Freud and Breton, published the journal Légitime défense, in which, among others, René Ménil (the future co-founder with Césaire of Tropiques) was already calling for the search for an expression of 'millenarian revolt' as far as could be from a Caribbean literature in imitation of the West, and of 'needs fundamentally condemned simply because they are not found in European literature' (Ménil 1978, p.8).

And even if René Ménil, in his 1978 preface to the re-issue of Légitime défense, deplores the presence in it of 'poems not rooted in this society, poems from nowhere, poems by no one' (ibid. , p.8), it is certain that all of this testifies to a climate of agitation which will not be without influence on Césaire who, from 1935, began a long ascent into himself. And this would merge with the re-conquest of the most denied aspect of a collective and individual memory, and lead to the invention of negritude, the result of a triple racial, social and ontological realisation: of being black, of being in the world and of being of the world.

What is extraordinary is that this was done not through theoretical reflection, nor a manifesto, but through a poem, 'Cahier d'une retour au pays natal', published in 1939 in the journal

Hervé Télémaque
The Voyage of Hector Hyppolite to Africa 2000
Musée d'Art moderne, Paris

Volontés. It is also extraordinary that Aimé Césaire, while splendidly giving form to the notion of negritude, here reinvented the very notion of subversion. And André Breton, who was first to discover Césaire in 1941 during his stay in Fort-de-France, was not deceived in celebrating 'the word of Aimé Césaire, as beautiful as oxygen in a nascent state' (quoted in Henry-Valmore et al. 1993, p.167).

Hence the originality of Césaire's conception of negritude, which comes from the most profound sense of existence, leading him (in the opposite direction to his friends Damas and Senghor) to refuse to appeal to any idea of *métissage*, even in cultural terms, which he considered a snare. Because for him, whether light or dark of skin, the Caribbean is above all a negro, whose alienation consists in the denial of this origin.

Nevertheless this did not for all that lead him, like Senghor, to seek a biological root for negritude, as he felt it useful in 1962 to clarify: 'There is no pre-determined negritude, nor is there a substance; there is a history and a still living one' (ibid., p.166). In 1969, he added: 'I do not in the slightest believe in biological permanence. My negritude has a ground. It is a fact that there is a black culture; it is historical but there is nothing biological about it' (ibid., p.167).

And no greater distance could be marked from essentialism than when Césaire, refusing any metaphysics of cultural or racial identity, took the trouble to add: 'I am for negritude from a literary perspective and as a personal ethic, but I am against an ideology founded on negritude' (ibid., p.167).

It is in fact the poetic origin of Césairian negritude which guaranteed the liberty of its development. Because if in the *Cahier* Césaire succeeded in undermining the foundations of western mastery (let's recall, 'Because we hate you, you and / your reason, we claim kinship / with dementia praecox with flaming madness/ with tenacious cannibalism': Césaire 1969, p.55), it must be recognised that this is reached at the price of an implacable movement of subversion in the literal sense of the word, to deploy a scorned possibility beneath what is unacceptable, to allow with each word the multiplicity of denied and mutilated presences annihilated by colonisation to return – whether we are talking about people, animals or plants.

We should not then be amazed that Césaire quite naturally recovers what, in the great insubordinate tradition of western poetry from Rimbaud to Lautréamont, fundamentally brings that which exists into question. Until in 1943 he would declare poetry accursed 'because [it is] knowledge and not entertainment. Accursed because it lifts the prohibition of the black seas. Accursed because it is in the wake of Prometheus, the thief, and of Oedipus, the murderer. Accursed in the wake of the discoverers of the world' (Césaire 1943).

And this was so true that among the worlds Césaire discovered was the Caribbean, which had never before been seen in this way. And it is difficult to understand how Césaire can today be attacked in the name of a Creolism whose realisation in fact started with the *Cahier* for, as René Ménil much later remarked: 'Moreover, everyone in the Caribbean can testify to how in having read *Cahier* they saw it differently than before' (Ménil 1981, p.207).

This realisation was also pursued elsewhere through the founding work Césaire and Ménil directed soon afterwards, between 1941 and 1945, at the height of the Pétain era, proposing their journal precisely as an 'instrument making it possible for Martinique to realign itself'. Thus, as René Ménil declares in the first issue, 'We are the only ones who can express what makes us unique.' After which from 1942 he opens with Césaire a dossier on 'Martiniquan folklore', coupled a little later with the sustained publication of articles on Caribbean fauna and flora, amounting to a symbolic re-appropriation of the innumerable forms of life that colonisation had annihilated.

All that is just to recall what should not be forgotten: this quest for a Creole diversity, which some people declare that they have discovered fifty years later, had actually been undertaken long before.

And it is in the light of all of this that the aberrance of the accusations directed against Césaire can be measured – first of all for having hidden the Caribbean to extol Africa. Because, to found the notion of Creolism, its ideologues (Bernabé, Chamoiseau and Confiant) started by declaring themselves in their 1989 manifesto 'forever Césaire's sons' (Bernabé et al. 1989, pp.18, 80). And this was because they then considered the negritude forged by Césaire 'gave Creole society its African dimension' (ibid., p.18). 'To the point', they again say, that they feel summonsed 'to free Aime Cesaire of the accusation – with Oedipal overtones – of hostility to the Creole language' (ibid., pp.18, 79).

This naturally leads us to wonder: what therefore freed them from this debt so that now they see Césaire's negritude as the instrument he used (I am citing Confiant) in order not to 'problematise his colonial inability to write in a minority language' (Confiant 1993, pp.75–6)? And how then is it that this negritude that they recognised in Césaire in 1989 as having conceived of 'the primal act of our restored dignity' has suddenly become by 1993 'the black way of being white' (ibid., p.57)?

One can certainly see that the more success the novelists of Creolism achieve in the white world, the less they tend to associate themselves with negritude. But things are also a little more complicated than that. I will go so far as to imagine that they did not at first realise the originality of Césairian negritude in relation to the one, manipulable in different ways, defined by Sartre in 1948 in 'Orphée noir', his preface to the *Anthologie de la nouvelle poésie nègre et malgache*. This is because, having been reviewed and corrected in the course of a laborious rationalisation by Sartre, negritude is there presented on the one hand as a transitory stage ('the crisis point in a dialectical progression') that had to be resolved in the future in a world without race. This is already a justification of Creolism even if, on the other hand, Sartre (striving to translate the poetic expression of negritude into concepts) manages to derive from it a black mentality that is highly contestable, one that Senghor subsequently laid claim to.

The result was a negritude that should not be confused with the one conceived by Césaire, that much is clear. For even if he did not openly differentiate himself from it, he still felt it necessary in 1978 to declare without any possible ambiguity: 'If blacks were not a people, let's say a conquered, ultimately an unhappy, humiliated people, etc. ... let us reverse history and make them a people of conquerors, I believe personally that there could be no negritude at all – it would appear to me untenable' (Césaire 1978, p.xxi).

This could not be clearer, but at the same time it enables us to understand better the tenacity of Césaire's enemies: their aim is not to attack a man or a thought but, through both, a way of existing that is incompatible with ordinary ideological recipes. So much so that in this affair Césaire's revelatory strength becomes remarkable: in fact it is by the attacks that Creolism generates that it is revealed to be the opposite of what it claims. Namely that this ideology – describing itself as thought of the diverse, of tolerance and of the whole world – is in reality as we will now see an ideology of the same, with totalitarian tendencies, but whose novelty is camouflaged in cultural packaging.

An ideology of the same. This can be proved simply by considering the litany of critiques made of Césaire's poetry, all of which denounce his non-conformity to Creole experience, which can obviously only be judged by its ideologues.

Thus, under the pretext that, to quote Confiant referring to

Michel Leiris and the Césaire
children, 1959.
Reproduced in Le Brun's article.

Bernabé, 'the central core of the Creole dictionary is structured
from the vocabulary of sexuality' (Confiant 1993, p.76), Césaire's
poetry becomes suspect because it is not sufficiently impregnated
with this atavistic sexuality. And that when sex appears it is
'disembodied, without any attachment to the historical and social
reality of the Caribbean people' (ibid., p.78).

And we then witness the absurdity of a reader seeking to
locate within Césaire's texts 'isolated sexual organs', 'disincarnated
acts of love', solitary pleasure 'celebrated', as so many divergences
from the norm of a Caribbean sexual practice – as though such a
thing existed.

Be that as it may, in the name of a sort of Caribbean socialist
realism, it is easy to conclude from this that Césaire is evidently
not 'Creolism correct'. All the more so as in the name of this
ideology of tolerance no occasion is lacking to deliver the message
that anything Creole is in essence beautiful and true, at which point
Césaire's crime has been not to have said often enough (I am
quoting Confiant) that 'we are beautiful, simply beautiful' (ibid.,
p.46). And doubts then have to be raised about this ideology
which claims to be a 'non-totalitarian consciousness of a preserved
diversity' (Bernabé et al. 1989, pp.28, 89) when they announce to us
at the same time that 'expressing Creolness will be expressing the
very *beings* of the world (ibid., pp.52, 113).

A strange diversity which proves to be totalising to the point
of tolerating everything in itself without the slightest critique, no
doubt in the hope finally of imposing its unblemished positivity

upon the whole world. They actually tell us – as far as we can tell – that 'the world is turning into the state of Creolism' (ibid., p.50).

Unfortunately, this is not simply applied from a theoretical point of view since, for having dared to doubt this Creolism by defending Césaire (and, what is more, publicly, during lectures in Fort-de-France and Pointe-à-Pitre in February 1995), in articles and radio and television broadcasts, Chamoiseau and Confiant challenged my very right to speak. And for the clearly formulated reason that I was neither 'Caribbean, nor African, nor a black American' – in other words, because I was white. To this was added the discredit of being an inevitably 'neurotic' woman, and inevitably 'motivated by the quivering of her ovaries', as the Prix Goncourt winner wrote; I could go on…

I then learned through my Caribbean friends that I was not being given preferential treatment, but that this was how Creolism's advocates treated all those who do not recognise their truth. Thus, over the years Césaire had been treated in turns as a 'black negro', a 'mulatto', a 'head without a body', and a 'petty bourgeois negro'. Moreover, this made it unsurprising to find this ideology of *métissage* also setting itself against the supposedly mulatto entourage around Césaire, as Chamoiseau has done in his novels, and something which gave Confiant a pretext to declare during an interview in 1993: 'I detest the mulatto spirit, the *mulâtraille* … the mulatto spirit must be destroyed with napalm. Creolism is an anti-mulatto ideology' (Confiant 1993b).

It fell to René Ménil to recognise immediately what was at stake. 'Raphaël Confiant knows perfectly well that what napalm kills is first of all the body. This cynical and indecent racism justifies itself as best it can … What can the mulatto spirit really be, good Lord? And all that in the name of Creolism: Racism + napalm = a more modern Macoutism' (Ménil 1993).

Unfortunately all of this is only too true when, while staying in Martinique, I learned about the anti-Semitic campaign by *Antilla*, the journal of Creolism, led in 1983 on the pretext of anti-Zionism, a campaign which quite simply argued that Hitler was right in persecuting and massacring the Jews. As it happens, Roland Suvélor, a friend of Césaire's, and moreover a mulatto, made the mistake of being shocked. Confiant was the one to reply to him, only too happy for the chance at the same time to smash mulatto and Jew in terms which left no room for ambiguity. And this was not just an error of youth, as some might argue, because in 1991, during the fifth centenary of the Conquest of the Caribbean by Columbus, the same Confiant leapt at the chance to accuse the Jews, with the 'yich man Rotschild' as they say in Creole, of an innate marketing sense: '[of having] managed to place the genocide of their people in the top 50 of world genocides' (quoted in Plenel 1991).

As an ideology Creolism is revealed at a stroke to be a lot less vague than one might believe. Its multiform activism is worthy of the racism from which it is nourished. A multiracial racism which has the advantage of being able to accuse any enemy, whether black, mulatto or white, of not being the right colour. It would be vain to continue to seek the tolerance and opening up that Creolism claims to oppose to the abstract rigour of universalism.

This is all too consistent, from the nature of the attacks on Césaire to the terroristic refusal of any criticism, by way of the practices of a populist party, the Modernas (Movement of Democrats and Ecologists for a Sovereign Martinique), founded by ideologues of Creolism, which loses no opportunity to use its external impact to impress their troops. So much so that, using their metropolitan successes to the ridiculous extent of congratulating themselves on being acknowledged from *Minute* to *L'Humanité* (ah, yes), they sadly illustrate a new avatar of the phenomenon revealed by Frantz Fanon in 1952 in *Black Skins, White Masks*. For if the imperative today is no longer to deny any trace of belonging to Creole reality but, quite the opposite, to play upon it in the way Paris likes, it is by seeking the same recognition from the same Europe – even if this means once again performing their role as jesters from the islands.

In such a way that it would be difficult to find a better example of a double language between the populist discourse carried on in the Caribbean and the exclusively aesthetic productions by which Creolism is here manifested, like a new exoticism. But an exoticism whose novelty is paradoxically to claim not to be one, even in affirming itself as *the* cultural product from afar. This is the issue to which I would like to draw your attention in concluding.

No matter what they might have liked us to believe in the beginning, it has become difficult to ignore the way in which these Caribbean novels have been tailored and re-tailored by Parisian publishers, panicked as they have been as much by the crisis of the French novel as they were fascinated by the success of the South American novel.

This might even only be because a well-known critic like Bernard Pivot one day let the cat out of the bag when revealing, in a 1992 article published in *Lire* entitled 'And Finally Kundera also Gets the Goncourt', the sort of orchestration from which the prize attributed to Chamoiseau resulted. Still, the fact that the publisher Gallimard, just before the prize season, had widely distributed an article by Kundera – first published in *L'Infini*, a journal from the same publishing house – about the book in question, is of the order of promotional poverty. But the novelty is elsewhere, in the nature of Kundera's interpretation, in which he used all of his authority as a successful author to lay down directions for use of the product so launched – in other words, by explaining 'why the language used by the Caribbean writer is anything but a local colour', as was claimed in the margin of his reprinted article, distributed moreover by FNAC. And that with the aim of passing off what was nothing more than a little local linguistic colour as a style, since what was so extolled consisted in systematically studding a mediocre French with Creole expressions, or else adapting Creole turns of phrase into French.

Nevertheless the critics have taken Kundera's claims as a down payment, without even caring to consider the adulterated product resulting from their vulgar veneer, and without seeing that it would lead to the reverse of the result announced, as Édouard Glissant today diplomatically suggests in his *Introduction à une poétique du divers*: 'Creolisms, particularisms, regionalisms, these are ways of satisfying, on the scale of the hierarchy of languages, the great languages of culture' (Glissant 1996, p.123). This is what really confirmed the success of these Creole novels, indicating that such a point of *denial* will rarely have been reached. Should we then be amazed that the critics might have seen nothing but fire here, where this new exoticism, denied as such, seems to constitute the very example of the fictitious differences which this age exalts in order more effectively to elude its uniformising conformism?

Without a doubt, the insistence of the Creole followers on placing themselves exclusively on the aesthetic terrain is highly significant for the tremendous aesthetic interference in question here: 'Full consciousness of Creolism will be reserved for Art, for Art absolutely' (Bernabé 1989, p.29). Here is one of the key thoughts of *Éloge de la créolité*. This does not in itself mean very much – but it explains nevertheless that, apart from the attack on the universalism of which Césaire would be the formidable agent, one of the characteristics of this Creolism is not to formulate any genuine critique of the state of the world.

It is no longer even a question of speaking of class or race. Thus Saint-John Perse is allowed a licence in Creolism that is denied to Césaire, even though this means forgetting the extent to which the author of *Vents* aimed to realise the universal that is so hated, and especially as his work is inseparable from the *béké* ideology of the great white landowners. This is nevertheless not the least interesting thing in this slippage into the cultural field where, by instigating confusion as a principle, they succeed in forestalling any awareness of the forces present. And from this point of view, one cannot fail to notice the analogy between Creolism and the fashionable ideas about diversity, moreover of western origin, all of which have in common the fact of favouring a generalised depoliticisation.

From this to making small formal freedoms appear to be freedom is no more than a single step for the critics to take with an ease that is all the greater for having killed two birds with one stone. Because, on the one hand it will have strengthened to the point of derision a phenomenon Marc Augé had already located fifteen years ago: 'The western gaze on others has ceased to be scornful only to become aesthetic' (Augé 1982, p.11). But also because, on the other, it confirms the fact that, by an interesting boomerang effect, this is henceforth valid *for the whole world*, the excessive increase of the cultural field being one of the privileged paths of a generalised depoliticisation.

Because in the end is not this Creolism the very example of a recourse to the aesthetic which, in this case, exalts the diversity of the world so as to be better able to ignore the fact that its shattered state results above all in population displacements, the expropriation of entire peoples, ethnic cleansing and so on...

populations that rebel less and less? And these populations rebel less and less because they have been rendered unnameable, in every sense of the word, as we appear above all to be incapable of apprehending them through words. Faced with recent political catastrophes, as in former Yugoslavia and Rwanda, have we not heard about 'tribal hatreds' and 'ancestral struggles', in the absence of any means or desire to formulate their political stakes? Whatever the case, it is remarkable that no one has noted how, in both cases, language has skated over the horror of the situation.

Well, we are a long way from Creolism, you'll say. I don't believe so, since it is constructed precisely from a large-scale falsification of language which results in camouflaging the totalitarianism, racism and larbinism which constitutes it.

Yes, larbinism, a word invented by Césaire, which refers of course to a black sensibility inherited from slavery, but one that Creolism has reactivated, by proposing it as a model of acquiescence to what exists, in exchange for some linguistic fantasies.

It is the renowned style vaunted by Kundera, enlisting words so as to make them vehicles of this internalisation of exoticism through the language of which I have spoken. In other words the very example of what is opposed in principle to the free surging of words that occurs in the Cahier, where those, as René Ménil remarked so well, call upon us 'at every moment, with every sentence … to pass from one image to another, from one affective theme to another', in calling on us ceaselessly to 'look onto something elsewhere, something unknown, something original, in the sentence and in ourselves' (Ménil 1981, p.210).

And even beyond the confrontation between negritude and Creolism the opposition between novel and poetry here assumes a particular meaning. There is something emblematic about this era's choice in favour of the novelists of Creolism, and against the poetry of Césaire: a case of preferring the Club Med to vision. Because if the Creolists speak of themselves as specialists of the 'Whole World', drawing upon a notion forged by Edouard Glissant who does not seem to see any drawback in it, it is all the same curious that they cannot show us anything other than the worst illustrations of an otherwise bygone world, as ridiculous for West Indians as they are exotic for Europeans.

For these scribblers there is no danger that their productions might become, as Raphaël Confiant reproaches Cahier with being, 'the text that may be claimed by any suffering people' and this under the comical pretext that 'if Québécois adopted it in the 1960s it was because it was not profoundly marked by the Caribbean' (Confiant 1992).

In fact, it is not in the Caribbean, nor in Europe, nor in Africa, that negritude takes shape for Césaire. It is in the depths of existential revolt, clearing a path through the turbulences of poetic freedom, that it was formed, as Césaire wanted it to be, as a 'flag of rage and renewal'. It lies at the greatest remove from aesthetic preoccupations, where words are so many modes of expropriation, by which life seeks to recuperate its wealth under the compartmentalisation of beings and things. And Césaire said nothing other in the *Cahier*: 'words, ah yes words! but / words of fresh blood, words which are / tidal waves and erysipelas / malarias and lavas and bush-fires, / burning flesh / and burning cities' (Césaire 1969, p.62).

This is really what they cannot pardon him for: for making negritude return (beyond its African roots and its Creole interlacing) to that obscure spring where freedom merges with our infinite power of negation. Because, it should be made clear, there is no essential difference between the *Cahier* and the *Discourse on Colonialism* or the 'Letter to Maurice Thorez', in which Césaire resigned from the Communist Party in 1956. Thus, when today we seek to confine sensibility to the aesthetic field, as the realm reserved for tastes and colours where anything goes, what is evidently not wanted is this fundamental revolt, in that it is of a nature not to recognise the order of things as innumerable forms of separation which follow between beings and things.

Everything unfortunately leads us to believe that ideologies of diversity constitute the best means of justifying the new diversity of this separation. And Creolism, as an identity of synthesis (within which the disappearance of the individual is moreover to be measured in terms of profit and loss), is the example we are presented with, so as to hide, and thereby aggravate, a catastrophic and perceptible separation of being with itself, as though in the end replacing ideological blindness with aesthetic blindness was more efficacious.

And, as a matter of fact, as can be seen in this case, this aesthetic blindness – as it ceaselessly testifies that everything is at a standstill – can be opposed only by poetic intuition. And that awareness of this coherence is alone able to restore to movement what is at a standstill, to shake what is stultified and to rouse whatever is petrified. Is this still possible? This question is posed to everyone and perhaps you would be more able to respond to it, you whose interest is borne towards other worlds.

Only, it is important never to forget what Césaire remarked in *Discourse on Colonialism*: 'A significant thing: it is not from the head that civilisations decay. It is above all through the heart.'

References

Augé, Marc. *Génie du paganisme*, Paris: Gallimard 1982.

Bernabé, Jean, Patrick Chamoiseau and Raphaël Confiant. *Éloge de la créolité*, Paris: Gallimard 1989.

Césaire, Aimé. 'Maintenir la poésie', *Tropiques*, nos.8–9, 1943.

Césaire, Aimé. *Return to my Native Land*, trans. John Berger and Anna Bostock, Harmondsworth: Penguin 1969.

Césaire, Aimé. 'Entretien avec Jacqueline Leiner', in *Tropiques*, reissued ed., Paris: Jean-Michel Place 1978.

Confiant, Raphaël. *Le Monde*, 6 December 1992.

Confiant, Raphaël. *Aimé Césaire, une traversée paradoxale du siècle*, Paris: Stock 1993.

Confiant, Raphaël. *Antilla*, no.56, 1993.

Confiant, Raphaël. 'Les Élucubrations de Dame Lebrun', *Antilla*,
   no.619, 1995.
Glissant, Edouard. *Introduction à une poètique de divers*, Paris:
   Gallimard 1996.
Henry-Valmore, Simonne and Roger Toumson. *Aimé Césaire,
   le nègre inconsolé*, Paris: Syros 1993.
Ménil, René. 'Généralitiés sur l'écrivain de couleur antillais',
   in *Légitime défense*, 1932.
Ménil, René. *Tracées*. Paris: Robert Laffont 1981.
Ménil, René. *Justice*, no.50, 1993.
Pivot, Bernard. *Lire*, December 1992.
Plenel, Edwy. 'Voyage avec Colombe', *Le Monde*, 23 August 1991.

René Alleau
The Exit from Egypt

Following the dissolution of the original Parisian surrealist group in
1969 and the subsequent realignments that took place during the
1970s, Vincent Bounoure organised a series of discussions devoted
to the then current position of surrealism in the face of the notion of
civilisation itself, the results of which would be the volume *La
Civilisation surréaliste*, published in 1976. This essay by René Alleau
takes up the challenge by making an analogy between the state of
civilisation and the development of an individual (something Pierre
Mabille had extensively explored in his 1938 book *Égrégores ou la vie
des civilisations*), diagnosing its current state as profoundly disturbed.
In his wide-ranging and complex examination, Alleau draws upon
Joseph Gabel's extensive elaboration of the idea of false
consciousness to show that this disturbance is principally the result
of an inadequate conception of reality, one that tries to dominate the
surrounding world and make it conform to its own exigencies. Seeing
little long-term hope in such a world, Alleau calls for a new exodus
from Egypt – one that would re-form civilisation on the basis of a
harmonious reconciliation between waking and dream, action and
contemplation, and reason and intuition.

First published in Vincent
Bounoure (ed.), *La Civilisation
surréaliste*, Paris: Payot, 1976.

Archaeologists have exhumed from between the paws of the
Sphinx a vast granite flagstone on which an inscription relates a
dream of Thutmose IV, a pharaoh of the 18th dynasty. Before his
reign, in the course of a hunt, the prince decided at the siesta hour
to rest in the shade of the solar genie which protected that sacred
place. During his sleep, the Sphinx appeared to him and promised
him the crown of Egypt if he would clear away the sands which
already covered almost her whole body. The last part of the
inscription is no longer readable. We assume that it mentioned
the accomplishment of this divine command and how, when
he awoke, the king found the terrestrial recompense of his

faith in the truth of the celestial dream of the sleeping hunter.

This distant adventure, on the frontier of shadow and light, of the desert and its mirages, where the calls and replies are found of the pursuit of game and the desire to rule, the human illusion of glory and the divine nightmare of oblivion, and the need to be visible and the fear of being buried, seems to me to signify fairly well a central enigma which the Sphinx still poses to us about the history of civilisations.

If homo sapiens, according to generally accepted evaluations, is sixty thousand years old, then its current situation can be compared chronologically to that of someone sixty years old, in relation to the way the duration of his life is distributed between waking, sleep and dream. On average, specialists divide this into forty years of physical and mental activity and twenty years of sleep, interrupted by five years of dreams. The proportion of this periodicity varies very slightly according to the individual, reverie not being taken into account in this calculation and the memory being more or less capable of retaining dreams upon awakening.

On the scale of the evolution of the human species and its current norm, this distribution reveals a past of forty thousand years, devoted principally to the reception, processing and interpretation of information coming from the external world, as well as to the realisation of conduct necessary to conserve collective, individual and physical life, but also of twenty thousand years without conscious contact with the visible universe. In this state, for at least five millennia, human beings would have witnessed and participated in the oneiric unfolding of innumerable scenes of its nocturnal theatre alone. Thus a history which claims to be 'positive' and only considers the events of the waking state to be of interest is completely unaware of all of those of dream and the duration of a human experience longer than that of ancient and modern civilisations, from the time of the Sumerians and the invention of writing to our own time.

However, the uncontrolled cerebral activity to which each of us is subject for an important part of our existence cannot be assimilated to a slower functioning of the cortex. It is rather the contrary: the most recent scientific research shows that the dream is announced at once by the disappearance of muscle tone and the appearance of rapid cortical waves and high voltage 'spikes', at the level of the reticulated pontiac formation, just below the mesencephalon. These waves are typical of a clearly characterised 'state of vigilance'. Thus, through a curious encounter, the data from neurology and modern neuro-chemistry confirms the ancient division between the traditional theory of the three distinct states of waking, sleep and dream, with dream being as different from sleep as sleep is from waking.

The still unexplained singularity which the association of rapid cortical waves with a deep sleep presents, at the same time as the growth of the intensity of stimulations then necessary when the sleeper wakes, has led specialists to name this phenomenon of a periodic type (with rhythmic intervals, of a specific oneiric activity accompanied by a notable augmentation of internal exchanges and metabolism) 'paradoxical sleep' (REM sleep). The dream thereby appeared as *a genuine bodily experience*, which the unconscious ocular movements which, for example, accompany the viewing of a tennis match or the respiratory pause and cardiac activity are enough to prove – these phasic phenomena linked to the dramatic intensity of the scenes the dreamer really witnesses, whether he is someone fighting bandits or a cat chasing mice.

So these are not only five thousand years of insignificant reveries, with neither consequence nor significance, which the 'positive' history of civilisations forgets, as it improperly over-estimates the value of events in waking state alone, but also the whole duration of the experience of *another state of vigilance* to which the effects and repercussions of waking itself should be added.

Nothing seems to me to prove that dream, as an autonomous conflicting source, might not be the origin of specific neuroses which it would not be possible to explain simply by the analysis of the events of the history of a waking individual. If this hypothesis is accepted, it would contrarily be the external event rather than the dream that should be considered psychoanalysable as an expression of a liquidation of the tensions and conflicts of a purely oneiric order. Moreover, is not the intensity of the scenes experienced in dream easily enough to convince us that they may leave traces as durable as (and sometimes more profound than) those of waking, and the generally calm and often monotonous habitual course of external existence?

This actually experienced difference of intensity has struck all of the specialists who have noted physiologically a state of considerable excitement of the majority of cerebral neurons, including the motor neurons, while in contrast, the motor efferents are blocked by a mechanism producing a sort of paralysis in the sleeper. In this respect a 'veritable cerebral storm' has even been evoked in the dreaming state, in the course of which recordings by micro-electrodes have shown that the nervous cells show an excitement analogous to that of the *most intense waking state*. This is why, if one manages to suppress the inhibiting mechanisms exerted over the driving efferents, then nothing else prevents *the physical externalisation of dream*. In these experimental conditions conducted with animals, spectacular behaviour of defence engaged against enemies, of pursuit or aggression, has been witnessed. These movements, on average lasting from five to six minutes, generally end in an abrupt awakening, characterised by a sudden dilation of the pupil when the animal again becomes calm and goes back to sleep.

Oneiric perceptions therefore do not in any way involve weakened or diminished cerebral and physical experiences in relation to those of waking, as classical psychology mistakenly affirms. Moreover, biochemical tests have established that substances needed for the individual's growth are liberated within the organism during dream and not during waking, in such a way that *a biochemistry of dream* may be scientifically conceived, entailing consequences for the behaviour of waking individuals and their state of physical and mental health. These phenomena suffice, it seems to me, to show that sleep is only an intermediary stage between two perfectly distinct states of vigilance, one external, the other internal – but one that it is no longer possible to oppose in the name of a criterion of reality which gives the waking state alone, with its forms and objects *and with their history*, a disproportionate importance in relation to the total experience, diurnal and nocturnal, of the living being.

This disequilibrium between the values of two equally necessary functions is so much less justified if we consider the primordial role of dream in the genesis of the body and the personality of the infant, the child and the adolescent, in a way that is largely independent of relations with the still misty and distant external world of the waking state. Everything seems to happen as if consciousness, which is initially fluid and mobile in the nascent state, was in some way coagulated and fixed around the objects of the external world by a series of successive crystallisations. In solidifying it, they also imprison it in the limits of its adult form and principally in the spatio-temporal categories from which dream, no matter what Kant thinks, continues trying each night to free us *a posteriori*, as it did well before our first metaphysical temptations.

The alienating consequences of a choice of civilisations marked by an excessive development either of the *will to power over the waking state*, or *the capacity of presence in the dream state*, thus still need to be questioned, a distinction which seems to me more accurate than that of their capacity for material production and social organisation. In other words, a given type of civilisation depends upon the predominance of diurnal or nocturnal experience for its production and values, but also for its conflicts and its neuroses. From this perspective, primitive and ancient societies may be just as much characterised by alienation as modern societies, but *by reason of an inverse disequilibrium*, provoked by the relative closure of collective and individual consciousness to the experience it diminishes or rejects, all the better to augment and integrate more profoundly the intensity of the one it prefers to explore and understand. It is therefore really desire which constitutes the principal driving force in the history of civilisations, a desire to which its own accomplishment is always opposed, thus compelling the people of any period sooner or later to burn their idols, whether they want to or not. Moreover, do we not see as we study the history of civilisations that there has not yet been one capable of harmoniously reconciling waking and dream, action and contemplation, reason and intuition?

Among other examples of a disequilibrium due to an excess of the capacity of the presence of dream, I will limit myself to those of Australian Aborigines and the Maya. Symmetrically in a way, at the other pole of history, our own civilisation is marked by an inverse alienation: that of the *over-estimation of events in the waking state*, resulting in what could be called without paradox a contemporary 'primitivism'.

Two equally inverse attitudes characterise the nocturnal or

diurnal predominance of civilisations. According to the first, by reason of the spatio-temporal freeing that constitutes the oneiric experience, the driving force of understanding is deliverance from the 'temporality of waking', considered as 'profane' in relation to the return to pure interiority, to its 'suspended' and 'matrix' time, considered as 'sacred'. By contrast, in the second, the engagement with historically experienced periods tends to absorb human faculties and powers entirely, to the extent of a complete extraversion expressed by the ideal type of the 'contemporary in every respect'. In the first case the radical cure for existential suffering seems to be obtained by returning to the 'absolute beginning of all birth' according to the expression in the *Rig Veda*, 'Finding myself in the matrix, I have known all the births of the gods' (IV, 27, 1), or the Buddhist notion of 'those who remember births' (*Jâtissaro*), or, as ancient therapies testify, by trying to return the sick man to the initial plenitude and intact energy reserves of the new-born, by getting him to participate in primordial cosmogonical myths. In the second case, in contrast, the future alone is imbued with all the soteriological powers of cure and renewal. Ultimately 'the future is already here' and allows the poverty of the present and the pains of the past to be forgotten.

It should be remembered that the myth of 'perfect beginnings', the memory of the lost 'golden age', lost thanks to the mistakes of 'civilisation' and the nostalgia for a 'a simple and vigorous life in the heart of nature', are not aspects of modern nostalgia. We find them expressed in Hesiod as well as by the most ancient Chinese chroniclers. The belief in human spiritual beatitude before the fall, and the myth of the 'noble savage' and 'lost paradise' are only variants of the same tendency towards primordial regression and blessed fusion within the 'Great Nocturnal Mother'.

The consciousness of waking life, in contrast, essentially means being integrated into time as active and virile. It explicitly condemns or implicitly scorns anything that might diminish it: feelings, inspiration, intuition, imagination, 'feminine' qualities. That is why the diurnal predominance in a civilisation is necessarily marked by phallocracy, by the development of the will to rational power and social success, as well as by a parallel regression of affectivity, going as far as the armed and policed justification of the rights of the strongest, and leading to the systematic elimination of the 'weak' or the 'helpless'.

The history of civilisations in fact finds nothing more in its field of investigation than values and hierarchies of values in which the people of a particular age have believed. From this perspective, if history claims to be capable of anticipating future values or, as pedants say, the 'axiological future system', nothing supports the deduction from this that it will be any truer than others. Or rather the philosophy of history needs, through a type of metaphysical hypostasis, arbitrarily to conceive of an ideal object, in a rationally unjustifiable way, as the bearer of imperfectly realised attributes in the empirical world of events. By reason of its anthropocentric nature and its anthro-pological orientation, this philosophy of history is thereby caught in the paradoxical obligation of hypostasing the social object quasi-theologically and privileging all values in relation to individual objects.

Even if history were limited to making the individual aware of the major importance of social life, how could it affirm that it really raises humans above the animal since nature gives us enough evidence to show that the collective imperative is imposed on it with much more power than on ourselves? What is more, no one has yet been able to demonstrate the existence of a definite agreement between the ends of the history of societies and the aims of the history of individuals. Many arguments can even be opposed to this thesis, beginning with the fragility of any system of this type, whether it is a question of an initial and pre-established harmony, or a final harmony.

These difficulties perhaps result from a general logical paradox: any science, including that of history, is obliged to operate with a certain number of concepts it can justify neither by deduction nor by induction, given that they will form the basis of its own operations. When the physicist ensures that he 'defines' force as being of a magnitude proportional to the product of acceleration and mass, he is stating nothing more than an operative, purely formal, rule allowing the observance in a particular case of whether the phenomenon in question is present or absent, whether it has produced itself, in what conditions and to what extent.

In this respect it is perhaps useful to recall that all science is founded on the relations intelligence has established between two or more systems of the concordance of coordinates. The universe cannot constitute a system of laws unless phenomena respond to rational networks, filtered and constituted by logical operations capable of linking the observation of phenomenal successions to the abstraction of their causal relations. One could no doubt assume that this intelligence would be that of a real being, infinitely superior to man, and capable of founding the materiality of things at the same time as it links them together intellectually. This *ontological a priori* has been that of classical religious philosophy but, since Kant, modern scientific philosophy has preferred an *epistemological a priori*.

So it is, for example, that the cosmological theories of Eddington and Milne are entirely deduced from *a priori* epistemological principles. Starting from these principles, with the aid of definitions relative to scientific method alone, what is proposed is not the discovery of the structure of the universe 'in itself' but only the means by which human intelligence proposes to analyse and conceive this structure. Eddington expressed himself very clearly on this subject: 'We must now show,' he said, 'not that there are n particles in the universe, but that anyone who accepts certain elementary principles of measurement must, if it is logical with itself, *believe* that there is such a number of them.' This is why Eddington, in his 'Fundamental Theory', argues that the very idea of measure necessarily implies *a determined structure* of human thought which, when applied to the analysis of natural forms, produces, so to speak

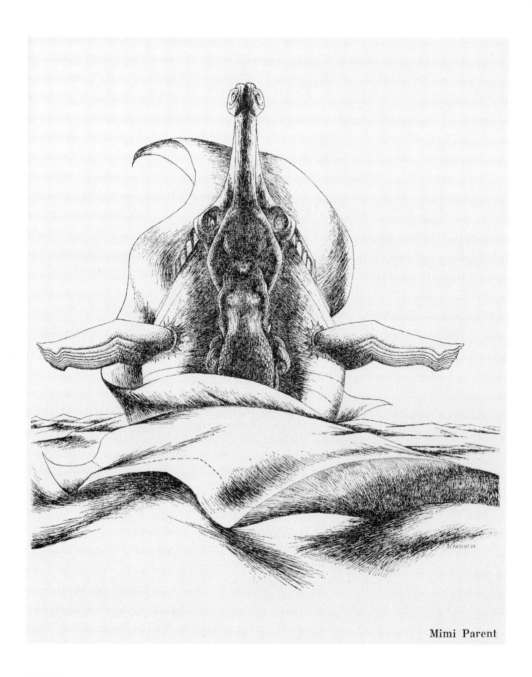

Mimi Parent
Reproduced in *La Brèche: action
surréaliste*, no.7, December
1964

automatically, the form of the quantitative laws of gravitation, electro-magnetism, and so on. According to Eddington, all measurement puts *four entities* at stake: two for the measurement of the observable, two for the standard with which it is compared. For example, for a length, it is necessary to associate its two extremities with at least two marks on a ruler, in such a way that all of our physical measurements are in fact just readings of reference points. The importance of the *conceptual quaternary* as a form imposed *absolutely* on any possible metric conceived by our intelligence and responding, in some way, to the very structure of our thought is no less evident in the theory of general relativity: 'We make four spatio-temporal variations $\times_1, \times_2, \times_3, \times_4$, correspond in the totality of events,' says Einstein, 'in such a way that at each event-point, a system of values of the variables $\times_1, \times_2, \times_3, \times_4$ corresponds.'

Eddington maintains that since the primordial intellectual entity possesses only the attribute of existence or rather of non-existence, the fundamental measurable quantity is necessarily determined by the four extreme entities from which the attributes of existence are, in principle, independent. Yet, this quantity exists only on condition that these four entities all exist together. Hence, Eddington deduces a type of 'associative linear' algebra which counts sixteen fundamental numerical operators from which *the structural motif* of the principal laws of physics can be conceived. In other words, the *epistemological a priori* of scientific thought, based on an abstract structural model, consents to a sort of conceptual and metrical net to be to constituted, allowing the results of the observation and the experiment to be *filtered*. Eddington himself compares the scientific method to a 'fishing line' and observes that if the logical meshes of this line are properly studied, the characteristics of the fish which will be held by it and caught can be anticipated. The unexpected characteristics are considered to be of no interest for physics; only precedents are *significant*. The possibility of comparing several 'models of the universe' comes from this, without allowing ourselves to be stopped by the limits of any single one of them. Thus, in its totality, scientific thought is freed from the limits of classical realism and the so-called evidence of common sense. Contemporary philosophy, and principally that of history, is very far from testifying to such a freedom of the intelligence and the creative imagination.

Nevertheless, it is not logically forbidden to propose *a priori* a 'model of reality' in the sense in which physicians understand a 'model of the universe'. In starting from this model, from this *pattern*, its properties can be analysed and the consequences deduced from them, while being careful to accord this schema an existence 'in itself', independent of the dialectical operations in respect of it.

For example, any 'factual' fact or event can be considered as the product of a constant and reciprocal adjustment of the series of internal relations, translated into the terms of the consciousness of a subject, with a series of external relations, expressed in terms of the experience of an object. The idea of a *real* subject or a *real*

44 Rudolf Carnap (1891–1970), philosopher who belonged to the Vienna Circle and was an advocate of logical positivism [trans.].

object leads in both cases to connections of *really coordinated* facts. Moreover, these can no longer be such in the case of disorders intervening either in their external relations or in their mutual adjustment. The experimental illusion produced in the relations with phantasmic objects, substituted for those of habitual perception by hallucination does not however entail a diminished sense of reality in relation to the consciousness of the subject, which we know gives, for example, an intensity and authenticity to the sufferings of alcoholic disorder that is unfortunately only too evident. We see clearly in this case that any notion of reality really depends upon a constant and reciprocal connection of internal relations with external relations, even in the case of madness, rather than of the subject 'in itself' or the object 'in itself', whose existence independent of their solidarity it is strictly impossible to demonstrate, being at once abstract and concrete. Thus, man and his external and internal worlds cannot be separated, isolated or substantified arbitrarily, by either the dogmas of idealism or by those of realism, although as distinct perspectives these conceptions both reveal important truths. They only translate a reality which, being at once one and the other, *cannot be either one or the other*, into a different language which is sometimes objective and sometimes subjective.

'The subjective and the objective elements', declared the great logician Henriques, 'are not two irreducible terms of knowledge. They form its two aspects resulting from the relation which is established between them and other knowledges of one or several persons touching upon one or several objects. We encounter the objective element when there is *an agreement of prevision*, whatever the means employed by one or several people to acquire it. The subjective element appears in the plurality of these possible means'.

In these conditions, it should be admitted that, from the point of view of the most rigorous logic, the notion of *event* or *fact* is really, as this quotation from Henriques underlines, far from attaining the ideal of a definitive determination from which either the logic of Russell or the 'logistic realism' of Carnap[44] and the Vienna school at times claimed to be able to construct the conceptual content of the scientific approach in a totally rational way.

Consequently, if history wants to be scientific, it must understand that it studies only relations between facts and the values accorded subjectively to these facts, and not 'objective' events. No other historical critique is possible or real other than that of these complex relations which are necessarily conscious or unconscious or *falsely conscious*. This is why an event has meaning, on the whole, only once it has been analysed and interpreted, *in the same way as a dream*, except that this is a collective dream, comprised of a minimum of communicability and uniformity in its process of manifestation.

Likewise, in many areas of the most advanced historical research, the careful and often hesitant attitude of specialists faced with documents which relate events experienced by their authors

45 Ferdinand Gonseth (1890-1975), Swiss philosopher and mathematician [trans.].

46 Joseph Gabel, *False Consciousness: An Essay on Reification*, translated by Margaret A. Thompson with the assistance of Kenneth A. Thompson. Oxford: Blackwell, 1975. In it Gabel extends the Marxist notion of false consciousness into the realm of psychotherapy [trans.].

increasingly resembles those of psychoanalysts in the presence of dreams or even, to use a less noble comparison, that of a rag-picker rummaging through and excavating the nocturnal remains of a banquet in the shadow of time. Why are the jam jars and bottles not equally empty? Why did they prefer this one to that? Who really wore this gold paper crown? Are these letters that are tied together with a ribbon more important messages than those torn or burned papers? Is what an age reveals of itself, what it has adorned with its favours, less significant than what it has disguised, rejected or excluded *from its own memories*? What compensation would it seek in the images of its grandeur and powers? Mysteriously, everything unfolds as if, in order really to die, the past expected us to understand it as it would have understood itself. An age to which history has thus not in some way restored its authentic form and real consciousness has not yet been fully concluded or, dare I say, been fully experienced. Thus we are, contrary to the so-called evidences of common sense, the *fathers of our fathers*: we owe them only our birth, but they owe us their true life, as brought back to life by the distance of our gaze. Only very recently has the medieval period started to be understood: before that people thought they knew it but, like a nebula in the telescope, it was not yet really visible. From that point, how do we dare to think that we know, from the events we observe, who we are here and now: *it is much too clear around the hour which strikes*.

Moreover, no scientific reality corresponds to a given factual immediacy. The mathematician Gonseth[45] has said: 'We perceive that it is far from possible to recognise as such everything that definitively or temporarily bears the seal of scientific reality in an immediate mental approach. Quite the contrary, reality is recognised as such in the changing aspects of what is apparent only thanks to the constantly renewed intervention of an active critique'. And Gonseth proposes an admirable definition of knowledge: 'In sum, ' he said, 'to know, *it is necessary to insert subjective necessities into objective necessities*'.

Here we are a long way from the alleged 'immediate objectivity' dear to naive realists and all those who endlessly crush us under the weight of the 'eloquence of facts'. But we also find ourselves much closer than could be thought to true dialectic, when it is no longer enclosed in the processes of reification and alienation so effectively denounced by Lukács and well analysed by the still too-little-known work of the philosopher and psycho-sociologist Joseph Gabel. For it is to Gabel that we owe a discovery I consider brilliant which, going beyond and deepening the superficial opposition between the conscious and unconscious, proposes a third term, the 'false consciousness', perhaps the most profound and serious evil of our times.[46]

There are multiple forms of 'false consciousness' of the history of civilisations. For instance, the one repeated since Valéry that although they are mortal they are forever dying and do not cease to haunt our museums, clutter up our flats and vampirise our archaeologists. Then the one which arranges civilisations in

Indian file, with one politely following the other like a line of schoolchildren, with pupils preceding adults. The one which classes them according to the tools they used, taking no account of the genius of the hand of the artist and the artisan. The one which admires all of their works on condition that they are monumental and forgets about the fate of their workers. The one which confuses civilisation with society (a widespread error in our age when humans are relatively less civilised than in other times while being, on the other hand, far more socialised). Indeed, we cannot forget that the human sacrifices in our time have numerically far outstripped those of the blindest and bloodiest idolatries of antiquity. And the false consciousness, finally, which promises us justice and order for tomorrow on condition that we accept injustice and disorder today, considered provisionally necessary for our evolution.

Let's rather pose the fundamental problem of an adult consciousness of the history of civilisations, whether they are diurnal or nocturnal, ancient or modern. *Is it really a question of reigning over Egypt or rather of exiting from it?* Of dominating the earth and mankind by science or magic, or rather of preferring freedom to any power over things and beings? A life which unconsciously consumes itself in order to defeat its father or mourn its mother, through conquests of external objects or through its absorption into the internal objects of waking and dream, no longer finds enough strength in itself to rise to its maturity, by illuminating the mind with the fire of awakening, the only thing able to free it from the parental possessions, projects and powers which burden and shackle it. Historical consciousness, as useful as it may have been for the evolution of the intelligence in revealing the power it can exert over the external world and its transformations, tends now to become a mechanism used for blocking and paralysing the highest functions of consciousness, when it inhibits and paralyses in some way our divination of the infinite and eternity. In order to know the human, the world and nature, penetrating into the depths lying under their appearances is insufficient. Much less to reconcile them in their intimate solidarity and in their perpetual nuptial exchanges. Far from opposing the relative to the absolute, illuminated knowledge sees the absolute not as what excludes the relative but what includes it, what integrates it through love and song into the smallest of its parts. This reintegration, closed on all sides to historical consciousness, is open to the divinisation of the heart and to it alone. This is why the first true civilisations will be neither magical nor scientific, but *necessarily poetic*. Liberated from the double mask of the real and the dream, it will be appropriate for us finally to celebrate *the surreal resurrection of the dead and the sleepers.*

Hans Bellmer
The Little Girl and Death 1963
Reproduced in *Obliques*, special
issue on Bellmer, 1979

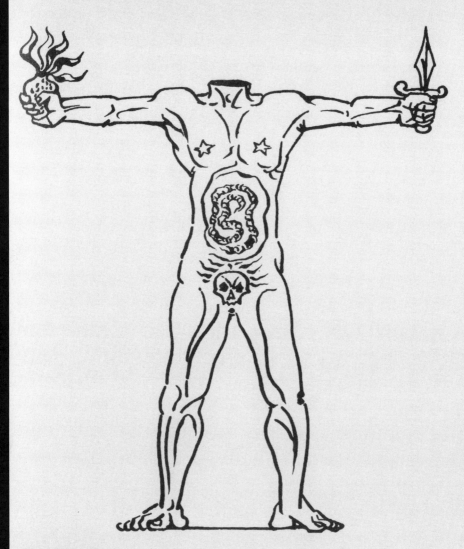

ACÉPHALE

RELIGION SOCIOLOGIE PHILOSOPHIE REVUE PARAISSANT 4 FOIS PAR AN

NUMÉRO DOUBLE — *NIETZSCHE et les FASCISTES* — 21 JANVIER

6 frs — *UNE RÉPARATION* — 1937

PAR G. BATAILLE · P. KLOSSOWSKI · A. MASSON · J. ROLLIN · J. WAHL

Acéphale, 21 January 1937
Front cover by André Masson

Part 3
The Moral Imperative

numéro 4

transmutation
du langage

S.U.
RR...

S.U.RR..., no.4, Spring 2003
Front cover, reproducing
Kathleen Fox, *Inside Continent*
1988

The Moral Imperative

Although Breton, in defining surrealism in the First Manifesto, placed automatism itself 'beyond moral considerations', it is now clear that surrealism has above all been a moral sensibility. Indeed it may be the major, if not the only, genuinely moral sensibility to have emerged during the twentieth century. The morality surrealism espoused was of course anti-bourgeois, anti-Christian and anti-rationalist and is a morality that may not be perceived as such – or may even be regarded by some people as the contrary of what is moral because it is founded in fundamental revolt, a refusal of the given, and opposition to all fixed forms. Surrealism has perhaps been unique in seeking to found morality not in conformity to any set of rules but in revolt and as a realisation of Marx's precept of engaging in 'merciless criticism of everything in existence', a process Charles Fourier called 'absolute divergence'.

The morality which has determined surrealism emerges from and relies upon a notion of freedom that has never been made explicit, but which initially emerged from Breton's and especially Aragon's reading of Hegel and Schelling. This 'freedom' is not of the sort promoted by liberal democracy – that is, one based on 'rights' and respect for the law. It is freedom in a much broader sense, one that cannot be limited or defined by juridical sanction. Freedom in surrealism is not something given to us but is rather a moral commitment to and responsibility for freedom in general. It is not therefore a specific responsibility to one's fellow humans, or to particular individuals, but to freedom as a totality; there is thus no relative freedom, the 'moderantism' Aragon caustically speaks about in his text below. Rather, each person is responsible for the freedom of all and it is only when this responsibility is assumed by all that freedom itself is realised. This is why freedom cannot be conceptualised in law (which is an abdication, allowing us to shrug our shoulders as an abstraction assumes what should be our responsibility). By the same token, freedom is not an individual right given to us, because any such freedom may impinge upon that of others. Genuine freedom can only be recognised in relation to necessity, its dialectical complement. As such, we need always to be responsive not simply to our own desire for freedom, but also to the ways in which our apparent freedom may be contrary to greater demands of freedom itself.

The texts in this section address issues of freedom in modern societies in different ways. Aragon's two texts set the scene by succinctly raising the dilemma that any liberal notion comes up against: that one cannot be free to act against freedom.

Humour, and the release of laughter that follows, is one of the few markers we have of freedom. But humour comes with a caveat, since it can be used to diminish and trivialise. This is why the surrealists have extolled Jacques Vaché's notion of 'umour' which builds its charge by bringing the fact of our existence into question, undermining our seriousness and placing our very being at stake. This form of humour is always 'black' and raises moral questions which Yugoslav surrealist Marko Ristić addresses in his essay.

Writing in 1938, on the verge of the Second World War and at a time when the revolutionary movement that had culminated in the Russian Revolution and partly impelled the development of surrealism had stalled, Nicolas Calas tries to understand the crisis in its socio-cultural frame, and especially in terms of what we would now call 'sexual politics' in a way that still has relevance even if his terms of reference may appear somewhat naïve today.

The Second World War also caused the surrealists to re-examine their own assumptions and some of the limitations of their pre-war positions. The Nazi phenomenon revealed that placing too much faith in irrational forces could be as dangerous as a rigid adherence to positivist rationalism, while the degeneration of communism into Stalinism showed that revolutionary upheaval did not necessarily result in a greater realisation of freedom. Breton himself looked more closely at theories of cosmic unity such as those developed by Charles Fourier as well as more ancient methods of investigation like alchemy. This led him to make a distinction – crucial to surrealism – between liberty and liberation, the substance of which is expressed in the extract given here.

Among those associated with surrealism, no one more than Georges Bataille recognised the fresh crisis into which consciousness had been plunged by the lead up to and enactment of the war. His essay here addresses the disturbing complicity existing between victim and executioner in the context of the experience of the concentration camps. The ramifications of the Nazi period are taken up in an essay from the mid-1960s in which Elisabeth Lenk weighs in with an early intervention into the Heidegger controversy (more than two decades before the controversy broke with

the publication of *Heidegger and Nazism* by Victor
Farias (1987). In a witty, Adorno-influenced critique,
Lenk provides us with a distinctively surrealist
understanding of what is at stake in the moral problem
raised by Heidegger's position and his association
with Nazism.

Freedom in its broadest perspective is
considered by Georges Henein, in an important and
far-reaching essay that directly addresses the post-
war context in ways that are just as relevant today
(perhaps even more so) than they were when he was
writing in the 1960s, especially in his analysis of the
progressive dehumanisation of modern society as
leading towards insidious forms of totalitarianism in
ways that anticipate concerns taken up more recently
by theorists such as Giorgio Agamben.

Philippe Audoin's essay continues the critique
of technology with a prescient discussion of the
managerial revolution that has since then transformed
life – but in a way that might be said to be the exact
opposite of the transformation surrealism sought.

With Gérard Legrand's essay, we look at the
specific position surrealism holds as an intellectual
current. With his book *The Philosophy of Surrealism*, the
philosopher Ferdinand Alquié had sought to defend
surrealism from charges of anti-humanism, made
most notably by Albert Camus in his 1950 book *The
Rebel*. Legrand insists, on the contrary, that surrealism
has to be considered outside the humanist tradition
and that Alquié makes a fundamental error by trying to
place it within the philosophical tradition, from Plato
to Kant, that extols the rational.

The text by Pierre Mabille brings together the
themes of this section by a dismantling of what he
calls the 'paradise complex'.

Louis Aragon
It's Up to You

These two early texts by Aragon are significant in the evolution of
surrealism towards a non-humanist, non-rationalist sensibility.
He strongly asserts that freedom can only be absolute and therefore
cannot contain within it anything that is contrary to freedom. It
follows that genuine freedom lies in the recognition of a lack of
freedom and cannot be contained by notions of right or embodied in
law (because if one's freedom is dependent on something outside of
itself it cannot be freedom). Indeed, it cannot even be contained in
language. Ironically Aragon would be the surrealist who, more than
any other, betrayed these very precepts, when he abandoned
surrealism to follow the diktats of Stalinism. Indeed, by later
excoriating Aragon, the surrealists were only following his exigency:
no freedom should be given to the enemies of freedom.

First published in *La Révolution
surréaliste*, no.2, 15 January
1925; reprinted in Louis
Aragon, *Chroniques du siècle*,
vol.1: 1918–1932, Paris: Stock,
1998.

No freedom for the enemies of freedom

Freedom... after a thousand vicissitudes, major disruptions, and the
failure of its most basic approaches, humanity shrugs its shoulders
in dismay. This word irritates like fire. You don't need two eyelids to
look freedom in the face.

At first the individual does not suspect his dependency. He
evidently knows that he can stretch his arms if he chooses. For him
everything is an object of will. Over just a few centuries doubt
appeared, became more defined, and the person was born into the
absolute determinism into which he eventually fell. This is where
we stand, at this moment of human meditation. And yet how could
the mind possibly have found its goal in a single place –there as
elsewhere limiting itself, apparently with good reason, to a vague
feeling raised to the dignity of an idea? How could a belief check the
movement of the mind? Will a new affirmation of freedom not
emerge from determinist dogma? Freedom transfigured by its
contrary, on the shores of these troubled waters I wait for its divine
features to show through beneath the widened ripples of the
inevitable, beneath the loosened chains which were hiding its face.

Freedom with wide eyes, like a streetwalker she might return.
It will no longer be the freedom it once was after having known
Saint-Lazare. Its bruised wrists... how could you have believed
that a single mental act could annihilate an idea? The word, even
as it is dishonoured on your public pediments, has remained in
your mouth even if you were saying you have crazily banished it
from your heart. And, thus denied, freedom finally *exists*. It emerges
from the night into which causality constantly ejects it, enriched by
the notion of the determined and completely enveloped by it. How
then are the contradictions of freedom resolved? What is perfectly
free, and at the same time determined and necessary? What draws
the principle of its freedom from its necessity? Such a being which

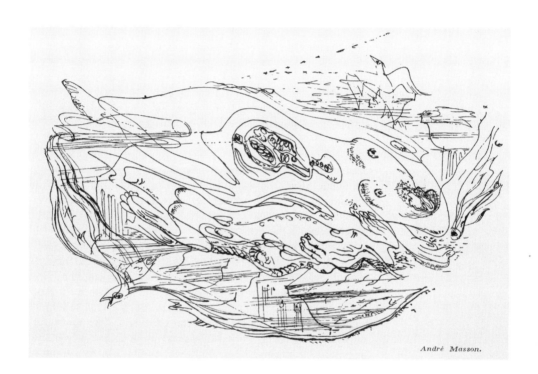

André Masson
Untitled automatic drawing
reproduced in *La Révolution
surréaliste*, no.3, 15 April 1925

has no other will but its becoming, which is subject to the development of the idea, and could imagine nothing but this, identifying itself with the idea, going beyond the person, it is the moral being, that I conceive at its extreme, which wishes for nothing but what must be, and which, free in its being, becomes necessarily the development of this free being. Thus freedom appears as the true foundation of morality, and its development implies the very necessity of freedom. There could be no freedom in any act turning against the idea of freedom. One is not free to act against it, that is to say immorally.

All of the above implies the condemnation of metaphysical considerations in the realm of sociology. This equality of disposition in the face of contrary notions, which in politics passes for broad-mindedness and which allows this continual reconciliation of the irreconcilables by which social life is improperly perpetuated, is due only to a primary error over the implications and significance of the transcendental dialectic. That the freedom of each might define the freedom of all by that frontier is a formula which has gained ground without our imagining that we could dispute its absurd terms. It is to this false freedom that our *philosophers* of government refer. This is the basis of all moderantism.

Oh moderates of every hue, how could you remain within this vague morality, in this haziness in which you take delight? I do not know what to admire most, your impartiality or your inanity. Morality and freedom are part of your vocabulary. But we would seek in vain to have you extract its definition. This is because the only morality is the morality of Terror, the only freedom the implacable dominant freedom: the world is like a woman in my arms. There will be irons for the enemies of freedom. Man is free, but men aren't. There are no limits to the freedom of one, there is no freedom for all. *All* is an empty notion, a clumsy abstraction, until one finally finds one's independence lost. Here ends the social history of humanity. Fishermen in troubled waters, your sophisms will not prevail: the movement of the mind is not indifferent, is not indifferently directed. There is a right and a left in the mind. And freedom is what draws the compass needle towards this magnetic north, which takes the heart's side. Nothing, neither catastrophes, nor people's ridiculous considerations, could shackle the accomplishment of becoming. The mind sweeps everything away. In the midst of this great plain where man lives, where, in the dried-out pools several suns have extinguished themselves one after the other, this great wind of the sky rages, the idea rises above the fields and overturns everything. Everything is to be gained from the greatest loss. The mind lives from disaster and death.

    * * *

Those who die moderately for their fatherland... those who sleep moderately throughout the day... those who moderately, but this is really true for you, radically, turn the divergences of thought into simple powerless misdemeanours, would these polite and tolerant hosts, these dilettantes of morality, these jokers, these playful sceptics, be *our* masters for long, do they still exercise oppression through their smiles? It is inconceivable to exalt man's minor faculties, for example sociability, at the expense of his major faculties, like the faculty of murder. A leap of conscience in that tiger, the ringed stripes of whose coat have been taken for prison bars will suffice for him to be raised to the moral notion of its freedom, and he might then recognise the enemies of morality. Then, oh moderates, there will be no further refuge for you in the streets, in the houses, in the temples, in the brothels, in the innocence of children, or in the blue tears of women, then tyrannical freedom will suddenly pin you (owls and rhetoricians) to your doors, then it will throw its name at the universe with a great burst of laughter, and the universe will go along saying that freedom is now called perpetual Revolution.

Louis Aragon
Note on Freedom

First published in *La Révolution surréaliste*, no.4, 15 July 1925; reprinted in Louis Aragon, *Chroniques du siècle*, *vol.1: 1918–1932*, Paris: Stock, 1998.

Freedom, entirely enfolded in its consequences which commit it only to the idea, its shadow, and the mechanical 'so what?' immediately pronounced whenever it arises, all this skein of notions ready for parade drives simple folk to representations of its terms, without their first having formed any concept which assembles them and testifies to their reciprocal subordination. Where there is no philosophical system, the word freedom becomes meaningless. Show me, in fact, any point of the mind that does not assume a philosophical system. And I would even say: precisely where there is a philosophical system, no matter what kind of a system, even a new one I haven't envisaged, the word freedom once more assumes a meaning, and not just any meaning but a meaning that is always the same and unique because any system, however contrary in appearance it might be to it, is only ever an elaboration of the idea, an ideation, and therefore it assumes what is beyond the suppositions of the idealist system, with its developments, its reversals and its solutions, in which the idea's light gives rise to the idea of freedom, which is freedom itself. (You should note that reasoning in this way for each idea, I affirm that there is no other philosophical system than idealism, or that words must no longer contain meaning, and then be quiet.) Everything I say about freedom is therefore irrefutable and absolute. It follows that freedom is a limit, that it is absurd to envisage freedom other than as a limit. If what I am saying about freedom is absolute, freedom as it appears in language always has a uniquely relative quality, and it is this confusion between two terms that are really distinct, the alternative use of these two terms, which engender the representations to which I was referring and which I was ridiculing.

It follows that whenever necessary I will commit any kind of outrage against the freedom of others, with respect to freedom. The free man is the one who can will nothing but that which contributes towards the idea. The perfectly free man is perfectly determined in becoming it. Death to mechanics that stem the tide!

Marko Ristić
Humour as a Moral Attitude

Humour was one of the cornerstones of the surrealist attitude, but this was black humour – the 'umour' identified by Jacques Vaché, one that is objective and disinterested. It is on this basis that Ristić can see it as fundamentally revolutionary and raise its relationship with morality. Just as only what is revolutionary is moral, so humour cannot be placed in the service of a cause. It is not therefore simply what is funny but, like poetry, what brings us face to face with the unacceptable aspects of reality. It is by this that it becomes moral, a morality that is against whatever is existent. Humour's task, therefore, is to restore life's freshness. Ristić's essay is part of the important but little-known research conducted early on by the Yugoslav surrealist groups. Ironically, Ristić will be among those who after the Second World War will betray this revolutionary morality to serve the repressive Yugoslav state, although not quite as unconditionally as his collaborator Koča Popević who would become for a time President Tito's right-hand man.

First published in *Le Surréalisme au service de la révolution*, no.6, 15 May 1933.

(Response to the enquiry 'Is humour a moral attitude?')
What is the relationship between humour and poetry, between humour and morality, between humour and death?

It is above all a new way of envisaging reality and of an attitude towards it (but from this perspective objects themselves show themselves in what is really the aspect of the modern within them), being the case when the machinery for disordering and denying humour does not work, or after the brief moment of its fleeting functioning. I mean that I am discussing humour in a humourless way.

The four pages of the publication *L'Impossible* (Belgrade, 1931) which, under the title *The Alarm Clock*, represented an initial attempt to establish experimentally the relations between poetry and humour, have been totally misunderstood by bourgeois intellectuals. In the light of these relations, it nevertheless appears very clearly that humour is, in its essence, an intuitive and implicit critique of the conventional mental mechanism, a force which extracts a fact or a group of facts from what is given as normal for them, in order to cast them into a vertiginous play of unexpected and surreal relations. By combining the real and the fantastic,

Lee Miller
Portrait of Space 1937

1 Jean Frois-Wittmann
(1891–1937) was originally a
cubist painter but in the 1920s
turned to psychoanalysis and
collaborated at a distance with
the surrealists during the late
1920s and 1930s [trans.].

beyond the limits of everyday realism and rational logic, humour
and humour alone gives what surrounds it a grotesque freshness,
a hallucinatory character of non-existence, or at least a doubtful
and contemptible objectivity and a ridiculous importance,
alongside an exceptional and ephemeral, but total, *over-meaning*
[*sur-sens*]. In contact with poetry, humour is the extreme expression
of a convulsive inadaptability, of a revolt for which any restraint or
restriction only adds to its strength.

According to Freud, humour has a 'grandeur in it [which]
clearly lies in the triumph of narcissism, the victorious assertion
of the ego's invulnerability. The ego refuses to be distressed by the
provocations of reality, to let itself be compelled to suffer. It insists
that it cannot be affected by the traumas of the external world;
it shows, in fact, that such traumas are no more than occasions
for it to gain pleasure.' [Freud 1961, p.162].

As a refusal to accept or recognise reality and its seriousness,
humour satisfies certain 'playful and regressive tendencies towards
pre-logical and pre-realist ways of thinking'. This is how Jean
Frois-Wittmann[1] draws our attention to the relations existing
between jokes and humour on the one hand and the poetic image
on the other, thereby reaching conclusions which are those of
purely poetic experience.

Psychoanalysis shows us how the transformation of feelings
accumulated during humorous pleasure render all effective
externalisation momentarily superfluous.

Humour is also in a certain way a mask stamped and
approved by the super-ego, which displays the unconscious so as
to be able to act as a stowaway evading the control of this very
super-ego.

And now, what are the relations between humour and
morality, between humour and a moral *attitude*, which rightly
assumes this constant, conscious and active reaction which
humour dispenses?

In our *Sketch of a Phenomenology of the Irrational*, Koča
Popović and myself, after having rejected bourgeois normative
morality – a disgusting set of rules and regulations, a codification
which, however much it may vary on either side of the Pyrenees,
no less remains a codification, and not only of right and wrong, *in
abstracto* but of human behaviour, of man and woman in love
(the normal and the perverse, the permissible and the forbidden,
procreation and the sixty-nine…) – made a distinction, on the one
hand, between real morality (the process of the realisation of
concrete, irrational and individual desire, the expression of the
direct demands of the unconscious, of instincts, of 'reasoning',
outside all systematisation) and, on the other hand, *modern morality*
(a stage of this development, a relative system, an *attitude*
conditioned by the exigencies of categories that the real, individual
and inapplicable morality in current society, such as categories of
'judgement', of rational conscience, of chronology, history and
society), cannot, by definition, take into account.

For want of a dialectical conception, the notion of morality

Opposite:
Georges Malkine
Ecstasy
Reproduced in *La Révolution
surréaliste*, no.7, 15 June 1926

would appear to us to be situated on two irreconcilable levels. On the first – already contradictorily, but at least on the same level – we should consider morality as a *system* which must at all costs be abolished and, at the same time, as the very condition of this abolition, as the negation of this system. On the other of these two levels, being the irreducible and wholly arbitrary exigency of the individual's personal freedom, desire's right to realise itself, morality appears to us as the personification of what is desystematised within *desystematisation* itself. The distinction of terminology proposed by the *Sketch* seems to me sufficiently justified in order to avoid this confused paradox.

If we take account of the distinction outlined above between real morality (the morality of desire) and modern morality (the revolutionary attitude 'dependent on the social dialectic'), the response to the question of whether *humour is a moral attitude* is *negative*, whereas to the question of whether *humour is moral* the response is *affirmative*. For, by the very fact that humour is perfectly amoral, it can be said that it is perfectly moral, given that by itself it does not fall under the categorisation of the moral and the immoral, which can only be concerned with the practical *consequences* of humour. Nevertheless such humour 'in itself', outside of its determination and results, whether or not it is usable in a revolutionary way, cannot be conceived except in its full unlimited and phenomenological development, which is unthinkable in the current state of our consciousness – or rather in the infinitely brief fulguration of an eternalised present; in other words in both cases beyond time. But we are in time, and how! And in what a time! If therefore we conceive that here, in the implacable light of wakefulness, in the midst of the class struggle, the word 'morality' uttered out loud (I am not alone in the world, you are not alone in the world, someone speaks to someone else, someone explains himself to someone) means *in conformity with the exigencies of modern morality*, for the statement gives words a social meaning, it then becomes clear that only what is revolutionary is moral. It is *revolutionary* because it is moral, moral because (perhaps considered as) revolutionary: it is by its consequences and its results that the morality of an initial fact can be judged. Because it leaves no centuries-old inscription, no corner stone of the amphitheatre of eternal wisdom, in peace, humour is moral, just as madness, poetry and love are (the affirmative response). Moreover, could it be that a thing which *ideally* is identified with the disinterested realisation of the unconscious, in other words with the real morality of desire, that such a thing might not have moral consequences? But that still does not mean that humour can be a moral attitude. 'Humour would be anarchy if it could be an attitude. But it exists only instantaneously, no matter how far its consequences might lead, consequences for which it is not responsible and that it has not been able to foresee' (Koča Popević).

Humour as a vital attitude is untenable.

Jacques Vaché killed himself, as did Jacques Rigaut.

L'EXTASE

Georges Malkine

Persistent humour could be the morality of solitude, but solitude has condemned itself to death (or rather is forced to transform itself into action, in other words to deny itself), hurled towards its unique resolution, towards self-destruction and definitive solitude. Nihilist humour tends regressively towards its own annihilation, towards the intra-uterine peace of isolation, non-participation and irresponsibility, towards the humoral withdrawal of the embryo.

Humour cannot by definition choose or commit itself, because it neither admits nor accepts the reality in which its choice, its decision, should be exercised. Its *supreme irony* is in reality a blind indifference. *In opposition to every possible fact about social reality*, generalised and perpetuated humour is incompatible with every decision, with every possible social adequacy... And, as indifference, humour is neither vital, nor viable; mankind's life as particularised in matter cannot be indifferent (*Sketch*, pp.170-1).

The times are too harsh and pressing for anyone at all to hope to scrape through by means of the artificial conservation of an illusion, under the fuzzy thatched roof of humour, in the solitary dead windmill of humour, in the extinguished lighthouse of humour. The disenchanted humorist (I'm not speaking about journalists), wrapped in the illusory cape of fatalism, squats at the summit of the highest haystack (whose base is on fire), without a smidgen of illusion (and entirely devoted to an illusion), without hope but without a creative bitterness, without a single gesture of active revolt, without movement and without effectiveness. 'Sensation – I was going to say a MEANING of the theatrical (and joyless) uselessness *of everything*' (Vaché): a feeling that doubts everything ('O ABSURD GOD!') – because everything is contradiction – isn't it? – and will umour be the one who is never taken in by the hidden and SHIFTY life of everything? – O my alarm clock'. 'A sensation of the theatrical uselessness of everything' ('... and the one who will feel the lamentable optical illusion of universal simile-symbols will be umorous') [Vaché 1995, p.228; translation modified]): the confused and ashen dawn of Dada. To feel the lamentable vanity and absurd unreality of everything is to feel one's own uselessness – is to be useless. So one must either annihilate or transform oneself, go beyond oneself through a substantial negation: Vaché killed himself, Dada became surrealism. The indifference of humour is a repressed expansion force, whose virtual power of explosion is clarified by another real and determining power, that of the present time, in the light of the decision and the action: the hidden energy, particular to that shackled indifference, thereby becomes a motor of action.

And for that, I bow very low to the virulent miasma of humour.

Psychologically, a man, through his 'humoristic attitude', shows that he wants to know nothing about the attacks of the external world, and he transmutes his traumas into motives for humoristic pleasure. But no one is mithridatised against the opaque and perfidious poison of the reality of its disasters. It is true that in its active moments, humour is a more secret, subtle and corrosive poison. In certain precise cases (for instance when

POÈMES   11

Quand je ferme les yeux des floraisons
phosphorescentes apparaissent et se
fanent et renaissent comme des feux
d'artifice charnus.

Des pays inconnus que je parcours en
compagnie de créatures.

Il y a toi sans doute, ô belle et discrète
espionne.

Et l'âme palpable de l'étendue.

Et les parfums du ciel et des étoiles et le
chant du coq d'il y a 2.000 ans et le cri
du paon dans des parcs en flamme et
des baisers.

Des mains qui se serrent sinistrement dans
une lumière blafarde

et des essieux qui grincent sur des routes
médusantes.

Il y a toi sans doute que je ne connais pas,
que je connais au contraire.

Mais qui présente dans mes rêves s'obstine
à s'y laisser deviner sans y paraître

Toi qui restes insaisissable dans la réalité
et dans le rêve.

Toi qui m'appartiens de par ma volonté
de te posséder en illusion mais qui
n'approches ton visage du mien que mes

yeux clos aussi bien au rêve qu'à la
réalité.

Toi qu'en dépit d'une rhétorique facile ou
le flot meurt sur les plages,

où la corneille vole dans des usines en
ruines,

où le bois pourrit en craquant sous un
soleil de plomb,

Toi qui es la base de mes rêves et qui secoue
mon esprit plein de métamorphoses et
qui me laisses ton gant quand je baise
ta main.

Dans la nuit, il y a les étoiles et le mouve-
ment ténébreux de la mer, des fleuves,
des forêts, des villes, des herbes, des
poumons de millions et millions d'êtres.

Dans la nuit il y a les merveilles du monde.

Dans la nuit, il n'y a pas d'anges gardiens
mais il y a le sommeil.

Dans la nuit il y a toi,

Le jour aussi.

SI TU SAVAIS

Loin de moi et semblable aux étoiles, à la
mer et à tous les accessoires de la mytho-
logie poétique,

Loin de moi et cependant présente à ton
insu,

Loin de moi et plus silencieuse encore
parce que je t'imagine sans cesse,

Loin de moi, mon joli mirage et mon rêve
éternel, tu ne peux pas savoir.

Si tu savais.

Loin de moi et peut-être davantage encore
de m'ignorer et m'ignorer encore.

Loin de moi parce que tu ne m'aimes pas
sans doute ou, ce qui revient au même,
que j'en doute.

Loin de moi parce que tu ignores sciemment
mes désirs passionnés.

Loin de moi parce que tu es cruelle.

Si tu savais.

Loin de moi ô joyeuse comme la fleur qui
danse dans la rivière au bout de sa tige
aquatique, ô triste comme sept heures du
soir dans les champignonnières.

Loin de moi silencieuse encore ainsi qu'en
ma présence et joyeuse encore comme l'heure
en forme de cigogne qui tombe de haut.

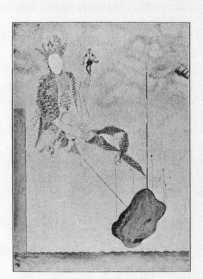

Yves Tanguy

Yves Tanguy
Reproduced in a page from
La Révolution surréaliste, no. 7,
15 June 1926

confronted with a priest), without taking account of the narcissistic nihilism which is generally appropriate for it, not only is it morally justified, but its reactions are once again identified with those of the modern morality of the revolutionary. But this could not become constant and could not objectively be prolonged.

Humour becomes immoral as soon as it tries (even unconsciously) to dress up its incapacity for durable validity by *a systematisation* that is no less immoral than all those wrongly operated over the subversive aspects of the mind, *with the conscious and consciously relative and practical exception of modern morality*. Generalised in a static way to narcissistic and illusory ends, humour is no longer the disinterested and direct expression of the unconscious. Betraying its own concrete and irrational particularity, neither is it any longer a necessary rational systematisation, with an objective, in other words revolutionarily efficacious, aim; it reduces itself to nothing. It is no more than a desertion, an alibi, and it hides all compromises.

For the freedom of desystematised life to become universal, a systematisation is needed (the very opposite of the generalisation of certain *individualised* elements) which includes all present and incomplete elements and, no less than the others, those of humour, the fleeting image of the unfettered and arbitrary.

Surrealism goes straight to the forbidden zone. But if, in its specific experimentation, it could not in any way be rationalised, it is, on the other hand, placed in the service of a cause – the only historically inevitable and decisive one – which requires a rational organisation of thought. Surrealism is placed in the service of the revolution which itself, by working to transform the material conditions of human existence, is in the service of a concrete and certain freedom whose elements, as far as is currently possible, are already incorporated into surrealism, placing itself at their own service. Humour, for instance, can be a weapon not to be neglected. But the fatalism (which becomes its fact as soon as it is generalised) has nothing in common with the determinist character of the moral attitude of the revolutionary. A revolutionary knows that freedom is gained only through the knowledge of necessity, and that one does not sidestep responsibility in the face of the necessity for that knowledge and action with which it identifies itself.

Nicolas Calas
Love of Revolution in our Time

Given the extent to which sexual roles have changed over the past seventy-five years, this analysis by the Greek surrealist Nicolas Calas of sexual roles in relation to changing socio-political conditions may seem at best rather quaint. And certainly it is true that its interest is principally historical, showing how the surrealists had in the 1930s anticipated the later notion that 'the personal is political'. It should not for all that be dismissed. In identifying the crisis of European society at that time – involving a fundamental moral breach into which fascism was able to install itself not simply as a political ideology but more significantly as a religious sensibility based upon a desire that is insatiable but divested of erotic content (or at least in which the erotic content is diverted away from any affective sensibility to satisfy a hierarchical order at whose summit is the leader) – Calas is raising an issue that still has resonance today.

First published in *Minotaure*, no.11, Spring 1938.

1. The Industrial Revolution and the crisis of love

The more civilisation develops, the more acute the contradictions at the heart of society; the more class antagonisms increase, the more the inequality of the sexes is accentuated. As Engels notes, the bourgeois family is now opposed by the proletariat, for whom the family has become merely a legal convention. The 'Industrial Revolution', by destroying the worker's home, liquidated domestic work, that form of division of work between man and wife which had always existed. Once the wife left home for the factory, her situation became identical with that of the husband and the struggle for a higher salary and a reduction in working hours became the basis of the movement for the emancipation of women. Equal in poverty, male and female workers now struggle side by side for liberty, equality and fraternity. Mary Wollstonecraft's *Vindication of the Rights of Women*, published as early as 1792, marked the beginning of women's political campaign. But we know women's poverty will not be abolished through the socialisation of the means of production; only social transformation will tear the power from the father in whose service both children and women alike are crushed.

For the moment this struggle against private property and the bourgeois family, a struggle in which the whole world is engaged, engenders a profound moral crisis which is reflected in all of the manifestations of the superstructure in today's society.

The social crisis affects the bourgeois family, disintegrating it by attracting two of its constituent elements – wife and child – towards different points of polarisation. The ever-greater power of the father, made possible thanks to the accumulation of capital and the way prostitution was given a new lease of life by industrialisation, favoured male polygamous tendencies. For the bourgeois woman, monogamy therefore became more than ever a sign of social inferiority. Unconsciously a female fraternity began to develop. The bourgeois woman recognised in the new situation of the worker's wife only what seemed to her to be an advantage: equality with the male. The bourgeois woman equally sought to free herself and establish equality with the male, represented for her, of course, not by the worker but by the bourgeois; and what the bourgeois woman wants is not an equal salary but the right to polygamy. What she wants is not money but the right to do what she wants with her money. The woman worker wants a salary; the bourgeois woman wants adultery. What the bourgeois woman sees

as the distinctive sign of individuality is the right which the male
has always reserved for himself, the right to polygamy. The woman,
in her struggle for emancipation, seeks to conquer individuality.
Naturally, since she has not yet obtained it, she can do no more than
copy the only form of individuality she knows, that of the male. For
the woman worker a man is someone who has a higher salary than
her; for the bourgeois woman it is a man who has more women.
But individuality is an attitude of fraternity – it is the attitude of the
boy against the father.

　　During the nineteenth century, for the first time in history,
woman demonstrated a tendency to detach herself from the father
so as to be closer to her brother. Feminism today for women is what
Socratic humanism was for the Athenians of Peracles: a movement
directed against the father. O'Neill, in his play *Mourning Becomes
Electra*, tries to modernise the famous ancient drama, but his
conception of modernisation remains very elementary, for the only
new thing he brings is a different setting for the same action. If he
had been more perceptive he would have recognised that the Electra
of our age would not call upon Orestes to avenge Agamemnon,
because what she wants is to kill her father, and to do this she needs
no help from her brother since she identifies with him. The modern
Electra is Violette Nozière:

> *Violette dreamed of ridding herself.*
> *To rid herself*
> *Of the horrible vipers' nest of ties of blood* (Éluard)

Today's woman in relation to man is in the same situation as the man in the Renaissance was in relation to woman. Fifteenth century man made the Madonna, a virgin, from a mother; the woman of the twentieth century turns the father into a brother.

Emancipation is thus produced by identification, which is not without risk, particularly for the bourgeois woman. Since the worker possesses nothing apart from his chains, when the female worker identifies with her brother she can ask for nothing much apart from a salary. But identification for the bourgeois woman is richer in content. And historically it seems to be formed of two stages. The first is the period of adultery, described in literature from Balzac to Anatole France. The woman of this period is Madame Bovary. The second stage pushes identification even further. One might say that the woman unconsciously feels that the right to adultery, which the new morality tolerates and accepts, does not give her that equality her being claims. She does not suspect that the path upon which she has embarked is false and she does not understand how contradictory this identification is. Equality does not mean identity. Equality means abolishing property, but the bourgeois woman is, because of her class, opposed to such abolition. What she wants is identification with the rich man. This contradiction between identity and equality only exists for the female worker, because when she seeks to identify with the male (given that the proletarian has no more individuality than the slave) she can only identify with something she conceives through anticipation: an increase in salary. When experience reveals to the bourgeois woman that adultery does not give her the equality she demands, and since she cannot (as she remains bourgeois) find the way to obtain it, when she neither wants to nor is able to stop her expansiveness, she finds herself forced to push her identification with her brother further still. What she now wants is not to be as polygamous as the man, but to love what the man loves. What the woman desires is therefore no longer a male lover but a mistress.

After the century of Balzac and Flaubert, we arrive at that of Marcel Proust. Woman, having been Beatrice and Madame Bovary, becomes a heroine of *Sodom and Gomorrah*. To please the woman, the man becomes effeminate, while the woman imitates a man to please her brother.

2. Love and fascism

The disintegration of the family also occurs by means of another constitutive element, the son. The class struggle, becoming more violent each year, reinforces class consciousness and brings the bourgeoisie together. This augments their tendency towards class fraternity. Paternity inevitably finds itself weakened by this movement. The camaraderie which fascism tries to exalt is in

André Masson
Heraclitus
reproduced in *Minotaure*,
no.11, Spring 1938

violent contradiction to the ideal of the family. Nevertheless the bourgeoisie cannot escape this impasse. For to abandon the family would be to abandon the principle of authority on which its domination is based. Without the sublimation of the idea of the father, without a leader, no authority is possible; but on the other hand, the need to close ranks so as to struggle more effectively against the class enemy obliges the bourgeoisie to exalt fraternity.

There is a second element which completes this fascist complex, which is the bourgeois man's attitude towards woman. Since the capitalist is in favour of the family in principle, he is against any genuine emancipation for women. At a time when he feels that the family is in danger he tries to save it by proclaiming the necessity for women's return to the home – only the bourgeois woman, of course (the female worker returns to the home in fascist as in other capitalist countries only during periods of crisis). Thus, when fascism speaks of the family, it means a family for the woman, camaraderie for the man. But this camaraderie without women can only be a homosexual camaraderie.

The affective evolution of the bourgeoisie these days follows some very odd paths. When it is liberal it becomes feminist and develops a lesbian sensibility; when it is fascist it replaces this attitude with behaviour tending towards homosexuality. But bourgeois feminism, just like fascism, is not the sign of female freedom, but simply a symptom of the impasse into which the bourgeoisie has been driven.

It should not be thought that this fascist homosexuality signals a return to Plato's morality. Homosexual philosophy and morality in Greece was humanist, whereas fascist morality is religious and makes the homosexual fixation a subject of adoration and not love.

We have already said that the bourgeoisie today becomes

2 Daniel Guérin (1904–1988), an important French anarcho-communist writer; Calas incorrectly called him 'René Guérin [trans.].

3 Nikolai Alexandrovich Berdyaev (1874–1948), Russian Christian philosopher [trans.].

reactionary because it feels that its progressive role has ended. It is obliged to replace reasoning with faith, and science with religion. Fascist religiosity, in appealing to authority, returns to the principle of the father; but since the strength of fascism does not reside in the family, as was the case for earlier religions, it must rely on camaraderie. This is why the fascist leader wants to have the authority of the father and the attraction of the brother. The ideal fascist leader must be young and old at the same time; he wants to be lover, brother and father. The Leader, the Duce, the Führer must all incarnate an analogous contradiction to that which Christianity has known and expressed with its myth of the Virgin-Mother.

It is the religious spirit of fascism that gives its homosexuality a sacred quality. The love of the leader must be exclusive; this is why all homosexual love not directed towards the leader is severely persecuted in fascist countries.

If the leader is not simply a father, but also a lover, it must mean that his authority cannot be based on the Oedipus complex; it must also depend upon a neurotic sublimation of homosexual love. Yet on the other hand, however loved the leader will be, his power remains far greater than anything known by tyrants in former ages ever was. The power of a Führer lies in the greatest of forces, on the most affective and intense connection, on the love of the lover. But if the leader one day loses this love, if he ceases to symbolise the lover, if he grows old, he will no longer be loved, for fascism will not be content with the idea of a wise leader (supposing it might be possible for a fascist leader to be wise) as wisdom is not a virtue of the Lover but of the Father. In a very interesting study entitled *Fascism and Big Business*, [Daniel] Guérin[2] suggests that if the bourgeoisie wants to survive it will one day be forced to repudiate fascism for economic reasons and return to the monarchy in which it will try to find the guarantee of durability and stability which fascism and its adventurous politics does not offer economic life. The conclusion to which our analysis of fascist psychosis leads perfectly accords with this economic perspective. The instability of the affective State, as in all amorous states, will inevitably force the bourgeoisie, once it loses confidence in its lover, to look for a stability which violent passion cannot accord it. It is therefore more than probable that after this period of love, if it survives a world cataclysm or, if this cataclysm does not happen, it will have recourse to the calm authority of the Father as symbolised by the monarchy.

Fascism, with its return to faith, presents analogies with the Middle Ages. Is this the Middle Ages the renegade Berdyaev[3] spoke about? For my part I think the analogy between fascism and the Middle Ages is not without foundation. But this fascist Middle Ages is not a Middle Ages any more than the fifteenth century was a renaissance of antiquity. By its tendency to rediscover individuality, the Renaissance marked a return to Antiquity. Likewise the new Middle Ages seems to indicate a return to the faith analogous to the time of St Paul. But the new Middle Ages is no more a Christian faith than the individuality of the Renaissance was the same as that of Plato. For the Renaissance individuality was woman; for fascism, faith is the lover divinised. This is why, after communism, fascism has no worse enemy than the Christian church. At the level of the superstructure a struggle to the death is in process between fascism and Christianity. Viewed in this light, as strange as it appears, the struggle of the Führer is one of the son against the father. But this war between fascism and Christianity at the level of the superstructure cannot interest the communist, since both the fascist and Christian solutions to the spiritual problems of our age constitute responses of a neurotic nature.

To conclude these remarks, let us simply add that the fascist attitude presents infinitely more serious contradictions than those Christianity has tried to resolve, and this is easily explained if we consider that fascism has set itself the task of finding solutions to a situation engendered by a reality far more contradictory than that which faced the people of the early centuries of our age. The great danger of the current situation for fascism on the affective level, like any attitude which appeals to the mass, results from the fact that its sexual attitude is a direct attitude. But, as Freud says in his remarkable study of the Leader, 'direct sexual tendencies retain a certain character of individuality even in an individual absorbed in the mass. When this individuality goes beyond a certain degree, the collective formation is threatened with falling apart.'

Camaraderie depends upon individuality; if fascism destroys it then it will destroy the camaraderie on which it bases itself, but if it develops the spirit of camaraderie, then, following Freud's principle, it will risk disintegration.

André Breton
Liberty versus Liberation

André Breton wrote *Arcane 17* in 1944. In this passage from the last part of the book, he clarifies the crucial surrealist distinction (which underlies all of the essays in this section of our anthology) between freedom and liberation. Here again the influence of Hegel is probably determining in Breton's thinking as he asserts the limitations of the notion of negative freedom (that is, freedom *from* rather than freedom *for*) at the very moment being enshrined in the Universal Declaration of Human Rights as a universal principle. Freedom in Breton's sense is dynamic and continuous, something always in process and on a par with the fact of living itself; it is not a cause to be taken up in the name of some (or any) goal. This gives substance to the surrealist watchword, 'Freedom is the colour of man'.

First published in *Arcane 17* (1944), which was reprinted in 1971 by Jean-Jacques Pauvert, Paris.

[...] There is unfortunately a [...] risk, for all those involved in the resistance movement in France and elsewhere, that they will have limited their perspectives to the liberation of territory. The effort of liberation coincides only in a partial and accidental way with the struggle for liberty. Today a very precise distinction between these two terms is called for when some people are ready to take advantage of the confusion between them at the expense of liberty. The idea of liberation has the disadvantage of being a negative idea, of having only momentary value in relation to a clearly defined act of despoilment which has to be rectified. Any such idea, containing nothing inherently constructive (as was clearly seen in pre-war anti-fascism, for instance, which was entrenched in the rut of pure opposition), has only a mediocre significance. The idea of liberty, on the contrary, is one that is fully master of itself, reflecting an unconditional view of what *constitutes* humanity and alone attributes an appreciable meaning to human becoming. Liberty, unlike liberation, is not a fight against sickness, it is *health*. Liberation can cause us to think health has been re-established when it is only a remission of the sickness, the disappearance of its most manifest and alarming symptoms. Freedom, however, escapes all contingency. Freedom, not only as an ideal but as a constant re-creator of energy, as it has existed among certain people and can be given as the model for all, must exclude any idea of comfortable balance and conceive itself as a continual *erethism*. The now widely felt primordial need for liberation and the love of freedom, which one cannot ignore as being far more elective, owe it to the rigours of time that they march side by side.

André and Elisa Claro Breton at Saint-Cirq-La-Popie, c.1960

Georges Bataille
Reflections on the Executioner and the Victim[4]

This text, like so many of Bataille's critical writings after the war, is ostensibly a book review – but one that goes far beyond its brief to touch upon concerns of intimate significance for him. The review is devoted to David Rousset's *Les Jours de notre mort* (1947), a novel of the experience of concentration camps;[5] Bataille uses the book as a springboard for considerations of evil and our complicity in it. There is continuity here with surrealist moral concerns, in Bataille's determination to confront the implications of the concentration camp in a way that goes beyond their particular situation as manifestations of Nazi terror to engage in general with the human capacity for inhumanity. A refusal to engage with this issue is, Bataille implies, to participate in it through cowardice. The moral issue raised here conjoins with the questions of freedom raised in the other essays of this section: freedom only becomes meaningful if it is the freedom of all, something which would make such inhumanity impossible (since the torturer would need to recognise the extent of his own suffering is contingent upon that which he inflicts on the tortured).

First published in *Critique*, no.17, October 1947; reprinted in Georges Bataille, *Oeuvres complètes*, vol.11, Paris: Gallimard, 1988.

'For the four weeks since we left Helmstedt, we have gone to the extreme limits of ruins. The society of the camps has come undone and people have then broken through every barrier. Myself, us, all. What we have been able to know in abjection will never be spoken about. Such as we are, so wretched and appalling, we still bear a triumph, well beyond ourselves, for the whole human collectivity. Never have we blasphemed against life ...' (p.760).

   If an extreme possibility was given to life, not in the furtive time of normal death, but in an infinite repetition that the gathering of hundreds of thousands of prolonged death agonies offered him, it is surely the one of which David Rousset has made himself the chronicler. He tells us in what the singularity of his experience consisted; it is that while being obliged to observe it, he remained its guinea pig. We see that in the end the guinea pig triumphs and when it is put to the test, staring death and misfortune in the face, it affirms the victory of life.

* * *

But the insolent conclusion of Rousset's book does not remove a value of negating contestation from his experience. 'Ordinary people', he tells us 'could never understand. They live on the surface. Not only of social conventions. But of others still more profound. Ones that are unsuspected. The conventions whereby the most intimate life endures itself. To tell them: the truth is that, like the executioner, the victim was vile; that the lesson of the camps was the fraternity of abjection; that if there were those who did not behave with the same degree of ignominy, it was only

4 'This book has been constructed with the technique of the novel'. The author, who has to find in it the richest means of expression and a subordination of language to the life which is not available to the historian, moreover adds: 'Fabrication has no part in this work. The facts, events and characters are all authentic. It would be puerile to invent when the truth goes so far beyond the imaginary [...]'.

5 Rousset, a survivor of Buchenwald, would later be the first to expose the horror of the Soviet gulag; his novel has not been translated into English [trans.].

Emila Medková
The Explosion 1959

because there wasn't enough time and the conditions were not
absolutely right; that only a difference of rhythm exists in the
decomposition of beings; that the slowness of the rhythm is the
prerogative of great characters; but that the compost, what there
is beneath us and which rises, rises, rises, is absolutely, frightfully,
the same thing. Who will believe it? All the more as those who
escaped did not know it either. They too will create Epinal images'
(pp.587–8).

* * *

In truth it is not the author who is speaking here but one of the
deported, whose meditation he is reporting: '... An enormous farce.
His own definitive way of reducing it to nothing'. Such, according to
Rousset, is the conclusion of the unfortunate individual who at the
last moment prefers poison to torture. But nothing is clear. And it
seems to me that seeking in the depths of reflection for a thought
which was possible in the mind of Pröll, who was about to die, the
author only came up against this fundamental difficulty: we can
never *establish* the limit; as soon as a person advances far into
suffering, he can no longer *be assured* that even one barrier which
has resisted might be broken. And what can precisely be admired
in the fact of the proof surmounted and in the victory of life is that,
discovering itself in the power of horror and knowing itself to be at
the mercy of physical misery, life nonetheless *assures itself* that,
through an excess of steadfastness in the face of filth, it will make
it prevail over the whole. But in the universe of suffering, baseness
and stench, each might have the *leisure* to measure the abyss, the
absence of limits of the abyss and this truth which obsesses and
fascinates.

* * *

One of David Rousset's most surprising reactions is the exaltation,
almost the euphoria, at the idea of participating in an outrageous
experience. Nothing more virile, nothing more *wholesome*. The
depth of horror – the suffering on one side and the debasement it
entails, and on the other the vile cruelty of the executioner, opening
onto a beyond of infinite possibilities – the depth of the horror of
things is offered to the human being as the truth to be discovered. In
other words it is still necessary for man to know, beyond the normal
state, the distant limit of the possible. But its price has to be paid...

* * *

But the one who recoils and does not want to see is hardly a man:
he has chosen as his foundation not to know what he is. In a sense
he knows it: he turns away from it! But he *does not want* to know it.
This negation of humanity is hardly less degrading than that of
the executioner. The executioner debases himself as he debases
his victim, especially because he strikes only in a cowardly way,
through ignorance (no one can, unless he is *inhuman*, reduce
himself to the state of blind nature; a torturer *is unaware* that he
is striking at himself, and adds to the suffering of the victim the
annihilation of the idea of humanity). But a *sensitive heart* is still
more cowardly and without doubt more formidable: his weakness
extends this ridiculous region in which humanity comes undone,

is no more than error and vanity, and asserts a garrulous foolishness.

* * *

Horror is evidently not truth: it is only an infinite possibility, having only death as a limit (death in fact has this significance in that being the termination of pain, it confers a definitive and inordinate meaning on it: it remains within us the impossible to the end, it suppresses any other possibility but pain and, to the extent that it limits it, it shirks consciousness). But man is formed from a possible abjection, his joy formed from possible pain; and if abjection and pain are not fully revealed to him by some means, this is only someone spineless disguised as a man, a pharisee, a clown or an old maid, just some stiff and tell-tale untruth, deadening the conscience with a failure.

* * *

Nausea is not at all what reveals things but the world is given to us only in contained nausea.

* * *

If this realm, that of the possibility of pain, were to be cut out of us, there would be a world of *milk and honey* that no one would laugh at any more. But in the end pain is there, the disgust of which determines us. And the knowledge of possible pain *humanises* us: it is what makes us so tender and hard, so cheerful and so thick with silence.

In this sense, David Rousset represents very precisely the point at which humanity fulfills itself: coming out of the test without hatred or complaint, with as much humour as lucidity.

* * *

What is worst in these sufferings of the deported is not the pain endured but the pain furiously desired by others. The pain that results from sickness or accident does not seem so horrible: the depth of horror lies in the resolution of those who require it. A world in which great pain strikes so many individuals but where the concordance of all would work to do away with them would be soothing. Multiplied debasement, ignominy and cowardice (gradually destroying the dread that is reason founding the civilised order) strikes us more harshly than naked suffering.

Yet the difference concerns the victim's suffering less than our own. We are threatened more if the barriers which opposed reasonable order to cruelty give way.

* * *

But this is not all.

We cannot be *human* without having noticed within us the possibility of suffering, as well as of abjection. But we are not simply the possible victims of executioners: the executioners are our fellow men. We still need to ask ourselves: is there nothing in our nature which might render so much horror impossible? And we really have to respond that in fact there is nothing. A thousand obstacles within us are opposed to it... Yet it is not impossible. Our possibility is therefore not just pain but extends to the torturer's rage. All these booted and bludgeoning killers, all of them cowardly and inexorable

6 The relevance of these names is unclear. They may have featured in contemporary news items, or possibly they were characters in the novel being reviewed [trans.].

7 Of course, I do not at all claim, proposing to go from this book to the limits of reflection, to have exhausted the interest of a work which is in truth a whole universe. The subject of Rousset's next book, *Lazare réssuscité*, will be the return from this other world to the normal world. How could the dark and immense experience of the camps not have brought everything into question? It is in every way and incessantly that one must return to it.

– the Toni Brunckens, the Heinzs, the Popenhauers[6] – are there to tell us with their irrefutable rage that cowardice alone is often the limit of violence and that there is no limit to cowardice.

And how would we not see, in the most painful silence, that such a possibility is only the most distant one, as well as the most inconceivable, but that it is *ours*? Nothing within us can be isolated, so that we might set it aside and which might allow us confidently to say: this was impossible, in any event. In any event? What we are has been dependent on circumstances which might have been very different: which might, for instance, have been those whose effect is Toni Bruncken.

* * *

It is clear that life is not reducible to the absurd and that nonetheless mankind's possibility overflows the limits of reason in every way. A sequence of reasonable acts is only ever one possibility among others, and the man that reason illuminates always perceives within him, at the same time, what is reasonable and beyond, but still within himself, which brings the reasonable into question.

It is then the essence of reason to be contestible, but the essence of contestation to be an effect of reason. Ultimately reason is probably only an insoluble investigation for itself and it can then seem that of itself it gives way to the absurd. It is nothing of the sort if one wants to see fairly dispassionately (perhaps also painfully). The reasonable is in fact what the absurd cannot destroy in that, of itself and internally, reason operates what the irrational does from outside: its unreserved questioning. But it is precisely there that man gets the upper hand over negation: he does not do so in some decisive victory, after which rest and sleep will be given to him; he does so through the doubt that it is the *awakening*.

Would it only be awakening if it illuminated nothing but a world of abstract possibilities? If it did not first of all awaken to the possibility of Auschwitz, to a possibility of stench and irremediable fury?

* * *

And in a given form of moral condemnation there is an evasive way of denial. On the whole we say: this abjection would not have happened if there had been no monsters. In this violent judgement the monsters of the possible are taken away. They are implicitly accused of going beyond the limits of the possible instead of it being seen that their excess precisely defines this limit. And it is no doubt possible, insofar as language is addressed to the masses, that this infantile negation seems effective, but fundamentally it changes nothing. It is even as vain to deny the incessant danger of cruelty as it would be to deny that of physical pain. Its effects are hardly obviated if in a banal way one makes this the prerogative of parties or races which, one imagines, have nothing human about them.

* * *

And of course, the awakening requiring a consciousness without respite of the possible horror is more than a means of avoiding it (or, when the moment comes, of being worthy of it). *Awakening* begins with humour, as well as with poetry. (And it is not the least significant meaning of Rousset's book that humour is also affirmed in it and that the nostalgia that emerges from it, never that of a sated happiness, would be that of movements drunk on poetry.)[7]

Gérard Legrand
Is Surrealism a Philosophy?

Ferdinand Alquié's book *The Philosophy of Surrealism*, published in 1955, was the first to treat the philosophical underpinnings of surrealism. It was greeted with two critical reviews in the journal *Le Surréalisme, même*, this one by Legrand and another by the philosopher Aimé Patri. Alquié himself was a professional philosopher who had been close to the surrealists since the late 1920s and, as Legrand notes, was respected by them for his intelligence and integrity. The book, however, disappointed the surrealists as they considered it to contain some fundamental misunderstandings if not wilful tendentiousness. This was especially so in not taking the surrealists' interpretation of Hegel seriously and in the way Alquié treated surrealism as a dissident part of humanist tradition rather than as a fundamental break with it. As in the other selections in this section, Legrand insists upon the absolute and even totalitarian quality of freedom which in fact is not just a human concept and should not exclusively be understood in human terms – it extends to the whole of existence (and, as Legrand states, it can even be understood in the absence of the human altogether).

Published in *Le Surréalisme même*, no.1, October 1956.

The *ambiguous* nature of surrealism (which has always seemed to me to be the clearest sign of its 'verisimilitude') could not be better illustrated than by the title of Ferdinand Alquié's book, *The Philosophy of Surrealism*. The author has long been familiar with surrealist thought and has repeatedly encountered it at the level of ardent action. A philosopher by profession, Alquié justifies his title by explaining it from the perspective by which he has placed himself to examine surrealism. But why end by discussing a 'Metaphysics of Absence', which one guesses to be his own concern, before concluding that 'Surrealism can lead to such a philosophy. But it is not the philosophy of surrealism'? This implies that somewhere there really is a philosophy of surrealism to be discovered, since it cannot be what Alquié explicitly claims as a point of observation.

Reading the book plunged me into great discomfort. Alquié never departs from the most sympathetic attitude towards the poetry and the vital attitudes of the movement. But, whenever he grapples with the theoretical problems which matter to him, a singular short-sightedness seems to seize one of us in respect either of his or my understanding of what I believe surrealism to be.

Alquié opposes 'authenticity to discourse (?), being to the object, the certain to the probable'. He believes that poetry recovers

8 And after the failure of the
marvellous 'Terror' of the
French Revolution.

the schema of a critical metaphysics derived from Plato, Descartes
and Kant. Is it not rather hasty to place not only Kant, indeed
Descartes, but also Plato, whose *conceptual mythology* so strongly
affected German romanticism, under the same sign? It is a haste
witnessed by reference to Spinoza's expression, 'at the level of God',
of the principle *Omnis determinatio [est] negatio*. This definition is
contained in the second book of the Ethics, and since Alquié sees
Spinoza above all as a 'Cartesian', he might have imagined that
it is only in the fifth book with the geometric method that the
great optician was led to the level of the Absolute. Yet *Essentia
particularis affirmativa*, the key formula of the fifth book, radically
contradicts what came before. As a philosopher of the will, as well
as of absolute ideality, Spinoza thus proves that the mind can attain
its essential quality (and therefore its universality) without for all
that ceasing to be individual.

But above all Alquié tries to separate surrealism from its
most important philosophical respondent: Hegel. According to
Alquié, surrealism is opposed to dialectical mediation, and its
vision of human 'indefinable reality', of which 'poetry is the direct
expression', is *Cartesian* without knowing it. Alquié even devotes
several pages to proving that Descartes is the precursor of the total
freedom of man proclaimed by surrealism, which cannot therefore
be found at the heart of the 'prisons' of Hegelianism.

Since the author is a friend of our movement, it pains me
to write that these pages recall what is worst in *The Rebel*, that
deplorable book by Albert Camus. The illusory fixation on the
dialectic at the 'master-slave' stage and the reduction of this stage
to certain uses made of it after Hegel constitute two 'errors' of
which our age is constantly guilty. It means forgetting that, as a
Marxist like Kojève confesses, Hegel died convinced that History
was dying with him (and from a certain perspective it could be
argued that nothing but a bloody and stagnant chaos has followed).[8]
It means neglecting how 'theological' and Marxist tendencies
have stifled part of the Hegelian left (Stirner, Feuerbach) from two
extremities. Finally it means to posit the principle of a posthumous
philosophical responsibility, a principle which appears to me at the
very least contestable.

Let's go further: even in the eyes of those who fight against
them without renouncing the Hegelian method, Stalinism and
fascism have a legitimate existence *in law*. Benjamin Péret has
written an admirable poem *against* the Tour de France: dialectically,
one could argue that the sporting event in question has a legitimate
existence, since only this existence rendered its negation, the
poem, possible.

The real philosophical reason for Alquié's antipathy to
Hegel is that he sees in the Absolute of the *system* a final synthesis
which 'retains all the determinations it has posed' and that it
is thus carried along by the flux of history without any possible
transcendence. But, aside from the fact that the whole of
Hegelianism ought not to be considered as simply a function of
Jena *Phenomenology*, it should not be forgotten that the dialectic

Is Surrealism a Philosophy?
Reproduced in Legrand's article

9 Thus, Spinoza's *Ethics* describes a 'progressive march' to the Absolute, while the *Treatise on the Improvement of the Understanding* proves that it is necessary first to install oneself, through a *leap* comparable to Gnostic 'revelation', within absolute rationality.

10 One in the Other: surrealist game in which one thing is described in terms of another; it is based upon the medieval theory of correspondences, which is that everything is contained within everything and that there is a fundamental unity to the universe [trans.].

has its inverse reflection in Gnosis, which begins with the Absolute and describes its disaggregation. Moreover, Hegel was convinced of the circularity of his system.[9]

Without therefore believing that Hegelianism might be the *only* philosophy utilisable by surrealism, I will remind the reader that the mediation which guarantees the richness of the concept is the same as that which presides over objective chance, in which natural necessity makes its way through the unconscious to coincide with the human necessity of desire (whose role in the *Phenomenology* is well known). The game of One in the Other[10] gives a poetic realisation to this duality.

Has Alquié not been duped by the mockery which Hegel heaped upon the ontological dogmatism of his predecessors? The synthesis admits a greater co-efficient, an increase of the consciousness of consciousness, which results from the 'father of all things' conflict. This is not simply descriptive, but creative, and from out of the heart of the immanence surges the transcendental song, when humanity grasps the Absolute in its irreducible duplicity. At the end of the *Encyclopedia* the 'proper division of the Idea' is unified in self-knowledge, 'in such a way that it is the nature of the thing, the notion which moves and develops, and that this movement is just as much the activity of knowledge: it is the eternal Idea, existing in and for itself, which is manifested, engenders itself eternally and eternally plays upon itself as absolute spirit'.

Alquié moreover challenges the surrealists' claim to the hyperlogical 'Knowledge' which crowns Hegelianism: in fact, Breton has never taken a position for or against this 'Knowledge'. He has never disapproved of the end of the *metaphysic* other than by charging it with having a religious meaning. He contented himself – in relation to the 'sublime point' of *Amour fou* in which certain pernicious antinomies are cancelled out – with declaring that one could not permanently remain there, something which in fact would be a biological impossibility.

If I can intervene here with my own personal experience, I will say that I am a surrealist precisely because 'I believe' in the legitimacy of an atheist metaphysic and the possibility of *Absolute Knowledge*. I 'believe' in the apprehension of a superior *empire* in which reason is annihilated, but annihilates itself only in its own admiration of needing to abandon explanation so as to be better able to 'contemplate' and *exist*. As an adolescent I found myself responding with the greatest distrust to philosophers until I discovered the Greeks, Spinoza and Hegel, who alone seemed to me not to be lovers of abstract psychology or the positivist citadel. At that time I had only a vague idea of surrealist poetry, but what struck me with Hegel was not the discovery of becoming but the will to grandeur and universality, something almost unknown since the Ancients. It was moreover in this way that his adulators and detractors of the years 1860-70 (Taine, Vacherot and even Fouillée) considered him and who, closer to him than we are, were more struck by the titanic aspect of the monument. If this uncompleted monument has collapsed, surrealism might be 'the appearance of ivy within the ruins'.

It is not by chance that I just mentioned Albert Camus. At the root of the hostility Alquié manifests towards Hegelian philosophy there is a *certain* conception not only of surrealism but of all thought. Admittedly, Alquié sincerely loves poetry and revolt, but he participates in that same state of mind which treats the *human* (understood in the vaguest sense) as the golden rule of all estimation. It is symptomatic that he prefers to consider surrealism as a 'conception of man' rather than as a 'vision of the world'. Alquié was recently defined, in the conclusion of a book on *The Desire for Eternity*, as giving an equal share to the absolute and the relative in the life of 'the one who proposes to be a man'. This definition is more philanthropic than philosophical.

At the risk of amazing even some of our friends, I formally contest the fact that surrealism *could be* any sort of humanism (or 'super-humanism'). I argue that freedom can be considered and even conceptualised entirely without taking into account the *human*, a hybrid of medieval Thomism, post-Renaissance scepticism (Montaigne) and the 'open' morals of academic syncretism. Surrealism is not a philosophy: it is the crossroads, the castle in which several philosophies meet and which have significance only as they are mutually completed before the blazing hearth of poetry. However, if it might in particular circumstances coincide with contemporary humanisms for the defence of interests and values belonging to 'the mind', it is not because humanity bore these values, but, in my opinion, for these values and the mind itself. Surrealism is well and truly an order of *totalitarian* thought; its experience is that of the Absolute, with all the approaches and consequences this implies, and, in this capacity, Hegelian philosophy is its essential aid. Placing no particular faith in man, at best it repeats in common with Stirner: 'I am a man absolutely as the earth is a star. It would be just as ridiculous to force the earth to be a true star as to give me the task of being a true man'.

Georges Henein
Freedom as Nostalgia and as Project

At a time when freedom is today invoked as strongly as ever in service of servitude, this important essay from the mid-1960s by the Egyptian surrealist Georges Henein remains resonant as well as prescient. The development of technology has not followed quite the repressive path he expected – at least insofar as the development of the internet has in some ways made the sort of State control Henein denounces untenable – but it has served other, arguably more insidious, forms of control, and it can hardly be denied that the processes he describes have become more entrenched in the intervening years. His insistence that our emphasis should be on preservation rather than development is one that is barely heard let alone heeded, notwithstanding the economic crisis that has made the consequences of relying on ever greater growth clear. Even though he was writing before the neo-liberal diktat was imposed upon us (placing economic striving above human needs), Henein's warning that 'to produce, no matter at what price, most often signifies to produce at the price of humanity' could now hardly be starker. Like Bataille, Henein locates moral responsibility in recognition of our own complicity in inhumanity, something which requires from us a refusal to look away. We need rather, as he says, to inscribe freedom within our lifelines.

First published in *Les Cahiers de l'Oronte*, Beirut, 1965; reprinted in Georges Henein, *Oeuvres: Poèmes, récits, essais, articles et pamphlets*, Paris: Donoël, 2006.

Our age is founded on a disposition towards misunderstandings. For a long time we have been committed to a kind of political Pirandellism by which we agree to name things by what they are not, so as not to have to think we have been deserted by the truth. Internal being and being in the world no longer communicate other than by the intervention of *neutral* words, words that have become at once incantatory, necessary and vain, and which are like a waiting room for multiple possible meanings. This language of absence is, in certain respects, crueller than falsehood.

This is the case for the two terms 'liberty' and 'liberation', constantly linked as they are in discourse, but even more often dissociated in reality. Liberation is a labour, liberty a state, a sovereign disposition of existence. It is more natural for labour to engender other forms of labour in constantly renewed fresh struggles, rendered common to any struggle by internal logic and constraints, than for it to cross the point of mutation, the point at which the accumulation of effort should lead to a non-partisan exaltation of life.

We are contemporaries of at least three great revolutions:

- in the realm of the psychology of behaviour, the Freudian revolution sought to free man of his inhibitions, obstacles and internal demons;
- in the social realm, the Marxist revolution (or what was more or less generally inspired by Marxism) claims to free man from economic exploitation;
- in the scientific realm, the Einsteinian revolution, by focusing on the sources of energy, by effecting the fission of the atom, has opened a decisive breach in the unknown and endowed humanity with powers which, like the secrets of ancient religions, arouse as much devotion as terror.

The moment thus seems to have arrived for us to ask ourselves to what extent these successive (and sometimes concomitant) revolutions contribute to freedom as such, or even if they have contributed to it at all.

Freudianism has advanced knowledge and has rendered the individual attentive to that fringe of night in which his life replenishes the stock of delirium and desire, but he has also

16

Robert Lagarde
Reproduced in *Le Surréalisme,
même*, no.5, Spring 1959

11 Kitman, or 'ketman': lying by omission; an Islamic notion which justifies lying to unbelievers in order to defeat them; in modern usage it tends to refer to occasions when people say one thing in public while believing the opposite (especially as a means of survival in totalitarian regimes) [trans.].

instituted a discipline, with its formulae, instructions and projects, and from this no doubt we get that mannerism of authorised neurosis which refuses to leave the stage and in the end usurps the place of true problems.

Marxism has produced combative organisations and, where it has triumphed, immense administrations of society.

Science proliferates its laboratories, gets carried away and gets frightened. And it seems to me that every morning many scholars have to examine their hands as though expecting to see the stigmata of consuming knowledge appear.

It has fundamentally been a matter (from the poetic tumult and great refusals of the nineteenth century onwards) of unleashing a new man: not a superman who will fulfil the void of legend, but someone with mastery and clarity whose existence would no longer be caught up in the internal knots and be humiliated when faced with the money or opacity of the world. This movement has undergone alterations which render it unrecognisable in our eyes and which force us today to pose problems no longer of development but of preservation. This concern is manifested, moreover, in a half-conscious way, in the initiatives of certain international organisms like Unesco which strive to save the original forms of expression by which the personality and the continuity of ethnic groups is constituted from annihilation. But to pose the question in this way at the level of folklore or specific cultural signs is to avoid the key question: that of the general restoration of freedom.

What has occurred since the beginning of our adventure? The method and the means put to work have closed in again on the intelligence and have given birth, one could say, to an intelligence of the inside which, on awakening, has known nothing but ever more extended requirements of methods and means – man himself henceforth being considered as secondary. The interpretation of these requirements acts more *upon* man than *for* man. If we might desire, when the time comes, to inflect or nuance this action (or more simply still to avoid it) then the method becomes a demand, instrumentation becomes structure and the work of deliverance becomes a work of conditioning.

The word 'freedom' resounds almost everywhere in the world, in public squares and in grand ceremonies, and the whole force of the word constitutes a watchword, in other words a commandment. But, almost everywhere, just as much, by a sort of dialectical precaution, we witness a conditioning of humanity, a predetermination of its projects and actions, and, in the end, but only in the end, of its silent thought, of its share of silence, of its 'kitman'.[11] The reduction, the casting of individual thought, represent the last phase of the apparently free man's intoxication.

Let's pause for a moment at an idea which has assumed so much importance in the debate which concerns us. It is the idea of alienation. In the nineteenth century we found out that man does not belong to himself. By selling his activity and his intelligence, man introduced a devouring foreign power into his life. Hegel, Marx and Stirner all effectively recognised that there is something here which goes further than deformation or mutilation – something exclusive, which could be soothed only by dispossession. They saw that by alienating a part of himself, in certain economic conditions, man was condemning himself to alienate everything. It then becomes the entire person who becomes debased to the rank of merchandise, who is manipulated, treated, augmented, diminished, sold off and exported like a sack of coal.

This affirmation summarises and defines a situation which is not disorder, but reversed human order, the Law of the absurd.

'The liberty of humanity in the face of the universe', wrote Ernst Jünger, 'is attested first of all in the word; the gods get their name from mankind and it is mankind that calls them by this name'. I will add that the liberty of mankind in revolt begins at the moment he clearly sets out, for himself and others, the origin of his misfortune and the monster against which he lays down his challenge. The revolt which has arisen in the footsteps of Marx is presented, in its first phase, as a Spartacist uprising of those who want recognition as combatants, as founders of free life. Events become complicated from the moment revolt appropriates the apparatus of power, enters the crucible of the State and, without renouncing its own aims, agrees to hand them over them to organisms which would only know how to obey their particular laws of propulsion and expansion.

The State, invested with these aims which are generous but apt to become blurred, disalienates in its way and according to the degrees of urgency and duties of which it is the sole judge. According to many indications, we can then see that to disalienate does not, for all that, mean to give humanity back to itself. We do not willingly restore so precious a good. And if History is an accomplishment of the Idea through the mastery of things, if it progresses to supreme unity along the ways of the Universal State, it is quite evident (and this is its great art) that man must at once be conquered and enlightened, for he is the one, once and for all, who will build the monuments of power. Conquered and enlightened, he undertakes works before which critical reason would perhaps declare itself incompetent, precisely because they overwhelm his freedom, because they return him to a position of submission. Clearly what then intervenes is a substitute for the sacred. An amazing thing: never since the desacralisation of society has the notion of sacrifice been so pathetically invoked as today. Sometimes five or six years of one life, sometimes a whole generation, is consigned for sacrifice and, beyond the inevitable appeal to historical development, we believe this sacrifice is entirely aimed at a whole background of religious emotionalism which the decline of the sacred had made redundant.

Man therefore steps aside, and yet this expression does not sufficiently account for the change which takes place and which is above all a change of assignment. He became transferable, inarticulable and easy to exploit. Here we see him fortified because rendered significant again, exalted by the newly acquired sense of

Anthony Earnshaw
Reproduced in *Les Lèvres nues*,
no.10 (new series), August 1974

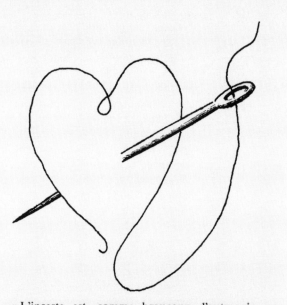

« L'inceste est, comme beaucoup d'autres in-
corrections, une circonstance très poétique. » —
Percy Shelley *(Dessin d'Anthony Earnshaw)*.

its historical function. He was, according to the former analysis, an object with a vocation to exist. Today he is a being called upon to objectivise himself in the State. We are entitled to a lengthy examination about the real condition of the 'disalienated'. There seems to be, for this man freed of his masters, a melancholy of freedom which authorises more hope for the future than the theoreticians of renewal can squander.

The theme of alienation finds its ultimate illustration in the hecatombs signed by Eichmann.[12] Eichmann had no ideas about man. Every idea comprises a possibility of diversion. Philosophy, in a certain sense, is the alibi of vagabonds. For Eichmann, anguish began with man's uselessness. And it is a State anguish, as there are State reasons. As gross matter, man must serve grossly. It cannot be a matter either of distracting him or of amusing himself with it, but of fixing the rate of exchange of this common currency. If a man is exchangeable with a car wheel, ten or a hundred men, according to their age and degree of vitality, with a completely new lorry, or a thousand with the latest locomotive model, then all is well with the world. This is the decisive bartering, the placing of existence in indifference, the insertion of human unity into a system conceived for its annulment.

We know that these practices have been tarnished and declared abominable. Let's not be too relieved, however. The Eichmann case is somewhat similar to the scandal which shamed the families of whose horrors we were unaware because they lived with curtains drawn. But the scandal having passed, are we

---

12 Adolf Eichmann (1906–1962), Nazi SS officer, one of the major organisers of the Holocaust; snatched by the Israeli secret service in 1960 from Argentina, where he was in hiding, and condemned to death for crimes against humanity following a sensational trial [trans.].

guaranteed that the spirit of economic lynching which had for once been brought into the open will not rage again (perhaps more warily) in other places and on other occasions? How can we convince ourselves that the period of these hideous operations is forever over?

The desacralisation of the world which has continued every day since 1789 has not, as one would like to think, entailed the radical repudiation and eradication of the great tutelary myths (including, for example, the myth of original sin), but rather their transformation, their fall to earth. One could almost speak here of relay or relief, so upsetting is it to see the way so many modern States subscribe to the 'myth of production'. When economic fact becomes an absolute, the effort of work becomes, by the same token, a just punishment. To produce, no matter at what price, most often means to produce at the price of humanity. And henceforth this will leave us dangerously close to this same notion of barter even though we now know the extremities to which it is at risk of leading.

Myths transform themselves. The power they were immobilising is doubtless liberated but immediately moves towards new centres of use. The problem of free choice is precipitously conjured away, and humanity finds itself either faced with a set of commandments, or entangled in a net of conditioning, each thread of which is strained to serve its purposes.

Today authority is the result of injunction and suggestion. And the principal suggestion consists in persuading even those who submit to authority that this is at once their emanation and their strength – that it is, in other words, the projection of the freedom they do not exercise.

There are thus two ways in which freedom is lost. There is a violent deprivation, a wrenching, where there is tyranny. And a conventional deprivation, if I may call it this, through the transfer or tacit assigning of freedom to another (in other words, the State) where there is an enveloping of consciousness, multiple or incessant entreaties in the name of an experience or a myth, set in play by History or to be undertaken in the future. But while on the one hand freedom is not an endorsable cheque (a negotiable deed which one can renounce but not exorcise without return), on the other hand, rare as times of complete respiration, of unequivocal freedom, have been in the annals of the human species, these moments suffice to nourish a tenacious nostalgia against which no amount of violence can hope to prevail.

It is often said, we hear it a lot: why should we be concerned about the freedom of one or another people, when these people have never had the slightest idea of its meaning? According to this argument, freedom would be the reflection and accompaniment of an enlightened civilisation. In this way, some human beings have no interest in freedom, never having conceived of making use of it and not suspecting its significance in the slightest. Nothing is more arbitrary than such a classification which responds to the criterion of morose respectability of minds beribboned in their comfort.

13 Raymond Abellio
(1907–1986) was a French
esoteric philosopher who
collaborated at a distance
with the surrealists during the
1950s. Despite the importance
Henein attributes to it, *La
Fosse de Babel* has never been
translated into English – in
fact none of Abellio's works
appear to have been published
in English [trans.].

14 Meister Eckhart
(c.1260–c.1328), German
theologian, philosopher and
mystic [trans.].

Freedom has no age. It is not the fact of colour or reason. Neither is it the sign of a particularly remarkable evolution. It belongs to a person as much as the sound of his own voice. It is, at the level of the immediate gesture, his means of choosing one path rather than another, his attitude faced with a landscape. It is his poetry and his portion of mystery and his difference from his brother. There is no one who is outside of freedom or who might not be called upon one day – even if only for a single moment – to meet with it and to grow within it.

Conditioning has just been mentioned. Like the total war of which it is one of the most evil continuations, the work of conditioning implies the constant, co-ordinated and simultaneous recourse to all available means (news, radio, television, school, spectacle, cultural activities and so on) to orient the will of the citizen and mobilise his energy. In this respect, as we are passing through a rather dark period, many things warn us. Let us take, among a thousand possible examples, a novel that is exceptionally important both for its quality and the density of the content it proposes. In 1962 *The Babel Pit* by Raymond Abellio[13] is a book of testimony, much as Andre Malraux's *The Human Condition* had been in 1932. At thirty years' distance, it is not a matter of comparing talents, but temptations. In *The Human Condition*, man finds his freedom in the total and fiery risk of revolutionary action into which he throws himself with his heart bared. In *The Babel Pit*, in contrast, everything occurs in an intelligent phenomenological coldness. The combination of Husserl, esoteric science and the most modern terrorist spirit clearly leaves little place for freedom. Its spontaneity is decapitated by calculation. Here death loses its aura of tragedy, abandoned as it is to the rigour of killers. In it, thought's objectives are nothing but the organisation of invisible centres of omnipotence, the acquisition of powers, acting from a distance over others and introducing themselves into their existence in order to dominate them in some way.

These bold speculations of characters who seek a ferment of constraint in doctrines and stay in the mind as in a principle of terror, might have seemed rather gratuitous in times other than ours. For these conspirators readily invoke Meister Eckhart[14] before sullying their hands. From the first pages of the novel, we are, moreover, informed about the nature of the action Drameille, the authorising officer of this conjunction, proposes to take: 'To participate in the burning of the world, to aid it, to bring light to these underworlds where, not yet having been received as light, it will be transformed into flame'. And this, which is equally explicit: 'Fundamentally playing on the future unification of knowledge, Drameille invented a game which would integrate all games... accept all motives, giving preference to none, and espousing only an ultimate and apocalyptic image: the fight of all against all in the full consciousness of all'. From this perspective, the few people who refuse just to be simple spectators of violence lend their passion to the development of powers and constitute themselves less as a secret society than as an egoistic caste of acting thinkers.

By silencing this tumult for a moment, the underlying theme could be isolated roughly as the following: since terror is henceforth installed in the world, it is important not to leave it exclusively to mediocre practitioners and uninspired hangmen. And in this we see a coupling which belongs most particularly to our age and which will perhaps define it becoming clearer: that of knowledge and terror. Admittedly, terror is not a recent phenomenon. Concentration camps, deportation and torture have a long history which is lost in the gleam of ancient pyres. It is the unending history of the hunting of humans. What is new, on the other hand, is the Hiroshima bomb, which is the apparition of a sort of objective terror which reaches into consciousness even before grazing bodies, which engenders fright even though it is only latent – an electronic, nuclear, spatial, terror, which is supported by scientific knowledge, from which it draws its prestige. In this respect a complicity is intertwined whose unravelling no declaration of intent will allow. Knowledge, in general, reaches the culmination of its Faustian movement. From control of man to the transformation of life, to the rupture of the world, it maintains a superior and confusing efficacy in the face of which wise people reflect and simple people give way to panic, like those peasants in India who hastily abandon their houses and run to the mountain because something tells them that we are on the brink of the apocalypse.

In this bruised and divided universe, where the needs of organisation are transformed into reasons for oppression, in which intelligence, to remain effective, assumes every means so as no longer to be itself but just one means among others, in which everything becomes possible and in which so few things are allowed, in this amazing and provincial universe in which optimism and panic are twinned to the same extent as knowledge and terror, what has happened to freedom and how can one be a free person?

Perhaps, to incarnate freedom a little, it is necessary for people today (against the solicitations of all kinds of which it is the object) to rediscover solitude – that is, their autonomous strength of thought and action. And not by withdrawing from the world, which would be ridiculous and unworthy, but on the contrary by living intensely each moment of the world as a whole, by bringing critical contestation where uniformity tends to be established, by situating oneself at the cutting edge of research but without hesitating to smash this edge as soon as it forms itself into a conformism of knowledge.

We have already noted how, in certain circumstances, liberty is reduced to its own caricature when it is not sacrificed, quite casually, to the imperatives of production and planning. For the complete interventionist, freedom is a luxury which complicates the ordering of human affairs. He considers it natural that it, along with consumer goods, spare time and travel, should be rationed. The satisfactions it procures can be adjourned, postponed for the day when the city will be constructed, which would no doubt be an acceptable perspective if freedom were just a source of satisfactions.

----

15 Giovanni Gentile
(1875-1944), Italian
neo-Hegelian Idealist
philosopher and
politician. Described as 'the
philosopher of Fascism', he
wrote A *Doctrine of Fascism*
(1932) for Mussolini [trans.].

For the same reasons, the attitude of those who seek to
preserve their capacity for resistance, their right to think on their
own, is considered seriously suspect. People laugh when this
solitary person goes by. They speak of ivory towers. They impute
him with the prejudice of non-participation in the common destiny.
The spirit of participation means, in effect, that each person is
founded in a current of organised life, in the general enterprise in
which everyone finds themselves shoulder to shoulder. But, what is
more, the experience of a mass regime which lays claim to this
fusion in a militant whole helps us to establish an essential
distinction between the idea of solidarity and that of participation.
The withdrawal enacted by the person who insists on thinking
alone does not release him from his duty of moral and affective
solidarity towards his brothers. To participate is another thing.
When the mind and the heart are at peace with the world, there is
no problem in participation. There is, in contrast, one (and a
singularly dramatic one) when to participate means to consent to
enter into the mechanisms of an action to which others are already
committed, but which is clearly judged from the start as being
conceived for oppression and not for freedom. Placed in such a
situation, anyone who preserves any moral concern is better able
to serve his brothers from without than from within. And by not
participating he undergoes trial by laceration, but remains, in spite
of everything, in a small zone of clarity. And this clarity is the token
of a return to enlarged debate and the condition, for others, of a
new freedom.

Participation is bitter but it may nevertheless sometimes
have advantages – especially for intellectuals. Freedom is difficult,
at least as difficult as its indissoluble partner, truth; because there
is no freedom in falsehood, no more than there is in compromises
with conscience or in shades of complacency which allow one to
serve power well without losing one's own self esteem.

Around the Mediterranean (the great reservoir of creative
nostalgia) there have been and remain many exemplary individuals
whose attachment to freedom continues to call for long reflection.
It is enough for me to evoke here the memory of two men, unequally
known, who, in the night of oppression, each marked out his
glimmer of light: Benedetto Croce and Lauro de Bosis.

The personality of Benedetto Croce is too well known to need
repeating. A philosopher, a historian, critic, publicist, Croce would
not have been the complete humanist worthy of our respect if he
had not affirmed, in every circumstance, his need for freedom, had
he not in anticipation challenged all knowledge which was not
founded on the exercise of freedom. Turning away neither from the
real nor from what was actual, Croce never separated knowledge
from the event. Brought up a Hegelian, he retained, in essence, the
ideological structures of Hegelianism, but knew how to forestall the
possessive idea of the State, which spared him in time from the
temptation of recognising a phenomenon responding to the will of
History in fascism. Another Italian philosopher, Giovanni Gentile[15]
(equally moulded by Hegel) succumbed to this temptation when, by

an intellectual process which was the inverse of Croce's, he made freedom an attribute of the State. The abyss which opened between the two thinkers who had, so to speak, worked at the same construction site, exalted the same masters and originally assumed the same positions, is tragically revelatory of the ambiguity that the destiny of intelligence suffered in the twentieth century. Hegel, Marx, Nietzsche and Sorel catapulted thought towards the horizon; they armed generations of theoreticians, but these weapons have not only served to destroy ancient conventions, they have also exacerbated the real civil war which sets their own disciples, their faithful interpreters, against one other. In witnessing this unleashing, which sometimes goes as far as murder (Trotsky and Gentile were both assassinated), we understand better how freedom might be celebrated equally by regimes which have nothing in common other than their vocation for political nominalism and their shameful exploitation of vocabulary. Confronted with the confusion so many partisan exegetes maintain, freedom today must be inscribed in a lifeline – failing which it will no longer exist anywhere. Freedom that is given by the law and taken away by decree, the freedom of mass gatherings to cheer the right leader at the right time, the freedom of carefully selected folkloric specimens to announce to the tribune their joy at being free is really of no interest to anyone: between that freedom and lived freedom there is as much difference as between criticism and self-criticism. If falsehood darkens humanity, parody debases it. With freedom to order, with self-criticism, we are entering the realm of simulacrum. The words that have been spoken in this, the gestures that have been made, have lost all relation with what should be their true object. Or rather, a final relation subsists, and it is a tarnished relation. With spontaneity abolished, all that remains is to humiliate through parody the nostalgic image of a possible freedom, or rather this faculty of judgement which one is first of all invited to turn against oneself according to a gymnastics whose rules are fixed on high.

Benedetto Croce had no interest in parody and simulation. His lifeline is hewn neither from denials nor from compromises. It is not erased in the dust. While the full weight of fascism dominated Italy, he refused honours and employment, maintained his rigour, continued to publish a more or less private critical bulletin, constituted around him a circle of attentive friends, and initiated young people who approached him in a spirit of debate. This man – bent with age himself – alone represented the health of his country. He was alone, isolated, under surveillance; what he could still say, he said not in the name of a party, but of the intelligence which rebelled and retained its pride. But Croce's privilege, like that of Pasternak later, both of whom were deprived of all means of retort, is to fascinate the adversary, to place him in a state of moral inferiority.

The most amazing and significant episode of Croce's life was what occurred in September 1943. It was the moment of the armistice concluded by the Badoglio government when the greatest

confusion prevailed over the country. In the depths of this
confusion, certain individuals suddenly acquired an extreme
importance, among them Benedetto Croce. From one day to
the next he became a strategic objective. The two incumbent
commanding officers, Allied and German, stuck little flags on
the map to devise the best way to effect his kidnap. Gangs of
commandos were prepared for this operation. Finally, the British
commandos landed on the Sorrento shore, ending up in Croce's
villa, carrying off the old philosopher and getting him to safety.
The episode is remarkable in showing the extent to which a
solitary person – but someone who has taken up the burden of
freedom and had, in some way, given it a home – concerns the
whole world.

In contrast to Benedetto Croce, the figure of Lauro de Bosis
is blurred and distant, threatening to slip away into an unjust
oblivion. His poems are now hardly ever mentioned, here and
there appearing in a few obscure anthologies, and only if those
chronicling resistance to fascism grant him a space in their works
(though they often don't).

Like Croce, Lauro de Bosis operated freelance, without any
relationship with organised parties. As a poet, fascist violence
seemed to him an unacceptable outrage against the poetry of life.
He still believed in the illuminating clarity of the individual gesture,
in the crazy contagion of hope. Acting alone, with few resources at
his disposal, he spent months patiently learning how to pilot an
airplane. By getting help from friends he managed to put together
the amount he needed to buy a small tourist plane. Then, one
October afternoon in 1931, de Bosis, all alone this time, climbed
into the cabin of his tiny machine parked on a Corsican field, and
calmly flew towards Rome. He would take his personal challenge
to the power whose progress nearly all of Europe then viewed with
benevolent interest. It was the period when people were amazed
that the Italian trains ran on time. As they say, nothing beats
exactitude. De Bosis was also exact in his own way. He flew over a
twilit Rome. Looking down, he could recognise gardens, fountains
and ruins with their long dislocated arms. He descended to roof
level and, above the Corso, scattered the amazed passers-by with
multicoloured papers which they were too afraid to pick up. And
then, his mission accomplished, Lauro de Bosis vanished into the
distance, lost in the night, between Posillipo, perhaps, and the
Italian sea.

They never found the body of he who died in this way, not as
the poet of freedom (because poets of freedom abound and are
generally well paid) but as a shooting star, as a pure explosion of
being which signs its death with an ardent and free hand.

When the reasons for pessimism appear to us overwhelming
in the world we pass through, we should think again about Lauro
de Bosis and tell ourselves that no matter how many attempts are
made to reduce human stature, there are still people, as numerous
as they are unknown, who refuse – people who perpetuate the
meaning of this necessary challenge.

René Magritte
Reproduced in
*Variétés: Le Surréalisme
en 1929*, June 1929

If freedom exists in the shadow of nostalgia, it also exists in a state of project. Because the moment is approaching when the enormous enterprise of organisation under development almost everywhere and which seems to be the major ambition of our time, will pose more problems that it will solve. With or without the aid of electronic automatism (and if this aid is required it is really a belated defence mechanism) there is a point of organisation one cannot go beyond when, becoming too vast for humanity, it condemns itself to sterility and decline. Such a crisis point represents the possibility for freedom to be inserted in tomorrow's universe.

For the moment, we are still in the heart of tragedy. Intelligence has launched itself. It has knocked over the barriers, flattened the enclosure walls and approached the threshold of the absolute. From Leonardo da Vinci to artificial satellites, a crazy lurch carries humanity ahead of itself. To the question, 'where are we, really?' we have to reply: 'ahead.'

We may today be able to dominate things, as though from an eagle's nest. And yet, to the extent that our inventions release us from our gangue of ignorance and immobility, other shackles form and multiply and hold us in a trap. The vulgar absurdity of modern state control resides in this. Between the eagle's nest and the mousetrap, I am convinced that anyone totally conscious at once of his past and of its intoxicating novelty, has a certain vocation for the eagle's nest.

I do not exclude the likelihood that the situations we face may, for a time, darken still further. It is possible that freedom will be encircled by mystery and assume the (doubly difficult) character of an initiatory virtue. But I will also say that people, solitary but numerous, who know how not to weaken in their thinking, who struggle, each according to their ability, so that the spirit of contestation is not extinguished, so that formal rituals, especially those that are avant-garde, are not substituted for the incessant critique of the movement, I say that these people are preparing a great clarification. They are preparing the rediscovery of freedom, whose youth is only just beginning.

Elisabeth Lenk
The Hidden Being

Over the past half century the Heidegger controversy has constituted one of the most significant debates concerning intellectual responsibility and the nature of freedom. This essay, published in the surrealist journal *La Brèche* by a student of Adorno, is a further contribution towards understanding the moral parameters of surrealism. Lenk opens her text with a quotation from the eighteenth-century writer George Christoph Lichtenberg. Another of his aphorisms, used by the surrealists to introduce the first issue of *La Brèche*, is equally pertinent here: 'Judge people not by their opinions, but by what their opinions make of them.' This succinctly expresses the surrealist refusal to separate theory and practice and sets up the backdrop against which Lenk makes her critique of Heidegger, precisely that he separates them so as to play one against the other.

First published in *La Brèche: action surréaliste*, no.6, June 1964.[16]

A madman who imagines himself to be a prince does not differ from the prince who is in fact mad because the latter is a negative prince, while the former is a negative madman. Considered without their insignia they resemble each other (Lichtenberg)

In our century unreason appears to have recourse to ruses once – according to Hegel – used by reason. Hardly had France been freed from the Occupation than it reappeared where one least expected it: at the very heart of ideas which had been the intellectual armour of the Resistance. It was discovered, not without embarrassment, that Heidegger, the spiritual father of so many humanisms, had been a Nazi sympathiser. Did this represent just a momentary error of a great philosopher or the failure of a philosophy? This question has left European philosophical thought with a wound which reopens whenever it is touched.

Heidegger himself was the first to be ready to pour on the balm. In an interview accorded to Alfred de Towarnicki in 1946,[17] the philosopher renowned for his flights above the clouds of the 'One', was unembarrassed about entering into very down-to-earth details. He detailed heroic actions (such as sending flowers to the Jewish Husserl in 1933, accompanied by a very kind letter from Mrs Heidegger, or the removal, on his instructions, of an anti-Semitic poster put up within Freiberg University campus) in order

16 This essay elicited replies from Aimé Patri and Jean Beaufret, which were published in no.8 of *La Brèche* along with a response from Elizabeth Lenk and an editorial comment under the title 'Suite de l'affaire Heidegger' [trans.].

17 *Les Temps modernes*, no.4, 1946.

18 See *France-Observateur*, 12, 19 and 31 December 1963, 9 and 23 January and 6 February 1964.

19 Étiemble (1909–2002), French essayist and novelist [trans.].

20 *France-Observateur*, 16 January 1964.

21 See 'Letter on Humanism', translated by J. Glenn Grey, in Martin Heidegger, *Basic Writings*, ed. David Farrell Krell, London: Routledge, 1993.

22 Alfred Grosser (born 1925), German-French sociologist and political scientist [trans.].

23 The second part of the book remains in manuscript form.

24 A Nazi institution corresponding to the STO in France [STO: Service du travail obligatoire, the body set up under the Vichy regime to oversee the deportation of French workers for forced labour in Germany – trans.].

25 *Les Temps modernes*, no.14, 1946.

to prove that only 'responsibility to the West' had forced on him the sacrifice of retaining his chair in spite of his 'increasing opposition to the regime'.

Today, at the time of a recrudescence of the Heidegger debate,[18] M. Beaufret repeats this version. Not content with having sent three letters to *France-Observateur* on the subject, he announced 'a publication bringing together all of the texts on the controversy which followed Étiemble's[19] article in *France-Observateur* of 28 November 1963 and which will be subjected to the reader's good sense'.[20] Without otherwise taking a risk, M Beaufret might have been expected to try at any price to save a reputation which to some extent has been linked to his own ever since the 'Letter on Humanism' Heidegger sent him in 1945.[21] In the meantime, it seems useful to recall – if only briefly – the facts to which Alfred Grosser[22] and Armand Ettedgui have alluded to and to consider their significance.

In 1927 Heidegger, then a student of Husserl, published *Being and Time*, an event which classed him as the master thinker of a new philosophy. Emerging from then current academic trends (Husserlian phenomenology, Neo-Kantianism and *Lebensphilosophie* or the philosophy of life) he intended not simply to continue them but to effect the 'destruction of the history of Ontology'. Going back to pre-Socratic sources, Heidegger claimed to have wrenched the fundamental question, that of Being, out of its millenarian oblivion. If this philosophy evokes phenomena as concrete as anguish, anxiety and many others, this should not be misunderstood. It is not a question of purely ethical and psychological categories as French existentialism understood it but of milestones on the path towards Being. It follows that politics has no place in this philosophy, as it has been given to us.[23] We find here the 'poverty' of the German ideology denounced by Marx, and in this Heidegger conforms to the observation made by Hegel.

An abyss separates the spirit of the world from realisations. To reach one from the other there remains for Heidegger only the leap of 'resolution' (*Entschlossenheit*) which, like any dangerous leap, must be made with eyes closed.

In May 1933, Heidegger leapt. Having never been interested in politics and (let's give him the benefit of the doubt) without having read even a sentence of *Mein Kampf*, he took the step of joining the National Socialist party and, as elected rector of Freiberg University, delivered his infamous lecture, 'The Self-affirmation of the German University' in which, with the certainty of a sleepwalker, he began from the outset to use a Nazi tone, while remaining true to the categories of his philosophy.

Karl Löwith, one of Heidegger's students, said of this discourse: '"labour service"[24] and "military service" overlapped with "knowledge service", in such a way that at the end of the lecture the listener hesitated about whether he should open Diels's *Pre-Socratics* or sign up to join the ranks of the Stormtroopers'.[25] Heidegger called upon German students to leave the freedom of the university and subordinate themselves entirely to the Führer.

26 This speech was translated in *Médiations*, no.3, 1961. Jean-Pierre Faye translated several Nazi texts by Heidegger for this book. Earlier signs of his Nazi leanings are to be found in the bibliography by Pierre Trottignon, 'L'Oeuvre de Heidegger', *Revue de l'enseignement philosophique*, vol.14, no.2, December 1963 – January 1964.

27 Albert Schlageter (1894–1923) engaged in a campaign of sabotage in the Ruhr (French-occupied German territory) after the First World War, for which he was executed. He was later lionised by and became one of the heroes of the Nazi Party [trans.].

28 *Freiburger Studentenzeitung*, 3 November 1933.

29 'The Heidegger Case', *Les Temps modernes*, no.22, 1947.

30 In Germany this sentence had, in 1953, provoked a discussion. Jürgen Habermas, a philosopher of Adorno's school, attacked Heidegger in the *Frankfurter Allgemeine Zeitung* while Mr Lewaiter defended the philosopher in *Die Zeit* and finally Heidegger himself concluded in a letter sent to this weekly: 'It would have been easy to cross out for the publication the phrase chosen at random, as well as others. I did not do so. On the one hand, historically, the phrases belong to the course, on the other hand, I am convinced that the course supports the said phrases' (see the book by Paul Hühnerfeld, *In Sachen Heidegger*, Hamburg, 1959).

The freedom he called 'inauthentic' would be replaced by links to which services correspond.[26] The lecture ends on a note of pathos with a very free translation of a Platonic sentence: 'All grandeur lies in the storm.'

Throughout that year Heidegger repeatedly lent his prestigious voice to National Socialism. So he extolled the German student Schlageter[27] who, during outrages conducted in the Ruhr in 1923, was arrested and shot by the French authorities. Heidegger considered that Schlageter had suffered 'the greatest and most difficult death' for the fatherland. Moreover, his 'strength of the will' came to him from the 'stone of origins' of the Black Forest from where Heidegger also no doubt draws his spiritual energy. Mention should also be made of 'the philosopher's appeal' to the university and to the German people at the moment of the elections and to his 'Appeal to the Students' in which we can read: 'It is not theses and ideas which should be the rules of your existence. The Führer himself and he alone is the present and future German reality and its law'.[28]

In February 1934, Heidegger resigned from his post as rector. Beaufret relies on this fact in order to suggest that, three months after his ardent electoral manifesto, Heidegger would turn full circle and oppose the regime. He writes: 'in February 1934 Heidegger publicly recognised [...] an error in his political choice by resigning from the post of Rector, which had been carried by the unanimous vote of his colleagues, and by refusing all promotion in such a way as to conceal his withdrawal'. In truth Eric Weil has given the reason for this resignation: 'As we know, there had been a quarrel, but not as Heidegger has claimed. He did not obtain what he asked for, at least implicitly: the position of Führer of the German spirit.'[29]

Heidegger nevertheless continued to teach: if he was forced to interrupt his courses in 1937–8, due to the hostility of certain 'philosophers' like Ernst Krieck who were entirely manufactured by the Nazi party, he was able to resume and continue them in the midst of the war.

In one of his courses given in 1935 and published in 1953 with the title 'Introduction to Metaphysics', the disappointed philosopher said what was on his mind: 'What is today marketed as the philosophy of National Socialism, but which has absolutely nothing to do with the internal truth and grandeur of this movement [sic!] ... goes fishing into the troubled waters of these "values" and "totalities"'.[30]

But Heidegger can have no further complaint. Not having obtained the prestige to which he aspired under Nazism, he had his revenge after the war. There is no intellectual elite which does not use his name for its own philosophy, whether we are speaking about atheist or Christian Existentialists, Personnalists, Phenomenologists or certain academic Marxists. This miracle could not have been effected without cost. Thus those who were not satisfied with the philosopher's self-defence have had to sacrifice Heidegger the man in order to save his philosophy.

'We do not in any way intend', said Alphonse de Waehlens for

31 *Les Temps modernes*, no.22.

32 Jean-Paul Sartre,
Existentialism and Humanism,
trans. Philip Mairet, London:
Methuen 1948, p.31.

example in 1947, 'to make pronouncements about the *personal* attitude of Martin Heidegger towards National Socialism. For us what alone matters is whether Heidegger's philosophy is intrinsically linked with National Socialism or whether it leads logically to it, abstracted from the auspicious or unfortunate, just or unjust, coherent or incoherent, heroic, cowardly or criminal personal reactions of a private individual'.[31]

This separation of the man and his work is all the more striking if one wants to see in the aforesaid philosophy a humanism which (like Sartrean existentialism) bestows upon man 'the total responsibility for his existence'.[32] If we are to believe Waehlens, Heidegger was a humanist in spite of himself. 'It is very clearly apparent that for Heidegger, as for the young Hegel of the *Phenomenology*, the crucial problem of being-in-common and the true meaning of history must be to make possible the recognition of man by man'. Such an exegesis is able to furnish great satisfaction to those who want to be at the same time Heideggerians, Hegelians and Marxists. But unfortunately Heidegger himself put an end to this euphoria. He is opposed to any attempt to class his philosophy among the humanisms. In his 'Letter to Mr Beaufret', he claims to have surmounted them, for the good reason that, like Hölderlin, he conceives 'the destiny of human essence from the outset as more than this "humanism" can accomplish'. To the thesis of Sartre, 'we are precisely at a level on which there are only people', he opposes the antithesis: 'we are precisely at a level on which there is principally Being'. It hardly needs saying that at such a level, human action (even if of the most erroneous kind) has little significance; all that matters is the '"ekstatic" relation of human essence to the truth of Being'. The philosopher, having left his realm for a period of time which (on the scale of Being) is not even equivalent to a second, has returned to it and has since removed himself from any 'purely human' interpretation and critique.

How then to gain access to his City of Clouds? How do we know whether he is really the great philosopher he claims to be and to whom our intellectual elites of the left as well as the right pay homage? Some remarkably intelligent people have compared Heidegger's adventure with those of Plato, Fichte, Hegel and Voltaire. Thus Aimé Patri, in his article 'Heidegger and Nazism', wrote: 'Heidegger could imagine that he was hailing Hitler after his political victory, as Hegel welcomed Napoleon after his military victory. Hegel had been wrong not to have anticipated Waterloo, as Heidegger was in not anticipating Stalingrad'; and 'the encounter between the philosopher and the tyrant has more ancient sources than Fichtean nationalism or Hegelian historicism. We could evoke Plato or Voltaire at the courts of Denys or Frederick the Great respectively.'

What is striking in these analogies is how Hitler is at least implicitly elevated to the rank of a Denys or a Napoleon.

In truth, just as Hitler was only the sad caricature of a great politician, is not Heidegger simply the bizarre imitation of a true philosopher?

33 See note 21.

34 Ibid. In the introduction to *Being and Time*, he had already said that being [*l'être*] demands notions which differ essentially from those designated by being [*étant*].

35 Heidegger uses the word 'Dasein', which Sartre translates as 'human reality'. Heidegger expressly refuses this translation which rather marks, according to him, Sartre's incomprehension of his philosophy. In its place he proposes the expression 'le-là' (the there) which met with approval from Munier and Beaufret.

36 René Crevel, 'Individual and Society', *Soutes*, July 1953, no.2.

37 In the 'Letter on Humanism', alluding to the second part of *Being and Time*, as yet unpublished, he speaks of a 'thought which itself runs aground', and he continues: 'If such a thought could be given to a man, there would be no misfortune in it, but to this man would be made the only gift that might come from Being to thought'.

38 It is in the exaltation of the will, the last weapon of a self which is no longer able to master existence by rational means, that Heideggerian sur-humanism and existentialist humanism meet. According to Sartre, man is 'not only how he conceives himself, but how he *claims* to be, and as he conceives himself after existence, as he *claims to be* after this dash towards existence...' (1947, p.30).

39 Lucien Goldmann (1913–1970), French philosopher and sociologist; Kostas Axelos (1924–2010), Greek-French philosopher [trans.].

40 Adorno, the only philosopher in Germany today with followers, is the very opposite of Heidegger.

Even if he might be protected against all moral criticism, there is according to Heidegger a level at which the authenticity or inauthenticity of a philosopher is revealed: in language. Language plays a central role in his philosophy. It is 'the house of Being'. 'Thinkers and poets are the guardians of this shelter'.[33] According to Heidegger, the vocabulary of traditional philosophy blocks the view onto Being. To express the truth of Being. Heidegger thus sees his vocation as the creation of a new language. 'What matters is solely for the truth of being to accede to language and for thought to attain this language.'[34]

Where can these fresh words which would break with conventional language be drawn from? For Heidegger there can be only one source: mankind,[35] which itself claims to draw its language from itself. But this very curious phenomenon then appears: isolated 'Dasein' poses and reposes the question of Being, but Being does not respond. The man who believes he is authentic in the solitary prison of his self finds himself cut off from those creative sources he never stops talking about. 'The harpsichord of the senses, ' René Crevel said in relation to Heidegger, 'persists in believing that everything that happens in it, will no longer understand anything in it: That is a fact and this fact is enough'.[36] But Heidegger, who moreover admits that there was a failure here, although it was an authentic failure,[37] is not satisfied with this. As Being does not unveil itself spontaneously to him, violence must be used. The despotic ego – cut off from all 'natural necessity' – wants to grasp it through 'strength of will'.[38] In fact Heidegger handles the German language, as well as the Greek, in an arbitrary way that is unprecedented in the history of philosophy. It is tempting to exalt him by applying the words he found for Hitler: 'Heidegger himself and he alone is the present and future German language *and its law*!' In such linguistic despotism, Being can only become an empty formula which, since it means anything one wants, no longer means anything. This formula seems to be metamorphosed into a phantom of unreason. It has sown a great confusion of tongues among those who used it: those who speak about authenticity and want to speak about Being do not understand each other.

Heidegger said 'Being' and wanted to designate some sort of mysterious source in the Black Forest. Marxist academics like Goldmann and Axelos[39] speak about 'Being' and understand it to mean totality. Sartre and Simone de Beauvoir, even as they invoke Being, have in mind the existence which precedes essence. Finally there is in Germany a whole choir of professional Christians who, with the aid of the magic formula of Being, hope to rouse a God which has for centuries withdrawn from all ecclesiastical affairs. The philosopher Adorno has diagnosed this parasitical excrescence of the German language as the 'jargon of authenticity'. For him, this jargon is 'sacramental without sacred content', an 'effect without a cause' and he sums this up: 'Where the Holy Spirit is extinguished, we speak mechanical languages' [Adorno 1973].[40] But not content to mystify its adulators by playing at Tower of Babel, the phantom

41 To repeat the words of Aimé Patri. See his article, 'An Example of Commitment: Martin Heidegger and Nazism', *Le Contrat Social*, no.1 ,1963.

Being hides away so as to amuse himself behind the most diverse political movements and, whenever intellectuals devoured by 'the appetite for commitment'[41] rush upon him, he draws back and restores them, stupefied, extinguished and disappointed, to banality. Did not Being, which attracted Heidegger towards National Socialism, also haunt the Resistance *maquis*? Has it not given Stalin a shabby halo as has since been shown intermittently in Algeria and Cuba? Is he going to emigrate to China?

Purification ceremonies are vainly repeated each year to cleanse the Heideggerian house of its Nazi features, but the phantom of unreason will continue to haunt those who seek a shelter in it, for the very construction of this house, a structure built of banality and turgidity, attracts them.

Philippe Audoin
Festival Mood

42 James Burnham (1905–1987), American political theorist who, as Audoin states, turned from Trotskyism to argue that the coming revolution, which would bring an end to capitalism, would not be led by the Proletariat but by Managers, who would institute themselves as a newly oppressive class. His subsequent hostility to communism made him a hero to American neo-conservatives, although Audoin here implies that Burnham was warning against the very mechanisms that neo-conservatives would rely upon to impose their vision of a market-led world [trans.].

One is often struck, in reading surrealist texts, by their prescient quality. This essay, written for the catalogue of a major exhibition organised by the surrealists in 1965 and devoted to the theme of consumer society and the way it had been able to utilise desire to its own ends of consumption through the 'artificial creation of needs', penetratingly exposes the insidious effects of the mechanisation of modern society. Paralleling some of the arguments being made at the time by Marcuse and Debord and anticipating Foucault, Audoin in some ways goes beyond them by locating this not as logical consequence of capitalist development but as a revolution within it, one all the more insidious for being silent. In drawing on Burnham,[42] Audoin was able to put forward a distinctly surrealist critique of what at the time was still a nascent revolution and whose full realisation would not be put into place until the 1980s. And this managerial revolution serving the cause of efficiency and effected through technological advances would be all the more insidious in the way it made all of us complicit with it.

Published in the exhibition catalogue *L'écart absolu* (Absolute divergence), XI International Exhibition of Surrealism, December 1965.

The revolution which will end the capitalist regime and the society which will take over from it will be neither proletarian nor socialist... This is one of the least provocative conclusions of a book written almost a quarter of a century ago: *The Managerial Revolution: What Is Happening in the World* (New York: John Day Co., 1941). The author, James Burnham, a former militant of the Fourth International, from which he had just resigned, affirmed that the real power had already slipped out of the grasp of those who theoretically owned the means of production, and was passing into the hands of a historically predestined class: that of the 'managers' who in fact technically, administratively and politically controlled the whole economy. This class asserts itself just as much in totalitarian regimes as it does in those that claim to be liberal. What motivates it is not so much profit as the frenzy for efficiency and organisation – in a word, for power – and the tyranny it is preparing to exercise over the population of the States (or Super-States) it controls will concede nothing to that which had instigated the first industrial revolution. Although they have been known in France since 1947, these theories were neither examined nor seriously discussed. Debate was limited to denouncing the author (not without some justification) as an 'agent of Yankee imperialism' and it seems that the less said about it, the more social structures, in the East as in the West, evolved in directions which appeared to confirm his direst prophesies.

The word 'Technocracy' is recent. Everyone uses it today without it occurring to them that it thus describes the very type of society whose advent Burnham announced. This is because the 'directorial' revolution is carried out silently and, one might say, painlessly. Those who lead it have hardly any awareness of their probable 'historical mission' because as far as they are concerned the notion of efficacy is drained of any political content so as to be identified – as it once was for 'legitimate' profit – with Wealth and Progress.

This illusion is moreover not the only achievement of the new ruling class: it is largely shared by the managed masses, to the extent that the technocratic society has known how to create or develop a relative abundance of goods and to organise their distribution in such a way that the least fortunate have something more to lose than their chains.

'Consumer societies' can be predicted gradually to abandon traditional forms of coercion so as to place their faith exclusively on the intimate complicity of their slaves. To be convinced of all we have to do is to consider the set of means put to work just in the realm of 'lifestyles', which moreover tends to annex all others to itself. The artificial creation of needs (which in the course of production have to be satisfied before they have even been felt) by means of advertising drivel, the delirious promotion of the everyday object, the hypnotic effect of 'audio-visual' media, is no doubt the most striking example of this. The same line is followed by a vacant and cheerful conformism and tendentious or disproportionate news stories; the huge mystification of competitive sport or the space race; directed leisure; the absurd invention of the 'second sex' which does not for all that free woman of her reproductive functions; a falsely beatifying culture dispensed by the 'contemporaries of the future', and so on... All of this contributes to diverting Desire from its own ends towards substitutive satisfactions which claim to bring happiness. Happiness is no longer a new idea; it is now on special offer.

The knowledge acquired since Freud, bearing upon the structures and mechanisms of the unconscious psyche, far from advancing as we had hoped towards the liberation of mankind, are in fact being used for its more effective mastery. The Libido, the dark and scandalous deity which once still scared us, presently

43 Jean Servier, *L'Homme et l'invisible*, Paris: Robert Laffont, 1964.

44 Raymond Borde, mainly known as a film critic, was an associate of the Surrealist Group. *L'Extricable* was a political tract published in 1966 (Paris: Eric Losfeld) [trans.].

serves the obligatory distribution of riches. Seduced and invested, it is imperceptibly led, by means of a quasi-pathological transfer, to valorise the erogenous qualities of any product, star or celebrity; it's all the same. The old bogey man with a foghorn head flickers in rhythm with the traffic lights, endlessly repeating idiotic slogans, dreaming of falling in love with a winsome washing-machine or a virile electrical gadget and, in the general euphoria, reaching the sublimity of cretinisation.

These processes are still vulgar enough for many lucid spirits to be aware of them and to try to avoid them. The majority are satisfied with a summary refusal of their time and exhibit an exasperated or angry obscurantism. An example is the recent publication of Jean Servier's essay *L'Homme et l'invisible*,[43] in which the modes of thought and knowledge of so-called primitive societies are preferred to the values of the West. The positive aspects of the work are the public reparations made to these societies, but its reactionary content is still unavoidable. Evidently humans are unable to escape contemporary conditioning just by exalting bygone structures, and it is in the very heart of these times, in their grip but also *in gear* with them, that there is some chance of glimpsing a way out. One man alone cannot claim 'salvation'. It rests with some – or more – people to try to 'be absolutely modern'. This attitude, which does not separate the everyday from 'true life', is specifically the one that surrealism demands. If it endorses and if necessary takes to the level of paroxysm every will of opposition to the new operational forms of alienation (of which proof enough is Raymond Borde's essay *L'Extricable*,[44] which could be compared to 'a gust of non-conditioned air') it tends, and in the same movement, to go beyond this negative humour through the affirmation of an 'elsewhere' which would be in an analogically inverse but necessarily ascendant relation with the contested object. Its denunciation of the contemporary universe has no nostalgic attachment to the past: each open breach in what is supposedly given must be a liberating vista onto a Marvellous which alone allows a glimpse of the 'accommodation of desires' and which is not an evasion but tends to become real. Any revolution which does not imply some vista (or divergence) towards these confines of the possible, which renounces its fires becoming perceptible for all, can be considered as void and already betrayed, even when it would flatter itself with being in accord with historical necessity.

'In order to reach a new continental world Columbus adopted the system of Absolute Divergence'. The spirit in which the XI International Exhibition of Surrealism invokes this statement by Charles Fourier and the system of thought it substantiates may be imagined. Admittedly it is a question of a readiness for combat, organised against a clearly situated form of social pressure, which intends to get the best out of any outburst of exasperation. But if the contested objects or processes are necessarily evoked in it (the meaning of the divergence is given from the point from which one diverges), by preference the accent has been placed on the distance to be taken and the horizon introduced. What is therefore being proposed is an operation of 're-orientation', most often by means of the very machinery which punctuates or indicates the path of the servitude. Moreover, a shifting effect has always been preferred to a simple opposition, by reason of the power that 'false' situations have to surmount the usual to-and-fro movement of the spirit, so as finally to orient them according to an unexpected result. In this way, in the face of the advertising operation which, under the pretext of finally welcoming beauty, claims to devote the work of art to the ornamentation of a ceiling or any other portion of a public monument, and does so for eternity, is *obliquely* opposed the ephemeral glorification of a stupid image, a ghost of an image of a ghostly place, an exemplary decoration whose bankruptcy of principle reminds us that artistic creation dries up and declines once it ceases to anticipate the expected awakening of the spirit and to prefigure the place of this awakening.

The noise of the century will only increase. It hides as best it can an alarming torpor that could be said to be formed from each person's denial. No matter how oppressive it might be and however overwhelming it might become, it is doubtless not vain once again to throw off the yoke of this new Destiny. Not only the works presented but also the 'climate' and the setting of the exhibition tend towards this. If didactic intention is entirely absent, it should be no less clear that it borrows from fashionable commercial shows only in as much as 'the festival mood' blows far enough away from them to raise the Cardinal Temptations of Love, Poetry and Freedom, precisely what, for want of being able to reduce them, they are today preoccupied with suborning. None of the luminous hoardings attain the splendour of this fleeting gleam, which shines only for the best of ourselves and from which we must more than ever not diverge 'and lose it from sight'. It still fringes the hazard of the streets and lifts up women's eyes. And it is the only day. It is also the arch of night.

Pierre Mabille
Paradise

We here return to an earlier period for an essay written during the Second World War, but which anticipates and summarises something that is central to most of the essays in this section in its refutation of the idea that surrealism is concerned with transcendence or discovering distant realities. On the contrary – by rejecting the myth of Paradise, which he sees as an inherent counterpart of the realist myth (that we need to work now to create a perfect existence in the future, whether in this world or in some other) Mabille makes it clear that for surrealists the only reality is what is existing here and now. This confirms the fundamental surrealist demand for the transformation of the world by changing life (and vice versa). With his rejection of the Russian Revolution on the grounds that it found itself trapped by the Paradise myth, Mabille, who is the most important surrealist theorist of the marvellous as a manifestation of material life, clarifies a frequently misunderstood aspect of surrealism: the revolution surrealism seeks will not be based on an ideal but will not occur by striving towards some pre-established end. Although social roles may today have changed radically from those described by Mabille, the thrust of his argument remains pointedly relevant.

First published in *VVV*, no.4, February 1944; reprinted in Pierre Mabille, *Traversées de nuit*, Paris: Plasma 1981.

Addressing a society infatuated with the sciences and modernism and eager for vitamins and psychological complexes, it appears necessary to bow to fashion and borrow from scholarly terminology in order to make myself better understood. I therefore propose to study what constitutes the Paradise complex in the individual and the myth of Eden in society.

This is a particular form which leads the normal reactions of existence into a struggle with the constraints which surround it, a deviation that concludes by constructing a different world in the future from the existing one, a diversion which orients personal and social behaviour, creating a sort of practical ethic.

For centuries millions of individuals have protested against the conditions of life they have been handed. Reduced to a more or less rigorous slavery the working masses have hardly any reason to rejoice, while the privileged minorities find serious motives for complaint in the sicknesses, emotional desperations and other catastrophes that afflict them. After all, the general opinion is that nature is not very well organised and that society is more detestable still. Even if this opinion draws its origin from immediate emotional reactions it is still supported by the work of the philosophers of the past. It considers the perceptible world, with its irregularities and incessant movement, to be a rather disagreeable accident and envisages a static order in which health would be perfect, love eternal, and where a friendly tranquillity would engender unlimited happiness as true reality. This world is regarded as the order of God, Paradise or Eden. Having created this duality, man strangely accepts as irrefutable evidence the fact that accession to the ideal life can only be the recompense for sacrifice.

Mystics immediately conclude that this sacrifice must be started without delay and be pursued with the most extreme vigour so as to attain the state of total and durable happiness as quickly as possible. Since terrestrial life is a test, since it is a brief passage through the vale of tears, there is no question of lingering there and taking the risk, by clinging to small transitory pleasures, of missing the infinite delights of Paradise.

This excessive behaviour is the actuality of only a few people. The great majority proceed with more malicious moderation. While counting on attaining celestial Paradise by observing religious rites, they do not give up the idea of sketching out paradisiacal existence on earth through a judicious arrangement of social conditions and through the utilisation of the principles of the Economy. The paradisiacal complex is manifested in what I call the philosophy of the jam sandwich.

Man convinces himself that Destiny distributes to each person his lot, comprised of a mixture containing joys and sorrows in set proportions, so that if the sorrows are first accepted, only the joys will remain. Destiny is seen as a sort of schoolmistress distributing sandwiches among the pupils at teatime. If the child is intelligent and moral, he will first eat the bread and then settle down in a comfortable corner to eat the delicious jam. The behaviour of the European bourgeoisie, which is what I particularly know, is typical in this respect. Life is a sort of masterpiece; its rules for success are strict. Upon emerging from military service, which marks the limit to which the eccentricities of youth are allowed, the boy must unite with an unblemished girl and immediately set to work. Boldly, without fearing the pain, one must get up at dawn, go to bed late, abandon pleasure, live without luxury, be sparing with food and clothes, and this will continue for twenty or thirty years. Children are brought up strictly and each month savings are deposited in the piggy bank and then in the real bank. Some are overwhelmed with a desire for power and constantly need to change social class and become bosses, but for the majority the aim of this immense sacrifice is to build up a reserve of jam and intelligently prepare a little paradise for themselves. This is what the spouses discuss in confidence every evening when the children are in bed; it is the secret sign of their understanding. They will build a house far away from the city.

Mrs: With flowers on the front steps, a veranda with roses.

Mr: The garden will look out over the river and we will set up a billiard table in the basement.

Mrs: We will finally have a radio good enough for listening to concerts. We'll have time to read.

Mr: We should also have a guard dog. We will call him Azor.

Once a year they will go on a trip.

And the children will come for lunch every Sunday.

This is what is said in the homes of the bank clerk, the baker and the greengrocer, the foreman and the postman, the teacher, the officer and the gendarme.

And, as though to speaking about it would bring misfortune, they each suppress this dream.

When the time comes the metamorphosis takes place, a curious inverse metamorphosis which takes the insect back to the larva, when it is time to retire. The house that is finally built is 'simple but to our taste'. The work clothes, the former uniforms of society life, are bartered for old rest clothes, 'the dress of those of private means'. The children are established: 'now that they are married off, they will work as we did'. And life in the suburbs begins, a suburb so reminiscent of the cemetery, the little quiet provincial corner with its crystalline stream, the reduced vision of the garden of Virgil's Gods ... far from noise and excitement.

Retirement is like a first, voluntary death, a death on a

Furies s'apprêtant à poursuivre un assassin par un clair après-midi d'automne.

Giorgio de Chirico
Reproduced in *La Révolution
surréaliste*, no.1, 1 December
1924

trial basis, with an incomplete Paradise, admittedly, due to the husband's rheumatism, and the wife's fibroma, but all in all rather a success, as they await a true and final Paradise. He, with his strong spirit, does not have so much belief in it but Madam firmly expects it because the priest says so, because the best books certify it, and because she gives an offering every Sunday during the collection at mass which is a bit like a registration fee.

The rules of this game exclude the worker who drinks, the person whose wife buys chickens from the market, the flirts who spend all their money on clothes, people with twelve children ('they breed like rabbits') unless they are rich enough (in which case they constitute a pious example), gamblers, pleasure-seekers, those who eat butter before bread, insatiable people who do not know how to retire when they should and work until their dying day without being forced to, because visions of grandeur are also a vice.

The demons and envoys of Satan must be severely punished and no penalty will be too severe for them: those who steal the savings, dishonest financiers, notaries who take to flight, adulterous women who break up marriages, corrupt politicians who talk about taxing income and deductions on capital, the shady world of international high finance which changes the value of money and provokes stock-exchange crashes, the revolutionary ogres 'who should work and economise like everyone', the idiotic politicians who by their lack of foresight bring war to the Homeland, while the other wars, those which happen distantly are rather amusing, like important football matches, and they are clearly a boon to business.

The whole world today is wildly battling in order to defend the rules of this game.

Not only has the Edenic myth engendered the bourgeois spirit, it has also contributed and it still contributes to the success of bellicose enterprises, because war pre-supposes the sacrifice of soldiers and this sacrifice would be inconceivable without the bait of recompense and without the attraction of Paradise.

For my part, I do not believe in the dominant role of sadistic and masochistic instincts in war. Admittedly they are unleashed during combat, but infinitely less than in other activities, such as police actions, for example. Historically, the courage of the soldier is in direct proportion to his belief in an Edenic future for himself or his kin. The Muslim is not afraid of dying in battle because he knows that he will immediately go to a shady garden where he will be served by forty young, beautiful and obedient slaves, a prospect that is singularly more delightful for him than lingering in a miserable life inhabiting a hut full of screaming babies, flies and lice. The Japanese soldier draws his heroism from a certainty of the same order. Poetic descriptions of the Waal have long excited German enthusiasm. In all religious wars death ensures salvation and the God one serves cannot do less than reward his herald with a privileged entry into the Elysian Fields. In the contemporary age, the soldier justifies his sacrifice by the fact that thanks to him a stable order and definitive peace will be established. Every war is announced as being the last. Politicians never fail to promise that the treaties and organisation which would be their work will form the beginning of a golden age of justice and general prosperity, for the victor will forever be able to live contentedly off what the vanquished will have to pay. The very feeble level of aggression of the French in 1939 came precisely from the experience they had undergone in the previous war, which divested them of their faith in this type of illusion, while the Germans were convinced of being able, thanks to a new technique, to provide themselves with a pleasant Paradise of Lords ruling over an entire world reduced to slavery.

It cannot be doubted that the international revolutionary movement has very widely been contaminated by the Edenic mystique. The progressive diminution of religious faith had provoked a transformation in the psychology of the masses. They understood that they were being mocked in the way they were being extensively swindled by the requirement that the proletariat work ever harder on the strength of a simple promise of rest in the afterlife. The financial operations which characterised the nineteenth century, the result of which has been periodically and scientifically to cheat the small investor, have divested the worker, who even now cannot possibly live on his salary, of the slightest hope of ever receiving any annuity. What is more, analysis of the conditions of production and exchange has caused many to think that the inhuman severity of work in factories arose from the number of idlers and profiteers and from the bad organisation of the voluntarily instituted society. Gradually the idea became established that capitalism is a sort of apocalyptic monster responsible for all suffering, a sort of half-abstract and half-concrete demon which the revolutionary party, like a modern-day knight, must kill. With the hydra dead, the earth liberated from evil will experience a Paradise in which machines will work for people who have become masters of their destiny, having barely two or three hours of labour each day. In this golden age the rest of the time will be occupied in a healthy and idyllic collective rejoicing that is little different from that dreamt of by the annuity holder. In the wake of the Russian Revolution, we have witnessed the emergence of a propaganda literature and a great number of films whose explicit theme is the Soviet Paradise: *The Good Life*, *The Road to Happiness* and so on. Intellectuals went to the USSR with the hope of finding a garden of the Hesperides but returned exasperated, thereby testifying to the fact that in their naivety they believed that the revolution had effected the conquest of Paradise.

It is time to put an end to this foolishness. If our age has a meaning, and if, as I think, profound mutations are in the process of operating within human mentality, one of the obstacles which must be overcome is certainly the Paradise complex.

The repeated failure of treaties for lasting peace, the acknowledged nullity of solemn contracts, the results of the Russian Revolution are so many experiments capable of developing a clearer consciousness of reality in many minds.

We are among those who categorically refuse the illusion of a Paradise in the beyond, the tarnished tranquillity of those who live off annuities, the infantile belief in a golden age that is always promised and forever postponed until later.

We intend to live from today. Of course the future must be prepared, but what better means of doing so than the present?

As far as we are concerned the dialectic is not a struggle between hero and monster or between good and evil; it is not a struggle that must result in the definitive extermination of the bad, in other words making room for recovered, static and ecstatic unity. The dialectic is the indefinite co-existence of contradictory and polymorphous forces whose conflict engenders life and whose good or bad meaning is only valid for a given being at a precise moment of his existence and has no general absolute character. The dialectic thus ceases to be an intellectual speculation, to be intimately incorporated into our everyday consciousness. We have surpassed linear and even circular reason for more complex forms, the simplest of which is the twin-centred ellipse.

With respect to ethics, we refuse any longer to accept the neurotic game of sacrifice and recompense; we struggle against the hysterical deviation of social relations leading to accumulation and capitalism, and against the systematic deformation of the natural conditions of life. We would like each day to be struggle and rest, desire and pain, and all of this conducted in the maximum of consciousness.

The revolutionary impulse merges with the permanent will to ensure the triumph of life over death. It does not date from yesterday, it is not the prerogative of any party, and it does not tend towards the constitution of an ideal state. No one can make themselves its guardian and no one can lock it within a closed system for it is unlimited in time, aiming at once at every domain – in other words, it cannot be satisfied by an action simply directed towards a single political, economic, religious or artistic goal.

We do not doubt that a certain strategy would be necessary to terminate aggression, just as techniques are useful in all aspects of activity. But we know the dangers of this strategy. In incessant movement, yesterday's liberatory force may rapidly be transformed into an oppressive force, and in the course of a prolonged assault the enemy may be behind rather than in front of us. As we have learned that oppression can at certain moments be diminished but will never be destroyed, we would like to recognise it in the multiple forms it can take and to this end each day to refine our lucidity, to submit the collective strategy as well as our own to the permanent control of consciousness. Our abandonment could never be complete.

Mindful of struggle but not of sacrifice, condemning holocausts, expecting nothing from eternal rest, we think it is important to normalise life by fostering rest, solitude and relaxation each day, and like any other Prometheus, regaining contact with the self.

Anthony Earnshaw
Reproduced in
Les Lèvres nues, no.10 (new
series), August 1974

Life ceasing to be systematically condemned to benefit the illusory conditions of contentment, we would like to undergo the apprenticeship of this contentment in everyday action.

In effect, the negation of Paradise does not lead us to a stoic attitude. If surrealism has a meaning, it is really that of having re-introduced the marvellous into everyday life. It teaches us that if reality appeared so deadly and banal and man so feeble, it is because we did not know how to see, that our viewpoint was limited by the aesthetic censorship of earlier ages, which we did not know how to hear, refusing to listen to our internal voice which, at each moment, dictates the poem when we would really like to impose silence on the hubbub of the most stupid society. Thanks to automatism it promises the springing up of the prophetic and emotional possibilities which remained hidden and seemed forever extinguished in each of our beings. In indicating the paths of permanent miracle, surrealism has shown that the marvellous was not foreign to life but could and should be incorporated into it. It is in part thanks to it that we can accept existence each day, in consciousness, each day in struggle, each day in rest, mobile in a moving world.

Anthony Earnshaw

LE SURREALISME
en octobre 1967

L'archibras 2

L'Archibras, no. 2, October 1967
Front cover, photograph by
Marcel Lannoy

Part 4

The Tasks of Art and Poetry

ANALOGON 19

SURREALISMUS - PSYCHOANALÝZA - ANTROPOLOGIE - PŘÍČNÉ VĚDY

MENTÁLNÍ MORFOLOGIE

Analogon, no.19, 1997
Front cover, featuring
Panák 1959 by Emila Medková

Introduction

Part 1
The Annihilation of Self-Identity

Part 2
The Challenge of Otherness

Part 3
The Moral Imperative

Part 4
The Tasks of Art and Poetry

Biographies
Journals
Bibliography
Index

The Tasks of Art and Poetry

Surrealism was born in poetry – and in making a
distinction between art and poetry the title of this
section is perhaps un-surrealist, since for the surrealists
these were one and the same, poetry being the aim and
rationale that united all art forms. From the beginning
of Paris Dada, those who would soon found the
Surrealist Group had already made a distinction
between poetry and literature in giving their journal
the ironic title of *Littérature*. 'Poetry ', they declared,
following Lautréamont, 'must be made by all, not by
one'; it required no special gift but was the common
property of humanity. And this was put into practice
by Breton and Philippe Soupault through the idea
of automatic writing in the 1919 text *Les Champs
magnétiques*. Though it lies at the heart of surrealism,
automatism has remained a contentious notion among
the surrealists themselves. Neither the Czech nor the
Belgian surrealists have shown very much interest in
pursuing processes of automatism and the major
theorists of their groups (Karel Teige and Paul Nougé
respectively) were highly critical of the notion, at least
as formulated by Breton. Precisely what 'automatism'
means, however, is by no means clear. Breton himself,

perhaps bedazzled by his initial experiments in automatic writing, expected too much from it and was unwilling to theorise it, content to leave it as a mysterious source of fecundity (by which he was nevertheless continually disillusioned). The issue of automatism is therefore a key thread of this section, not always being directly addressed but often remaining untheorised in the background.

A text by Breton and Éluard, 'Notes on Poetry', sets the scene. Although it doesn't directly address automatism, it tries to establish a poetics within which it could be grounded, by making a break with the symbolist tradition in which surrealism had its roots and which had reached its highest (and most intellectualised) point in the work of Paul Valéry. Taking their cue from Lautréamont, they challenged Valéry, who had been one of their early intellectual mentors, not by directly criticising or contesting his position, but by taking one of his own texts apart and subjecting it to derision. They were, however, not so much attacking Valéry as providing surrealism with a platform from which its own poetics could take flight. The aim, as Breton put it, was definitively to 'purge the literary stables'.

There are many complexities here, but perhaps the fundamental difference between Valéry and the surrealists was that he saw poetry as a precious treasure of humanity, something that was realised only through an immense effort and gave testimony to the triumph of the human will to greatness. Breton and Éluard advance the exact opposite: poetry is as natural as breathing; the task for the poet therefore is not to work hard to create something great but to become the conduit for a poetry that is itself seeking expression. The poet's task is to allow the universe to express itself through him and not to promote his own ego. Poetry is therefore neither precious nor in need of protection but is perfectly natural. 'Poetry is a survival', wrote Valéry; 'Poetry is a pipe', corrected Breton and Éluard. The allusion is no doubt to Magritte, whose first version of the famous painting *The Treachery of Images* ('Ceci n'est pas une pipe') had been realised the year that Breton and Éluard wrote their text.

Within surrealism the first major challenge to Breton's conception of automatism came from Salvador Dalí. In the first text he published in a surrealist journal, 'L'âne pourri', Dalí introduced what he called an active mode of thought, which he defined as 'paranoiac'. In this text he suggests that this could act 'simultaneously with automatism and other passive states' to 'discredit the world of reality'. Dalí has picked up the notion of discrediting the real world from Breton's *Introduction to the Discourse on the Paucity of Reality*, where it is seen as a function of the surrealist 'poetic' object. Later Dalí insisted more on the contrast between paranoiac thought, which actively interprets the world, and the passive state of automatism.

Perhaps taking a cue from Dalí, Roger Caillois set about trying to put some precision on an idea that had until then been fêted rather than analysed. The difficulty of conceptualising automatism arose from the fact that it was not a technique with a set aim. If it was not directed towards the writing of poetry it was equally not, as many critics have assumed, a way of mining the unconscious or seeking poetic inspiration. If anything it was more akin to a form of meditation (Octavio Paz once made this association), whose aim was to was to induce in the poet a state of receptivity that would allow him or her to be responsive to the natural poetry of the universe. As such it was also a form of confrontation with oneself and a confrontation with the world, an attitude of primary revolt. Caillois recognised these difficulties and 'Specification of Poetry' was the first of many essays in which he sought to establish a poetics of automatism based on scientific analogies. Caillois's rejection of any form of poetic lyricism has not found favour with all surrealists, although one has to say that it seems fully in accord with the basis on which surrealism was founded, and his contentions have yet to be properly analysed from a surrealist perspective.

Tristan Tzara's essay is an important one in the history of surrealism, if only for the distinction he draws between poetry as a 'means of expression' and as an 'activity of the spirit', even if, as we explain below, it is also problematic in many ways.

More general issues of poetry, especially in terms of the moral and political questions it raises in the pre-war context in which fascism had declared war on the sort of poetry surrealism upheld are taken up by Georges Henein, while Paul Nougé develops further the idea of a surrealist poetics in his 'Notes on Poetry' From the beginning of his involvement in surrealism, Nougé had been doubtful about the idea of automatism and like Caillois found it difficult to accept that poetry could emerge from a spontaneous engagement with phenomenon. On the contrary, he considered spontaneity to impose a certain servitude on the poet. Like Caillois he considered that the poet needs rather to establish a relationship with his or her material, though which poetry could emerge.

Language has been a central concern of the work of the surrealists in Czechoslovakia. In the 1930s they had close relations with the Prague Linguistic Circle. Karel Teige was part of this environment, having

Luis Buñuel
Publicity still for
L'Age d'or, reproduced in
*Le Surréalisme au service de la
revolution*, no.1, July 1930

friendships with Roman Jakobson and Jan Mukařovský and their concerns strongly influenced Teige's own work. Here he argues against the positivist view that there is a fundamental dualism between reality and the image, exploring the surrealist view that the image has its own reality. Vratislav Effenberger, who assumed Teige's mantle as the organising figure in the Czech surrealist group on Teige's death in 1951, takes up some of the strictures made by Karl Kraus in the 1920s about the way in which language was being constantly vulgarised in modern society, something that has damaging social and political implications. Effenberger therefore argues that a revitalisation of language should be a necessary task for us to undertake today.

Paul Nougé, in 'Inviolable Images', his other essay in this section, takes up issues of surrealist poetics in relation to vision, using Magritte's paintings as exemplars. He advances an important argument about the relationship between sight and reality. What we see is restricted neither to observation of the everyday world, nor to the purely visible; nor do we necessarily see what is there. The connection between mind and vision is complex, and its bearing on consciousness and the imagination is full of surprises. Nougé discusses the visual metaphors in Magritte's paintings in the light of the surrealist image, the bringing together of unrelated things, so that, for instance the dream is stone, the lips are coral.

Arguably visual artists affiliated to surrealism have gleaned more from automatic practice than the writers, as they variously devised means of exploring its possibilities in such diverse procedures as frottage, fumage, drawing, grattage, decalcomania, cameraless photography, etc. Adrien Dax, in 'Automatic Perspective', looking back on nearly thirty years of such experiments, links their 'mechanical' character to the forces and products of nature, such as crystals and agates.

In his essay, Vincent Bounoure draws upon his own expertise as one of the leading experts on the art of the South Seas to explore what has been at stake in the surrealist interest in 'primitive art'. This theme is further developed in the essay he wrote with Vratislav Effenberger considering the significance of the notion of 'magic art' advanced by Breton to designate forms of art that engaged the very essence of human expression against the dominant forms that art has taken in the west since the Renaissance, seen by Breton not at the beginning of art but the moment it lost its vital meaning. For the surrealists, the recovery of this vital spark is a crucial task to addressed in today's world.

André Breton and Paul Éluard
Notes on Poetry

This is a revision, or correction, of part of a text written by Paul Valéry entitled 'Literature', made by Breton and Éluard in accordance with Isidore Ducasse's dictum that good cannot be exchanged for evil and that an erroneous proposition has to be undermined in order to free the underlying concept concealed within it. In doing so, they defined surrealism against previous (especially symbolist) poetics, refusing the idea that poetry was the highest human aspiration which had to be protected from vulgarity, instead arguing that poetry came from elsewhere, in accordance with the surrealist idea that the poet was nothing but a 'modest recording instrument'. The fundamental difference is perhaps marked most clearly in the second statement. Where Valéry had written that 'Completely naked thoughts and emotions are as feeble as naked men. They must therefore be dressed', Breton and Éluard corrected: 'Completely naked thoughts and emotions are as strong as naked women. They must therefore be undressed.'

First published in *La Révolution surréaliste*, no.12, 15 December 1929; reprinted in Breton, *Oeuvres complètes*, vol.1, 1988.

Books have the same friends as man: fire, humidity, wild beasts, time; and their own content.

Completely naked thoughts and emotions are as strong as naked women.

They must therefore be undressed.

Thought has no sex; it does not reproduce itself.

Preamble.

The existence of poetry is in essence certain; this is something to take pride in. On this point poetry resembles the Devil.

One can be deaf to poetry, blind to Him – the consequences are perceptible.

But what everyone can confirm and something we want is for it to establish a nucleus and a powerful symbol of our lack of reasons for being what we are.

A poem must be a debacle of the intellect. It can be nothing else.

Debacle: a stampede, but a solemn and coherent one: an image of what one should be, of a state in which effort is no longer of any importance.

Something is ruined if it is accomplished or represented in its purest and finest state.

Here there is faculty of language and its *inverse phenomenon*: the earthquake, the identity of things that it separates. We isolate its everyday pranks. We completely overturn the possibilities of language.

After the debacle everything begins anew. Sand and oxy-hydrogen blowtorches.

In the poet:
> The ear laughs,
> The mouth swears;
> It is intelligence and awareness that kill;
> It is sleep which dreams and sees clearly;
> It is the image and phantasm which closes eyes.
> It is lack and lacunae which are created.

Some people have such a vague idea of poetry that the very vagueness of this idea among others is for them the definition of poetry.

Poetry

Is the attempt to represent and restore, by cries, tears, caresses, kisses and sighs, or through objects, *these things* or t*hat particular thing* which *articulated language obscurely tends to express*, in so far as it has an appearance of life or supposed intention.

This thing cannot otherwise be defined. The nature of this energy is to refuse to respond to what exists...

Thought has to be hidden in verses as nutritive values are not contained within a fruit. Fruit is not nourishment, but merely thought. No pleasure can be perceived in it, and no sustenance received from it. The fruit is enchanted.

Poetry is the contrary of literature. It reigns over idols of all sorts and realist illusions; it enthusiastically embraces the ambiguity between the language of 'truth' and that of 'creation'.

And this creative and real role of language (which itself is of mineral origin) is rendered as clearly as possible by the complete *a priori* non-necessity of the *subject*.

The *subject* of a poem is as inherent to it and has as little significance for it as his own *name* has for a man.

Some see in poetry a completely utilitarian occupation, a banal industry which will always flourish. The number of manufacturers of cars and artillery shells could always be increased.

Others see it as a manifestation of a very secondary property or activity, having no link with the situation of intimate existence between knowledge, duration, sexual relations, memory, dream and so on.

While the interest of prose writings lies in themselves and is born from the non-consummation of the text – the interest of poems is not inherent to them and can be separated from them.

Poetry is a pipe.

Poetry – in an age of the complication of language, conservation of forms and sensitivity towards them, in an age of busybody sensibility and specialisation – is an *exposed thing*. We mean that poetry, along with rites of all sorts, will be invented in today's society.

A poet is also someone who seeks the unintelligible and unimaginable system, the expression of which belongs to a fortunate accident of the chase: each word, each disharmony of words, each syntactical joke (each outburst) that has been encountered, awakened, stumbled upon on purpose, and barely noticed, due to his nature as a poet.

Lyricism is the development of a protest.

Lyricism is the type of poetry that assumes the *inactive voice* (a voice returning directly to, or provoked by) things that are not seen and whose absence is still felt.

The mind sometimes refuses poetry without reference to any spring or visible divinity.

But the ear does not demand some sound, when the mind insists upon some word whose sound does not conform to the ear's desire.

Never, never, never, never was the human voice the basis and condition of literature. The absence of the voice does not explain the earliest literature, from which the classics, and that sad *disposition*, took shape. There is nothing *below the voice*, torpedoing and drunkenness of the *idea*.

A day came when it became known how to read with the eyes, without it being spelled out or understood, and literature was really enlivened.

There were evolutions of the little maniac in the square des Arts-et-Métiers.

Voice-Poetry

The qualities that can be expressed by means of a human voice are the contrary of those that should, without being studied, be *received* in poetry.

And the 'magnetism' of the voice should not be transposed into the just or unjust and un-mysterious alliance of ideas and words.

The discontinuity of beautiful sound is essential.

The idea of *Inspiration* is contained in the following:

What costs thruppence is not worth most.

What is worth most cannot be evaluated in pennies.

And by this:

To be most glorified by what one is least responsible for.

The slightest erasure spoils the principle of total inspiration. Idiocy effaces what the ear had carefully *created*. One must therefore under no circumstances let it in, at the risk of producing monsters. There can be no sharing. Idiocy cannot be queen.

This great poet is just a brain full of contempt. There are those who acclaim him and play on the strange strings of genius. Others, who differ from them, appear as they are spiritual winnings and games of skill. This is when he does not want to reflect the former and take the consequences.

What pride there is in writing, without knowing what language, verbs, metaphors, changes of ideas or tone are; to be able to conceive neither the *structure* of the work's duration, nor the conditions of its end, and to be completely oblivious to the why and the how! Turn green, turn blue, turn white parroting everything.

Opposite:
Dorothea Tanning
Reproduced in
*Almanach surréaliste du
demi-siècle*, 1950

Rhetoric

The old rhetoric that considered those figures of speech and relations to be merely verbal ornamentation and artifice has finally been revealed by the increasing vulgarity of poetry to be the negation of its object. The progress of analysis has already found them to be the effects of ridiculous properties, or of what could be called worthless sentiment.

Two sorts of verse: verses and *arithmetical calculations.*

Calculated verses are those which are necessarily presented as *riddles.* Above all their initial condition is the command to stand to attention, and rhyme, syntax, and the grotesque meaning already set in train by these facts then follows.

We are always, even in prose, led and willing to write what we did not want and that perhaps we did not even want what we wanted.

An arithmetical operation. The vague idea, an intention, Jesuitical reticence adapted in numerous ways to regular forms, the puerile defences of conventional prosody, engenders old subjects or predictable forms. Nothing but tiresome consequences result from this accord between ulterior motive and calculation with the insensibility of conventions.

Rhyme has the great advantage of comforting simple folk who naively believe there is nothing more important under the sun than a convention. They have the elementary belief that any old convention *can* be more profound and durable... than some thought.

This is not the least of rhyme's disagreeable qualities, and the means by which it gives the least violent shock to the ears.

Rhyme constitutes a law on which the subject depends and it is comparable to a couple of slaps.

The never excessive multiplicity of images produces in the mind's eye a disorder eminently compatible with *tone.* Everything is made clear in bedazzlement.

To construct a poetry that contains only poems is impossible.

If something contains only poetry, it is constructed; it is a poem. It is not poetry.

Fantasy, even if it is strengthened and lasts for a while, does not forge organs, principles, laws, forms and so on for itself. Nor is it able to prolong itself, or assure itself of existence. Improvisation is not concerted, the spontaneous remains spontaneous, for nothing can remain, nothing can affirm itself and go beyond the moment, nothing happens from what allows the addition of instants.

The dignity or indignity of verse: a single missing word saves the whole thing.

A certain lapse of memory dismisses a word that is not the right one, because it is not the best one. Such a word would set a fashion, the confusion would become a system, a superstition and so on...

A correction, a false solution is declared thanks to a slow look at a page that is satisfactory and to be put aside.

Everything drowses. One was too involved. Everything withers away.

Dorothea Tanning.

The false solution paralyses a vital word and binds it. The same thing happens in chess when all one has to do to block this bishop or that pawn is to put it in one's pocket.

Without this move, the work immediately existed.

Through this move, it does not exist.

A work whose completion (the judgement which declares it complete) is uniquely subordinated to the condition that it pleases us, is always completed. There is an absolute rectitude of judgement which compares the last state and the final state. The standard of comparison exists.

Something that is successful cannot be the transformation of something unsuccessful.

A successful thing succeeds only through abandonment.

The author's own comments and variants

A poem is always complete – it can never be at the mercy of the accident that terminates it, in other words by which it is offered to the public.

Neither, as swine believe, can it be at the mercy of laziness, pressure from a publisher or the 'thrust' of another poem.

But the actual condition of the work (if the author is a fool), always makes one think that it could be 'thrust', changed, treated as a first draft, or made the starting point for new research.

As far as we are concerned the same subject and the same words must serve only once and not concern us for more than a moment.

'Perfection'

is *laziness*.

If all the research assumed by the creation or adoption of *content* were to be represented, one would never stupidly oppose it to *form*.

One is distanced from *form* by concern to leave as much scope to the reader (and even to oneself) for certainty and possible arbitrariness.

The worst form is a form we do not feel the need to change and do not change. Equally bad is a form that allows one to repeat or imitate it.

The worst form is essentially bound to *repetition*.

The idea of the new thus conforms to the desire for *content*.

Antonin Artaud
The Social Anarchy of Art

One of the remarkable essays Artaud wrote while in Mexico in 1936, this takes on the social responsibility of the artist, making clearer the extent to which surrealism renounced not only Enlightenment individualism but also the romantic notion of the inspired genius.

For Artaud, and for the surrealists in general, the great artist is not an inspired genius but someone whose self-investigation embodies and gives voice to the underlying and generally unrecognised conditions of the age. As Breton wrote in the *Second Manifesto*, 'inspiration is familiar'; the important quality is recognition of the signs and the message that passes through us.

First published in the Mexican newspaper *El Nacional*, 18 August 1936; reprinted in Antonin Artaud, *Messages révolutionnaires*, Paris: Gallimard, 1971.

The social duty of art is to provide an outlet for the anguish of its age. The artist who has not examined the heart of his age, the artist who is unaware that he is a *scapegoat*, that his duty is to magnetise, attract and bring the itinerant anger of the age down on his shoulders in order to discharge its psychological malaise, is not an artist.

Ages have an Unconscious just as much as people. And *those dark parts of the shadow* Shakespeare spoke about have also a life of their own, a proper life *that must be extinguished.*[1]

This is what works of art are for.

Today's materialism is in reality a spiritualist attitude because it prevents us from attaining those values which elude meaning in their substance all the better to destroy them. Materialism calls these values 'spiritual' and disdains them: they then poison the Unconscious of the Age. Then nothing of what can be attained by reason or intelligence is spiritual.

We possess the means by which to fight, but our age is perishing because we are forgetting to employ them.

In its beginning the Russian Revolution caused absolute carnage among artists, and everywhere people have risen up against this scorn for spiritual values that the executions of the Russian Revolution appeared to signify.

But, in looking at it closer, what was the spiritual value of the artists the Russian Revolution shot? In what ways did their written or painted works testify to the catastrophic spirit of the time?

Artists, today more than ever, are responsible for the social disorder of the age, and the Russian Revolution would not have shot them if they had had a real sense of the age.

In all authentic human feeling there is a rare strength which commands respect from all.

In the course of the first French Revolution a crime was committed of guillotining André Chénier.[2] But in an age of shootings, hunger, death, despair, blood, at the moment when nothing less than the balance of the world was at stake, André Chénier, led astray into a useless and reactionary dream, could vanish without harming either poetry or his time.

And André Chénier's universal and eternal feelings, if he experienced them, were neither so universal nor so eternal that they could justify his existence in an age in which the eternal faded away behind one individual with innumerable concerns. Art must precisely grasp particular concerns and raise them to the level of an emotion able to dominate time.

Not all artists are in a position to reach this sort of magical identification between their own feelings and mankind's collective rage.

1 We have been unable to discover where in Shakespeare these quotes come from. The only suggestion we have been able to come across is that they may be an idiosyncratic translation of these lines from *Macbeth*: 'Out, out brief candle! / Life's but a walking shadow' [the translators would like to thank Anthony Martin for this suggestion].

2 André Chénier (1762–1794), French poet caught up in the politics of the French Revolution and guillotined [trans.].

And not all Ages are in a position to appreciate the social importance of the artist and this protective function he exerts to the benefit of the collective good.

Scorn for intellectual values is fundamental to this modern world. In reality, this scorn hides a profound ignorance of the nature of these values. We cannot squander our strength in making it understood in an age which has produced a great proportion of traitors among intellectuals and artists and has engendered among people a collectivity, a mass which does not want to recognise that the mind, that is the intelligence, should guide the march of the time.

Capitalist Liberalism of modern times has relegated the values of the intelligence to the lowest rank, and modern man, in the face of the elementary truths I have just expressed, acts like a beast or like the terrified individual of primitive times. Being so preoccupied with them, he expects these truths to become acts, whether manifested as earthquakes, epidemics, famines or wars, in other words through the cannon's roar.

Salvador Dalí
The Rotting Donkey

This is Dalí's first attempt to define paranoiac thought in relation to his paintings, in which he was experimenting with double and multiple images. He drew his notion of paranoia from current psychology, which considered it in terms of delusional but systematic "mis-reading" of the world. Dalí's rejection of automatism, already apparent in his paintings from 1929, became more insistent in his texts of the 1930s. Breton was later alarmed at his use of the idea of 'discrediting reality', lifted from his own 1924 text 'Introduction to the Discourse on the Paucity of Reality', because Dalí called for a total overriding of the real world, while Breton believed the surrealist questioning of conventional categorical divisions between real and dream, etc. , embraced their interpenetration. The image of the 'rotting donkey' had appeared in paintings of 1927 and referred, among other things, to sentimental lyrical poetry.

First published in *Le Surréalisme au service de la révolution*, no.1, July 1930; reprinted in Salvador Dalí, *La Femme visible*, Paris: Éditions surréalistes, 1930. This translation by Haim Finklestein was published in *The Collected Writings of Salvador Dalí*, Cambridge: Cambridge University Press, 1998.

An activity having a moral tendency could be provoked by the violently paranoiac will to systematise confusion.

The very fact of paranoia, and, in particular, consideration of its mechanism as a force and power, lead us to the possibility of a mental crisis, perhaps of an equivalent nature, but in any case at the opposite pole from the crisis to which we are also subjected by the fact of hallucination.

I believe the moment is drawing near when, by a thought process of a paranoiac and active character, it would be possible (simultaneously with automatism and other passive states) to systematise confusion and thereby contribute to a total discrediting of the world of reality.

* * *

The new simulacra which the paranoiac thought may suddenly let loose will not merely have their origin in the unconscious, but, in addition, the force of the paranoiac power will itself be at the service of the unconscious.

These new and menacing simulacra will act skilfully and corrosively with the clarity of physical and diurnal appearances; a clarity which, with its special quality of self-reserve or modesty, will make us dream of the old metaphysical mechanism which has something about it that may readily be confused with the very essence of nature, which, according to Heraclitus, delights in hiding itself.

* * *

Standing wholly apart from the influence of the sensory phenomena with which hallucination is more or less taken to be associated, the paranoiac activity always makes use of materials that are controllable and recognisable. Suffice it that the delirium of interpretation should have linked together the sense of the images of heterogeneous pictures covering a wall for the real existence of this link to be no longer deniable. Paranoia makes use of the external world in order to set off its obsessive idea, with the disturbing characteristic of verifying the reality of this idea for others. The reality of the external world serves as an illustration and proof, and is placed thus at the service of the reality of our mind.

All physicians are of one mind in recognising the swiftness and inconceivable subtlety commonly found in paranoiacs, who, taking advantage of associations and fact so refined as to escape normal people, reach conclusions that often cannot be contradicted or rejected and that in any case nearly always defy psychological analysis.

* * *

It is by a distinctly paranoiac process that it has been possible to obtain a double image: in other words, a representation of an object that is also, without the slightest pictorial or anatomical modification, the representation of another entirely different object, this one being equally devoid of any deformation or abnormality disclosing some adjustment.

The attainment of such a double image has been made possible thanks to the violence of the paranoiac thought which has made use, with cunning and skill, of the required quantity of pretexts, coincidences and so on, taking advantage of them so as to reveal the second image (the image of a lion, for example) and thus in succession until the concurrence of a number of images which would be limited only by the extent of the mind's paranoiac capacity.

I submit to a materialist analysis the type of mental crisis that might be provoked by such an image; I submit to it the far more complex problem of determining which of these images has the highest potential for existence, once the intervention of desire is

3 I am thinking in particular of the materialist ideas of Georges Bataille, but also in general of all the old materialism that this gentleman senilely claims to be rejuvenating, while relying gratuitously on modern psychology.

accepted; and also the more serious and general question of whether a series of such representations accepts a limit, or, whether, as we have every reason to believe, such a limit does not exist, or exists merely as a function of each individual's paranoiac capacity.

All this (assuming that no other general causes intervene) allows me, to say the least, to contend that our images of reality themselves depend on the degree of our paranoiac faculty, and that yet, theoretically, an individual endowed with a sufficient degree of this faculty, might as he wishes see the successive changes of form of an object perceived in reality just as in the case of voluntary hallucination; this, however, with the still more devastatingly important characteristic that the various forms assumed by the object in question will be controllable and recognisable by all, as soon as the paranoiac will simply indicate them.

* * *

The paranoiac mechanism giving birth to the image of multiple figuration endows our understanding with a key to the birth and origin of the essence of the simulacra, whose furore dominates the aspect under which are hidden the multiple appearances of the concrete. It is precisely the violence and the traumatic essence of the simulacra with regard to reality, and the absence of the slightest osmosis between reality and the simulacra, which lead us to infer the (poetic) impossibility of any kind of *comparison*. There would be no possibility of comparing two things, unless it would be possible for them to exist with no links whatsoever, conscious or unconscious, between them. Such a comparison made tangible would clearly serve as illustration of our notion of the gratuitous.

It is by their lack of congruity with reality, and for what may be seen as gratuitous in their existence, that the simulacra so easily assume the form of reality while the latter, in its turn, may adapt itself to the violence of the simulacra, which materialist thought idiotically confounds with the violence of reality.[3]

Nothing can prevent me from recognising the multiple presence of simulacra in the example of the multiple image, even if one of its states adopts the appearance of a rotting donkey and even if such a donkey is actually and horribly putrefied, covered with thousands of flies and ants; and, since in this case one cannot infer the meaning of these distinct states of the image beyond the notion of time, nothing can convince me that this merciless putrefaction of the donkey is anything other than the hard and blinding glint of new precious stones.

Nor do we know if the three great simulacra, excrement, blood, and putrefaction, do not expressly conceal the coveted 'treasure land'.

Connoisseurs of images, we have long ago learned to recognise the image of desire hidden behind the simulacra of terror, and even the awakening of 'Golden Ages' in the ignominious scatological simulacra.

* * *

The acceptance of simulacra, whose appearances reality strives with difficulty to imitate, leads us to *desire ideal* things.

Perhaps no simulacrum has created ensembles to which the word *ideal* could apply so well as the great simulacrum constituted by the astounding art nouveau ornamental architecture. No collective effort has managed to create a dream world so pure and so disturbing as the art nouveau buildings, which, existing on the fringes of architecture, constitute in themselves a true realisation of solidified desires, and where the most violent and cruel automatism terribly betrays a hatred of reality and the need to find refuge in an ideal world, in a manner akin to the way this happens in infantile neurosis.

Here is what we can still like, this imposing mass of frenzied and cold buildings spread over all of Europe, despised and neglected by anthologies and scholarly surveys. This is enough to put up against our porcine contemporary aestheticians, defenders of the detestable 'modern art', and enough even to put up against the whole history of art.

* * *

It would be appropriate to say, once and for all, to all art critics, artists, and so on, that they need not expect from the new surrealist images anything other than disappointment, foul sensation and feeling of repulsion. Being quite on the fringes of plastic investigations and other kinds of 'bullshit', the new images of surrealism will more and more take on the forms and colours of demoralisation and confusion. The day is not far off when a picture would attain the value and only the value of a simple moral act, which would yet be a simple gratuitous act.

The new images, as a functional form of thought, will adopt the free disposition of desire while being violently repressed. The lethal activity of these new images, simultaneously with other surrealist activities, may also contribute to the collapse of reality, to the benefit of everything which, through and beyond the base and abominable ideals of any kind, aesthetic, humanitarian, philosophical, and so on, brings us back to the clear sources of masturbation, of exhibitionism, of crime, and of love.

The surrealists are Idealists partaking of no ideal. The ideal images of surrealism are at the service of an imminent crisis of consciousness, at the service of the Revolution.

Roger Caillois
Specification of Poetry

Roger Caillois was opposed to all lyricism in poetry. For him poetry was analogous to scientific exploration and needed to be pursued with a similar rigour. Caillois's strictures against lyricism go too far even for many surrealists, but they do go to the heart of what surrealism sought from poetry and from art generally, that it should reject personal expression and descriptive embellishment and devote its energy to exploring the nature and limits of language – thereby putting the boundaries of reality to the test.

First published in *Le Surréalisme au service de la révolution*, no.5, 1934; reprinted in Roger Caillois, *Approches de l'imaginaire*, Paris: Gallimard, 1974.

It is a fact that poetry continues to benefit from a dubious indulgence which tends to confer dangerous advantages on it by safeguarding it, under the pretext of a sacrilegious intrusion, from any critical examination no matter how lacking in rigour. Poetry has more to lose than gain from such complacency, for it is enough that were it to be assumed that poetry thrives on complacency then it might immediately be disqualified. The fact that so many works present themselves as poems when it is difficult to find in them anything but the most inexcusable sentimental, artistic or intellectual frauds, makes it impossible for a strict thought not to consider poetry as the right given to anyone at all to say whatever they like, without guarantee or obligation to account for it. This is why, at the slightest compromise, it falls into the rank of a (particularly literary) literary genre which barely commands attention, apart from a generally irritating typographical arrangement, a greater confusion and a greater audacity in inflation and jiggery-pokery. This state of things could thus be invoked by interested parties to try to justify the opposition they are happy to open up between the poetic as a special case of the imaginary and the real. It is nonetheless certain that this situation by itself alone risks cancelling out surrealism's claims to absolute objectivity and to compel it to consider itself as being in an unfair and unjustified competition with scientific activity (the prejudicial question relating to the true implications of this idea of unfair competition being placed to one side for a moment). On the contrary, it is precisely to the extent that surrealism has considered poetry as a fact and has systematically exhausted it as such by taking it to these extreme limits, limits which in their turn are poetic facts susceptible to a concentric development and so on, that it has with some validity earned the sole right to undertake the critique of the empirical imagination.

It is therefore a question of *organising* poetry. Under these conditions, the concept and the object are fundamentally equally valid application points, given that the same *concrete independence* and uneasy relations exist between the concept and the ensemble of singular adventures which support it affectively as between the object and its utilitarian role, a long way from glimpsing here and there the perfect coincidence that rational thought might assume that it contains. It is clear that the utilitarian role of an object can never completely justify its form, in other words the object always overflows the instrument. Thus it is possible to discover in each object an irrational residue determined among other things by the unconscious intentions of the inventor or technician.[4] Equally, any concept possesses a specific concrete value which allows it to be considered as an object and no longer as an abstraction. For example, as an abstraction, the word 'spider' can only pass for a

4 It would clearly be of enormous poetic interest to *isolate* this irrational residue. But in practice the operation proves extremely delicate. Only the simultaneous use of different methods will allow us to reach some certainty through the comparison of results. In spite of a certain lack of clarification, the surrealist enquiries are to be considered as a first means of investigation.

convenient and approximate means of expression. That is the
ordinary sphere of literature: it is therefore characterised by the
premature and ill-considered use of words, using what is most
superficial about them, most skeletal and least graspable, taking
them in their minimal representations, the impersonal as much as
the personal, the murky as much as the distinct which, moreover
without prejudice, renders its scientific interest practically
worthless. In contrast, poetry begins at the moment the word is
considered in the theoretical infinity of its representations, that
is, in the preceding example, the irrational concept of the spider
as an aggregate of empirical data. It is clear that the affective
independence of the concept in relation to the word which supports
it is determined both by the object, which is to say by its potential for
collective representations or excitement (thus psychoanalysis and
gestalt theory in different realms reveal the existence of symbols
and attractive forms of universal value), and by the subject, which
means the conscious and unconscious systematisation of
memories and tendencies, in a word, by its life – and finally by their
preceding relations, by the 'decor' of the occasions when they are
already in attendance: the spiders' webs destroyed in advancing
into the shadow, those which Heliogabalus collected in enormous
quantities before the end of the day, the legs of so-called harvester
'spiders' which move around an open hand for a long time, erudite
works about spiders, spiders that prisoners keep as pets in their
cells, spiders and somnambulism, spiders and dishes that must
be eaten cold.

We notice on the other hand that this mediation of the
irrational concept, in which the complete history of the individual
intervenes, abundantly justifies the fundamental role surrealism
has assigned to automatism in poetry.

Finally, and especially, the opposition between the poetic
and the real has become difficult to maintain. It could be admitted
if necessary that to benefit its very specific interests an industrial
civilisation casts discredit on manifestations of reality (dream
and madness for example) which from its perspective are less
immediately of use and so it consequently places them in categories
like those of the unwonted or the abnormal, at least to the extent
that they imply only a statistical or commercial judgement. But at
the moment when an excessive deviation has managed generally to
impose concepts of appearance and subjectivity, in other words to
select a certain number of its manifestations in reality and declare
them less real than others for the sole reason that they are less
apparently dependent on all the other representations, that they
are only of interest to the individual consciousness or, to crown it
all, that they result from chance, according to the circumstances a
hypocritical confession of ignorance or a convenient flat refusal, it
becomes indispensable to denounce such arbitrariness and affirm
once and for all that in a philosophy which assigns no special value
to the mind, concepts of appearance and subjectivity can have no
meaning.

That said, surrealism's efforts will perhaps be more easily

situated: it has been thought to have striven to bring reality into disrepute, or more precisely, with the benefit of evidence, to place all objective solidity in doubt. This proposition is precise only dialectically, in other words if the antithetical aspect of this effort is considered at the same time: to accredit everything that industrial and rational pragmatism has attempted to remove from reality without ever appreciating the pretentious absurdity of such a suppression. Surrealism can thus take as a maxim of its experience Hegel's very obvious aphorism: 'Nothing is more real than appearance considered as appearance'. This is also the epigraph for all poetry which refuses to take advantage of its artistic privileges if is to be considered a science. It is thus in principle violently unilateral in the sense of the marvellous and the unwonted, and applies itself independently of any other consideration and using any available means of taking into account what is irrational in the object and the concept, but there is nothing it should not subsequently take account of according to the strictest of methodological critiques.

On this path, the otherwise so useful presence of mind gives way to a mysterious *absence of mind*, as does the supposed and otherwise so brilliant but illusory freedom of mind to the necessity of mind – which is less forgiving and knows better. Poetry has no right to autonomy.

Tristan Tzara
Essay on the Situation of Poetry

This essay is important for the distinction Tzara makes between poetry as an 'activity of the spirit' and as a 'means of expression', something fundamental to surrealism. His supporting arguments, however, are problematic and contentious, especially as related to his other distinction, drawn from Jung, between directed and non-directed thought. Indeed this directly contradicts another fundamental of surrealism expressed by Benjamin Péret – that 'thought is ONE and indivisible' – and Nicolas Calas subjected Tzara's use of this distinction to some withering criticism (see Calas 1937, pp.18–20). By 'non-directed thought', Tzara was probably intending to signify something akin to automatism, and his notion of poetry-activity of the mind or spirit is opposed to poetry as defined by formal means of expression. In fact, by combining these two distinctions and making non-directed thought the characteristic of poetry-activity of the spirit, Tzara seems even to undermine his own argument that the latter is part of a recent development within poetry. Written at the time of surrealism's uneasy alliance with communism, Tzara's essay is also unusual within surrealist writing for its optimistic, not to say naïve, faith in the progress of thought. Tzara was probably keen to contribute to debates about the role of art and literature as he underlines the dire state of 'poetry as means of expression', and how the 'refuge' it offers will disappear with the end of bourgeois society.

First published in *Le surréalisme au service de la révolution*, no.4, December 1931.[5]

This is about assembling, through an inextricable jumble of facts and emotions on which human diversity hungrily feeds with the aim of baffling the most lucid, a schema of poetry valid for the present period which, in spite of the glacial aridity into which we have been placed by science, may be able to aid us to recover a co-efficient which tends perceptibly to decrease. It is about analysing, in the light of new data, now that anticipation of the consequences becomes possible – those who have felt that a bridge of light links us, my friends and myself, to the beginning of a vast enterprise, are still not very many, because a centenary for pigs served up by swineherds all too content with the setting up of their literary pig farms, in the end has disrupted the true sense of romanticism – now that the anticipation of the consequences of an activity of which we constitute only a link becomes possible, I say that it is about separating the good coal from the clinker, by the only light science currently places at our disposition: dialectical materialism (the help of psychoanalysis will be more efficacious when it comes to *explaining* poetry, a subjective phenomenon). There are others more qualified than I am to evaluate the choice of this method, in terms of its value in current society, the critique it offers and which supports that of our own, the confirmations it has received and, to mark more effectively the stage of passage in a continual becoming, *the reasons it has given us to live*, the help it brings to us, after incalculable neglect, to become aware of these reasons.

I would like to give more emphasis to a principle dear to me, *the provisional*, but a provisional solidly founded on a continuation which can no longer escape us, necessarily linked to other past provisionals, responding to the needs of others to come, a *provisional state aware* of its extreme importance, closing off the paths from which it comes, and hastening to leave behind as much as possible of the successive states in a given direction. I have never been able to accord any other importance to facts which have occurred or in the works I love than that which, at a level at which they could be maintained as *signs*, as *testimony*, as marking posts in a continual transformation, was measurable only on the scale of their becoming. Their explosive content – the door broken down, the step crossed, their degree of indifference to any static attitude (meaning masterpiece) – the advancement in a determined direction, the relation between the point or step takes as its point of departure a terminal of another step crossed so as, in its turn, to cross a fresh step and this newly acquired point constitutes for me the unique value I lend it. And if the door is wide open, if the distance crossed is great (in the age in which the fact occurred) it is because a considerable explosion has preceded this memorable fact, the maximum imaginable in time at the level familiar to it and, preserving all proportion regarding its becoming, a knot,

5 Contrary to one of our principles in editing this anthology, we have on this one occasion abridged this text – Tzara's original article is extremely long and includes a lot of historical detail which is no longer necessary to his argument. It should be noted that the always problematic translation of the French word 'esprit' (mind/spirit) presents special problems in this essay – by 'poetry-activity-of-the-mind/spirit', Tzara is invoking the idea of a poetry that comes both directly from the individual mind and is a representation of a collective spirit (Lauréamont's 'poetry must be made by all, not by one' invoked by Tzara at the end).

6 It should be understood that for convenience I am using this terminology only in a provisional way, by opposing two different terms within a single proposition.

a revolution, were brilliantly produced: here is the origin of my emotion. It is not to be confused with its assimilation by simple minds to emotions of an artistic order for which long ago I had already spared neither my scorn nor my disgust.

What I am talking about is poetry and I'll try, with the means I possess and certain that others will do better, to demonstrate that poetry, as I will later define it, *follows a direction along an existent path*, and that, consequently, as with any phenomenon, Hegel's law of the *nodal line of measure relations* may be applied to it, while foreseeing the possibilities, in a new society, to which its transformation from quality into quantity is linked. This obscure language will become clarified in the course of the journey, because it is, almost, with the same phrase that my demonstration will end.

* * *

Despite this poorly defined, living flame, the poetry which continues to gleam more and more intensely (the very indifference that opposes the so-called public to those whom today's society obstinately calls poets, aggravates the reactions to it still more) a doubt about the very efficacy of poetry eats into the secret construction which, for centuries, has not been able to impose its reality, although its intention to participate as an active element with other intellectual forms might so often be demonstrated with a tragic ardour. Let us as rapidly as possible dispel a misunderstanding which claims to class poetry under the rubric of a *means of expression*. Poetry which is distinguished from novels only by its external form, or poetry which expresses either ideas or sentiments, no longer interests anyone. To this I oppose poetry as an *activity of the spirit*.[6] Recent ravings about pure poetry do not situate the debate. It is accepted today that someone can be a poet without ever having written a verse; or that there exists a quantity of poetry in the street, in a commercial spectacle, no matter where, the confusion is great, it is 'poetic', Proust went out of his way to find it in public urinals, which led to the dawning of a new generation of seekers of poetry at any price and everywhere, applying it to their own dramatic productions or those of others and find it again at the end of this excremental chain where justice ignominiously couples with the church. The same confusion concerning painting had already occurred in another period: the quest for the gleefully recalled picturesque. It will easily be understood that neither this poetry, nor this painting, taken in the sense of a topic being able to serve to..., of a subject or vague quality not committed to anything, could contribute anything of interest to my outline. In recent times painting, sculpture and even the novel has been subordinated to poetry – this attempt should be seen merely as a poorly assimilated expression of certain Dada principles.

The primacy of the poetic taken in its sense of quality proves once more the impotence of situating on the ideological level a multiple activity which is actually at variance with current society, but which one tries to integrate rather than opposing it to that society. In the principles of beauty, static and immutable beauty

7 It should be understood that the framework of poetry-activity of the spirit should also include painting and sculpture (see also the surrealist objects described by Breton and Dalí), as can be seen most clearly in the context of Dada and surrealism.

(from this the notion of the masterpiece is only spitting distance away), we find what have always been considered the unshakeable foundations from which to build the house of cards – knocked down and rebuilt so often – of what is called art. It would be completely inadmissible that, in the name of dialectical materialism, theoreticians should adopt wholesale a notion whose very bases are idealist, which by its essence is idealist in its turn, without seeking further its sources or its base, to adapt it and give it a stimulus in the 'framework' of dialectical materialism. We would not be amazed if such confusions led their partisans to quite absurd results.

* * *

[...] The idea which has guided us and which from 1916 received fresh verification has been that of poetry pursuing a development whose sense of direction has been given by the line connecting poetry-means of expression with poetry-activity of the spirit, that tendency being repeated within poetry, is the very one poetry as a whole will follow. To put this another way: despite all the intermediary steps, poetry-activity of the spirit grows quantitatively and progressively over time to the detriment of poetry-means of expression. Poetry *tends to become* an activity of the spirit. It *tends to deny* poetry-means of expression. That today it might in part be a means of expression, is determined by its liaison with language, in other words its form. Poetry will therefore only be able to become uniquely an activity of the spirit by freeing itself from language or from its form.[7] How might it do this?

* * *

It is not through some trick of the trade that I want to gain acceptance for my proposition that the form of poetry should be identified with language. (In some ways it is a matter of what I will crudely call logical language, and not of words or concepts).

Two ways of thinking exist and confront one another. If the tip of one is represented by dream, it is easy to locate so-called 'directed' or logical thought at the tip of the other.

Without according great importance to the vocabulary employed by Jung, I will use it to give a general sense of the distinction between 'directed' and 'non-directed' thought. (See the chapter in *Psychology of the Unconscious: A Study of the Transformations and Symbolisms of the Libido* devoted to the two forms of thought).

Thought defined as directed is a psychic process of adaptation into the milieu. This form of thinking, says Jung, 'working for communication with speech elements, is troublesome and exhausting; [... It] creates innovations, adaptations, imitates reality and seeks to act upon it' [Jung 1991, p.20]. We think in words. As though it were a matter of convincing someone, we recite thought to ourselves. Language is at each stage of civilisation the sum total of past human knowledge sifted from collective experience. Directed (or logical) thought engenders scientific progress; it is productive. Being a process of adaptation to the milieu, it would correspond in psychic life to the function of vital work in biology (and productive work in economic life, one might add).

The form of non-directed (or associative or hypological) thought 'turns away from reality, sets free subjective wishes, and is, in regard to adaptation, wholly unproductive' [ibid., p.20]. This thought consists of an apparently arbitrary sequence of images; it is supra-verbal and passive, and the dream, fantastic and imaginative thought and diurnal reverie lie in its domain.

I have no illusions about the confusion that may result from the introduction of this new element into the debate. It has value only as a comparative term.

In a study I am currently writing, 'On dream in the thought of primitive peoples', I propose to demonstrate that 'non-directed' thought so dominates what has improperly been called 'primitive mentality' that it would be possible to envisage a pure state of it in which the break that the passage from the dreaming to the waking state represents for us might vanish completely. Just as notions of work, laziness, proletariat, and so on assume a completely different aspect, a new specific content, in a communist society, in primitive society the states of dreaming and waking are not measurable by the knowledge at our disposal. Jung affirms that the form of 'directed' thinking (which engenders the development of the sciences) is a relatively recent acquisition of humanity. But Jung does not show us how it developed over the course of history by expanding so extensively to the detriment of 'non-directed' thinking. It seems undeniable that this would be intimately linked to the development of economic conditions and the passage from primitive to capitalist society, a point we will have occasion to return to. Historically, the process of the mode of thought follows a direction in a way given by the line linking 'non-directed' to 'directed' thought. The elements of the former still existing as a residue in 'civilised mentality' (it is not without a certain irony that I use this term) are dream, diurnal reverie and fantastic thought. It seems to me that in this activity of the spirit, poetry, as Breton has related it to dream through automatic writing and surrealism, finds an entirely natural place.

Perusing once again a historical outline of poetry will easily allow us to appreciate how 'directed' thought corresponds to poetry-means of expression while 'non-directed' thought corresponds to poetry-activity of the spirit: we will see on one side the preponderance of systematically logical language, thinking in words, the instrument of this thinking within which it is perfected, and on the other side the characteristics of thinking which consist in a succession of images.

Poetry follows, at a completely different level, a direction contrary to that of forms of thinking. But from the development of the latter as they are reproduced individually within each of us, going from the unconscious to the conscious and from infantile to logical thought, it would be easy to establish the attitude of opposition and contradiction, that the two developments of ways of thinking and of poetry-dream are allocated mutually within the general sphere of human thought.

* * *

8 A few idealistic fools, perhaps unaware of the role they play in bolstering bourgeois culture, have attempted to oppose the *spirit* to the *machine* (Werfel), forgetting that the latter's role is to *serve* and not to enslave. Haven't I recently heard a celebrated muddle-head, one of those professional falsifiers of history (Barbusse), say that only total realism (!) ('I have added a bit of social extension to realism' are his very words) is capable of leading to the Revolution? Basing himself on Comte's frankly reactionary positivism, he was demanding freedom for the people! Incredible, but that's how it was.

[...] No creation of the spirit, as expression of this spirit, would be able to elude the reigning ideology, itself resulting from class antagonism. Work that is considered 'art', in any period, reflects a historical fact engendered by social and economic relations. Note that, within the framework of poetry, the contribution of poetry-means of expression or the influence of a bourgeois ideology needs to be revealed, while the contribution of poetry-activity of the spirit completely eludes this grasp. Through a long succession of plastically demonstrative acts (Dada) and verifications with a real concern for scientific method (surrealism) – I'm speaking of poetry – these influences are reduced to the minimum in direct proportion with the reduction of the quantity of poetry-means of expression.

If in current society poetry constitutes a *refuge*, an *opposition* to the bourgeoisie as the dominant class, in the future society in which the economic antagonism of classes will vanish, poetry will no longer be submitted to the same conditions. The poet (for want of another name, I am forced to use this inadequate word, however true it is for us that the terminology is no longer adequate to the new content), takes refuge in the realm of poetry because he assimilates his opposition to the capitalist class with opposition to 'directed' thinking, which has engendered science and today's civilisation and is in hock to the bourgeoisie.

Just as work in a socialised society is no longer what today we consider as such, just as the proletariat no longer being the exploited loses the meaning accorded to it, can we predict that poetry, which will lose even its name by pursuing its historic development, will be transformed into an activity of the collective spirit (just as the dream is), following the law of the nodal line of measure relations and that in these terms Lautréamont's motto 'poetry made by all' will become a reality?

Theoretically we can admit that, just as a primitive mentality could exist, one whose characteristic was non-directed thought in a relatively pure state, something difficult for us to conceive, a new state could be born in a communist society in which every relation of value is new, a *poetic state* dominated by non-directed thought superimposed on the structure of civilisation and its indestructible conquests. It can no longer, for us, be a matter of any sort of retrenchment and of regressing to a primitive state for instance, as certain eighteenth century authors wanted, but of establishing a *superstructure* of a psychic order over an existing mass. It would also be anti-dialectical to want in any way to retrench within an activity which, historically, is justified perfectly as a continual progression and to return either to a form of poetry which has already been overcome, or to the ends of education or propaganda that, through its evolution, poetry has eliminated as anti-poetic.[8]

Engels said: 'We have already seen earlier ... in connection with this Hegelian nodal line of measure relations – in which quantitative change suddenly passes at certain points into qualitative transformation ... one of the best-known examples – that of the change of the aggregate states of water, which under normal atmospheric pressure ... so that at both these turning-points the merely quantitative change of temperature brings about a qualitative change in the condition of the water.' And further on: 'In proof of this law we might have cited hundreds of other similar facts from nature as well as from human society. Thus, for example, the whole of Part IV of Marx's *Capital* deals, in the field of co-operation, division of labour and manufacture, machinery and modern industry, with innumerable cases in which quantitative change alters the quality, and also qualitative change alters the quantity, of the things under consideration; in which therefore... quantity is transformed into quality and vice versa' [Marx and Engels 1987, p.117].

Is it possible to apply this law to poetry? I firmly believe it is. The quantitative increase of the role of poetry-activity of the spirit within the generalised sphere of poetry will render necessary the leap from the qualitative to the quantitative: the poetry which will be born from it will appear quite different from the one we now know.

Poetry-activity of the spirit *denies* poetry-means of expression. The vital demands of the Revolution (we see the conflict occurring at present) demands from poetry a participation it cannot grant without risking its death, the crushing of a long activity whose development is well established in a given direction. In its turn it is *denied*. A new poetry must be born from this negation of the negation, raised to a power that could only be found at the psychic level of the collectivity.

Once more we have to turn to Engels and consider his example of the grain of barley which, denied (not destroyed), might disappear as such if it falls on favourable ground, under the action of moisture and heat, to germinate and be replaced by the plant born from it. Through certain specific metamorphoses, this plant eventually produces fresh barley grains and is in its turn denied. We obtain the primordial, but *multiplied* barley grain. In some plants we obtain qualitatively improved grains and 'each fresh negation of the negation enhances this process of perfection', says Engels who also applies the principle to mathematics, geology, history and to philosophy. He shows how the negation of the immediate materialism of the Greeks by idealism is, in its turn, denied by modern materialism. Thus it is no longer the same as that of two thousand years ago (even though the latter contained its germ); it is multiplied, given potential by the new contributions to human understanding brought by the evolution of the two thousand years which have passed.

A disturbing fact that archaeologists and pre-historians have never explained in a satisfactory way, a mysterious point, a break it has not been possible to bridge occurred in the study of every ancient civilisation. Excavations, in Egypt, for instance, bring to light a very *reduced* number of prehistoric objects, rudimentary results of a primitive culture which extended over a quite considerable period of time. On the layers just above them (in chronological correspondence) we find, after a phase of some improvements, a *great quantity* of objects whose improvement

9 Vestiges of the preceding age remain in an embryonic state (dreams, reveries), in an attitude that is oppositional even if it is creative and liable to development.

continued over brief periods. A leap occurred. Over a long period, the material civilisation was manifested by a minimal and slow evolution of barely differentiated man-made objects. The dominant form of thinking is what we have called 'non-directed' (containing the seed of 'directed' thinking). Having reached the end of an evolution, which might be the realisation of 'directed' thought, provoked by new economic relations, a sudden surge occurred which, through the abundant vestiges of a material civilisation, their rapid evolution and improvement hastened at an increasingly accelerated rhythm, giving us a glimpse of the importance this new way of thinking assumed in a new society whose result, through the sciences, is today's civilisation. This phenomenon of 'rupture' is recorded, in different periods, wherever systematic excavations have revealed the existence of a prehistoric culture, except where this has continued over a long time (Australia, Oceania, Africa) and where we collect its last remains.

In a schematic way it could be affirmed that 'non-directed' thought is denied (in other words verified, conserved and elevated at the same time, *aufgehoben*) by phenomena of an economic order: the predominance of 'directed' thought is born from it.[9] We currently live in an age whose products, mechanism, standardisation and so on are perhaps its final stages. Communism will now place them in service of humanity. It is currently possible to foresee the effect this new fact will have on 'directed' ways of thinking. It will be denied in its turn and a new way of 'non-directed' thinking will be born from this negation of the negation, which will not simply be prehistoric non-directed thought, but what the latter contained in germ (let's say crudely, dream projected onto reality), multiplied, elevated to the power of lessons of thousands of years and the additions which constitute logic, science and so on. Without wanting to prophesy, I link the development of poetry in the future society to this destiny.

* * *

If surrealism, as a whole, as Aragon judiciously noted, is opposed to bourgeois culture and must, consequently, be placed in service of the Revolution, poetry, whose cycle surrealism must moreover lead it to perfect, cannot act on reality, for it is its share of poetry-means of expression which would be alone necessarily capable of this, and this must tend to diminish progressively.

Only a manifestation whose supreme aim is *freedom* is worthy of aspiring to a conscious and sustained development, and this is why it does not seem possible to me to conceive, starting from different postulates, any other course for poetry, providing the dialectical method of a becoming in formation is admitted as alone being valid. To simplify, I have not studied the problem of poetry in foreign languages which, in spite of the play of reciprocal influences from one country to another and following the ideological development and historical circumstances peculiar to them, anticipates or lags behind us; it nevertheless seems useful to me to insist on the fact that the step followed is parallel to that of French poetry which serves me here as a standard.

Marcel Duchamp
Female Fig Leaf 1950
Reproduced on front cover,
Le Surréalisme, même, no.1,
October 1956

One remark of a technical order is called for. Ever since Dada, under an elliptical and intentionally obscure style, many elements of poetry-means of expression had been superficially veiled and their elimination was merely apparent. Gratuitousness, like the arbitrary and the absurd, is ungraspable in the *pure* form Dada granted it. It is therefore necessary today as much as possible to objectivise that element of the means of expression, so as to be able to bring out poetry-activity of the spirit more effectively.

It is only to the extent that influences operate over its social and economic form or the remnant of a bourgeois ideology in the world of feelings that poetry has not yet reached total independence, just as the dream, however autonomous in its functioning, still represents in its images the reflection of a bourgeois life to which it is opposed. It is nevertheless likely that the transformable matter of poetry plays only a minimal role if one compares it with poetry's aspirations to independent sovereignty, a poetry whose character has been given ever since Dada. It is a matter of limiting more closely the differences between *dream* properly speaking and *poetry* (*dream projected onto diurnal life*) as well as their specific characteristics.

The complete meaning of *laziness* will be born from the study of their functioning. 'The right to laziness', as Lafargue said, 'is sacred' – but this laziness is one of the elements of the struggle for the reversal of social values, for once it has become a real conquest of the Revolution, it will cease to exist as such. What will it consist of when productive work is reduced to just a few hours? What will be the orientation of the leisure resulting from it, so that it will not create fresh needs which, in their turn, would quantitatively increase work hours to the detriment of this very leisure? By what means would we prevent productive work from resembling what we have become accustomed to calling laziness and leisure to become virtually work?

Poetic activity alone is capable of giving a *human* conclusion to *liberation*. Dream, laziness and leisure should be organised with a view to communist society; this is poetry's most current task. It will succeed only by refusing all temporary concessions and, by doing so, serving as an example and point of departure for those who would subsequently know how to make practical and assimilable to the masses a process of activity that, for the moment, few people admit, which is *quality* and which, in communist society, can be transformed into *quantity*.

* * *

An irreducible *emotional element* is born within the majority of us from the unease created by the poorly defined positions of several activities, from the non-concordance of their developments, from spiritual interests, some being manifested with greater intensity than others, successively taken as a focal point, then abandoned, taken up again, interlacing, crossing each other in parallel, moving away from each other, some towards the appeals of reason, others towards the seductions of the mind, in a continual struggle, interspersed with weariness (for this too is virulent and contains the seeds of unforeseeable activity). Let us without delay analyse what separates and what unites the surrealists, and accept once and for all the image which currently becomes increasingly valid, of an emotion resulting from battles between desires and satisfactions, attempts and uncertainties and even insufficiencies, human emotion in the first degree, which has never failed to help us out of the often painful blind alleys in which the whole future of group activity is played out.

I know how cruel the cold application of laws to a phenomenon which intimately affects us can be. I am the first to be tempted to cry out: at this price poetry does not interest me. A poetry acting independently and detached from the entirety of the phenomena of life... can one devote one's life to poetry when the slightest movement in the street, a little livelier than ordinarily, gives you a start, making you believe that all hope is not lost? To act, to really act! But the facts are there in their bare cruelty. More than once they confront us with the dilemma: to abandon or continue our efforts. The social Revolution does not need poetry, but poetry needs the Revolution.

To tend, with all its strength, towards the accomplishment of the Revolution, by pursuing in parallel poetic activity which is justified from the perspective of dialectical materialism, this it seems to me is surrealism's historic role: to organise leisure in the future society, to give content to laziness by preparing the realisation on scientific bases of the immense possibilities contained in Lautréamont's expression:

'POETRY MUST BE MADE BY ALL, NOT BY ONE.'

Paul Nougé
Inviolable Images

Nougé promotes the idea of seeing as an act, a dynamic action. Apparently influenced by gestalt psychology, the text was written at the time Nougé was challenging the psychology of sight with his project of the subversion of images. 'Vision is discontinuous', he tells us. Basing his argument on René Magritte's painting, Nougé also helps to explicate the painter's work, concerned as it is with the enigma of the way we see the world. Nougé was the first person to write about Magritte and he still has much to say to us both in terms of Magritte's own aims as part of the Belgian Surrealist Group and more generally about what surrealism expected of painting: not beauty but 'illumination' and 'revelation'.

First published in *Le Surréalisme au service de la révolution*, no.5, 1934; extended version in Nougé, *Histoire de ne pas rire*, Lausanne: L'Age de l'Homme, 1980.

Observation

No matter what it may appear, the pages that can be read or perused here are not constituted by 'thoughts'. They have no secret pretension to this, no indulgence, brilliance or rigidity. They are notes, fairly careful ones, to be sure, but destined for some unwritten coherent discourse, the author having a dread of the type of implacable cement used to make eternal monuments and tombs.

The author has rejected the conveniences of the language of philosophers and psychologists, at risk of finding himself being reproached for a certain clumsiness. It is rather to be regretted that he has so often had to have recourse to the words 'consciousness' and 'mind'; he has however tried to give them a reasonably precise content, which is unusual.

In the same way, the pleasure of originality has always given way to the desire to proclaim those propositions which merited and continue to merit being repeated.

These notes have a common object, a peculiarly difficult one, which it will probably be barely possible to reduce, one which will always elude us along some short cut. To get closer to this object it was decided to use various means, including some which have been greatly disparaged, classical analysis and traditional logic. We hope to have handled them with sufficient tact and care.

Among all the snares in the tricky domain into which he would have ventured, abstraction has seemed to the author one of the most formidable. This is why, in the course of his work, he has continued to rely on an eminently concrete given: the painting of René Magritte. Among several names which could be mentioned here (de Chirico, Max Ernst) the fact of having specifically fastened upon Magritte will be sufficiently explained in a moment.

The tone and appearance of some of these pages remain to be excused; it was a question of pressing on quickly and going reasonably far. At times a rather dogmatic appearance may not have been avoided which seems to contradict their true meaning, that of necessarily limited propositions, partial propositions in which some not insignificant aspects of the problem have only been touched upon lightly while others have been accentuated to serve the investigation.

However they seek to engage the reader, as they engage he who wrote them.

Moreover, the author believes they are susceptible to dialectical transformations and resolutions worthy of some care.

Vision thwarted

A general theory of vision which would not be in flagrant contradiction with the facts of everyday observation would be desirable...

The eye which still sees that which no longer exists, the star or the vanishing image on the screen; which does not see what goes too fast, the shot, this smile; which does not see what goes too slowly, the grass as it grows, ageing; which recognises a woman and finds she is someone else, a cat and it is a shoe, his love and it is the void: the freedom of the eye should long ago have put us on our guard.

It would be worth profiting from this freedom which has continued to be exercised at our expense.

TRANSFOR MAcTION
9

THIS IS NOT A MAGRITTE

This Is Not a Magritte
Front cover of *Transformaction*,
no.9, January 1929

Conjurers have dreamt of this, without too much precision perhaps, but they have succeeded.

Thus, to make invisible, to become invisible, this old hope is perhaps not as illusory as might be thought. But the solution does not lie in the direction of Arab stories. If I burden your arms with a sack of lead, then the captivating garden you will then cross will not in all reality exist for your suddenly petrified eyes. And you yourselves are invisible in the light of this woman beautiful enough to gratify all gazes.

... There is also that story of the strangely enlightening purloined letter.

Anatomy and physiology can play dirty tricks on those who follow them a little too closely; abstract psychology and the science of optics blind us.

The assimilation of the eye to a mirror, to the darkroom, is not without its disasters.

The fact that an illuminated object exists in front of the open eye does not mean that we will see it.

Objects are not imposed on our eye; at most they solicit it in a more or less confused or insistent way. Passivity is not appropriate here. To see is an act; the eye sees as the hand grasps. Our hand can pass within reach of many things it is not led to grasp; our open eyes pass over many things which remain, in the *physical* sense of the term, *invisible*.

Vision is discontinuous.

We see only what we have some interest in seeing. Interest can be born suddenly, which reveals to us what we might have rubbed shoulders with for years. And it is really a question of *seeing*, not of *looking*. Terror brutally illuminates the object, or desire, or pleasure, and we will speak of threat, charm or disgust when it is necessary for us to account for it later.

What is true for objects also holds for their image. We desire to enter this forest, whether it is real or painted. We see it only at the price of a similar desire. And not experiencing this desire, not seeing this forest, in some circumstances, reveals the kind of person you are.

What is true for vision is also so for the other senses. We hear only the words we have some interest in hearing, in a public place, those of people who are known to us or are in some way interesting, and not those we are indifferent to. There is a meditative solitude in very busy cafés...

It is thanks to a rending memory that we suddenly perceive that faint scent of roses.

We have felt nothing of this shock, but we did feel the imperceptible brushing of that delightful hand.

For us to see an object it is not enough to create it, it is not enough for it to exist. It has to be shown to us, that is, by some artifice, to excite the spectator with the desire and need to see it.

Fortunately it is here that arise those intimate banal things, certain figures and some movements closely implicated in the whole of human existence, certain points of departure which always and so easily engage us.

In this respect, we need to address ourselves to the flirts, the swindlers, the fairground vendors and tradesmen. They will inform us more accurately than painters.

Man beset by images

The first feature of painting is evident to the point of passing unnoticed: painting proposes to us certain isolated images in the midst of the unbroken images of the universe.

Isolated; in the most subtle or vulgar way, no matter. The wooden or gilt frame, the more or less emphasised rupture with the environment, the countryside in the heart of the city, snow in the midst of summer. Or if Apelles can for a moment lead birds astray, it no less remains that the image of a grape is not the same whether it comes from the bunch or from Apelles. And by falling prey to it from the outset the isolation of the image is subsequently accentuated.

If the image is isolated, how does the mind respond?

The mind desires nothing so much as to abandon itself to its initial movement; it likes nothing as much as its well-trodden paths. For as long as painting has existed, the majority of painted images strangely flatter this deep-rooted taste for facility. As is usually the case, in the course of the discourse and the current through these landscapes bereft of surprise, why shouldn't the imagination follow that woman who is a little too beautiful to evoke love? In the end a memory of the stroll barely remains.

But sometimes painting does not offer such convenience. Far from benignly opening up familiar perspectives, the image blocks the mind from all restful paths.

Rather than offer the mind a series of very logically inferred images, with the first image evoking its successors by ceding its place to them, the immobile painting sometimes settles down in consciousness – and remains there. Just as it has arrested the eye, the painting arrests the mind.

But the same thing may happen to consciousness concerned with a single image, and which lasts, as happens to the eye fixing upon a single object. The eye gets confused. Consciousness dims. The eye becomes blinded, and as for consciousness...

The person who stares for a long time at a brilliant mark happens to become lost to external reality, or else reality begins to die around him. Voices rise from some depth, voices he himself had until then ignored. For this sleeping man, walls and heads become transparent. Secret thoughts and hidden treasures spring up.

There is no need to go as far as hypnosis. Certain isolated images that painting presents to us are capable of latching onto clear consciousness to the point of making it coincide with them, thereby stopping the flow of words and phantoms, the immense *flight* which normally constitutes it.

But a resistance is not really opposed to the mind. For the mind immobility merges with death. The enormous dark river which tirelessly rolls along in our depths breaks its banks and suddenly overflows in bright sunlight. It constrains man to see, think and feel what he believed himself forever incapable of experiencing or wanting.

This would explain the only power painting has which might not be unworthy. We can speak here of 'illumination' and 'revelation'. We know precisely enough what it means to speak.

The birth of images

One would wish that an image would support images.

If painting exists, we know how it treats the spectator. One can however worry about the moment in which this painting did not yet exist. And the painter comes into play.

It could not be a matter of a forest of symbols but of the singular contact of some object and the mind in the midst of the incessant and fleeting images of the world.

Whether it is a banal or exceptional object that the gaze encounters very particularly or which raises an object which owes its virtue of attraction to its particular properties from some silent eddies of the memory or sees this virtue conferred upon it by the thought it fascinates, doesn't matter here.

The object, separated by some mysterious operation of the tangled universe to which it still belonged a moment ago, the strangely fluid object caught up in living as days and sleep go by. A measureless space is filled up with unknown figures, which create a void around themselves. The haunted shadow makes itself less transparent. This is the decisive hour and second. And suddenly the mind sinks into miracle. The marvel takes shape. Unforeseeable evidence joins its scattered limbs with a bond of flesh and blood. This, sometimes, is how painting exists.

The thousand events which make the painted work the physical and mental object it is – one that is eminently complex, a singular crossroads of more or less deliberated memories, desires, pleasures and intentions – are situated between that decisive moment and, delivered up to itself, the palpable surface saturated with all its colours, as it is in some way imposed on the consciousness of the painter.

But, as we can see, neither a programme, nor a preoccupation of a plastic order decides the essential element.

... On either side of the painting the portrait of the painter and the portrait of the authentic art lover can still be seen coinciding very curiously.

Metaphor transfigured

To transform the world to the measure of our desires assumes the belief that people, as a whole, are animated to various degrees by the same profound need to elude the established order. The validity of the enterprise is linked to the existence of such a desire.

It is therefore essential to indicate its complete extent and it is in this way that Magritte observes that a certain linguistic figure, the metaphor, could testify to it on condition of taking it in an uncommon direction.

The metaphor would not arise from a difficulty in naming the object, as some people think, or from an analogical slippage of thought. It should be grasped in its literal meaning, like the mind's wish that what it expresses should exist in full reality, and further, as belief, in the moment it expresses it, in this reality. Thus we have hands of ivory, eyes of jet and lips of coral.

But there is hardly any sentiment that does not double itself up to some degree with a contrary sentiment; the desire for it to be like this is thus undermined, for the average person, by fear - fear of the consequences. One will only consent to see metaphor as an artifice of language, a more or less precise way of expressing oneself, but with no repercussions on the mind which uses it or on the world to which it is addressed.

In this way one can wish for a *lasting* metaphor, a metaphor which removes from thought its possibilities of return. The only poetry we recognise as valuable tends in this direction. And the painting which confers on the sign the concrete evidence of the thing signified, evidence it will no longer be possible to dodge.

Means and ends

Refusal of the established order, the will to destroy current values or to introduce new ones into them, the essentially subversive aim must be to use every available means according to circumstances. And if circumstances require it, such a vigorous will should not hesitate to use even the most disparaged of these resources. The moment confers a unique grandeur on them. Thus the one who can, when appropriate, play at will upon the highly subtle and complex scope of the word, will if necessary write the indispensable page in terms of a political log. Sometimes abuse and trivial insults mask their youthfulness. Its language no longer contains any *divergence*.

Painting needs to invent images equivalent to such writing, images that must be experienced with the naked eye. Hence Magritte's paintings *The Three Priests* and *The Inverted Virgin*. Scandal consecrates such enterprises. And we are entitled to require a sufficient freedom of the painter from the point of view of painting for him not to give such paintings a lesser value than any other of his canvases.

He will also completely refute the hierarchy proposed to him by aesthetes and art lovers. For he knows what it conceals, what it tends towards, and the fact that ultimately it is only an ambiguous weapon wielded by a class which refuses to die.

He knows that the revolutionary spirit which animates all images he happens to present to the world, from the poorest to the most refined, confers an equal and sufficient dignity upon them.

Such a sentiment still makes living possible.

Roger Caillois
Systematisation and Determination

Upon joining the Surrealist Group in 1933 at the age of nineteen, Roger Caillois brought with him a determination to subject the phenomena of the world to a rigorous examination that would disclose the true nature of things. In particular he considered that the task of the poet had to be analogous to that of the scientist, something which precluded any form of personal expression or sentiment. This was in accord with basic surrealist precepts, but no one was as severe as Caillois in seeking to establish a poetic attitude that would make lyrical flights of fancy unsupported by empirical evidence redundant. This also led Caillois to an understanding of automatism very different to how it is generally understood, in which what is at stake is a provocation of the mind, such that the idea of the freedom of the mind is replaced by a necessity of mind. From a surrealist perspective, what is crucial in Caillois's examination is the determination to treat poetic (and by the same token artistic) creation as a methodology and not as an aesthetic.

First published in *Intervention Surréaliste*, 1934; reprinted in Roger Caillois, *Approches de l'imaginaire*, Paris: Gallimard, 1974.

All human attempts at knowledge seem to be reduced to seeking invariance in a fluctuating world.[10] I will admit that personally I am not, in effect, able to stay within the common antinomy, since I perceive no appreciable difference between the known and the unknown. I think it is enough to pay a little attention to this subject, providing that it is outside of any theoretical set purpose, so as to understand how minimal is the division separating them. There is neither scepticism nor excessive ambition in this. I merely wish to say that knowledge and ignorance appear as equally imperfect and, so to speak, incomplete, as the one accommodates itself equally well to the most acknowledged insufficiency as the other to the most compromising behaviour, and that in this respect it is easy to recognise that words here hide two clearly equivalent aspects of the same situation. The opposition between the diverse and the identical, the moving and the motionless, and the Other and the Same, appears a more precise approximation. Science is fairly accurately defined as research into the unity of the cause behind the multiplicity of effects. That no disciple might fail to complete this enterprise in every realm with the aid of a principle which seems only to relate to one alone constitutes a disturbing fact, singularly going beyond the slightest circumspect expectation and precisely

10 C.J. Keyser, *Mathematical Philosophy: A Study of Fate and Freedom*, New York: E.P. Dutton & Co., 1922; Émile Meyerson, *Identity and Reality*, translated by Kate Loewenberg, London: G. Allen & Unwin; New York: Macmillan & Co., 1930.

seemingly unable to be explained except in terms of the hypothesis of a systematic over-determination of all the elements. Everything in fact occurs as though the mode of explanation of each specific science was an *organisation of plausibilities* constituted from one poorly defined fact or group of facts and, due to the continuity of the universe, susceptible to a sort of indefinite concentric extension into all other realms, which of course would be to the detriment of the rigour of its comprehension. In fact the explanations of science overlap to such an extent that each deludes itself that it is even able to account for the existence of others. Thus we currently see historical materialism and psychoanalysis, for instance, reciprocally relating their constitution to the principle they have respectively adopted, each of these systems considering the other as a specific, easily reducible fact.

Even mathematics allows itself the boldest intrusions and finds the most precise verifications where they are least expected, in botany or zoology, for example. Likewise, in a general way, it is legitimate to affirm that the experimental data can be deciphered on the basis of several keys and systematised from several perspectives whose number is not *a priori* determinable and each of which constitutes a particular method of knowledge, which because of this appears to be a systematisation. This thereby leads us to pose the problem of the value of the lyrical imagination in the same terms and to examine whether it can render the same service in the realm of affective representations and emotional themes as what is, for instance, rendered elsewhere by geometry and dialectics whose triple genetic, absorbent and systematising character is manifest. *On the whole, it is a question only of translating the fact that comprehension always more or less comes down to integration*; from this perspective, the perfect science would be nothing other than effective awareness of the multiple coherence of the elements of the universe, an apperception which very probably would lead not only to highly significant modifications in the way of seeing and feeling (it is does not seem arbitrary here to play on the double, abstract and concrete, meaning of certain words) but also the possession of a genuinely moral, if not metaphysical, position. This is the content I agree to give to the idea of salvation, for which there should be no excess of honours and which deserves more in any case than the indignity in which one is currently more or less obliged to maintain it (due to its ideological inconsistency) if one takes indulgence to the point of not judging the tree by its fruits.

Whatever the case, and to return to the focus of the debate, I would be content if it is granted that the above lines have identified the problem of the value of lyrical thought in the clearest light and most fitting situation. I have not the slightest illusion about the response I will get to this. More than anyone I recognise how limited my research has been: its results are hardly decisive and its approximation is wide. On the contrary, I think I can obtain my own evidence by affirming that if lyrical thought holds no interest in respect of the systematisation I expect it to have, it cannot have any interest at all - or none of value, I mean.

The work is more than half done for dream. Indeed, if one agrees to consider the mechanisms that psychoanalytic research has if not disclosed then at least defined (condensation, over-determination, transference, and so on) as *processes in the affective systematisation of representations* which, as a result of the necessities of action, at first appeared disparate (and it seems difficult to assign them any other role), it is clear that, even if there

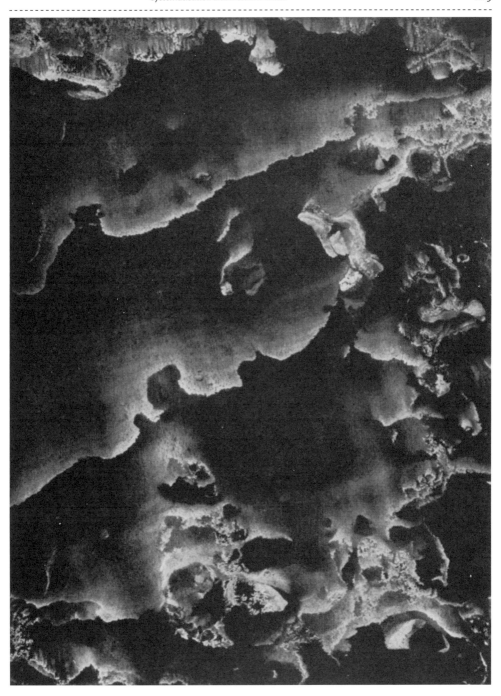

Marcel Jean
Decalcomania
Reproduced in *Minotaure*, no.8,
June 1936

might be different kinds of dream, oneiric indications are less negligible and moreover they constitute especially reliable documents, elaborated as they are according to relatively autonomous processes.

It is not the same for lyrical thought, whose means of access are far from being above suspicion and for which there is no reason to think it responds to an initial necessity rather than to laziness or abuse of authority. However, it should be pointed out that the example of dream, a phenomenon I drew upon earlier to recall its elementary and independent character, shows that the mind's necessity is capable of identifying or associating the representations appropriate to it by itself, in such a way that one is led to wonder if *the function of lyrical thought in waking life is not to figure in a similar way any given element whenever it is felt necessary*, in other words when some multiple representations have already over-determined its content, a content that is best capable of filling the ideogrammatic role of systematisation which pre-existed it and to which, in the final analysis, its advent is exclusively due. Thus several irregular stones carelessly gathered together leave a certain gap between them whose form is precisely designed in such a way that the block which would fill this gap is strictly determined beforehand, this determinism of the negative space being as rigorous as any other. Similarly, it seems that an accumulation of convergent representations pre-determines all or some of the conditions which will have to be fulfilled by the content of what they need in order to present an unbroken coherence. It follows that this exists virtually, due to the existence of what came before it, and that it will be established in consciousness at the initial and contingent appeal, passing from power to the act.

Such at least are the thoughts which occurred to me in the course of analysis of a recent example of non-directed associations. While waiting for a train, my eyes fell on a sheet-metal plaque (perhaps marking a junction) with a white 'M' painted on it. I realised that this letter was curiously the first name initial of the only three women with whom my relations had assumed a character of exceptional gravity and of the nickname I had given to one of them; I then considered the test of the inverted 'M' in the hand (an expression that appeared to my very disjointed attention to bear sufficient evidence in itself). I pictured a wound in the form of an 'M' on which vinegar was being poured, a torture in an initiatory ritual, while I had a rather clear visual image of a hand opening and revealing to me an 'M' in its palm which, because its ends were being turned towards the fingers, appeared as a 'W'. Without lingering over the strangeness of this vision, I let my thoughts wander and noticed that 'W' and 'M' were the initials of a lady to whom I had that very morning sent a book and that these two interlaced letters formed a monogram which appeared on the dining room chairs at my parents' home – a sign with a cabalistic aspect which had made a strong impression on me as a child. I asked about their significance over and over, but was never satisfied with the very reasonable response given to me that they

11 René Guénon, *The King of the World*, translated by Henry D. Fohr, Hillsday, NJ: Sophia Perennis, 2001 [trans.].

12 I am alluding to the fact that some days later, and in relation to something completely different, it occurred to me that as a child I had read in an illustrated magazine the story of Ismail the Bulgarian who carved a cross on the hand of his prisoners with a dagger. The image of the hand may have been produced by the memory of this torture, although the arrangement of the fingers themselves into an 'M' and the fact that this letter is at the same time the initial of the word *main* [hand] may have been enough to over-determine its apparition.

were simply the initials of the furniture's previous owners. I nevertheless felt I had glimpsed the monogram more recently and indeed I hastened to recall (although doing so brought an end to the association) that the previous day I had noted a not very different motif presented as a condensed sign of the sacred monosyllable AUM in a work by René Guénon, *The King of the World*,[11] the impression of which I had wanted to compare with that of the book I had just sent to the woman I mentioned and whose initials were precisely 'W' and 'M'.

I enjoy the fact that this is nothing more than the most banal experience: it becomes all the more important to account for the unexpected representation which occurred at just the right moment so as to unite the other elements and for which I could find no precise substratum, no matter how deeply I examined my memory. Admittedly it could still be a matter of a memory of an unidentified dream or some deformed hypermnesic image *whose deformation would moreover still be significant*.[12] It seems a lot more economical to assume that it might have been a sort of ideogrammatic crystallisation (and in this particular case having a slightly hallucinatory character) destined to associate the multiple cross-references which immediately came to the fore and whose existence alone determined and implicated the content, assigning it as a necessary and sufficient property for its explanation as much by perception as by reflection the fact that an inverted 'M' is a 'W', and at the same time to show the two signs united. As for the word 'crystallisation', it is not at all chosen at random: indeed how can one fail to notice that the bizarre situation of these images between virtuality and reality, their latent existence and in some way its solution, is analogous to those unstable states studied in chemistry like phenomena of over-saturation, in which a minimal but well-defined stimulation, condensed and appearing as if a precipitate of the dissolved invisible substance, suddenly sprang up from nothing? But instead of extending the comparison to the circumstances of production (here, the rising of temperature and slow cooling; there, accumulated and satisfied emotions) whose sweep is clearly identical, it is undoubtedly wiser to draw attention to the facility with which such analogies become specious when more is asked of them than the modest and empirical services of reciprocal clarification they can render.

On the whole, I would be satisfied if the preceding analysis had cast some light on the means by which lyrical thought can fulfil its systematising function. Thus the value of the synthesis we have witnessed it carry out could at least be approximately measured. We are in the presence of an irreducible effort towards this perfect affective lucidity, whose consequences, as unforeseeable as they might be, could only be very great and which one could not discredit without discrediting oneself at the same time. What is called poetic activity, supported by objective over-determination of the universe, was viable; itself an over-determination, and one of the most effective in this realm, it now appears, to the extent that it is exercised as it should be, in other words according to a

13 These considerations characterise my position within surrealism. Desiring to situate them in a precise way, for instance in relation to ideas expressed in the *Surrealist Manifesto*, I would readily compare them with the following lines: 'By slow degrees the mind becomes convinced of the supreme reality of these images. At first limiting itself to submitting to them, it soon realises that they flatter its reason, and increase its knowledge accordingly. The mind becomes aware of the limitless expanses wherein its desires are made manifest' [Breton 1969, p.37] or again, this definition: 'Surrealism is based on the belief in the superior reality of certain forms of previously neglected associations, in the supremacy of dream and in the disinterested play of thought' [Breton 1969, p.26; translation modified].

methodological and not aesthetic attitude, neither replaceable nor devoid of validity.[13] It follows that the advantage drawn from a sequence of lyrical associations is measured by the increase of the immediate sensibility following from its assimilation and that it is also a function of the number and intensity of representative focal points which it condenses and over-determines in a personal myth. These focal points being indefinitely contagious due to their epidemic character, it is not difficult to conceive that these two scales coincide among all individuals sufficiently driven to *occupy* the synthesis they appropriate. In this light, the expression 'the beauty of a poem' has hardly any appreciable meaning. On the contrary, we will validly know the lyrical power or objectivity of a representation or a given association from the strength, stability and generality of its use and particularly, in relation to each, from the greater or lesser necessity for its integration in personal affective development.

More profoundly, in fact, it is what is really at stake and perhaps a more decisive study could be tackled by following this path. I noted earlier the serious consequences which for my part I was expecting from it, definitely situated beyond the two terms of the central problem of the necessity or the freedom of the mind.

It is a question of systematisation, of knowledge, and of knowledge of necessity. Is it consequently a question of freedom, as a certain well-known proposition affirms, which could, it seems, rank among the worst errors? One would not dare make this claim. When it is lucid, consciousness is as much in the determinant as in the determined, to which, as ignorant, it was relegated. It is therefore a question only of determining for oneself, of identification with determination itself.

So I would give some indication of what it is to me…

Georges Henein
The Subversive Function of Poetry

For the surrealists poetry was both revolutionary and the focus of a quest for the original meaning of language. In this affirmation of the power of poetry as understood within surrealism, written at a dark period of European history as it was about to enter into a new world war, Henein asserts the always trenchant surrealist demand for poetry's autonomy even, or especially, at times of crisis. This demand would be developed controversially by Benjamin Péret in his pamphlet 'The Poet's Dishonour' attacking the poetry of the French Resistance, especially that of his former comrades Louis Aragon and Paul Éluard. This ties in crucially with the texts in Part Three, since for the surrealists poetry is the only realm in which we can genuinely assert our freedom. The affirmation of poetry's status as the embodiment of freedom is the poet's moral responsibility, which can admit of no compromises.

First published in *Grande Erg*, Oran, no.1, Summer 1939; reprinted in Georges Henein, *Oeuvres: poèmes, récits, essais, articles et pamphlets*, Paris: Denoël, 2006.

Of all the judgements brought to bear on the poetic function, I remember one by Hegel that is more valid than ever. First of all a very general formula: 'anything able to interest or occupy the mind in some way' can become poetry. And Hegel's inventory includes 'every object of the moral world and nature, events, histories, actions'. But he adds that 'this very rich and varied material is not poetic just because it is conceived by the imagination … Actually it is not imagination in itself which renders a subject poetic but only the artistic imagination, which must', Hegel tells us (and this is crucial), 'be its own end, remain free and fashion everything it conceives towards a purely artistic and contemplative end, like a world that is complete and independent in itself'.

Everything contained in these lines that is strictly speaking revolutionary should be underlined in an age when all sorts of sordid prescriptions still lurk within poetry, in which the modalities of versification continue to define the poetic act for 'connoisseurs'. Hegel speaks to us of a 'world that is complete and independent in itself'. It involves searching the depths of this idea, clarifying where this world comes from, following its development and studying its uncompletable course.

The story of the magic carpet is nothing but a colourful protest against the laws of gravity. People divert their unemployed energies from immediate reality to serve the constant elaboration of an internal universe in exact proportion to the way human volitions are checked and thwarted by the rigour of physical laws. And what at the start had been simply the expression of a utilitarian will becomes, as soon as reality is opposed to the exercise of this will, a sort of gratuitous and ideal demand, one that is generative of poetry.

Moreover, the unformulated ambitions of broad anonymous humanities, which practical reason has reduced to silence, become condensed into a sort of exceptional spirit and become the prime matter of its poetic genius.

A work which obediently aligns itself with the order of existing facts, society, moral norms, oppressive processes and everyday servitudes, a work which accepts the human condition, in other words, using clear language, the condemnation of man by the world, has not the slightest claim to poetry. Every poem in some way militates against a certain state of reality that restricts what can be brash and exemplary about the poetic vocation. When Baudelaire puts a head of hair centre stage, it is for him only a pretext for other rarer and more difficult possessions. In it and from it, he grasped enormous desired spaces, he grasped the entire ocean.

Affirming this is neither to speak in jest, nor even is it paradoxical: poetry consists in denaturing nature. Because this is really where the complete revision (if not abolition) of logical criteria, in terms of which we classify things perceived, is leading. One should not say 'this cloud resembles a camel', but on the contrary, that 'this camel resembles a cloud'. And Lautréamont took the experiment to its necessary conclusion when he declared with the very tone of certainty: 'I've seen a fig eat a donkey'.

This approach is merely a response and an opposition to the aberrations perpetrated by some of the least worthy romantic writers. Their whole creative activity was in fact limited to forming a modest stock of landscapes suited to just so many duly catalogued states of the soul. According to the time and mood one will be able to settle down in landscapes of anguish or serenity or hope and so on. A convenient and comfortable attitude. The result is a code of utterly inept affective reactions – a similar mechanism occurs in both cases, whether the conformity of pure civility requires degrees of joy on the occasion of a marriage or a birth, or of sadness when it is a burial. To seek at any price and unfailingly to reveal a synchronism between internal events and external things, considered as interchangeable and irremovable, amounts to levelling the course of our subjective life by harmonising it with pre-established rhythms with which it has little or no concern. I consider a poem like Lamartine's *The Lake* as the most abject example of this sort of literature, a type of sentimental tourism.

Let's now move on to a poetic ensemble of the stature of Arnim's *Strange Stories*. Here the imagination determines its own course of action entirely on its own terms: it boldly composes its own setting, the only possible setting for the projected adventure – consider the opening pages of *Isabelle of Egypt*. The same thing goes for the *Chants de Maldoror*. The poet uses every element inherent to reality and external matter with absolute freedom. He de-crystallises them and, if I can venture the term, he 'de-paralyses' them, tearing them from their usual destination and arranging them at his entire and unique convenience.

All the unsatisfied desires, all the unrealised intentions of being, and finally everything within man that is less learned, less imported, of greater importance, finds a place in this spontaneous gushing forth of an autonomous world.

It is false and ridiculous to claim that poetry, especially as we understand it, is without social resonance, that to detach the poet from his time, from everything that is actual and concrete, renders his manifestations of conscience sterile; that the intelligence of a lyrical work being 'in principle' reserved for a minority of beautiful souls means that there is no question of acknowledging its genuine subversive significance.

Poetry is the contrary of an ivory tower. Poetry is not only a refusal of obedience served on all existing censorship and tyranny or the most elevated form of non-resignation to the summary explanations of our terrestrial destiny. It is also an ever-increasing knowledge of the self, an uninterrupted discovery of new human regions and a necessary renewal of the bases of life. Poetry, and this is where the whole extent of its role becomes apparent, has the power to transport what was just a way of dreaming into a way of being. Or more precisely – it exalts this power within us.

Baudelaire's famous poem *Correspondences* is in fact simply an inspired anticipation of the victories of the modern sensibility, a manifesto for the individual's sensual enrichment and the proclamation of a stage that can now be declared surmounted.

Clovis Trouille
Reproduced in *Le Surréalisme au service de la révolution*, no.5, May 1933

The only possible conclusion is that Baudelaire, like Rimbaud or like the poet per se, must figure as one of the most important builders of the future.

And the word 'revolution' gleams greater and purer deep within the word 'future'. Freedom and necessity, which determine in equal measure the situation of the work of art, share the common outcome of permanent revolution as inseparable from human becoming. I am effectively saying that there is a total symmetry between the free development of the artistic imagination to which we owe our principal reasons for writing and the necessary adaptation of regimes and things to the growing needs of man, for which we have only too many reasons to fight. And a blatant solidarity at the level of action to this verifiable symmetry corresponds at the level of the idea. Wherever the vital needs of the species are, at the current time, repressed and insulted, everywhere in which the sinister watchword 'Guns, not butter!'[14] prevails, the rights of poetry are humiliated, just as are the fortunes of art and thought, and it is impossible for art's fortunes to grow. The bullets of Franco's killers know how to find the chests of poets and the voice of General Millán-Astray[15] drowns out the din of execution squads as he utters this unforgettable rallying cry: 'Death to the intelligence!'

How can we not agree with André Breton and Diego Rivera when they declare in their manifesto of 25 July 1938: 'We have too high an idea of the role of art to deny it an influence on the fate of society. We believe that the supreme task of art in this day and age is consciously to take an active part in preparing the revolution' [Breton 1996, p.33].[16]

Literary and artistic creation, for all that it constitutes a sum of

14 A reference to Hermann Göring: see John Heartfield's photomontage *Hurrah the Butter Is Finished!* [trans.].

15 José Millán-Astray y Terreros (1879–1954), founder of the Spanish Foreign Legion who also coined the Fascist watchword 'Long Life Death!' In 1936 he shouted 'Death to intelligence! Long live death!' in the course of a seminar chaired by Miguel de Unamuno, one of Spain's leading intellectuals. Millán-Astray's outburst was against Unamuno and in support of a call by one Professor Maldonado for the extermination of all Basques and Catalans [trans.].

16 As is now well known, this manifesto was actually written by Breton and Trotsky [trans.].

autonomous ideas and forms that are not derived from the system of causality and values established by any given society, ends up by becoming unacceptable to that decadent society which demands that art and literature justifies its own existence, for want of being able to find it within itself. To break with society is nothing; breaking it is what is needed – it is to break within it all that is opposed to the obstinate march of man towards 'more light'.

If directed poetry appears as absolutely inadmissible, there is not the slightest doubt that what is at issue in the above-mentioned passage from the Breton–Rivera manifesto is to bring to its point of culmination the natural conflict which raises all poetry that is released from social constraint against a certain society which can no longer live except through constraint.

Karel Teige
On Surrealist Semiology

As in many of the texts in this anthology, Teige is concerned with the nature of the image and its relation to the 'reality' it represents, or more precisely: what is the reality that is inherent to the image itself and how does this correspond to its referent? Refusing the dualistic separation of image and reality Teige, like all surrealists, insists upon the polysemous quality of the image as it acts through the imagination not simply to reflect the world but to take an active part in its creation.

This text is assembled from a manuscript written in 1945 as a preface to the work of Toyen. Published in *Change Mondial II*, no.25, December 1975.

Imagination turns the represented thing into a symbol, which is at once an independent reality and a sign, filled with images, of all the realities to which desire links it through secret connections. It does this in such a way that, in addition to its apparent meaning, it contains a certain number of latent meanings which are inaccessible to consciousness.

It is the perpetual and fundamental impulse of our representation. The symbolic object or representation is the content of consciousness, which discloses hidden unconscious processes in the background. The realist technique of the imitation of nature, which effaces the frontiers between the thing and the image, is not used here in the service of realism or the principle of reality alone. When the image becomes a thing and the thing becomes a sign full of images, exchanges between psychic and material realities are arrived at in the course of which the psychic world, which is originally the reflection of the material world, makes this material world its reflection and image, the illustration and *manifestation of its desire*. The realist technique of imitation becomes a magical technique of the conquest of the real and the magical technique is submitted to the pleasure principle, creating a new poetic reality which is not dependent on the interdictions and laws of the apparent world, but of infantile, narcissistic and still eternally human and revolutionary omnipotence, of the desire which changes the impossible into the possible and the possible into the real.

The imitative drawing obeys the reality principle, in as much as it organises the liaison between image and thing; however, when it creates a new poetic reality on the surface of the painting, by such means it offers, precisely thanks to its magical nature, a gratification of the libidinal tendencies normally excluded from the content of consciousness, and submitted to the domination of the pleasure principle. The pleasure principle and the reality principle interpenetrate and are reconciled in the poem, the painting and the drawing. The world of imagination, assimilated into the material world thanks to this imitative drawing, is saturated with a strongly affective charge and the personal message assumes a meaning for collective life. The suppression of the barrier between the painting-sign and the thing allows not only the substitution of the painting for the thing represented and *an exchange between psychic and material realities* but also a collapsing of the barrier between the self and the author and that of the spectator.

* * *

The mirror certifies reality and deceives us about it. Infantile and poetic thought believes in the real existence of the image, in the identity of the thing and the representation, and it wants to dominate reality through representation. Rational thinking shows the virtual and immaterial character of the image, proves the duality of the thing and the image, and thereby constitutes two spheres, one of which is the appearance of the other: either perceptible objects alone are real, of which our representations are only immaterial reflections, or the empirical world is only the image of the spirit of the world. The surface of the painting and the mirror is the frontier between two universes and the miraculous land is always situated on the other side, relegated to the domain of the virtual, beyond the terrestrial world.

Surrealism goes beyond this duality. Without refusing either the reality or the primacy of the external world, it equally recognises a reality and an efficacy in the mental representations which result from them. It destroys the wall separating dream and reality, subject from object, representation from real, and imaginary representation from real perception. It not only wants to translate real life by means of a painting or a poem, but intends to *change it* through the realisation of a pan-human dream. Magic thinking is to the poem what dialectical logic is to scientific knowledge. In the domain of the spirit, it is the reconciliation of the two fundamental antagonistic forces of psychic life, the reality principle and the pleasure principle.

The thought that a repugnant world has aroused in the human mind and heart is that of denying its inhuman

LES MOTS ET LES IMAGES

Un objet ne tient pas tellement à son nom qu'on ne puisse lui en trouver un autre qui lui convienne mieux :

Il y a des objets qui se passent de nom :

Un mot ne sert parfois qu'à se désigner soi-même :

Un objet rencontre son image, un objet rencontre son nom. Il arrive que l'image et le nom de cet objet se rencontrent :

Parfois le nom d'un objet tient lieu d'une image :

Un mot peut prendre la place d'un objet dans la réalité :

Une image peut prendre la place d'un mot dans une proposition :

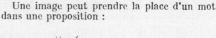

Un objet fait supposer qu'il y en a d'autres derrière lui :

Tout tend à faire penser qu'il y a peu de relation entre un objet et ce qui le représente :

Les mots qui servent à désigner deux objets différents ne montrent pas ce qui peut séparer ces objets l'un de l'autre :

Dans un tableau, les mots sont de la même substance que les images :

On voit autrement les images et les mots dans un tableau :

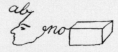

Une forme quelconque peut remplacer l'image d'un objet :

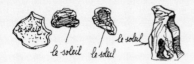

Un objet ne fait jamais le même office que son nom ou que son image :

Or, les contours visibles des objets, dans la réalité, se touchent comme s'ils formaient une mosaïque :

Les figures vagues ont une signification aussi nécessaire aussi parfaite que les précises :

Parfois, les noms écrits dans un tableau désignent des choses précises, et les images des choses vagues :

Ou bien le contraire :

René MAGRITTE.

René Magritte
Reproduced in *La Révolution surréaliste*, no.12, December 1929

[text reads, down the three columns:]

Words and Images

[*Column 1*]
An object is not so bound to its name that another might not be found that would better suit it.
[*image*]
There are objects that do without a name:
[*image*]
At times a word only serves to designate itself.
[*image*]
An object encounters its image, an object encounters its name. The image and the name of this object happen to meet one another.
[*image*]
Sometimes the name of an object takes the place of an image:
[*image*]
A word can take the place of an object in reality.

[*Column 2*]
An image can take the place of a word in a proposition:
[*image*]
One object implies there are others behind it.
[*image*]
Everything leads us to think there is very little relation between an object and what it represents:
[*image*]
Words that designate two different objects do not show what can separate these objects from one another.
[*image*]
In a painting words are of the same substance as images:
[*image*]
We see images and words differently in a painting,

[*Column 3*]
Any form can replace the image of an object.
[*image*]
An object never acts as its name or as its image.
[*image*]
The visible contours of objects, in reality touch one another as though they formed a mosaic:
[*image*]
Indistinct forms have a meaning as necessary and perfect as precise ones:
[*image*]
Sometimes names written in a painting designate precise things, and images indistinct things:
[*image*]
Or the contrary:
[*image*]

condition: acting in the spirit of this negation, as a real force aiming at the destruction of the world, it denies itself as thought, transforming itself into the reality of a new, humanised world. Surrealism's magic images neither illustrate nor take the place of reality, but act upon it, freeing the power of our unconscious desire, of our total and bare life. Painting and poem influence the human soul and operate a transformation of life, doing so not through propaganda or their latent content, but by the magic action of symbols inhabited by complex meanings and unfathomed tendencies. The surface which reflects the world is the burning material of human desire and immemorial dreams; it sends back its images, transformed by the desire developing within them, to the real world.

* * *

The nature of the symbol, as Hegel and Freud understood, always contains a plurality of meanings or, at least, a visible and existing thing that should not however be apprehended simply in its immediate existence, in itself, but in a more general and figurative sense, as a sign of another thing or other things and the representations it evokes, even if very vaguely, by means of certain of its properties. Of course, the idea or the representation symbolised transcend their apparent existence, overflowing the object by which they are manifested and which cannot absolutely enclose them within itself or make them disappear. The thing that carries the symbol equally contains qualities within itself that are different from those that express the meaning of the symbol in question.

      The mystery of symbolic works, which resists lexical, conceptual and rational explanation, the impossibility of responding in a completely exhaustive and precise manner to the question 'what do paintings of this type represent and mean?', stems from the fact that the symbol is never identical to its meaning, that the symbolic painting always represents something other and *in addition to* its meaning, while remaining a direct sign, bereft of images, of the thing in question. Moreover, if the particular elements and motifs of the painting are considered, we can start to doubt whether their material forms should be considered as symbols or not. Any depicted object can at the same time signify itself and symbolise something else; secondary meanings and representations, that are for the most part imprecise and contradictory, operate in the background of all depicted objects. What is gathered (by these meanings) as they become established behind the depicted thing and join with its properties, are all the richer and more numerous for the representation of the object being more realistic and exact. Rough drawings, plastic shortcuts that come closer to ideograms make the thing above all a sign: the only qualities of the thing in question which remain in it are those which translate the intended meaning. The naturalistic approach elaborated in details conserves all of the sensual qualities of the object, whether it is real or spectral, to which can be added various and innumerable representations, memories, feelings or unconscious tremors.

* * *

Neither detailed semantic explanation, nor a vast psychological analysis(which moreover is always incomplete and is never certain about its verification of biographical elements) can completely enlighten the painter's work in all of its dimensions and depth, can give a conceptual transcription of it or reveal the nature of its radiance. The latent content of the dream which can, after detailed analysis, be summed up in a few sentences, constitutes dry information about the terrifying, rending and fantastic drama which is the waking dream. The emotional power of the work resides in the disturbing mystery of this internal tension between the different signifying spheres whose convergences provoke discharges of lyrical electricity which run between its two poles.

The polysemous quality of the poem's cryptogram is never completely deciphered in its depths.

René Magritte
The Sense of the World

In this short text, René Magritte succinctly sums up one of the central aims of both his own work and that of surrealism as a whole, which is to promote the freedom of thought through provoking simultaneously the senses and the understanding (throughout the text, Magritte is playing on the various meanings of *sens* as sense, meaning, understanding, direction).

First published in the catalogue of the exhibition *Magritte*, La Louvière, Maison des Loisirs, 1954; reprinted in René Magritte, *Ecrits complets*,Paris: Flammarion, 1979.

Sense is the Impossible for possible thought.

To think of Sense means, for thought, to free oneself from the states which habitually characterise it. These states, which make thought coincide with *what does not concern it*, owe their relative value to an oppositional energy. Such is the belief in the necessity of glory or, again, the passion for questioning, the 'effects' of which are obtained 'outside'. Such is not the idea of Creation without Creator nor, again, the sympathy one can feel for a stone, the 'effects' of which are felt in thought.

Value is given by thought. Free thought alone has a value which does not depend on an opposition. The freedom of thought is the possible thought of Sense, in other words thought of the Impossible.

* * *

Possible thought is a means which cannot imprison free thought. The boundaries within which thought is imprisoned generally have no other horizons than those which are posed by a fastidious mode. In the realm of the arts, for example, a 'novelty' such as what is called abstract or non-figurative painting offers the Present only the substance of an exclusively superficial freedom. As for 'non-sense' and the impossibilities judged such by 'common sense' (the square circle, ghosts, scientific advances and so on), it is assuredly advisable to seek their origin in indulgence for the imagination and not in a will for freedom.

* * *

The freedom of thought is the possible thought of Sense, the Impossible for possible thought.

My paintings have been conceived to be material signs of the freedom of thought. For this reason they are perceptible images which are not unworthy of Sense.

To be able to reply to the question, 'What is the 'sense' of these images?', would correspond to reducing Sense, the Impossible, to a possible thought. To try to respond to this question would be to recognise it as having a valid 'sense'.

...The spectator should see these images in complete freedom, see *what they are*: they are HIS thought of Sense.

Adrien Dax
Automatic Perspective

Automatism was fundamental to the surrealist attitude, but how it was to be applied and what sort of results should be expected from its practice has always been subject to debate and disagreement within surrealism. In this text from 1950, the painter Adrien Dax takes stock of where automatism had taken the surrealists up that point and what could be expected of it in the future. His perception that one only advances over ruins is a key element of the surrealist attitude that sets it apart from the forward flow of most other currents of modern art.

First published in *Almanach Surréaliste du démi-siècle*, 1950.

Although it may not be acceptable to limit the intervention of surrealism in the plastic realm to the practices of graphic automatism alone, it is appropriate to note that often it has been able to affirm itself, and to do so in its most overwhelming aspects, through purely mechanical processes like those, for example, of frottage, fumage or decalcomania. In fact, from the surrealist point of view these techniques to a large extent - and sometimes to an extreme degree - have the incontestable advantage of reducing the conscious participation of the artist, who is thereby reliant upon a kind of chance, the auspicious character of which may be revealed as involving an augmentation of creative possibilities.

Beyond certain artistic approaches that are entirely valid precisely because of their contingencies of voluntary expression, for anyone who still remains attached to any exigencies, plastic creation very soon seems limited when it is conditioned by aesthetic preferences and subordinated to the will. At best, the artist can then exercise a disruptive influence by establishing new relations between the various events of a pre-existing world. It is a negative attitude - whose alignment with manifestations of the unconscious

17 Anton Prinner, lecture on printmaking. [Anton Prinner (1902–83) was a woman born in Hungary who, upon moving to Paris in 1927, pretended to be a man and established herself as painter, engraver and sculptor – trans.].

is flagrant – easily demonic in the eyes of Christian theology, admirable, no doubt, by reason of the sentiments of revolt it assumes but which brings only a desperate solution to the problem of creation, one above all characterised by the refusal of a certain order. The artist then constructs with borrowed elements and upon which this fragmentary character confers an unwonted aggression, a world of defiance whose insubordination and provocative value assumes all of its meaning only by implicating the confrontation with the initial order. In this respect, I cannot refrain from evoking the work of Bosch, in which the predominance of infernal subjects, even if only as a pretext, nonetheless remains symptomatic.

The practice of automatism can suggest the idea of a no doubt less dramatic but certainly more intransigent poetic attitude, to the extent that plastic creation is no longer exerted on the basis of an established or denied order, but more freely even beyond any intention of expression.

* * *

Most of the time the mechanical processes of graphic automatism have their origin in technical hitches, if not accidents, whose fortunate results, in revealing an unsuspected aspect of the possibilities of art, tend to cause us to reconsider the usual facts of the craft under the sign of a certain experimentation. Yet the utilisation of these facts to which the conscious reproduction of the conditions of the initial accident leads (a step which soon defines a particular process that is strictly determined by starting from a typical experience) may threaten the fortuitous character of the initial manifestation. In the course of a recent lecture on printing, Anton Prinner was able to reveal the multiple facts of this type, how their utilisation unfailingly assumes a formulaic aspect if one seeks to integrate them summarily with familiar techniques. Fortunately the aleatory character of the results does not always allow chance to operate in a direction which would soon lead to its most complete negation; and most often, within the limits of a particular art, the technical contribution is the weakest. Thus it is only a question of obtaining one or another 'effect' and so we are invited to consider these things solely in the light of studio 'tricks of the trade'.

It is rather within the frame of an entirely new art, no longer assuming any traditional technical considerations and defined solely by the generalised systematisation of an ensemble of experimental facts, that automatism has possibilities of revealing the significant means of action. In this sense, the research of Oscar Dominguez, more than bringing an augmentation of the possibilities of painting, helps us anticipate a whole art of printing, of which decalcomania is one particular aspect – one that Max Ernst has often used in a very free way, appropriate enough to be able to conceive a new attitude of the artist. 'In Hayter's studio, Max Ernst was the most astute in this type of experiment, arriving with pockets full of stuff he had collected on the way: leaves from trees, bits of toys, anything that came to hand. We were always intrigued to see what would come out of his pockets and then from the press.'[17]

18 Edouard Monod-Herzen, *Principles of General Morphology,* Paris: Gauthier-Villars, 1956-7.

In this way the whole unexpected aspect of these enterprises is underlined and their interest, beyond simple curiosity, often stems from the hope for a sort of miracle whose surprising results are sufficiently propitious not to make us reject any eventuality. In this case, works are above all else marvellous spectacles in which the eye can sally forth into a never before seen world, but envisaged from this aspect alone they soon lose their primitive seduction. In this sense we know the setbacks of decalcomania where in the end one just gets trapped in a devastation of the spirit in the same coral forest. It is only in proportion to their genesis and by reason of an activity that is constantly renewed in its means that these works manage to assume their full significance. One cannot remain constantly at the same window, even if it opens onto the most beautiful landscape in the world; it is surely vital to have the desire to open another one... always another one, to the point of the complete disappearance of a wall which, even if it is often that of Leonardo, nevertheless remains an obstacle.

Rather than drawing up a balance sheet of success and failure it is useful first of all to define the direction of a technical approach in which (in the light of acquired results) a disturbing analogy with natural processes of creation is hinted at. The testimony of Monod-Herzen, despite being oriented in terms of aesthetic considerations as opposed to surrealist preoccupations, here assumes its full value. We know the morphological law he wanted to formulate:

> *Relations of form and matter are the same whether matter is put to work by the play of natural forces or by man. And when a similar operation is applied to diverse material, the resulting transcriptions obey the same norm, whether the operating factor is an artist or nature.*[18]

Mechanical automatism, by the very fact of its character of involuntary expression, here finds an invaluable confirmation of its creative possibilities. In fact, the formal analogy between a natural object and any artistic creation could allow (with a measure of prudence so as to exclude any hasty deduction) the conclusion of a similarity of relations between the various specifications of matter and the generative processes employed on either side. In schematic terms, this could be expressed by a sort of equation:

NATURAL FORM = Matter (1) / natural action = matter (2) / human action = CREATED FORM

The results of automatism, provided that one seeks to appreciate them from a purely morphological perspective, illustrate this law. In this way grattage, for example, allows us to obtain effects that are quite close to those determined by the natural phenomenon of erosion. In sum, it is the same general process of wearing away which, making an abstraction of certain temporal conditions, is in play in both cases and that we will easily find by chance in surrealist paintings using this technique, the furrowing

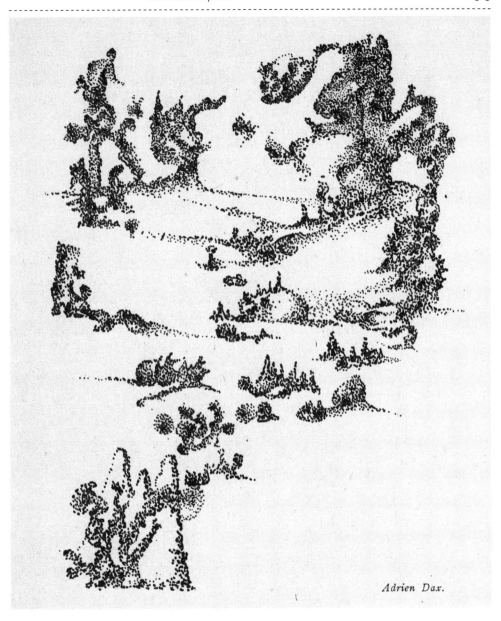

Adrien Dax.

Adrien Dax
Reproduced in his article

19 Stéphane Leduc (1853–
1939), French biologist who
sought to understand the
development of life through
experiments in which the
interactions of various
combinations of chemicals
were explored [trans.].

of dead wood and the disturbing surfaces of aeolian erosion.
However, it is useful to point out that in relation to grattage, one can
speak of formal creation only within certain limits; more precisely it
will be a matter of the modification of a given morphological state.
Let's all the same recall the analogy of the results. It is above all
with decalcomania that a less contestable manifestation of forms
created by an action exercised upon matter is revealed. The
procedure is well-known: it essentially consists in obtaining, by
applying pressure and peeling apart the damp gouache, images
that are varied but which affirm, regardless of how the technique is
modified, the persistence of certain structures characterised by a
sort of profusion of appearance that is at once vegetal and mineral.
In referring to a range of research into colloids (and precisely by
reason of the material employed) the morphological system
revealed by these images can easily be connected to a whole series
of natural creations. It can be affirmed that it is a question of forms
in their broad outlines determined through a colloidal action of the
material, fully comparable on the basis of figures of diffusion (of
which they are particular cases) in the dendrites Stéphane Leduc[19]
was able to provoke in the course of his experiments into
crystallisation, already a long time ago. The amazing kinship of
these dendrites with vegetal states assuredly testifies to a tendency
common to both inanimate and living matter, but it would be risky
to draw a conclusion too hastily from this relation. From this let us
just remember the fact that decalcomania can be integrated into a
whole series of natural phenomena from the birth of agate to the
appearance, at high altitude, of some mysterious arborescence
shaped by the wind and frozen mist.

Examples of this type of similitude could be multiplied in the
case of other automatic processes if one did not worry about thereby
crediting the simplified notion that these activities finally lead
merely to repeating forms that are actually revealed by nature. On
the contrary, nothing prevents us from thinking that one might, in
the course of a very open-ended research, arrive at a combination
of action and matter which achieves a form without any reference
to a natural aspect. The possibility of anticipating the unfolding of
natural creation can give a hint and this view indeed risks being
confirmed by the appearance of some unsuspected means of action.
There is nothing too utopian in this hope if for example one refers to
the birth of an invention like that of photography. Originally this
was nothing other than the idea of a painter for whom the camera
obscura's inverted landscape suggested that the art of drawing
could obtain every advantage from this optical phenomenon if only
it became possible to fix the image. All in all, it was just a matter of
compelling the light itself to outline the appearances it revealed; an
audacious idea for anyone satisfied with the means of painting but
which needed the encounter with the chemist to find a satisfactory
solution from which photography was born. A simple trick of
painting in fact, destined to make it appear incontestably real.
Today, some hundred and thirty years' distance reveals the extent
that has been crossed. A new art had been born, without its

20 Charles Cros (1842–88), French symbolist poet and inventor [trans.].

21 J.-Marcus de Vèze (E. Bosc), *La Transmutation des métaux: L'Or alchimique, l'argentoratum. Divers procédés de fabrication*, Paris: Dorbon aîné, 1902.

promoters realising it, and it was not long before it was able to improve in a barely conceivable direction: that of the registration and reproduction of movement. In the maturing of this fortunate hybrid and in the unforeseeable ricochets of its consequences there lay an invitation to explore every path, even if they only went to those suspect realms of invention which, in spite of valuable discoveries, often led Charles Cros[20] astray. The conclusion of these ambitious (to say the least) ideas was most often an incontestable failure, but it would be imprudent to judge them as always being chimerical; however, a disappointing result can present an unsuspected interest through a promising detour. It is in this light that it is useful to cite by way of example the incredible alchemical process developed by Strindberg.

Perhaps you are unaware that only a few things are needed to make gold. A sheet of paper, a few grams of iron sulphate, a little ammonia and a cigar are all that are required. The manipulations are very simple:

'Furnished with these ingredients, one takes a strip of paper, soaks it in the iron sulphate solution, and then holds it above the vapours rising from the flask of ammonia. This done, the sheet is left to dry in the cigar smoke one has smoked during the operation. Gold will appear after, at most, ten to twelve minutes of exposure to the smoke.'[21] Of course one should acknowledge the formation of an ammoniac iron sulphate whose molecular weight would correspond to that of gold chloride and to accord a surprising property to nicotine. Moreover, these things have no importance: alchemy did not make Strindberg rich, but these experiments allowed him to constitute his 'golden book' and by chance he discovered fabulous landscapes of fir trees in the brilliant stains with their metallic reflections which led his thoughts to a village in Bohemia to which he associated a happy memory. In spite of appearances, the transmutation had succeeded… it is at the level of the mind that the great work had been accomplished.

* * *

Considered from the perspective of their suggestive value, the results of automatism offer the eye, precisely because of their unexpected character, the possibility of escaping a common vision which, however objective it may claim to be, ultimately arises only from a collection of mental habits about whose value it is legitimate to have doubts. For the westerner of the twentieth century, the viewpoint, limited by the great convergent approaches of aesthetics and ethics, remains above all oriented simply by the utilitarian face of the world. Caught in this wire meshing, the eye is itself pragmatised and functions only as a filter in which a visual reality is elaborated, one that is reassuring as a working drawing but whose precarious quality is revealed by the unease man experiences whenever his vision operates beyond norms. If he then succeeds in overcoming his anguish, things are revealed to him under new aspects in which his most secret desires are objectified and he can form a vague sense of the full extent of his clairvoyant faculties, in spite of a long history of abdication and consent to the worst necessities which today have ceased to allow anything but sparse manifestations of them.

As a liberating re-education of sight, whose impact clearly goes beyond aesthetic satisfactions alone, the practice of automatism can reveal a close kinship with various divinatory processes. The invention of frottage as related by Max Ernst clearly unveils the interrogative character of the experience which it would be wrong to limit just to the level of art, and moreover one must agree that the marvellous illustrations of his *Natural History* are not so much pictures as doors flung open onto an unknown aspect of the real; their importance, otherwise great, confronts the possibilities they have been able to bring to the eye by tending to reaffirm the perfect coincidence of perception and representation, the very condition of clairvoyance.

At the origins of art, the mural paintings of the Magdalenian period appear in a similar landscape, provided we agree not to separate them from the rocky supports which most often determine their animal forms. The dark and mysterious cave in which the dancing gleams of flames brought about the strange blossoming of limestone concretions and the slightest projections of the rock in a living play of shadow and light have to be imagined in order for all the innumerable suggestions the wall could suggest to the people of that time to be understood. The bounding of the bison on the Altamira ceiling and the horse springing from the stalactites at Font-de-Gaume have an incontestable character of apparition; the hunter had only to define an outline and emphasise a detail in order to fix the strikingly truthful attitude of the animal suggested.

This human intervention tending to clarify the suggestion proposed by the external world finds an echo in some current attempts at interpreted automatism. But just as the prehistoric hunter knew how to see only animals in the rock face, today's artist seems only able to take advantage of suggestion to the extent to which it allows the projection of certain individual constants, rendered conscious by the very fact of interpretation and tending to create a visual habit that is soon limited to the same type of forms. Thus Hans Bellmer's beautiful interpreted decalcomanias are only particularly revealing of a persistent taste for the ambivalent body of an eternal minor.

The intervention of the artist would seem to gain by taking place more freely, and a new path could no longer be found in the inter-penetration of the results of automatism, which a certain practice soon makes deliberate, but rather in an attempt to steer the material reactions during the elaboration of the work. The not very easily controllable meaning of this approach (easily limited to an impulse) would, by constantly challenging the suggestive elements and interpretations they could have provoked, prevent any fixation on a predetermined meaning. From this perspective, the simultaneous use of two processes, such as grattage and decalcomania, has proved to have some efficacy.

If an overview of all of the various activities of mechanical automatism reveals, alongside some successes, a long sequence of failures, it nevertheless remains that the disappointing results may chance to be entirely valid, to the extent to which, no longer considered as ends, but rather as the bases of an imminent experimentation, they can maintain a certain irritation of the spirit, characteristic enough to engage us on a path along which one should expect to advance only over ruins.

Paul Nougé
Notes on Poetry

In this text Nougé emphasises several characteristic surrealist attitudes towards poetry, in particular the moral relation that exists between the poet and language which the poet should not abuse by trying to impose on it. Language is rather an object to be provoked by the poet into revealing *its* secrets, much as the scientist provokes the material world through experimentation to give up its secrets. Like Caillois, Nougé saw poetry as a form of science but where Caillois applied a largely phenomenological approach, seeking out the signatures of things from their general surroundings, Nougé was more concerned to draw out the hidden reality within phenomena itself by subverting our normal perception of it. This is a form of automatism, but one that is completely different from the spontaneous outpouring that so excited Breton. For Nougé spontaneity was actually the enemy; one had rather to interrogate phenomena in a deliberate manner until they revealed their reality.

First published in *Les Levrès nues*, no.3, October 1954.

An authentic poetic approach shuns the arbitrary. A metaphysical root can be found without too much difficulty within it: man, and consequently the universe, has not been accomplished; the pre-figuration of this accomplishment eludes us and one should not depend on an intellectual operation to discover its meaning or some abstract image or outline.

Nor can it be founded on a means of attentive passivity when confronted with the universe and oneself. There are no means which might be able to aid this accomplishment and which do not merge with action and adventure. If it is to be valid, poetic experience cannot be without risk or danger. The poet puts himself at risk and intends to guarantee the complicity of others. Thereby we realise that the poetic problem is inseparable from the moral problem.

It is useful to turn first of all to observation so as to have the firmest grasp on the problem and so illuminate its essential aspects.

The easiest examples to consider belong to the collection of written things we call 'Poetry'.

It is not too difficult to classify these objects according to easy to define types which respond to the intentions and practice of those drawn to create them.

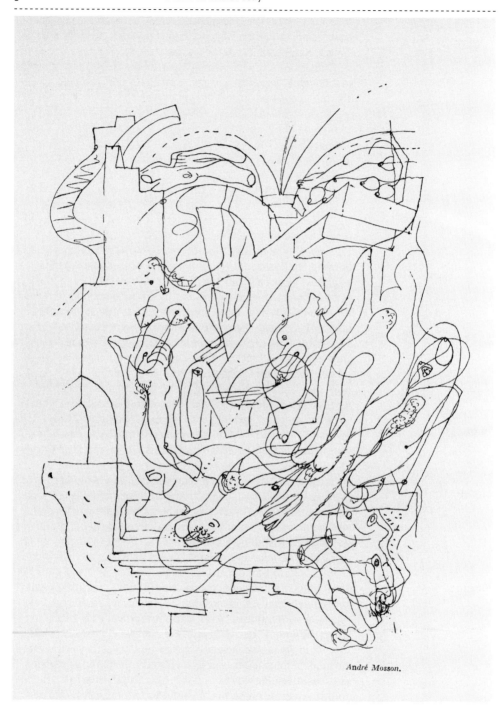

André Masson
Untitled automatic drawing
reproduced in *La Révolution
surréaliste*, no.3, 15 April 1925

1. Most authors have modest aims. They seek pleasure and especially the pleasure they take in using words to express and fix their emotions, feelings and thoughts.

The use they make of language arises from the habitual confidence we place in it to express ourselves. They are proud of being able to use words according to some instinct they recognise in themselves, which they claim to possess and which, notwithstanding the names they give to it and the assurance they place in their discourse, is nothing less than dubious. As soon as 'beauty' and 'sincerity' are stressed we have ceased to know what speaking means.

If they consider the reader, it is only so as to have him share this feeling of 'beauty', or to move him, or engage him through the image the poet presents of himself and in which he thinks he will not fail to find a little of himself.

It is therefore a matter of charming, with a charm identical to the one the poet feels, either of making himself hated or loved, which comes to the same thing.

2. There can be found among 'poetry' what seems to respond to different ends. The poet's effort is no longer governed just by his feelings and pleasures. He is concerned with more than being admired or disliked, or with communicating some aesthetic emotion to his peers. Or such preoccupations are, at the very least, subordinated to other concerns.

Moral preoccupations were absent from earlier output or came in only at a secondary level. Here we see them in a way take pride of place. The poet deliberately writes for others with the intention of affecting them in a certain way which he ordinarily imagines with the greatest precision. His human adventures, his happiness and unhappiness, have no place at all in his work or, at least, the poet will allow them to assume only a very relative importance, of such a nature that they will not upset the balance of the work to the point of modifying its expected effects. The poet writes for others, for he recognises a duty in relation to those others, a mission to be accomplished.

We owe 'epic' and 'didactic' poetry, as well as more disguised forms, such as prophesy, to such intentions.

In effect it is a question of placing the resources and charms of language in the service of a moral decision and a metaphysical, religious or scientific truth recognised once and for all, a language which the poets preferred to utilise to more or less personal ends.

It could be pointed out from the outset that these writers are eager to rid themselves of metaphysical problems and problems that arise from the very use of language. They hasten to find a solution to these problems that appears to them justified to the point of entailing a definitive commitment, and which consequently allows them to act with complete assurance.

How simple the philosophy of philosopher-poets and how perfunctory the morality of moral poets is has already been noted. In such a way poetic effort that relies on a metaphysic, religion or morality seems strangely to turn against them and ruin what appears essential in both morality and metaphysics. (And 'revolutionary' poetry is deployed against the revolution.)

We can also see that this 'poetry' intentionally assumes an oratory turn and often presents the formal coherence of discourses that follow closely the links of traditional logic. And, in fact, it is not a question of anything other than a lesson or a sermon adorned for the needs of the cause with all the politeness of language.

3. But a small number of poetic writings are finally discovered which manifestly respond to a different attitude and intentions. One quickly perceives that the desire to please, to charm in the usual sense, is absent in such poetry. They can do without approval.

The relations they maintain with their author are the secret ones which borrow as little as possible from the accidents and external forms of his life. His desires, hopes and misfortunes appear only as sublimated and deprived of their transitory qualities.

The metaphysical postulate is reduced to an immense and pure hope: that everything is possible for the universe and for man.

This moral imperative, always present and inflexible, establishes a duty, a severe duty upon the poet to neglect nothing, to set everything to work in order to advance, support and hasten such accomplishment.

Having reached this point in our search, we may wonder if what is no doubt essential in the scientific approach, in other words the spiritual habits it sets in train, would not be of such a nature as to furnish us with a doubtless rather coarse but still valid image of the poetic approach we have just indicated.

If we refer to the 'natural sciences', it will be noticed that, in the course of its development, 'experiment' plays the essential role. For scientists, experiment has assumed a very precise abstract role.

Faced with a given whole, the experimenter will try to recognise its elements and factors while being sure not to omit any, then vary one of the elements or factors, or introduce a new condition into it, so as to produce a modification of this whole as he tries to evaluate the effect properly.

We know the aspect experiment assumes when it becomes manifest in reality, and it will be useful to return to this later, for it seems that such consideration might disclose some priceless information from it.

But for the moment we will remain with its abstract and, let's admit, essential image.

The scientist is at once audacious and careful. Or rather, the experimental method he has once and for all adopted requires audacious prudence from the outset.

He is attached to 'hypotheses' (which resemble metaphysical systems in more than one feature) only in as much as they serve him on the path he has marked out; he considers them instruments and is always ready to abandon them if they cease to be profitable.

At the root of his approaches a sort of metaphysical prop and moral imperative can also be found.

An engagement with being and a taste for risk can be observed among some scientists which also links them with some poets.

Maurice Henry
Reproduced in *Almanach
surréaliste du demi-siècle*, 1950

They have an equal desire to dominate the elements brought into play, neither to be duped by them nor to be their plaything. Finally, with an equal confidence, they have poignant recourse to the great dark powers of the imagination.

In this way we readily arrive at a discussion of experimental poetic approaches and a 'poetry of experiment'.

The means of poety

We deconsecrate language and forms of their usual functions and give them fresh missions.

The poem considered as *object*.

To reach a poem:

its elements:

words and groups of words, drawn from memory, invented (or thought to be); furnished by the dissection of texts (division, isolation).

Isolated words, abstracted from language.

Groups of words, fragments of language.

Isolated words rarely come to our minds. They are the result of an abstraction which deprives them of the only life they might be granted: the power to engender a movement.

Isolated words are generally obscure and inert.

The contrary is the case with groups of words, the living fragments of language, which retain the power to engender or sketch a movement in an almost always unpredictable direction in relation to the language from which they have been separated.

Isolated words must be forced, and the conscious use one wants to make of them almost inevitably commits us to paths traced by the habitual logic of anyone using them. And it distances him from discovery.

There is an empiricism of poets.

They trust in their *memory* and their *situation*.

There's nothing astonishing about the mind not retaining any real benefit from their practices.

Efforts to go beyond these crude means (whether real or simulated): the story of 'the raven' – Paul Valéry.

The ends of poets and a whole collection of prejudices habitually stand aslant from such research. Their preoccupations are rather more inclined to provoke states they consider favourable (excitement, reading, alcohol, opium and so on).

Language

Research, experiments and reflections about language and particularly written language.

The mechanism of language.

The dynamism of language.

Language, and especially *written language* takes as an *object*, no doubt an acting object, in other words capable at any moment of *making sense*, but an object *detached from the one who uses it* to the point that it becomes possible in certain conditions to treat it as a material object, a material to be modified, an experimental material.

The particular interest of *games* which have language as their principal element comes from this:

> word games,
> riddles,
> charades,
> games of consequences;

the interest of approaches which tend to situate language as an object to be analysed:

> grammars,
> syntaxes,
> semantics;

the interest of *its most detached* naive manifestations which the community of minds might be able to accept:

> slogans,
> anecdotes,
> fables,
> apologues;

or, to express it better, where the community of minds use it with *the greatest freedom*, solely concerned *with an effect to be produced* independently of any preoccupation with expression or veracity.

Two ways of using language can rather roughly be distinguished.

The first presupposes the confidence one has in it as the translator of a state, a thought or an idea which would be prior to it and that it would have a mission to express.

It entails the priority of the need for sincerity, truth, submission to a certain object which is precisely the state, thought or idea, considered as such, that is isolated and pure of all contact, and is defined or capable of a definition that records or that language helps to form.

For anyone subjected to it the second considers language as an object apt to provoke certain states, thoughts and ideas, and it treats it (by additions, suppressions, interpolations, inflexions and so on) as an object as modifiable as a material object, directed solely to producing a certain anticipated or foreseen effect – or one simply considered to be unforeseeable.

It assumes a confidence in a certain science, a certain ingenuity, a certain joy which is sometimes confirmed by experiment.

But it relegates the idea of truth and sincerity to the rank of superfluous preoccupations or absurdity.

On the contrary it keeps in the foreground the concern which guides approaches that treat language as their object, in other words a feeling that could be taken from the value and responsibility provoked by the effects obtained.

Vincent Bounoure
Surrealism and the Savage Heart

Many theories, some of them rather fanciful, have been put forward as to why the surrealists in general were not greatly attracted to African art, much preferring as they did the art of Oceania and pre-Columbian America. Bounoure implies that African societies in general, being peasant communities concerned with subsistence, and thus based upon market systems of exchange centred in barter (rather than the gift exchange largely found in Oceania and the Americas), were principally devoted to utilitarian concerns which left only limited room for the 'revolt against empirical existence' and engagement with the ineffable which Bounoure sees as the essential feature linking surrealism with the societies of Oceania.

First published in English translation (not used here) in the exhibition catalogue *Surrealist Intrusion in the Enchanter's Domain*, 1960; published in French in *L'Archibras*, no.2, October 1967; reprinted in Vincent Bounoure, *Moments du surréalisme*, Paris: L'Harmattan, 2001.

The storms of romanticism were no more adequate than its outpourings. Even as art was slamming the doors of the 'salons' where it had prevailed only by dint of embracing its less perverse but most richly endowed favours, it persisted in patiently satisfying the vanities of aesthetes, as it furnished the disillusion born of leisure fit for dogs. Art was a language. The mission of painting or sculpture was evocation. High society's hedonism found in it satin thorns for its faded roses; came nightfall the concerted futility of images took the place of the solemnity of stock exchange speculation. A rudimentary television allowed the enjoyment of the self. Nestled in armchairs of passivity, the spectator sometimes gained an exalted opinion of how responsive and quick-witted he was, at great cost but without excessive nervous expenditure.

When Guillaume Apollinaire undertook to make each of his poems a 'poem-event' and entirely revised the means of poetry, the event – not without some antecedents, but upon which he shone a new light – corrected the aim all too opportunely not to fuel surrealist speculations before long. This meant that value would be attached only to the mental operation of which the work of art is both the product and the opportunity and not to work and skill. From its very inception, surrealism refused the terms of reference in the dispute between figuration (painters of effusion or formal stylisation) and abstraction (supporters of a language by means of which they hoped to solve the antimony between the individual and the universal) that would drag on for a quarter of a century. Other artists, clearly loathe to consider themselves as such, who needed words and forms to modify their relations to the universe, if only for a moment, opposed this woeful quantity of barely adequate words that the artists in both cases made the bearers of its 'message'. The means and materials traditionally in use in the arts offered an almost virgin field of action to this elementary and irrepressible postulation. Modern art thereby made internal necessity the major criterion by which art should be judged. It couldn't fail to find, in its own pre-history, emblems of this explosive movement raised by the 'insane' and the 'wild'.

Yves Tanguy
Reproduced in
*Le Surréalisme au service de la
révolution*, no.3, December 1931

Weights and Colours
[*Text below first image reads:*]
The object above, the size of a
hand and as if it was kneaded by
it, is made of pink plush. The
five lower endings that fold
over the object are in pearly
transparent celluloid. The four
holes in the body of the object
allow the four large fingers of
the hand to pass through.

[*Text below second image reads:*]
In the group above, the object
on the left is made of plaster
painted with a zinzolin colour,
with the nail pink. It is weighted
at the bottom with a ball of lead
which, while allowing
oscillations, always returns it
to the same position.
    The very small object in the
middle, full of mercury, is
covered with braided bright-red
straw in order to appear
extremely light. The large object
on the right is of pale green
moist cotton, the nails in pink
celluloid. The last object on the
right is in plaster covered with
black ink and the nail is pink.

[*Text below third image reads:*]
The object on the left is in soft,
imitation-flesh wax. The piece
added at the top is loose and
more brownish in colour. The
three rounded forms in its
centre are in a hard, matt-white
material.
    The object on the right is in
sky-blue chalk. In the upper
part, some hairs. This object
should serve to write on a
blackboard. It will be used from
the base up, so that in the end
only the cluster of hairs at the
top might remain.

POIDS ET COULEURS

L'objet ci-dessus, de la grandeur de la main et comme s'il
était pétri par elle, est en peluche rose. Les cinq terminaisons
du bas qui se replient sur l'objet sont en celluloïd transparent et nacré. Les quatre trous dans le corps de l'objet
permettent d'y passer les quatre grands doigts de la main.

☞ Dans l'ensemble ci-dessus, l'objet de gauche est en plâtre
peint de couleur zinzoline et l'ongle rose. Il est lesté dans le
bas par une boule de plomb qui, permettant des oscillations,
le ramène toujours à la même position.
    Le très petit objet du milieu, plein de mercure, est recou-
vert de paille tressée rouge vif afin de paraître extrêmement
léger. Le gros objet de droite est en coton moulé vert pâle,
les ongles en celluloïd rose. Le dernier objet de droite est
en plâtre couvert d'encre noire, l'ongle est rose.

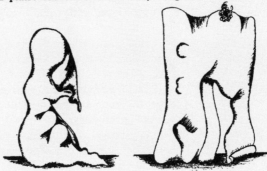

L'objet de gauche est en cire molle imitation chair.
L'appendice du haut est flottant et d'une couleur plus brune.
Les trois formes arrondies du centre sont en matière dure,
d'un blanc mat.
    L'objet de droite est en craie bleu ciel. Dans le haut, des
poils. Cet objet doit servir à écrire sur un tableau noir.
Il sera usé par la base, pour qu'il ne finisse par subsister
que la touffe de poils du haut.   Yves TANGUY.

We know painters and poets were among the first to cross the
fence on which specialists had always kept close watch in order
to keep from view those objects that, hitherto the preserve of
ethnographic data, were henceforth accepted as 'primitive arts'.
The twentieth century had not yet really begun. The aesthetic was
still a quality of the art of enjoyment. It required a diversion for the
sacred sculptures produced by supposedly 'primitive' cultures to
enter the art world: this meant that the magic power of which they
were the custodians could only be lost. This misfortune especially
affected African sculptures, some of which were complacently
exhibited. The plays of light on the ivory, the patient stylisation
of mass, even when it was a question of a ritual sculpture, bore
witness to a concern for form the Cubists didn't scorn. They found
in them the reflection of their descriptive concerns and their
desire for global representation. But from the time that surrealism
replaced the *interpretation of the world* that in various ways
characterised cubism with a will to *change life* by means of an
investigation bearing on the *actual functioning of thought*, the
criteria of classic aesthetics were shown to be ineffective. Instead
of formal perfection what mattered was the necessity that had
led to the dazzling manifestation of a functional principle. This
irrepressible moment of externalisation traced the odyssey of desire
among the forest of substances and play of images. Objects arrived
from the Pacific that the mirages of 'art for art's sake' couldn't
account for at all. Even more, they showed the powers in their
moment of blind concentration, at the moment they prepared to
break their chains. Spangled with deadly grins, they spoke through
birds' cries. The world into which they were born might be mistaken
for a nightmare thronged with night blue feathers. The entire fauna
of the Australian Great Barrier Reef had left its shimmering lights in
them, or lent them its creaking language. From the extreme north
arrived the resounding Eskimo laugh derived from the ten months
of the red moon, while, in cosmology of the Pueblos, the gods of
pre-Columbian mythology still swirled around. In the Amazon,
the parliaments of birds lived on, crazy levitations in complicitous
grace and glory.

Yet the collapse of aesthetic criteria didn't end there. As soon
as they became better known, the sculptures were grouped
according to the isles from which they came, so as to unite with
traditional types making the diversity of origins more apparent and
the particular acceptance of human life and the world to which it
responded more appreciable. We know that African statuettes
illustrated an animist conception that, in its operations, seeks to
perpetuate the constant order of the world through refinements
of polished wood. The static nature of such a conception properly
belongs to a civilisation of peasants, preoccupied with the fecundity
of their lineage and of their earth. African civilisations opposed
with all the power at their disposal the enemy forces that would
endanger this fecundity if they did not take care. If in Africa the
generality of such a perspective, to which we owe the delightful
finesse of Baoulé art, is tempered by many exceptions, the most

Hans Arp
Piano apocalyptique 1959
Front cover, *Le Surréalisme,*
même, no.5, Spring 1959

remarkable of which for the surrealists were the sculptures of the
Baga in Guinea, what was found in Oceania and the Americas was
an altogether different dimension of the mind. Following Indian
and Melanesian sculptors, it was a matter of venturing into the
jungles of dreams and bringing back from them, like trophies of
bird feathers, the patterns of a lasting enchantment.

From one shore of the Pacific to the other, from the Indian
Archipelago to Araucanía, by way of Melanesia, Australia, British
Columbia and the Pueblo Indians – excepting a few Polynesian
islands where no doubt a late autocratism transformed the
indigenous society – the same sort of understanding of the world is
apparent: a universe as passionate as can be, usually composed of
two complementary halves, a universe conceived as an androgyne,
not a primordial one as in the speculations of Mediterranean
antiquity, but current and active, whose main gestures are the
dramas of love. Whether the organisation of society reveals this
quality as more geometric, as in the case of the Navajo Indians
whose sand designs outline the compass rose of a sacred space or,
as more openly sexualised, as in Australia or Melanesia, it shows
the state of interpenetration of the social world and the natural
world as interpreted by cosmologies. No doubt this unity of level
was needed in every realm of human activity so that from one to the
other the same language continues to be current and to carry its
power of amazement into works that make manifest this high state
of consciousness. Perhaps surrealism has owed what it became

only to the skylight of the *malagas* whose branches allowed that nocturnal breeze to filter through the networks of lianas and snakes. Some oceans, deep within the dark night of man, have been explored over there by dug-outs with a human head or those wooden sharks in which Solomon Islanders would place the skulls of their dead. Here we become aware of the deficiencies of our senses: for a long time poets had, at times when 'pagan blood was returning' (Rimbaud), suspected how appearances could be imbued with profound and variable meanings. Totemist peoples have never been afflicted with the short-sightedness that takes out all perceptible value from forms so as to attribute to them a stability that is alone compatible with technical use. For them, as in critical-paranoiac activities, there is no reality that isn't on the point of slipping towards another one that is more revealing. Perhaps it is sculpture's task to confirm this. But whether or not the aim is purely ritualistic, what matters most is to see objectified in this way an attitude of everyday life that has always been that of surrealism. For, as [Breton] said, 'words make love', and it follows that the forms of the world are making love.

If appearances are a lot less simple than they seem, their existence is revealed only thanks to a unique distraction, to a necessary availability attentive to the reception of the internal message. It is no less necessary for the practice of automatic writing than to note the data of everyday magic or, on the Pacific shores, to recognise large pink lizards as the dead returning. Let there be no misunderstanding: wonder is attained only at the end, after stunning encounters at every turn of the path. Tree trunks are inhabited. Windows look out from the axils of the branches. The elders, who have been seen to release their living costumes and no longer frequent the village but the forest, wearing in turn all their finery, when the holothuria were celebrated or the dance of the shark, and sometimes war finery, which women can't resist. It doesn't matter if the injunctions of dream, eagerly discussed by those who are in touch with the spirits, are concerned mainly with the tribe's public business or the behaviour of individuals among the pitfalls of appearances, or just the erection of a ritual sculpture, which immediately takes its place among the major events of public life. When Dalí transposed the intentions of Oceanic and Indian sculptors through the *trompe-l'oeil representation of dream images* his painting tended to knock down the barriers that made surrealists' intentions the act of a very limited group of artists. But, for all that it is less discreet, the figurative representations of sculptors living on the shores of the Pacific is no less subject to public judgement, which evaluates their qualities with a legendary erudition. This is what maintains stylistic rigour in a still traditional art. The extreme freedom that visibly takes precedence within these completely dissimilar artistic domains rather defines them as territories that are each governed by a similar grammar of forms, which alone accounts for each people's spirit. Just as automatic writing integrally respects the syntax in everyday use, the spontaneous movement of Oceanic or American expression releases its booty of new inventions without apparent innovations in style. This is a condition of admissibility or intelligibility. It's really even more the practical condition outside of which fidelity to the internal message is inevitably lost. The artist's maternal language, the style imposed on him by the place where he was born is the natural substance of his action. This is the idiom to which he spontaneously has recourse when the explosive will towards expression of his race is incarnated within him, like a trap from which surge the most active spices of the public spirit.

The passing winds, the clouds and imperceptible currents that move the deep waters of the modern ocean, the migrations of birds at the equinox today cross their initials on these white pages that would be those that dare to bear witness to the powers of the mind. Their heritage is arrayed on the threshold along with school memories and the dead weight of the satchel. The house is open; so then the spirit's pretensions to behave wisely, which are only a miserly way of restraining one's bursts of excitement or to consent to one's servile training, are thrown into the litter. This is the sole criterion by which all cultural goods are evaluated. Hence each person is given the power to witness the misleading spurts of the blindest of human powers, that which overturns all thrones, speaks through the voice of all glorious rioters and shoots archbishops during the Communes, that which levels off the obstructions patiently erected over twenty centuries by the masters and their slaves and drops hard stones into the poet's hands on which the millstones of stale thoughts are vainly worn out. I can say that speculative activity and praxis should not be seen as opposed, as Manichean versions of marxism would have it. Its cries alone, from the depths of the ancient night to the latest jolts of recent history, still speak in humanity's honour. Its practical will, the gestures that escape it, the words it comes to utter, the emblems it raises alongside its path are signs equivalent to its fundamental protest. A certain number of years, a history squatting down on prayer mats, henceforth the waiting would suffice to sustain us with its cinemas of hypotheses! The dense calculations of plausibility will not vanquish the power of underground fire! It was an everyday evocation in those 'primitive' societies organised on a dialectical level. From them alone surrealism could reap a lesson that elsewhere was tarnished or stained by the regular subordination of free expression to the ends of differed efficiency or intellectual acquisition: all the property of the mind was sold off on the ruins of the future of vile repressions whose lot is not to extinguish the initiatory fire. Here opens a canopy of high foliage. The jackdaw will carry you on its wing.

Vincent Bounoure and Vratislav Effenberger
Magic Art and Revolution

In this essay, Bounoure and Effenberger seek to reconfigure, or to clarify in the light of the unfortunate history of the twentieth century, the surrealist use of the term 'revolution', linking it with the idea of 'magic art' as explored by Breton in his 1957 book of this title. In doing so, they also clarify a fundamental misunderstanding often applied to surrealism – that it promotes subjectivity and the irrational –by making explicit the fact (implicit within surrealism throughout its history) that irrationality is as problematic as rationality, of which it is the essential complement. As a result of bitter experience, surrealism learned that political revolution is not necessarily a prerequisite (or even a component part of) of the revolution they sought. It is rather through the reconciliation of objective fact with subjective experience, united through the imagination, and given expression in the transformative example of magic art, that a true revolution can begin.

First published in Vincent Bounoure (ed.), *La Civilisation surréaliste*, Paris: Payot 1976.

The imagination, even when it succeeds in liberating itself, when it escapes the double trap that castrating rationality and gratuitous irrationality sets for its energy, is still for all that unable to establish communication between individuals as long as they remain overwhelmingly prisoners of the static opposition between subjective and objective, as long as the operative value of signs remains inaccessible to them and the charge they carry through their circulation remains imperceptible. In philosophy as it is still taught, just as much as in everyday life, subjective and objective are described and experienced as enemy worlds separated by an irreducible antagonism. The official philosophy that forms the intellectual framework of technological civilisations presents what is in fact a fruitful complementarity of different aspects as an absolute opposition. In light of the balance sheet of this century's catastrophes it is permissible to think that so considerable a malpractice may not remain unpunished.

   The surrealists quickly renounced (if they ever shared) the illusions according to which a political and social revolution would suffice to put an end to this shattered mental situation. This is evidently the source of the endless misunderstandings which gravely affected their relations with the professional revolutionaries they had to oppose with a more global notion of the revolution and a more demanding usage of the word, one evidently incompatible with the common practices of journalism and ideological propaganda. In their mouths, the word 'revolution' gradually moved away from what they judged to be its increasingly debased common deployment. The means of the specialists in seizing power, subordinated to partial objectives, seemed unsuited to

José Guadalupe Posada
Calavera from Oaxaca

the revolutionary ends of surrealism. To reduce the antagonism between subjective and objective, affirmed by contemporary ideology to be inscribed in the nature of things, other revolutionary means than class struggle were necessary. Chance producing the event in the meeting between interior causality and exterior causality, the passionate harmony which reconciles the coexistence of individuals in society and the satisfaction of their instinctual energies, these singular modalities of everyday life – which is nothing if not that of the mind and where the unexpected sets foot on earth – mark out routes barely visible beneath the asphalt of urban crossroads and undetectable either to rationalist assumptions or metaphysical or aesthetic irrationalism. Recognising these routes and advancing along them is no less urgent.

In activities explicitly dedicated to individual expression, such as what are called the arts, the connection between object and subject, between the fixed sign and the being who brings it to light, is all the more obvious, constituting in itself alone the whole territory to which exploration rights are granted, for the opposition between them is more than elsewhere quite easily overcome. These fields of investigation, ever since the birth of rationalist civilisations and the accompanying rejection of the irrationality within superstructures, have thus assumed, on the map of psychosocial continuum that is without frontiers or relief, the distinct colours of an enclave. Does this mean that this kind of reconciliation is only possible in the domain of fiction, in that marginal world of illusion? Quite the contrary. Doubtless the social status of the arts is that of segregation, which is one reason why play should be one of the

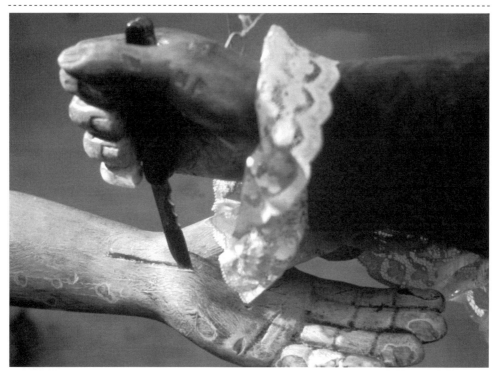

Jan Švankmajer
Film still from *Faust* (1994)

essential mainsprings, among those leading effectively to the liberation of the mind by carrying it to the plateaus of the most perceptive sensibility. The willing interest currently shown, by virtue of needs that are undoubtedly repressed by the practical rationalism of existence or disappointed by subjectivist irrationalism, in artistic forms where the most personal expression of sensibility and the transport of great quantities of the imaginary demand the designation of the most concrete objects, is significant. From Hieronymus Bosch to Breton, one need only name Novalis, Lautréamont, Jarry, Apollinaire, Chirico or Magritte as remarkable representatives of concrete expression nowadays capable of modestly relieving the spiritual dearth and returning meaning to language and fundamental human activity. The mind only reaches the object by making a sign for it, immediately integrated in the fable it utters. Through words and images, through things linked into the configurations where their names are found, the mind builds in its assemblages the meaning of objects which had no other than that of being there. It's because their signs are capable of being integrated into individual inventions and confabulations and of acquiring a characteristic value that is wholly dependent on the structure they come to inhabit, that the mind, even if it may not be very conscious of it, can reach a new objectivity that could just as well be called a subjectivisation of the appearances that then attain the reality of fact via the play of the mind. Why does the manipulation of signs affect things? Because the nature of the mind is to structure. Moreover it will not be surprising that when it rediscovers its true power, whose technical activity is only what a private realism (clouded by the 'notable quantities of no importance' and a naive belief that the object has a reality independent of the mind) allows to survive, the mind then grasps the instruments of magic. 'The imaginary is that which tends to become real. ' But there are degrees of reality: the imaginary is what establishes a real relationship with the object, a relationship which transforms the world, a magic gesture that induces a double evolution of the subject and the object whose connections henceforth inevitably elude repetition, because the given is a pure possibility accorded to the mind to command a world of signs, and because the great storehouses of the imagination are incessantly restocked with new experiences.

In the immemorial use of what Breton has called magic art, we see, like a phosphorescent ocean, the imperious appetite for human realisation infused and the prefiguration of its psychological and material future flow periodically back into view. The fusion of the interior and exterior worlds, outside any prediction, even if it slips unnoticed between the dead points of the future, no less gives concrete meaning to the history of the mind. It is from this perspective that surrealism, genetically determined and strengthened in its refusals by the current crisis of civilisation, opens up experimental routes which, starting from the modes of consciousness in artistic activity, go right back to the dynamic sources of real life which alone give meaning to the word revolution.

Vratislav Effenberger
On the Utilitarian Conception of Language

Throughout the history of surrealism the surrealists have seen the degeneration of language as a crucial marker of the escalating decadence of the modern world which underlies the increasing uniformity of societies resulting in increasing specialisation. Its revitalisation is therefore seen as one of the keys to the regeneration of society and has been a particular concern of the Czech surrealists throughout their history. In this essay Effenberger gives us a preface to one of the themes that will pre-occupy the Czechoslovak surrealists in the years after it was written as they tackled issues of inter-subjective communication through game-playing and collective investigation.

Published in Vincent Bounoure (ed.), *La Civilisation surréaliste*, Paris: Payot 1976.

The militant internationalism which can be seen as one of the constants of surrealism doubtless emerges from its political choices, but also from the current state of things of the mind. Within national entities, neither their 'traditions' nor their language guarantee the arts, for instance (or more generally culture), a clear-cut specificity, nor an internal homogeneity which, on the other hand, dislocates the autonomous development of artistic, technical, philosophical and scientific disciplines. Thus we witness, within social unities, a breaking apart through differentiation which, perceptible initially at the level of specialised thought, step by step reaches the deep layers of collective being, and as it does so dissociates the elementary functions of communication. The victim of a permanent prefabrication of thought, reduced to a state of increasing passivity, as much in respect of reflection as of imagination, the man in the street is henceforth revealed to be less and less able to describe the directions to take from one place to another in the city in which he lives and then demonstrates the gradual collapse of the imaginative energy necessary for the most summary forms of communication more openly than one would like. 'The tyranny of a thoroughly debased language', once denounced by Breton in 1953's 'Surrealism in its Living Works' [Breton 1969, p.298], unfolds from this piecemeal uniformalisation, and from the universality of this process of the alteration of thought which everywhere narrows the movement of the mind to the dimensions of a set of increasingly meagre images and ideas. Behind the façade of rationally prefabricated buildings made according to an identical process, the inhabitants of Paris, Prague or Moscow inhabit an internationalised universe, deprived of any particularising sign, in the heart of which the same conflicts emerge: at the windows everywhere the same bars form the same grid of rationality.

The specialised differentiation that marks contemporary intellectual evolution reinforces so many ideological axes which each person knows in its diverse contexts, in any given country marked by its language and heritage, the different growth patterns, like trees of similar species. Such was the history of the avant-garde from Impressionism onwards in particular. At the last stage of this history, surrealists treated all frontiers as null and void: they considered their first duty to be agreement, inferred notwithstanding differences of country or school, about the meaning of human activity. In what could be called the surrealist international, from group to group and within each one, in the consensus resulting from an identical judgement on the poverty of the language of rationality which expelled lyrical language from the public sphere and relegated it to a place of shame, nothing has been as fertile as linking them systematically. But this could not avoid rendering surrealism's segregation more severe by underlining what differentiated it from everything else, and especially from all dualist enterprises that were developing at the same time. 'Civilisation' defended itself against an operation of the de-specialisation of the mind by isolating it as the concern of specialists. We have good reason to believe that we are equipped to make a riposte to this show of summary categorisations. Independently of the stigmata of degeneration already being manifested in current forms of social existence (the deepening rift between exchange value and use value; the duality of rational expression and emotional expression; the blind faith sustained by the values of utility under the pretext of rationality, when it is only a matter of the preservation of current modalities of economic and social exploitation; the accelerating frustration of real needs in their universal and uniform formalisation, at the sight of so many stigmata announcing the liquidation of Empire) the surrealist objective is not just to hasten its collapse, but to contribute to the advent of a new state of individual and public spirit, illustrating the functional cohesion of unconscious impulses and their conscious development. The utility of language must no longer fool us at a time when its formalisation renders it unable to fulfil the integral nature of its functions, or even its most summary ones. The conditions have come together for the creation or restoration of modes of communication which are richer and whose functional efficacy can only grow in proportion to the continued 'unmasking' of formal pseudo-rationality.